Slavery, Race, and Conquest in the Tropics

Slavery, Race, and Conquest in the Tropics challenges the way historians interpret the causes of the American Civil War. Using Abraham Lincoln and Stephen Douglas's famed rivalry as a prism, Robert E. May shows that when Lincoln and fellow Republicans opposed slavery in the West, they did so partly from evidence that slaveholders, with Douglas's assistance, planned to follow up successes in Kansas by bringing Cuba, Mexico, and Central America into the Union as slave states. A skeptic about "Manifest Destiny," Lincoln opposed the war with Mexico, condemned Americans invading Latin America, and warned that Douglas's "popular sovereignty" doctrine would unleash U.S. slaveholders throughout Latin America. This book internationalizes America's showdown over slavery, shedding new light on the Lincoln–Douglas rivalry and Lincoln's Civil War scheme to resettle freed slaves in the Tropics.

Robert E. May is a professor of history at Purdue University. He is the author of *Manifest Destiny's Underworld: Filibustering in Antebellum America* (2002); *John A. Quitman: Old South Crusader* (1985), winner of the Mississippi Historical Society's book prize; and *The Southern Dream of a Caribbean Empire* (1973). He is editor of *The Union, the Confederacy, and the Atlantic Rim* (1995).

THE NEW YORK HERALD.

WHOLE NO. 9887.   NEW YORK, MONDAY, OCTOBER 12, 1863.—TRIPLE SHEET.   PRICE THREE CENTS.

THE FRENCH IN MEXICO.

Map Showing the Whole Territory of Mexico and the Portion Occupied by the French.

The Portion of the Mexican Republic Occupied by the French is Enclosed in Black Lines.

Slavery, Race, and Conquest in the Tropics

Lincoln, Douglas, and the Future of Latin America

ROBERT E. MAY

Purdue University

CAMBRIDGE
UNIVERSITY PRESS

CAMBRIDGE
UNIVERSITY PRESS

32 Avenue of the Americas, New York NY 10013-2473, USA

Cambridge University Press is part of the University of Cambridge.

It furthers the University's mission by disseminating knowledge in the pursuit of
education, learning and research at the highest international levels of excellence.

www.cambridge.org
Information on this title: www.cambridge.org/9780521132527

© Robert E. May 2013

First published 2013

A catalogue record for this publication is available from the British Library

Library of Congress Cataloguing in Publication data
May, Robert E.
Slavery, race, and conquest in the tropics : Lincoln, Douglas, and the future of
Latin America / Robert E. May, Purdue University.
pages   cm
Includes bibliographical references and index.
ISBN 978-0-521-76383-7 (hardback) – ISBN 978-0-521-13252-7 (paperback)
1. Slavery – Political aspects – United States – History – 19th century.
2. Slavery – United States – Extension to the territories.   3. United States – Territorial
expansion – History – 19th century.   4. United States – Civil War, 1861–1865 –
Causes.   5. Lincoln, Abraham, 1809–1865 – Political and social views.   6. Douglas,
Stephen A. (Stephen Arnold), 1813–1861 – Political and social views.
7. Freedmen – Colonization – Latin America.   I. Title.
E338.M338   2013
973.7′112–dc23   2013018644

ISBN 978-0-521-76383-7 Hardback
ISBN 978-0-521-13252-7 Paperback

To Jill

Contents

Illustrations and Maps

Acknowledgments

This project, though brewing in the back of my mind for many years, likely would never have been initiated had it not been for the encouragement of Eric Crahan, then a Cambridge University Press editor of history and politics, at a breakfast meeting during a professional conference some years ago. I owe Eric a tremendous debt for urging me to plunge into the already well-plowed ground of Lincoln–Douglas studies and to pursue my instincts about one of the still untold stories about their famous rivalry.

Although this book has benefited from discussions with and tips from many scholars, I owe particular thanks to U.S. expansion experts Amy S. Greenberg, the Edwin Erle Sparks Professor of History and Women's Studies at Pennsylvania State University, and David Narrett at the University of Texas at Arlington. Both Amy and David have read the manuscript and rendered thorough critiques, in the process guiding me to new sources, correcting errors, suggesting ways to improve the narrative's style, and helping me to rethink my original plans for its chapters and organization. My colleague and expansion scholar at Purdue, Michael Morrison, and Howard Jones, a close professional friend for many decades and University Research Professor at the University of Alabama, both gave me very important encouragement and advice when I was first conceptualizing this project.

Among the many archivists and librarians who have helped me locate materials for this project, I especially wish to thank Eileen A. Ielmini, Director of Archives Processing and Digital Access, Special Collections Research Center, University of Chicago Library, for her advice and access to the Douglas collection there at a time when that repository was planning to withdraw access to Douglas's papers temporarily so they could be digitized. The staff at the Abraham Lincoln Presidential Library and Museum in Springfield, Illinois, likewise did everything they could to assist my research and brought a number of very helpful documents to my attention. I am particularly indebted to James M. Cornelius, Curator; Bryon Andreasen, Research Historian; and Glenna Schroeder-Lein, Manuscript Librarian, for their guidance. One of my former Ph.D. students, Sean Scott, now on the faculty at Christopher Newport University, helped guide me to an important document at the National Archives. Bruce Kirby, Manuscript Reference Librarian, Manuscript Division, Library of Congress, went out of his way to help me.

I want to thank the Purdue interlibrary loan system for processing what must have seemed yet one more endless succession of requests from me for materials. I am indebted to the Purdue University Department of History for its continuing, consistent support of my research and writing. The department's lead secretary, Nancy Cramer, helped me tremendously in tracking down and arranging for reproduction rights for images in this work. My Department Head, Doug Hurt, has facilitated the completion of this book in countless ways, most importantly by his enthusiasm for the project. Ever since he joined the department some years ago, Doug has consistently encouraged me in my research projects, and I am deeply grateful for his unflagging support. Above all, I owe the most to my wife, Jill. This book, like my previous books, benefits from her suggestions and skilled copyediting. She also assisted me in locating documents on research trips. She easily wins its dedication.

Abbreviations Used in the Notes

AL   Abraham Lincoln

BBPC James J. Barnes and Patience P. Barnes, ed., *Private and Confidential: Letters from British Ministers in Washington to the Foreign Secretaries in London, 1844–67* (Selinsgrove: Susquehanna University Press, 1993)

CG   *Congressional Globe*

CWAL Roy P. Basler, ed., *The Collected Works of Abraham Lincoln*, 9 vols. (New Brunswick, NJ, 1953–55)

HSP   Historical Society of Pennsylvania, Philadelphia

JRMP James D. Richardson, comp., *A Compilation of the Messages and Papers of the Presidents, 1789–1908*, 11 vols. (Washington, DC, 1908)

LC   Library of Congress

RG48 Records of the Office of the Secretary of the Interior Relating to the Suppression of the African Slave Trade and Negro Colonization, 1854–1872, M160, National Archives, Washington, DC

SAD   Stephen A. Douglas

UC   Special Collections Research Center, University of Chicago

WHH   William H. Herndon

WHS   William Henry Seward

WRM   William R. Manning, comp., *Diplomatic Correspondence of the United States: Inter-American Affairs, 1831–1860*, 12 vols. (Washington, DC: Government Printing Office, 1932–39)

Introduction

Did she pay any attention to what the president actually said? On March 4, 1865, Cara Kasson, the wife of a Republican congressman from Iowa, made her way to the Capitol through Washington's muddy streets, as rain poured down, to witness the second inauguration of Abraham Lincoln. Later, when reporting her impressions of the day to a Des Moines, Iowa, paper, Mrs. Kasson was more effusive about the sun's appearance as Lincoln took his oath than his inaugural thoughts. Observing that the president delivered "his few clear sentences" modestly, she suggested that the timely breaking out of sunshine might be an omen that God was prepared to let Lincoln lead the nation to final victory in the Civil War.

Perhaps Lincoln's text sped by her too quickly to be absorbed. A mere 703 words, it was several times briefer than the inaugural in 1857 of his immediate predecessor, James Buchanan. Yet, within it, Lincoln boiled down to a few sentences what had caused the horrific conflict that had already taken hundreds of thousands of American lives. Asserting that everybody understood that "somehow" slavery was the problem, Lincoln explained why it so divided Americans: "To strengthen, perpetuate, and extend" slavery had been the purpose of southern disunionists, he contended, while he and fellow Republicans "claimed no right to do more than to restrict the territorial enlargement of it." The issue of slavery expansion, in other words, brought on the Civil War, not the actual situation of slaves already in the southern states.[1]

---

[1] "Miriam" (Caroline Kasson) to the (Des Moines) *Iowa State Register*, Mar. 6, 1865, "Source Material of Iowa History: An Iowa Woman in Washington, DC, 1861–1865," *Iowa Journal of History* 52 (Jan. 1954): 89; Ernest B. Ferguson, *Freedom Rising: Washington in the Civil War* (New York, 2004), 138; AL, Second Inaugural Address,

Lincoln's remarks did not specify the western frontier as the locus for this dispute, yet most accounts of Lincoln, his famous rivalry with the U.S. senator from Illinois Stephen A. Douglas, and the beginning of the Civil War treat the heated territorial controversy of the 1840s and 1850s as if it was *only* about the U.S. West. Neither Lincoln nor Douglas, however, nor their political parties, saw matters that way. As Lincoln put it at Peoria, Illinois, in October 1854 in one of his first outbursts against Douglas's controversial Kansas-Nebraska Act, Douglas's law not only extended slavery to Kansas and Nebraska but allowed its "spread to every other part of the wide world, where men can be found inclined to take it."[2] Lincoln's warning hardly had points north in mind; southerners never seriously entertained illusions of taking slaves to the cold climes of Russian Alaska or Britain's provinces in Canada. Rather, slavery expansionists had been trying to spread their labor system southward toward the Tropics, and from Lincoln's perspective and that of fellow Republicans, Douglas had been the South's accomplice in these efforts.

Slavery, Race, and Conquest in the Tropics is hardly the first book about arguably the most famous political rivalry in the history of the United States. Recent works such as Allen C. Guezlo's *Lincoln and Douglas: The Debates That Defined America* and Douglas R. Egerton's *Year of Meteors: Stephen Douglas, Abraham Lincoln, and the Election That Brought on the Civil War* are symptomatic of the fascination of historians, publishers, and the American reading public with not only the Lincoln–Douglas debates but also the decades-long rivalry itself.[3] It is almost impossible to conceive of Lincoln ever becoming president had not Douglas been his foil. Lincoln honed his policies and defined his ideals in response to Douglas's stance on the day's issues, especially slavery in Kansas. This book, however, is the first to explore the rivals' dramatically different ideas about the future of Latin America and why their competing visions help explain not only their bitter feud over slavery in

---

JRMP, 6: 276–77; Ronald C. White Jr., *Lincoln's Greatest Speech: The Second Inaugural* (2002; rpt., New York, 2006), 29, 31, 48, 52.

[2] Lincoln speech of Oct. 16, 1854, CWAL, 2: 255.

[3] Allen C. Guelzo, *Lincoln and Douglas: The Debates That Defined America* (New York, 2008); Douglas R. Egerton, *Year of Meteors: Stephen Douglas, Abraham Lincoln, and the Election That Brought on the Civil War* (New York, 2010); John Burt, *Lincoln's Tragic Pragmatism: Lincoln, Douglas, and Moral Conflict* (Cambridge, MA, 2013); Roy Morris Jr., *The Long Pursuit: Abraham Lincoln's Thirty-Year Struggle with Stephen Douglas for the Heart and Soul of America* (Washington, DC, 2008). The publication of a near-definitive edition of the debates further indicates continuing fascination with the rivalry: Rodney O. Davis and Douglas L. Wilson, *The Lincoln-Douglas Debates* (Urbana, 2008).

the U.S. West but also the breakdown of North-South comity that led to the Civil War.

The dispute began in the mid-1840s, when the positions of Lincoln and Douglas on slavery's expansion southward diverged in ways that became more pronounced as years passed. Prior to 1844, neither Lincoln nor Douglas said much of anything about foreign affairs, much less Latin America and slavery's expansion. The Texas annexation controversy and subsequent war with Mexico, however, changed everything.

Apathetic about the annexation of Texas and opposed to war with Mexico, Lincoln was dubious about the popular expansionist ideology of "Manifest Destiny," which celebrated U.S. territorial growth as a means of fulfilling the nation's promise. Rather than support U.S. diplomatic and military initiatives for new tropical acquisitions, Lincoln wished to foster democracy to the south by making the United States a model of progress and republican institutions – the "last best, hope of earth" as he put it in his second annual message to Congress in December 1862. In contrast, Douglas gained notoriety as Washington's most aggressive apostle of Manifest Destiny. An ardent champion of projects to extend the United States' territorial and commercial sway in Latin America, Douglas promoted the annexation of Texas, the absorption of the entire Mexican nation, U.S. acquisition of Spain's colony in Cuba, and territorial extension into Central America. At times he seemed to crave the whole hemisphere.

It would be simplistic to imply that Lincoln and Douglas invariably disagreed regarding Latin American issues. Both men critiqued Latin Americans for failing to achieve political stability in the decades after achieving their independence from Spanish and Portuguese rule. Both endorsed the Monroe Doctrine's strictures against new European colonies in the Western Hemisphere. Both favored growing U.S. trade with Latin America. If Douglas was more willing than Lincoln to use military muscle abroad, he nonetheless espoused the rhetoric of peaceful expansion, often dissembling that the United States had acquired its entire continental empire through honorable means. Douglas even shared an interest in colonization with Lincoln. Had he lived through the Civil War, he likely would have rallied to Lincoln's programs for voluntary black resettlement in Latin America as a means of resolving America's turmoil over slavery and race.

Still, Lincoln and Douglas differed fundamentally on Latin America's future, and their divergent perspectives became a subtext for their angry disputes over the West. Both men realized by the 1850s that the

Tropics were inextricably linked to the outcome of the slavery expansion controversy within the United States. When Abraham Lincoln and Stephen Douglas argued passionately about whether or not slavery should extend westward, they did so partly because Latin America lurked in the West's shadow.

Slavery, Race, and Conquest in the Tropics reveals a "Latin beat" modulating the rhythms of Lincoln's battle with his great rival Douglas over slavery in the West. Behind Kansas's curtain lay vistas of slave plantations in the Tropics.

I

A "Spot" for Manifest Destiny

Ambitious congressmen needed little prodding to join the army when war erupted with Mexico in the spring of 1846. Since the earliest days of the Republic, Americans had promoted war heroes to their highest office. Generals George Washington, Andrew Jackson, and William Henry Harrison all won election as the nation's chief executive primarily because of their military luster, and many other presidential contenders positioned themselves for presidential bids with martial exploits. No wonder, then, that a mere three days after Congress voted for war with Mexico on May 13 an observer in Washington reported some fifty congressmen had applied to the U.S. president, James K. Polk, for army commissions, in some instances on behalf of relatives, but many of them for themselves.[1]

Caught up in this *rage militaire*, Stephen A. Douglas joined the ranks of U.S. congressmen clamoring for a commission. Just before the war, Douglas had established a military record by participating in a volunteer militia campaign to pacify Hancock County (in west central Illinois), where disorder had erupted between Mormons and their neighbors. Douglas served there as aide-de-camp at the rank of major to his recent fellow Illinois congressman, the militia general John J. Hardin. When warfare erupted with Mexico, Douglas considered military service again, perhaps partly from a sense of personal responsibility. As chairman of the House of Representatives' Committee on Territories he had

[1] "Oliver Oldschool" to J. R. Chandler, May 16, 1846, in (Philadelphia) *United States Gazette*, May 18, 1846.

helped enact legislation annexing the independent Republic of Texas to the Union, a cause of the fighting since Mexico had never recognized the Lone Star Republic's independence and still claimed it. Already known as a strident expansionist, Douglas emerged as the war progressed as one of the country's most fervent apostles of Manifest Destiny – the new creed that God intended the United States, because of its superior democratic institutions, to possess the entire North American continent. Rather than campaigning with the army, however, Douglas remained in Congress, an arrangement that worked out to his political advantage. In midwar, Douglas gained advancement to the U.S. Senate, a decision then made by balloting of state legislatures, not by popular vote. Shifting to the more prestigious upper chamber in December 1847, Douglas became prominent in the "all-Mexico" movement, which sought to capitalize on U.S. defeats of enemy forces by completely absorbing America's southern neighbor. As the war wound down, Douglas supported an effort to amend the peace treaty so that his country would gain more of Mexico than it allowed.

The same month Douglas assumed his Senate seat, Abraham Lincoln arrived on the Potomac as a freshman congressman. Less outspoken on Texas than Douglas, Lincoln was ambivalent about adding it to the Union. Although southerners might now emigrate there with their human property, he reasoned, adding Texas would do nothing to increase the overall number of U.S. slaves. Still, he opposed slavery's spread, saying that the North should never allow its expansion if doing so would prevent slavery from coming to a natural end. Consistent with this belief, Lincoln supported banning slavery from territory that was gained by the United States as a result of the fighting in Mexico. Indeed, he felt the war should never have begun in the first place. Lincoln used his congressional seat to attack President Polk for starting an unnecessary war. Though he did not take as strong a position against Manifest Destiny as Douglas assumed for it, Lincoln argued that it would be a mistake for the nation to grow further. By the end of the Mexican-American War, Stephen Douglas and Abraham Lincoln had staked out different approaches to U.S. expansion and slavery's southward spread.

Had the young Stephen Douglas enjoyed carpentry and menial labor, perhaps he would have never become a leading apostle of Manifest Destiny. Douglas's work experiences, however, nudged him into the Democratic Party, America's most stridently expansionist national party, before the Civil War. Born in 1813 in Brandon, Vermont, not far from Lake

Champlain, Stephen Arnold Douglass[2] descended from Puritan New Englanders and was the son of a doctor who died the year Stephen was born. After her husband's death, Stephen's mother, Sarah, moved with him and his younger brother to a small family farm nearby that adjoined the place of her brother Edward. A studious child during the months he attended the local school, Stephen resented unpaid work required of him by his uncle the rest of the year. At fifteen, in 1828, he left for Middlebury to begin an apprenticeship in cabinet making, which also proved unsatisfying. He disliked being assigned menial jobs around the house in addition to his skilled work on washstands, bedsteads, and other furniture.

As Douglas told the story, while learning his trade he socialized with fellow apprentices and they initiated him into politics, encouraging him to pass many hours in political reading. He arrived in Middlebury during a presidential election, and his new comrades all strongly backed General Andrew Jackson of Tennessee in his successful campaign against the incumbent John Quincy Adams of Massachusetts. When Douglas moved in 1830 to Canandaigua in western New York, he remained politically active and defended Jackson in the debating club of the academy he attended. Douglas remembered how his initial political experiences "fixed" his party affiliation for life, meaning that he became devoutly loyal to the Jacksonian clique in U.S. politics, which morphed within a few years into the Democratic Party of today.[3]

What did it mean for Douglas to become a Democrat? In domestic policy, the party championed egalitarianism and political democracy for white males, adherence to states' rights, and suspicion of federal domestic programs such as national banks, protective tariffs, and federally funded transportation improvements, which Democrats feared might be manipulated by special interests at the expense of America's farmers and working classes. If Democrats were restrained when it came to government activism in the domestic sphere, however, they tended toward an expansive and often militarily aggressive approach to foreign challenges. In world affairs, Democrats inherited the traditions of the men they considered their party's founding fathers – Old Hickory (as Jackson was known) and Thomas Jefferson. These southern slaveholders not only

---

[2] This is not a misspelling of Douglass's name. He used this spelling until 1846, when he dropped the second "s." Robert W. Johannsen, *Stephen A. Douglas* (1973; rpt., Urbana, 1997), 876n. I use the "Douglas" spelling throughout this book, except when the original appears in quotations.

[3] "Autobiography of Stephen A. Douglas," ed. Frank E. Stevens, *Journal of the Illinois State Historical Society* 5 (Oct. 1913): 328–30, 342; Johannsen, *Douglas*, 5–13.

helped make the United States a continental nation by the late 1840s; they also articulated an ideology of American empire, a philosophy of national growth that had ramifications long after the nation completed its land acquisitions.

Jefferson held a mystical belief in the U.S. experiment in republican governance. His America, a bastion of human rights, would enlighten "other regions of the earth" with its traditions of "freedom and self-government." The "most expansion-minded president in American history" in the opinion of one historian, Jefferson believed Americans could launch an "empire of liberty." Eventually, the "rapid multiplication" of America's population would overrun all of North America and possibly South America too, so that the hemisphere would be dominated by English-speaking people and their democratic forms of government. Jefferson's Louisiana Purchase of 1803 spent more than $15 million (more than the year's federal budget) to double the nation. It acquired from France some 828,000 square miles of land including much of the terrain between the Mississippi River and the Rocky Mountains. Jefferson's administration also claimed a sizable swatch of Spain's North American holdings along the Gulf Coast from the Pensacola area in Florida's Panhandle to the Rio Grande River in the West, while extinguishing Native American title to vast land tracts in the South and today's Midwest.[4]

The year Jefferson purchased Louisiana, Jackson, at the time U.S. senator from Tennessee, told his colleagues that God and nature intended America's "natural bounds" to extend to the Gulf of Mexico and that the entire world could not keep "this great and rising empire" from its geographical destiny. In 1812, he predicted that war with England would result in U.S. "conquest of all the British dominions upon the continent of north America." Toward the end of his life, Jackson affirmed that

---

[4] Robert W. Tucker and David C. Hendrickson, *Empire of Liberty: The Statecraft of Thomas Jefferson* (1990; rpt., New York, 1992), 3, 7; Gordon S. Wood, *Empire of Liberty: A History of the Early Republic, 1789–1815* (New York, 2009); Richard W. Van Alstyne, *The Rising American Empire* (Chicago, 1960), 81, 88; Frank Lawrence Owsley Jr. and Gene A. Smith, *Filibusters and Expansionists: Jeffersonian Manifest Destiny, 1800–1821* (University, AL, 1997), 26–27; Alexander DeConde, *This Affair of Louisiana* (Baton Rouge, 1976), 181–87, 213–35; Bernard W. Sheehan, *Seeds of Extinction: Jeffersonian Philanthropy and the American Indian* (New York, 1973), 4, 8, 17–20, 42–43, 122, 125, 245–48; Robert V. Haynes, *The Mississippi Territory and the Southwest Frontier, 1795–1817* (Lexington, 2010), 94–96; Reginald Horsman, *Expansion and American Indian Policy, 1783–1812* (1967; rpt., Norman, OK, 1992), 137–38, 123, 143–57; David E. Narrett, "Geopolitics and Intrigue: James Wilkinson, the Spanish Borderlands, and Mexican Independence," *William and Mary Quarterly*, 3rd ser., 69 (Jan. 2012): 116–20, 128.

peacefully enlarging the nation's boundaries would grow "the area of freedom."[5] By then he had an expansionist résumé rivaling Jefferson's. Aptly characterized as the "tribune of democratic imperialism,"[6] he conducted military campaigns that further dispossessed native tribes in the U.S. Southeast, consolidated U.S. control over Spanish West Florida, and laid the groundwork for U.S. acquisition of what remained of Spanish Florida in the Transcontinental Treaty of 1819. In the Creek War of September 1813–March 1814, Jackson led Tennessee militia and U.S. infantrymen against the hostile Red Stick faction of the Creek nation, crushing their resistance at Horseshoe Bend on the Coosa River in today's Alabama. Promoted to major general in the U.S. Army, Jackson induced dispirited Creeks to sign away the largest cession yet achieved from the southeastern tribes – some twenty-three million acres constituting about a third of today's Georgia and approximately two-thirds of modern Alabama, in the Treaty of Fort Jackson. After the War of 1812, Jackson negotiated new land cessions from Choctaws, Cherokees, and Chickasaws.[7]

Jackson's invasion of Spanish Florida in 1818 exemplified his dramatic aggressiveness. He captured several Spanish outposts and eventually Pensacola, the capital of Spain's province of West Florida, without express authorization from President James Monroe. Not only did Jackson tell Monroe he believed U.S. possession of all Florida essential for frontier peace and "the future welfare of our country;" he deemed the Spanish island colony of Cuba essential to secure America's "southern frontier" and boldly asserted that with more troops and a larger war vessel he could take that island "in a few days." As president (1829–37), Jackson instructed U.S. diplomat Joel Poinsett to try to buy Texas from Mexico. Although the initiative failed, Jackson supported the Texas Revolution of 1836 and recognized Texan independence on his last day of office, a step toward U.S. annexation less than a decade later. Jackson's administration displaced thousands of Native Americans from ancestral lands by removing them across the Mississippi River to reservations. In some seventy

[5] *Annals of Congress*, 7 Cong., 2 Sess., 150; Fred Anderson and Andrew Cayton, *The Dominion of War: Empire and Liberty in North America, 1500–2000* (New York, 2005), 222; Andrew Jackson to A. V. Brown, Feb. 12, 1843, in James Parton, *Life of Andrew Jackson* (New York, 1861), 3: 658.

[6] Anderson and Cayton, *Dominion of War*, 209.

[7] Robert V. Remini, *Andrew Jackson and His Indian Wars* (New York, 2001), 130–62; Walter Nugent, *Habits of Empire: A History of American Expansion* (New York, 2008), 118–20.

treaties, Jackson's negotiators gained approximately 100 million acres of tribal lands in the East for some 32 million acres in the West.[8]

If the young Stephen Douglas found Democratic Party doctrine especially attractive, it was surely in no small part because of the expansionist accomplishments of the party's iconic figures. Douglas later claimed that from his youngest days he had "indulged an enthusiasm" for the "growth, expansion, and destiny of this republic," devoting careful study to the topography and geography of the continental stretch between the Mississippi River and the Pacific Ocean. Eventually, he familiarized himself with each western "mountain and valley, plain and river" as well as the landscape of the older states. Even if this remembrance, which he voiced at a public celebration in 1851, was hyperbole, it hints at what made the Democratic Party especially appealing to him, why he would say that the "best days" of his party occurred when it was "under a Jefferson or a Jackson." Douglas found inspiration in his party's expansionist roots, and his first major speech as U.S. congressman defended a measure to refund a $1,000 fine on Jackson during the War of 1812. It was characteristic of him to exclaim in 1844, when the United States and Britain were engaged in a serious dispute over their competing claims to Oregon, "Let us rather act upon the maxim of Old Hickory – 'Ask nothing but what is right, and submit to nothing that is wrong.'"[9]

Like Douglas, Abraham Lincoln may have drifted into politics as relief from demanding physical labor. The second child of Thomas Lincoln and the former Nancy Hanks, Abraham was born on February 12, 1809, in his family's one-room log cabin on a farmstead in northern Kentucky. He spent his early childhood in Kentucky, receiving meager schooling, until December 1816, when the family moved to southern Indiana at Little Pigeon Creek in Spencer County. In October 1818 Lincoln's mother died from milk sickness, a disease caused by drinking milk from cows that grazed on white snakeroot, a poisonous plant. A little more than a year after her death, Thomas Lincoln convinced Sarah Bush Johnston, a Kentucky widow with three children, to marry him and help keep his Indiana household and raise Abraham and his older sister, also named Sarah. Young Lincoln seemed built for manual labor, and he did plenty of it on his father's successive tracts in northern Kentucky, southern Indiana,

[8] Nugent, *Habits of Empire*, 122–27; Harry Watson, *Liberty and Power: The Politics of Jacksonian America* (New York, 1990), 111.
[9] *Springfield* (IL) *Daily Register*, Apr. 8, 1851; *Alexandria* (VA) *Gazette*, June 11, 1852; Johannsen, *Douglas*, 129 CG, 28 Cong., 1 Sess., Appendix, 600.

and then central Illinois, as well as for temporary employers. Tall and "big-boned" with a "frame of *iron*" in the words of William H. Herndon, later his law partner, the gangly Lincoln weighed more than two hundred pounds by his early twenties and stood six feet four, famously earning repute among his peers for his strength and prowess at wrestling. He never, however, took to agricultural labor. Once, later in life, when a close friend wrote to him about farming, Lincoln responded that he could not say anything because he had never owned a farm, had no intention of doing so, and had "not studied the subject enough to be much interested with it."[10]

Lincoln thought differently about politics, which he entered after moving in 1831 to New Salem, a village of only some one hundred residents in central Illinois's Sangamon County about twenty miles from today's state capital of Springfield. The following March, Lincoln announced what proved to be an unsuccessful candidacy for the Illinois state legislature.

Although he lacked any party affiliation at the time, the progressive developmental doctrines Lincoln endorsed resembled the "American system" of Kentucky U.S. senator and former secretary of state Henry Clay and anticipated doctrines of the Whig Party that Clay would soon help organize. Whigs like Clay favored government intervention in the economy, and Lincoln believed the Illinois state government should underwrite the educational improvement and economic growth his town needed, partly by providing state aid for widening and deepening the channel of the Sangamon River. The "internal improvements" Lincoln advocated promised local farmers a way to move their goods more quickly and less expensively all the way to New Orleans and even toward international markets, since New Salem overlooked the Sangamon, a waterway connected to the Mississippi River by way of the Illinois River. Though Lincoln's announcement never mentioned Clay, who was running for president that year, he surely knew something about the Kentuckian's domestic policies. Lincoln voraciously consumed newspapers and may

---

[10] WHH to Mr. Bartlett, Aug. 7, 1887, Emanuel Hertz, ed., *The Hidden Lincoln: From the Letters and Papers of William H. Herndon* (New York, 1938), 196; Ronald C. White, *A. Lincoln: A Biography* (New York, 2009), 23, 28; Lynn McNulty Greene to WHH, July 30, 1865, WHH interview of James Harriott (undated), John M. Rutledge to WHH, Nov. 18, 1866, *Herndon's Informants: Letters, Interviews, and Statements about Abraham Lincoln*, ed. Douglas L. Wilson and Rodney O. Davis (Urbana, 1998), 80, 402, 703; AL to Joshua F. Speed, Mar. 27, 1842, CWAL, 1: 282; David Herbert Donald, *Lincoln* (1995; rpt., New York, 1996), 32–37, 39; Richard J. Carwardine, *Lincoln: Profiles in Power* (London, 2003), 3–6. Lincoln's sister moved away to get married when he was seventeen and died in childbirth less than two years later.

have read a campaign biography of Clay. Soon, like Clay, Lincoln would consider himself a fervent Whig. Originating in meetings held in the winter of 1833–34, the Whig Party adopted its name, a throwback to the antimonarchical Whigs of England, as a repudiation of the nation's incumbent president. Clay and his party regarded Andrew Jackson, who vetoed more bills – including an ambitious internal improvements measure – than all his predecessors combined, as a power-hungry usurper of congressional authority.[11]

Lincoln's marriage in 1842 to Mary Todd of Lexington, Kentucky, whose family knew the senator, strengthened his identification with Clay. That year, as a member of the executive committee of Springfield, Illinois's "Clay Club," Lincoln joined eight other Whigs in inviting Clay to visit the "prairie-land" for a grand reception. According to an unverified reminiscence by one of Lincoln's Illinois contemporaries, Clay invited Lincoln to dine at his Ashland estate in Lexington five years later. Though questions remain about whether Lincoln and Clay had a personal relationship, there is no questioning the depth of Lincoln's devotion to Clay's political economy.[12]

Lincoln's fealty to Clay included the Kentuckian's foreign policy values. Perhaps more than any other nationally prominent figure, Clay

[11] Donald, *Lincoln*, 41–42; Paul Simon, *Lincoln's Preparation for Greatness: The Illinois Years* (1965; rpt., Urbana, 1971), 3–6; Carwardine, *Lincoln*, 6; William Gienapp, *Abraham Lincoln and Civil War America: A Biography* (New York, 2002), 8, 12; AL, Communication to the People of Sangamo County, Mar. 9, 1832, CWAL, 1: 5–9; Maurice G. Baxter, *Henry Clay and the American System* (Lexington, 1995), 25–32; Michael F. Holt, *The Rise and Fall of the American Whig Party: Jacksonian Politics and the Onset of the Civil War* (New York, 1999), 28, 35; Gabor S. Boritt, *Lincoln and the Economics of the American Dream* (1978; rpt., Urbana, 1994), 99. Most politicians in 1832 still considered themselves "Republicans," the name that Jefferson's party had gone by.

[12] Dennis F. Hanks to WHH, Dec. 27, 1865, Joshua F. Speed to WHH, Jan. 12, 1866, Usher F. Linder undated statement, 569, 146–47, 156, in Wilson and Davis, ed., *Herndon's Informants*, 569, 146–47, 156; George D. Prentice, *Biography of Henry Clay* (New York, 1831); Donald, *Lincoln*, 26; Douglas L. Wilson, *Lincoln before Washington: New Perspectives on the Illinois Years* (1997; rpt., Urbana, 1998), 8; AL to Dr. Edward Wallace, Oct. 11, 1859 (copy), Herndon-Weik Collection of Lincolniana, Division of Manuscripts, LC, Reel 1; Lowell H. Harrison, *Lincoln of Kentucky* (2000; rpt., Lexington, 2009), 69; Anson G. Henry et al., Aug. 29, 1842, *The Papers of Henry Clay*, ed. Robert Seager II (Lexington, 1988), 9: 760; Executive Committee, Clay Club, Springfield, to Henry Clay, Aug. 29, 1842, CWAL, 1: 297; Jean H. Baker, *Mary Todd Lincoln: A Biography* (New York, 1987), 34; Catherine Clinton, *Mrs. Lincoln: A Life* (New York, 2009), 11, 17; WHH to Jesse W. Weik, Nov. 24, 1862, Hertz, ed., *Hidden Lincoln*, 89. John Rowan Herndon, cousin to Lincoln's law partner, said that Clay was Lincoln's "favorite of all the great men of the Nation he allbut [sic] worshiped his name." John Rowan Herndon to WHH, May 28, 1865, in Wilson and Davis, *Herndon's Informants*, 8.

rallied to the support of Latin American revolutions against Spanish (and in the case of Brazil, Portuguese) rule in the years following the War of 1812. Clay applauded the insurrectionists in Congress, urged aid to them short of military intervention, and backed official U.S. recognition of the insurgents' regimes. In 1824, when fellow congressmen disapproved of an amended resolution declaring sympathy for Greek resistance to Turkish rule, Clay ridiculed their caution, saying that his own lips had "not yet learned the sycophantic language of a degraded slave." Following Clay's death in 1852, Lincoln would eulogize Clay, lauding him for championing freedom abroad: "When Greece rose against the Turks and struck for liberty, his name was mingled with the battle-cry of freedom. When South America threw off the thraldom of Spain, his speeches were read at the head of her armies by Bolivar," Lincoln reflected, in claiming Clay's memory for the world.[13]

What did Clay's story tell Lincoln about territorial expansion? Clay and other prominent Whigs generally did not oppose territorial growth in principle, and sometimes their expansionist rhetoric sounded as strident as Democrats'. Arguing for annexation of Spanish West Florida, Clay not only claimed U.S. title over it, but suggested that by principles of self-determination his country could seize any adjacent European colony whose transfer to another power threatened its stability. In the War of 1812, when U.S. House Speaker, Clay wished Canada retained if American military forces took it. Decades later, U.S. Senator William Seward of New York, one of the best-known Whigs in America, enthused excessively that American borders should extend to "greet the sun when he touches the tropics, and when he sends his gleaming rays towards the polar circle, and shall include even distant islands in either ocean"![14]

The difference between Democrats and Whigs had less to do with the desirability of growing the nation than its urgency. Whigs gave less priority than Democrats to expansion. They worried more than their rivals about incorporating foreign peoples, especially Catholics – who many Whigs feared were pliant tools of the pope – into the American body

[13] Arthur P. Whitaker, *The United States and the Independence of Latin America, 1800–1830* (1941; rpt., New York, 1964), 343–48; David C. Hendrickson, *Union, Nation, or Empire: The American Debate over International Relations, 1789–1941* (Lawrence, 2009), 78–79; *Annals of Congress*, 18 Cong., 1 Sess., 1170–78; AL, "Eulogy on Henry Clay," CWAL, 2: 121–32.
[14] Brian Loveman, *No Higher Law: American Foreign Policy and the Western Hemisphere since 1776* (Chapel Hill, 2010), 26; Ernest N. Paolino, *The Foundations of the American Empire: William Henry Seward and U.S. Foreign Policy* (Ithaca, 1973), 7.

politic and giving them the right to vote, hold office, and shape policy. Whigs also vexed themselves about the economic costs of waging war for empire and whether new territory might divide Americans over slavery's status in acquired regions. In his famous "Raleigh letter" of 1844, Clay opposed the immediate annexation of the independent Republic of Texas because of costs to the nation's treasury it would incur and because it would likely provoke war with Mexico (which still claimed ownership of Texas). But Clay hardly ruled out eventual U.S. possession of Texas; rather, he opposed taking it "at the present time." This gradualist approach was typical of Whig expansionism. In 1852, Millard Fillmore, America's last Whig president, would reject a U.S. "tripartite" guarantee – with Britain and France – of Spain's ownership of Cuba, because it would have tied U.S. hands in the long run.[15]

Being a Henry Clay Whig, therefore, nudged Lincoln toward an anti-imperial agenda, but not ironclad opposition to territorial growth. Still, it would be reductionist to imply that Lincoln's foreign policy thinking was simply Clay's. When Lincoln in his eulogy recalled Clay's inspirational, warmongering speeches in Congress prior to the War of 1812, he praised his hero for defying the "British Lion" and upholding America's honor but failed to laud Clay's wartime calls for Canada.[16]

Before the mid-1840s, neither Stephen Douglas nor Abraham Lincoln said much of anything about U.S. foreign affairs, much less Latin America, which is unsurprising since both men were state-level officeholders immersed in domestic policy matters. When Lincoln in an 1838 speech alluded to the military impossibility of foreign nations invading America and crushing its freedom, he tellingly predicted that even the combined "armies of Europe, Asia and Africa" commanded by a Bonaparte would be unable to accomplish such a feat – as if he was not aware of Latin America's existence.[17] On the other hand, both men staked out

[15] Major L. Wilson, *Space, Time and Freedom: The Quest for Nationality and the Irrepressible Conflict, 1815–1861* (Westport, CT, 1974), 94–119; Frederick Merk, *Manifest Destiny and Mission in American History: A Reinterpretation* (New York, 1963), 39–40; Michael Morrison, *Slavery and the American West: The Eclipse of Manifest Destiny and the Coming of the Civil War* (Chapel Hill, 1997), 72–73; Watson, *Liberty and Power*, 245; Glyndon G. Van Deusen, *The Life of Henry Clay* (Boston, 1937), 365–67, 373–76; Paolino, *Foundations*, 12–13. David S. Heidler and Jeanne T. Heidler, *Henry Clay: The Essential American* (New York, 2010), 315.

[16] AL, Eulogy, 127.

[17] AL, Address before the Young Men's Lyceum of Springfield, Illinois, January 27, 1838, CWAL, 1: 109.

preliminary positions on slavery, presaging their later differences about human bondage in Latin America.

Douglas had not remained long at Canandaigua, New York. Arriving there toward the end of 1830, he studied and apprenticed at law, but in 1833 he headed west, where it was easier to get licensed for the law than in New York. By year's end, he had settled in Jacksonville, a booming county seat in central Illinois. Douglas briefly earned an income as a schoolteacher in nearby Winchester and in March 1834 passed a ridiculously easy examination before a judge on the Illinois Supreme Court. This gained him a legal certificate despite having a rudimentary knowledge at best of the law. Immediately establishing a practice in Jacksonville, the curly-headed, stocky, tobacco-chewing Douglas identified instinctively with Illinois's mostly frontier, informal, nondeferential mores and plunged into local politics. Apparently his lifetime nickname – "Little Giant" (an allusion to his shortness, disproportionately large head, and formidable presence) – took hold as early as 1834.

Early on, Douglas mastered an unusually combative and sometimes demagogic speaking style (reportedly buffeted by imbibing quantities of alcohol), anchored in a mastery of numbers and details, as well as an egalitarian commitment to white political and social democracy. Once, he attributed his political success to his willingness to drink, lodge, hunt, and pray with constituents who lived in one-room homes, as well as to "eat their corn dodgers and fried bacon, and sleep two in a bed with them." Douglas's love of speechmaking and the give-and-take of politics became so legendary that one newspaper sarcastically explained that he attended a public funeral because an audience would be there he could harangue. Sometimes, Douglas played loose with the facts, but his speeches always projected an ability to process huge amounts of information and in 1835 he gained election as Illinois state attorney for its First Judicial District. That same year, Douglas helped organize the first Democratic Party convention ever in his county. In 1836, Douglas was elected to the state legislature for a term in Vandalia, the state capital, that December.[18]

By then, Lincoln was already a seasoned officeholder. Successful in his second legislative race in 1834, he served in the December 1834–February 1835 session. During the state's tenth legislative session in 1836–37, Lincoln and Douglas became acquainted, serving together on the House

---

[18] Johannsen, *Douglas*, 15–46, 79, 115–16; James L. Huston, *Stephen A. Douglas and the Dilemmas of Democratic Equality* (Lanham, MD, 2007), 5–6, 13, 18, 34; *Chicago Herald*, Feb. 25, 1845; *Augusta* (GA) *Chronicle*, July 7, 1840.

of Representatives' Penitentiary Committee and a special committee (chaired by Lincoln) to consider the creation of a new county. They also jointly attended a state education convention. During deliberations in the General Assembly, they found occasional common ground, but often disagreed, notably over banking measures but also on slavery's future in America and the legitimacy of the growing movement to abolish it.[19]

Slavery had plagued the American polity since the country's beginning, causing serious disputes at the Constitutional Convention of 1787 and intermittently dividing the U.S. Congress afterward. In 1819–20, such divisions threatened to break up the nation, when the Missouri Territory, originally a part of the Louisiana Purchase, applied for admission as a new slave state. James Tallmadge, a representative from New York, proposed an amendment to the Missouri enabling bill that would have gradually terminated slavery there, challenging a congressional tradition of admitting states that wanted to have slavery. That crisis was resolved by the so-called Missouri Compromise of 1820, which dropped the gradual abolition plan, paired the admission of Maine as a free state with Missouri's admission as a slave state, and drew a geographical line separating free from slave territory through the entire Louisiana Purchase. The deal stipulated that slavery would be prohibited in all remaining territory above the parallel of 36°30' (Missouri's southern border), implicitly blessing slavery below the line. Since most of nine future states lay in territory above the line and only what became Oklahoma and Arkansas lay below the line, the North got the better end of the bargain.[20]

Afterward, the issue of slavery continued festering, and when, because of the growing abolition movement in the North, it spilled over into the Illinois legislative session of 1836–37, Lincoln and Douglas felt compelled to take their first public stands on the issue. Earlier, it had seemed possible that U.S. slavery would gradually die out; many southern politicians had conceded slavery's evil nature, and the institution appeared economically unsustainable over the long run. This was especially true in parts of the Upper South where constant plantings of tobacco exhausted nutrients in the soil and caused slaveholders to turn to less labor-intensive crops like wheat. By the late eighteenth and early nineteenth centuries,

---

[19] Simon, *Lincoln's Preparation for Greatness*, 17, 27, 34, 56–57, 113, 115; Johannsen, *Douglas*, 30–31. Ronald White and Allen C. Guelzo differ on whether Douglas and Lincoln initially met during the 1834–35 session. White, *A. Lincoln*, 72; Allen C. Guelzo, *Lincoln and Douglas: The Debates That Defined America* (New York, 2008), 25.

[20] William W. Freehling, *The Road to Disunion*. vol. 1: *Secessionists at Bay, 1776–1854* (New York, 1990), 152.

slaveholders in states like Virginia and Maryland had emancipated thousands of their slaves voluntarily. By 1810, Maryland had more than thirty thousand free African Americans, amounting to 23.3 percent of its total black population. Afterward, though, as the impact of the cotton gin was felt, the southern emancipation movement seemed to stall. The abolition movement was as much a result of the failure of the southern emancipation trend as anything else.[21]

It gradually became apparent after the gin's invention in 1793 not only that southern planters could earn astounding profits from cotton crops where climate and terrain allowed, but also that Upper South slave owners had declining incentives to free surplus slaves. Why emancipate excess slaves who could be marketed to Deep South buyers desperate for more cotton laborers, a need exacerbated by Congress's decision in 1808 to criminalize the African slave trade? As evidence mounted that southerners might never end slavery voluntarily, abolitionism flourished in pockets of the North. In 1831, William Lloyd Garrison launched his famous abolition paper the *Liberator* in Boston, calling for an immediate start upon emancipation and invoking the Declaration of Independence's promise of equality for all men. Over the following winter, Garrison helped form the New England Anti-Slavery Society, which drew many northern free blacks as members, and this was followed by the founding of the American Anti-Slavery Society in 1833 and an explosion of state and local societies. In 1835, the American Anti-Slavery Society mailed enormous numbers of abolitionist publications southward in a futile effort to turn southern public opinion against slaveholding. On the heels of this effort, abolitionists flooded Congress with petitions asking Congress to end slavery in the District of Columbia. Abolitionists considered the capital a particularly egregious target, since slavery and slave trading there brushed the whole country with the South's sin. Furthermore, the federal district, like the territories, seemed more vulnerable to congressional dictate than the southern states themselves. Although slavery is not explicitly mentioned in the Constitution, several of its provisions seemingly upheld the institution at the state level. In contrast, Article I gave Congress power to "exercise exclusive Legislation in all Cases whatsoever" over the U.S. seat of government, and Article IV granted Congress the right "to dispose of and make all needful Rules and Regulations" for federal territory.

[21] Ira Berlin, *Slaves without Masters: The Free Negro in the Antebellum South* (1974; rpt., New York, 1976), 46–47.

What led Lincoln and Douglas into slavery politics in 1836–37 was the furious southern reaction to the antislavery campaigns. Unwilling to concede slavery's horrors, southerners damned abolitionists for what they considered tampering with their property. Abolitionists, in their eyes, spread subversive doctrines that would cause otherwise faithful slaves to become disloyal, even possibly to revolt. Nat Turner's rebellion in Virginia in 1831, the bloodiest slave uprising before the Civil War, erupted seven months after the *Liberator*'s first issue, and to southerners the timing seemed no coincidence. Abolitionists, therefore, needed silencing. Georgia legislators announced a $5,000 reward for anyone kidnapping Garrison to Georgia for trial. In 1835, a mob of angry Charlestonians confiscated from U.S. postal authorities and burned abolitionist literature arriving in the city. In 1836, southern congressmen and compliant northerners began stifling debate on the petitions for emancipation in the federal district by enacting procedural changes that collectively became known as "gag" rules. The House of Representatives provided that petitions relating to slavery be tabled without being printed or afterward considered; the Senate suppressed debate by tabling the very question of whether or not to receive antislavery petitions.

All this had repercussions for Douglas and Lincoln because southern complaints struck a sympathetic chord with conservative northerners who worried abolitionist provocations would estrange slaveholders from the Union, causing its dissolution. Mob persecutions of abolitionists occurred in several northern cities, and the antiabolitionist backlash infected Illinois. In the south Illinois town of Alton late in 1837, an antiabolition mob set on fire the building housing editor Elijah P. Lovejoy's antislavery paper, the *Observer*. Moreover, Lovejoy was shot and killed as he attempted to flee the burning structure.[22]

Trying to calm the waters, Illinois lawmakers responded in January 1837 to requests from southern legislatures and Connecticut that they act against the movement. Illinois's General Assembly passed antiabolitionist resolutions by an overwhelming vote of 77–6 in the House and a unanimous 18–0 in the Senate, which reassured southerners of their "deep

---

[22] William J. Cooper, Jr., *The South and the Politics of Slavery, 1828–1856* (Baton Rouge, 1978), 58–64; William Lee Miller, *Arguing about Slavery: The Great Battle in the United States Congress* (New York, 1996); Fawn M. Brodie, "Who Defends the Abolitionist?" in *The Antislavery Vanguard: New Essays on the Abolitionists*, ed. Martin Duberman (Princeton, NJ, 1965), 58; Daniel Wirls, "'The Only Mode of Avoiding Everlasting Debate': The Overlooked Senate Gag Rule for Antislavery Petitions," *Journal of the Early Republic* 27 (Spring 2007): 115–38.

regard and affection for our brethren [read this white slaveholding masters] of the South." The resolutions promised to assist southerners should an emergency arise and expressed strong disapproval of abolition societies and their doctrines. Lincoln cast the very first nay vote in the House of Representatives *against* these resolutions, eighteen votes after Douglas gave them his support. Then, on March 3, Lincoln unnecessarily but purposely drew attention to his dissenting position by submitting a formal written protest to the House (cosigned by a colleague). Conceding that Congress lacked power to make policy regarding slavery in the southern states themselves, Lincoln affirmed its right to end slave labor in the District of Columbia and condemned slavery as "founded on both injustice and bad policy." The statement included qualifications differentiating Lincoln from the very abolitionists his wording seemingly defended: it conceded southern arguments that abolition agitation was counterproductive because it made defensive southern slaveholders tighten up restrictions on slaves as precautionary measures, making their daily lives more difficult; it also urged that Congress refrain from abolition in the District of Columbia without the consent of its inhabitants. Still, Lincoln's censure of antislavery agitation stopped short of stifling abolitionists' right to speak, and he soon made another important statement on the topic.[23]

Around this time, Lincoln moved to Springfield (the new state capital by a state legislative vote in February 1837) and set up a legal practice in the village as partner of John Todd Stuart, taking a bed in a room above the store of Joshua F. Speed, a merchant and Kentucky native. Until 1841, Lincoln lived there, sharing the room with Speed and Speed's clerks, including William H. Herndon, with whom Lincoln would form a partnership in 1844. A year after arriving, Lincoln addressed the Springfield Young Men's Lyceum, a nineteenth-century version of today's adult education programs, on "The Perpetuation of Our Political Institutions."

The speech fascinates on many levels, partly for what it possibly says about his rivalry with Douglas. The previous month, Lincoln had expressed competitive attitudes about the Little Giant, noting in a letter that Whigs in Springfield had "adopted it as part of our policy here, to never speak of Douglass at all." What did Lincoln mean at the Lyceum

[23] William Lee Miller, *Lincoln's Virtues: An Ethical Biography* (New York, 2002), 116–18; Burlingame, *Abraham Lincoln: A Life*, 1: 122; White, *A. Lincoln*, 75. Noting that Lincoln waited until the end of the session to put his antislavery case on the record, precluding debate on it, Douglas L. Wilson emphasizes the weak nature of Lincoln's initiative. Wilson, *Honor's Voice: The Transformation of Abraham Lincoln* (New York, 1999), 164–66.

when he vaguely envisioned a particularly precarious time in America's quest for political liberty when "men of ... ambition" would arise to "strike the blow, and overturn" a government that for some five decades had been "the fondest hope, of the lovers of freedom, throughout the world"? What "man possessed of the loftiest genius" and "ambition sufficient to push it to its utmost stretch," he wondered, would aspire to become America's Alexander, Napoleon, or Caesar and in pursuit of fame try to subvert America's "government and laws"? Though historians have had a field day projecting all sorts of psychological interpretations on Lincoln's remarks, possibly his speech indicted Douglas without specifying him as a means of circumventing the Lyceum's rules against partisan content.

Whether or not Lincoln meant to besmirch Douglas, his address bears significance as an addendum to Lincoln's position on abolitionism in the legislature. In elaborating the Union's endangered state, Lincoln lamented a nationwide surge of mob violence, mentioning mobs' throwing "printing presses into rivers" and shooting editors – a barely disguised allusion to the persecution and killing of the abolitionist editor Lovejoy in Alton. Lovejoy's printing presses had been ruined three times by mobs prior to the fateful night when he was killed. Lincoln ingenuously argued it would be proper to take legal action against the dissemination of abolitionist doctrine *if* abolition doctrine was "wrong," but he emphasized that the "interposition" of mob action against abolitionists was always inexcusable and unjustifiable and maintained that abolitionists merited "the protection of all law and all good citizens" if what they wanted was "right within itself."[24]

Why Lincoln made his dramatic pronouncement against slavery in 1837, however hedged by qualifiers, remains a puzzle. Toward the end of his life, Lincoln said in a private letter that he was "naturally anti-slavery" and could "not remember when I did not so think, and feel," inferring that something in his childhood made him that way. Thomas and Nancy Lincoln had never acquired any slaves, even though Thomas was a relatively large landholder for his vicinity in Kentucky. In 1808, a year before Abraham's birth, Thomas and Nancy had joined a faction of congregants who split off from their church because of a dispute over

---

[24] White, *A. Lincoln*, 81; Burlingame, *Abraham Lincoln: A Life*, 1: 116–17, 131, 140, 311; AL, "The Perpetuation of Our Political Institutions," Jan. 27, 1838, AL to William A. Minshall, Dec. 7, 1837, CWAL, 1: 107, 108–15; Gerald Sorin, *Abolitionism: A New Perspective* (New York, 1972), 91.

slavery and founded a new church presided over by an antislavery minister. As Ronald White points out, it is not hard to imagine antislavery sermons being discussed in Abraham Lincoln's childhood home, perhaps affecting Lincoln's formative attitudes. Several Lincoln biographers have attributed Thomas Lincoln's move from Kentucky to Indiana to a desire to escape a slave society for a free one; Hardin County, Kentucky, where Lincoln spent his boyhood years, had 1,007 slaves as compared to 1,627 whites, according to tax listings in 1811. Though bordering on Kentucky, Indiana, like Illinois, fell under the antislavery Northwest Ordinance of 1787, and its state constitution of 1816, the year the Lincolns migrated, prohibited slavery. So did the Illinois constitution of two years later. Lincoln, however, never attributed his antislavery feelings to his father, though he autobiographically observed that his father moved to Spencer County, Indiana, in 1816 "partly on account of slavery" though the main cause related to the uncertainty of land titles in Kentucky at the time.[25]

Did Lincoln's reading or travel turn him against slavery? If we can believe a tentative remembrance by his stepsister, the young Lincoln read William Grimshaw's *History of the United States* (1820), which contained antislavery passages calling for the fulfillment of the Declaration of Independence's affirmation of human equality. However, Lincoln made flatboat trips to New Orleans for business purposes in 1828 and 1831, and they more likely molded his animus against slavery. Lincoln's cousin John Hanks, who accompanied Lincoln on the latter trip, told William Herndon during an interview after Lincoln's death that in New Orleans they had seen "Negroes Chained – maltreated – whipt & scourged," and that Lincoln had turned suddenly silent from his sadness over the sight. Hanks thought the 1831 trip generated Lincoln's hatred of slavery.[26]

Perhaps the most important conclusion to be drawn from Lincoln's stand in the 1837 legislature is that it foreshadowed the direction and limitations of his moderately antislavery career in the 1840s and 1850s, when he proclaimed his hatred of slavery without embracing abolitionism. In 1841, after visiting Joshua Speed's plantation near Louisville, Kentucky, Lincoln sent Speed's half sister a letter mentioning an incident on their return to Illinois, when aboard a boat going to St. Louis he

[25] AL to Albert G. Hodges, Apr. 4, 1864, CWAL, 1: 281; White, *A. Lincoln*, 14, 17; WHH interview of Matilda Johnston Moore, Sept. 8, 1865, Wilson and Davis, eds., *Herndon's Informants*, 109; White, *A Lincoln*, 33; Donald, *Lincoln*, 31; AL, Autobiography Written for John L. Scripps, c. June 1860, CWAL, 4: 61–62.
[26] White, *A. Lincoln*, 33; Donald, *Lincoln*, 31; Carwardine, *Lincoln*, 18; WHH interview of John Hanks, 1865–66, Wilson and Davis, eds., *Herndon's Informants*, 456–57.

and Speed had observed twelve slaves, chained together in two groups of six, who seemed remarkably cheerful for people being transported from Kentucky to a farm farther south. In reflections worthy of an abolitionist tract, Lincoln expressed empathy for slavery's victims, noting that they were in the process of being "separated forever from the scenes of their childhood, their friends, their fathers and mothers, and brothers and sisters" to labor in a region (Lincoln likely meant the Louisiana sugar-cane country) notorious for "ruthless and unrelenting" masters. Fourteen years later, Lincoln told Speed that the sight of the shackled remained "a continual torment to me." During a temperance lecture in Springfield, Lincoln imagined the glorious day "when there shall be neither a slave nor a drunkard" anywhere on earth.[27] But he never embraced the abolitionist crusade against slavery in the states where it already existed, deferring always to the protections for slavery within the U.S. Constitution; he took strong positions against slavery's claims only where it lacked constitutional insurance.

Conversely, Douglas indicated by his vote for the legislature's antiabolitionist resolutions that he cared more about the claims of slave owners than slaves' sufferings or their natural rights to freedom. Douglas's acquaintance George Murray McConnell claimed long after the Little Giant's death that during the winter of 1853–54, Douglas had privately stigmatized slavery as a "curse beyond computation" for *both* blacks and whites and even predicted the inevitability of its disappearance in his country. But Douglas never took meaningful steps toward its abolition, and if we credit McConnell's account we must also note he reported that immediately after denouncing slavery, Douglas remarked that since slavery was constitutional he saw no way to end it but through war. This he would shrink from since he regarded "the integrity of this political Union as worth more to humanity than the whole black race."[28]

Still, the Lincoln–Douglas gap on slavery remained narrow for many years, as became apparent just before and after Douglas's election as state Supreme Court justice by the legislature in 1841. Merely twenty-seven years old, Douglas had responsibility for holding court in the state's west central region, the Fifth Judicial Circuit, which included a couple of towns, Quincy (where Douglas took up part-year residence)

[27] AL to Mary Speed, Sept. 27, 1841, AL, Temperance Address, Feb. 22, 1842, CWAL, 1: 259–60, 259n, 260n, 279; AL to Joshua Speed, Aug. 24, 1855, Herndon-Weik Collection of Lincolniana, Reel 1.
[28] George Murray McConnell, "Recollections of Stephen A. Douglas," *Transactions of the Illinois State Historical Society* (1900): 49.

and Galesburg, where abolitionists were noticeably active. Meanwhile, Lincoln remained in the legislature until he announced in 1842 that he would decline running again. Instead, he set his sights on being elected in 1843 to represent the new Illinois Seventh Congressional District in the U.S. House of Representatives, a quest that failed when his backers were outmaneuvered at the Whig county nominating convention.[29]

Throughout this period, the Lincoln–Douglas rivalry simmered, though remarkably their strained relations never erupted in physical violence. In 1838, as an attorney for an accused murderer in a Sangamon Circuit Court case, Lincoln bested Douglas, the prosecuting attorney. The same year, Lincoln assisted John Todd Stuart's victorious congressional campaign against Douglas. Lincoln filled in for Stuart in a debate with Douglas when Stuart became ill and possibly authored pseudonymous letters attacking Douglas in the local *Sangamo Journal*. Late in 1839, Lincoln participated with other Whig politicians against Douglas and other Democrats in a series of debates, in the form of alternate speeches, in Springfield. In December, as the first legislative session held in Springfield convened, Lincoln alluded to Douglas's nickname in a barbed report to Stuart. He quipped, "The Democratic giant is here; but he is not now worth talking about." Still he reacted irritably when fewer people turned out for his (and the Whigs') final speech in the series than when Douglas spoke previously. During the 1840 presidential election, Lincoln debated Douglas on a couple of occasions to promote the Whig presidential candidate William Henry Harrison over the candidacy of the incumbent Democratic president Martin Van Buren, and sometimes the tension between them caught press attention.[30]

During the canvass, Lincoln retreated from whatever compassion he had earlier shown abolitionists when championing their free speech rights. The national election revolved primarily around economic issues and the politics of personality; this was the famous "Log Cabin" campaign when

[29] Huston, *Douglas and the Dilemmas of Democratic Equality*, 18, 21, 27–28; Johannsen, *Douglas*, 55–60, 64–68, 87, 93–97; Burlingame, *Abraham Lincoln: A Life*, 1: 119–23.

[30] Roy Morris Jr., *The Long Pursuit: Abraham Lincoln's Thirty-Year Struggle with Stephen Douglas for the Heart and Soul of America* (New York, 2008), 1–2; Guelzo, *Lincoln and Douglas*, 29–30; White, *A. Lincoln*, 82–83, 90; Burlingame, *Abraham Lincoln: A Life*, 1: 139, 142, 154–60; AL to the Editor of the Chicago *American*, June 24, 1859, AL to John T. Stuart, Dec. 23, 1839, CWAL, 1: 151, 152n, 159; Wilson, *Honor's Voice*, 198–200; *Sangamo Journal* quoted in Simon, *Lincoln's Preparation for Greatness*, 214. Speaking on banking policy in December 1839, Lincoln accused Douglas of false assertions and said Douglas "indulged himself in a contemptuous expression of pity for me." AL Speech on the Sub-Treasury, Dec. 26 [?], 1839, CWAL, 1: 160, 172, 173, 174, 177.

Democrats attacked Harrison with the fabricated claim that he lived in a simple log cabin and was too unsophisticated to serve as president, causing Whigs to respond that Harrison's very touch with the common man would make him a great president. Partisans of both men, however, appealed to northern conservatives and southern voters by casting the opposing candidate as being a racial egalitarian who sought slavery's abolition. Though born in Virginia, Harrison had become an Ohioan and was vulnerable to charges by Democrats, including Douglas, of being subversively abolitionist because he had favored colonizing slaves in Africa. Van Buren was smeared as championing racial equality because he had backed black suffrage at the New York Constitutional Convention of 1821 and because his partner on the Democratic ticket, incumbent vice president Richard M. Johnson of Kentucky, had lived openly with a mulatto woman with whom he had fathered children and had taken up with a mulatto mistress after the first woman's death. Lincoln claimed in speeches and debates that Van Buren was unsuited for the presidency because he had supported "Negro Suffrage under certain limitations." The New Yorker's "breath smells rank with devotion to the cause of Africa's sons," Lincoln charged, claiming Van Buren wore "the sable furs of Guinea." Douglas responded by denying Van Buren's support for black suffrage.[31] To carry Harrison to victory, Lincoln catered to rather than challenged the prejudices of Illinois voters.

Although some lawyers in Illinois welcomed litigation in which they could assist fugitive slaves (including William Herndon, who represented accused runaways on a pro bono basis), Lincoln was not one of them. There was barely any distance between him and Douglas over masters' claims to escaped slaves. In his new capacity as "Judge Douglas," a title that stuck, the young justice sustained slave owners' claims, as when an abolitionist physician in Quincy was arrested for helping a runaway evade capture. Douglas upheld Illinois's fugitive slave law as a legitimate exercise of the state's police power and assessed a fine against the doctor to dissuade others from similar conduct. Assisting slave owners in recovering legal property, however, was not the same as helping them to obtain illegal property. When Lincoln represented a black female child in the *Bailey* v. *Cromwell* case (1841) before Douglas's court, he claimed an attempt to sell her in Illinois was illegal. Douglas concurred, liberating

---

[31] Huston, *Douglas and the Dilemmas of Democratic Equality*, 21; AL speech at Tremont, Illinois, May 2, 1840, CWAL, 1: 210; Lincoln quoted in Burlingame, *Abraham Lincoln: A Life*, 1: 154–55.

her on the logic that Illinois law presumed "that every person was free, without regard to color" within state borders. Neither Lincoln nor Douglas fought Illinois's fugitive slave legislation. Six years after *Bailey* v. *Cromwell*, Lincoln was counsel for a Kentucky slaveholder named Robert Matson, who had been evading Illinois law against domiciling black slaves by working his Illinois farm with slave labor on a part-year basis but removing them back to Kentucky once the harvest was in. After an abolitionist harbored one of his slaves and her children to prevent them from being sold in Illinois and the slaves were seized and held in custody in the town of Charleston, Lincoln unsuccessfully argued Matson's claim to the slaves in court. He did this even though Matson was on shaky legal ground since the particular slaves in custody had been kept in Illinois continuously for two years *without* breaks in Kentucky. Lincoln's handling of such cases reflected his clients' interests, little more.[32]

In August 1843, Douglas won election to represent the state's Fifth Congressional District in the first session of the Twenty-eighth Congress, convening that December. By the time Douglas took his seat, the Texas annexation issue, simmering for nearly a decade, was threatening to overtake economic policy as the most heated dispute in U.S. politics. In 1835, Anglo-American colonists in Mexico's state of Coahuila and Texas, many of them from U.S. slave states, had become so discontented with Mexican customs regulations and other policies, including initiatives to rid Texas of slavery, that they began what morphed into a full-scale revolution for independence. After Sam Houston's army routed Mexican president, General Antonio López de Santa Anna's forces (and captured Santa Anna) in the Battle of San Jacinto on April 21, 1836, the rebels converted an interim government they had already established into a permanent one. That September, Houston won election as first president of their precariously established republic.

When Houston pursued annexation negotiations with the United States, which a vast majority of Anglo-American Texans favored, however, he got nowhere. Although U.S. president Andrew Jackson officially recognized Texas as an independent republic on March 3, 1837, his last full day in office, he deferred the annexation question, as did his Democratic successor, Martin Van Buren. Antislavery northerners were

---

[32] Eric Foner, *The Fiery Trial: Abraham Lincoln and American Slavery* (New York, 2010), 45–51; Johannsen, *Douglas*, 102–104; Donald, *Lincoln*, 103; Burlingame, *Abraham Lincoln: A Life*, 1: 250–52,

charging that Texas was part of a plot by the South's slaveholding master class – or Slave Power – to dominate the country, and the calculat-
ing Van Buren (the "Little Magician") feared annexation would risk war
with Mexico, jeopardize his reelection chances, and endanger the Union.
Meanwhile, slavery thrived in the new republic under a constitution that
prohibited legislation banning slave imports. Texans had never really
abided by Mexican restrictions on slavery anyway, evading them by sub-
terfuges like classifying new slaves as indentured servants. Independence,
though, opened the floodgates. What had been a black population of
about 3,000 in Texas before independence exploded to at least 12,570 in
1840 and more than 30,000 by 1846.[33]

The annexation stalemate might have lasted indefinitely, since the
rebuffed Texans withdrew their annexation bid in 1838, had it not been
for the policies of Van Buren's second successor, John Tyler, and southerners in Tyler's cabinet. Tyler, a former Democrat who got the Whig vice-
presidential nod in 1840, assumed the presidency in 1841 when William
Henry Harrison became the first U.S. chief executive to die in office. A
states' rights and limited government advocate and a Virginia plantation
owner who probably owned some seven hundred slaves over his lifetime,
Tyler recognized the institution's evils but never voluntarily freed a slave
and rested hopes for its disappearance on the murky theory it might gradually end on its own through diffusion westward: as the nation's black
population thinned out, masters supposedly would become less resistant
to voluntarily freeing their chattels.[34]

When Tyler alienated his party's leadership by vetoing Henry Clay's bill
for a new national bank, disillusioned Whigs began mocking him as "His

---

[33] Johannsen, *Douglas*, 116–22; David E. Narrett, "A Choice of Destiny: Immigration
Policy, Slavery, and the Annexation of Texas," *Southwestern Historical Quarterly* 100
(Jan. 1997): 274–302; John M. Belohlavek, *"Let the Eagle Soar!": The Foreign Policy
of Andrew Jackson* (Lincoln, NE, 1985), 233–34; Richard Bruce Winders, *Crisis in the
Southwest: The United States, Mexico, and the Struggle over Texas* (Wilmington, 2002),
17–28, 80–82; Timothy J. Henderson, *A Glorious Defeat: Mexico and Its War with
the United States* (New York, 2007), 58–59; Randolph B. Campbell, *An Empire for
Slavery: The Peculiar Institution in Texas, 1821–1845* (Baton Rouge, 1989), 21, 23–31,
40, 48–49, 55, 56; Joel H. Silbey, *Storm over Texas: The Annexation Controversy and the
Road to Civil War* (New York, 2005), 10–17; Sam W. Haynes, *Unfinished Revolution:
The Early American Republic in a British World* (Charlottesville, 2010), 220–21; David
M. Pletcher, *The Diplomacy of Annexation: Texas, Oregon, and the Mexican War*
(Columbia, MO, 1973), 74–75, 85.
[34] Edward P. Crapol, *John Tyler: The Accidental President* (Chapel Hill, 2006), 37–38,
58–63, 177–78; Holt, *Rise and Fall of the American Whig Party*, 104; Thomas R.
Hietala, *Manifest Design: Anxious Aggrandizement in Late Jacksonian America* (Ithaca,
1985), 47–49.

Accidency" for his unanticipated promotion to the presidency. Discovering he could not dominate the stubborn Tyler, Clay induced a caucus of Whig senators and congressmen to expel him from their party. Some congressional Whigs even labored to have Tyler impeached. Realizing his renomination hopes in 1844 needed a popular cause to champion, the president settled on Texan annexation, which he favored anyway. As Douglas entered Congress in December 1843, Tyler's secretary of state, Abel P. Upshur, was engaged in annexation machinations. Upshur negotiated a treaty with Texan officials, finalized in late February 1844 and sent to the Senate in April, by which Texas would accede to annexation if the United States afforded immediate protection against an anticipated Mexican retaliatory attack. Further, Upshur authorized diplomatic efforts in London to combat reported British tampering with Texan affairs. Rumor had it that Texas would end slavery in return for a British loan to help with the Republic's national debt. Additionally, the administration secured Andrew Jackson's endorsement of annexation and began lining up the required two-thirds Senate vote on behalf of Upshur's treaty.[35]

Unfortunately for Tyler, the manner in which his administration launched the Texas campaign jeopardized its success by reviving sectional tensions over slavery's expansion, mostly dormant since the Missouri Compromise of 1820. After Upshur's shocking accidental death in February 1844 (from a cannon blowing up on a U.S. warship), Tyler appointed Senator John C. Calhoun of South Carolina as his replacement. A notorious states' rights ideologue and vocal defender of slavery, Calhoun in April sent a letter to Britain's minister in the United States blasting British abolitionism that imperiled the Texas project once the press reprinted it. The letter attacked the rumored British scheme by which Mexico would finally recognize Texan independence if Texans concurred in abolition. Calhoun's letter also praised slavery for civilizing blacks and justified U.S. annexation of Texas as a necessary preemptive step. Were slavery ended in Texas, Calhoun predicted, abolitionism would infiltrate across its eastern border into the southern states.[36]

[35] Crapol, *Tyler*, 176–78, 182, 194–98, 201; Steven E. Woodworth, *Manifest Destinies: America's Westward Expansion and the Road to the Civil War* (New York, 2010), 112–14; Freehling, *Secessionists at Bay*, 1: 394–407; Haynes, *Unfinished Revolution*, 230–41; Morrison, *Slavery and the American West*, 15–16.
[36] Pletcher, *Diplomacy of Annexation*, 118–25; Crapol, *Tyler*, 197; Freehling, *Secessionists at Bay*, 388–410. Although Britain's government decided against actively promoting Texan emancipation, some Londoners, minor British officials, and British travelers in Texas had advocated abolition in the Lone Star Republic. Narrett, "Choice of Destiny," 285–91.

Not all the Democratic propaganda hyping Texas in 1844 was as obviously southern as Calhoun's letter. A twenty-six-page public letter dated January 8, 1844, by Robert J. Walker – Democratic U.S. senator from Mississippi – published in the *Washington Globe* in February, reprinted in other papers, and subsequently a pamphlet that circulated by the millions exposed Americans to a more national (but very racist) idea fundamental to later schemes of colonizing U.S. blacks in the Tropics. A holder of Texas land and a Tyler administration collaborator, Walker claimed annexation would benefit *all* white Americans by draining westward and southward their black populations into Latin America by way of Texas. First, slavery would die in the South, where the soil was already worn out and from which masters would flee if able to relocate in Texas's virgin lands. Then slavery would recede from Texas, as the same process inevitably repeated itself. Ultimately, virtually all American blacks, even those residing as free people in the North, would seek homes in the Tropics of South America, Central America, and Mexico, where the climate was suited for their African physiology and where they could experience equality. Walker enthused that because "colored races" made up 90 percent of the population in the Tropics, darker-skinned people there were not given the same "degraded caste" as they received in the United States. Without annexation, the same no-longer-needed southern slaves would instead migrate northward, driving down workingmen's wages and causing an upsurge in crime.

Walker's pamphlet helped sway many fence swingers into thinking that giving Texas statehood would benefit the country and not just the South – though not quickly enough to save Upshur's treaty, which failed overwhelmingly in a Senate vote in June. Tyler's second term hopes also faded over the summer. Although a tiny third party nominated the president for reelection, he dropped out of the race in August and endorsed the regular Democratic nominee, James K. Polk of Tennessee. That slaveholding former House speaker and Jackson protégé narrowly beat Clay in the fall 1844 election, running on a flagrantly expansionist platform linking northerners' territorial goals with southerners' Texas ambitions. The Democratic platform boldly posited that the country's "title to the whole Territory of Oregon" (which then extended much farther up the Pacific coast than today's state) was "clear and unquestionable" and that the nation ought to complete the "reoccupation of Oregon and the reannexation of Texas at the earliest practicable period" – an allusion to Thomas Jefferson's claim that Texas was within the Louisiana Purchase of 1803. Reannexation implied that Texas remained U.S. territory from the Louisiana Purchase until 1819, when Secretary of State John Quincy Adams alienated it in the Adams-Onís Treaty with Spain that acquired Florida. Thus, Texas needed to be repossessed.

Polk's ensuing close election victory created the necessary precondition for annexation. Creatively construing the election results as a mandate for Texas, the lame-duck Tyler recommended in his final annual message that Congress pass a joint resolution letting him implement the already-negotiated Texas annexation treaty, a clever way of bypassing the Constitution's required two-thirds vote for Senate ratification of treaties. Congress then passed a resolution allowing the president either to follow through with annexation or to negotiate a new treaty. Tyler chose the former. Just before leaving office in March 1845, he alerted Texas that it could now join the Union. Texas's Congress unanimously accepted Tyler's offer, and a specially convened Texan convention endorsed annexation on July 4. Finally, in December 1845, with Polk now in the White House, the U.S. Congress made Texas a state by joint resolution.[37]

When Stephen Douglas in 1844 realized the popularity of territorial expansion in his part of the country, especially among fellow Democrats, he identified himself with the cresting movement. Initially favoring former president Martin Van Buren for the 1844 Democratic presidential nomination, Douglas and many other midwestern Democrats grew disenchanted after Van Buren released a public letter in the *Washington Globe* on April 27 against annexing Texas unless Mexico relented in its opposition. This document devastated Van Buren's front-runner's status and helped pave the way for Polk's nomination. Prior to the Democratic nominating convention in Baltimore, which opened May 27, Douglas leaned to Lewis Cass, the expansionist U.S. senator from Michigan. Afterward, at a public meeting on May 31, he endorsed Polk and the party's expansionist agenda. In a House speech on June 3, Douglas defended American claims to the Oregon country, then jointly occupied with Great Britain. After explaining why Americans required the entire Oregon Territory because of its natural resources, rich soil, and strategic location in regard to trade with the East Indies and China, he turned to Texas. For the first time, Douglas presented himself as a nationalist expansionist ideologue

[37] Frederick Merk with the collaboration of Lois Bannister Merk, *Fruits of Propaganda in the Tyler Administration* (Cambridge, 1971), 23–24, 98–104, 221–52; Crapol, *Tyler*, 203–206, 218–20; Woodworth, *Manifest Destinies*, 121–22, 131–32, 139–41; Freehling, *Secessionists at Bay*, 418–20; Silbey, *Storm over Texas*, 33–35.

and strident Anglophobe. He also displayed sensitivity as a northerner for southern plantation interests.

Praising candidate Polk as a "zealous, firm, and unwavering advocate of reannexation," Douglas made a partisan, geographically constructed argument of national security in justifying his country's need for Texas. He dredged up evidence suggesting that Whig nominee Clay, who in April had issued his public letter ambiguously opposing annexation "at this time," suffered from a credibility gap since he had supported U.S. claims to Texas earlier in his career; and he lambasted remarks by former president John Quincy Adams, now a Whig congressman, suggesting that the United States would be unwise to wage war should Britain attempt to annex Texas and Cuba. Douglas argued that such weakness amounted to national suicide since U.S. navigation of the Mississippi River and commerce in the Gulf of Mexico would be at risk should the Texas Republic or Spain's colony fall into unfriendly hands. Britain already held sway in Oregon, despite America's superior claims, plus it controlled forts on the Canadian frontier and the Bahamas and Bermuda off the Atlantic coast. From Douglas's vantage point, the United States was already dangerously surrounded. Britain's next step would be to finish encircling America by dominating Texas, likely by offering Texans duty-free export of their cotton into English ports in return for Texas imposing no more than minimal duties on British manufactures. Though Douglas's remarks were calculated to appeal to northern manufacturers hoping to sell goods to Texas, they were especially aimed at cotton planters in the South, since Britain was the most important overseas market for slave state cotton. Dramatically, Douglas predicted that southern cotton planters would become uncompetitive and literally ruined if Britain took over Texas. Finally, Douglas called upon his nation "to embrace the 'present golden opportunity' to extend the principles of civil and religious liberty" over Texas.[38]

Douglas's flourish about his country's mission to give other places its political system and religious freedom anticipated the ideology of Manifest Destiny about to sweep the country (Figure 1.1). In backing America's claim to Oregon, he envisioned the entire area "peopled with American citizens, enjoying the blessings of equal laws and republican institutions." The concept that American representative democracy and

---

[38] Johannsen, *Douglas*, 143–47; *Washington* (DC) *Daily National Intelligencer*, June 3, 1844; CG, 28 Cong., 1 Sess., Appendix, 599–602; Woodworth, *Manifest Destinies*, 125–26, 132–36.

FIGURE I.I Stephen A. Douglas.
From Sara Agnes Rice Pryor, *My Day: Reminiscences of a Long Life* (New York: The Macmillan Company, 1909), p. 85.

religious traditions bested other forms of government and religious customs (especially Catholicism, which many Americans considered a repressive, exploitative faith), and that it was therefore obvious (or "manifest") that the United States had God's blessing to prosper and enlarge, dated to the earliest days of the American Republic. The specific term "Manifest Destiny," however, awaited the Texas annexation question's final stages. An unsigned article, "Annexation," appeared in the July–August 1845 number of the *Democratic Review* (formally the *United States Magazine and Democratic Review*), a Democratic magazine edited by John L. O'Sullivan and published in New York City, which contended that opponents of Texan annexation should cease obstructing it since other nations wished to thwart "the fulfilment [*sic*] of our manifest destiny to overspread the continent allotted by Providence for the free development of our yearly multiplying millions."[39]

During the heated political campaigns of 1844, besides campaigning, successfully, in Illinois for his own reelection, Douglas traveled to Nashville in August for a mass rally for Polk, giving political addresses in Tennessee before stopping at St. Louis for a three-hour speech on the way home. Again, he called for U.S. acquisition of Oregon and Texas, announcing belligerently that he would accept war with Mexico if caused by annexation of the Lone Star Republic. Then, three weeks after the Twenty-eighth Congress assembled for its second session on December 2, 1844, Douglas assumed a leadership role on Texas. On December 23, Douglas introduced a joint resolution for Texas's "reannexation" to the United States as the "Territory of Texas," which, in anticipation that disputes over Texas's boundaries might cause war with Mexico, authorized the president to try to resolve the issue through negotiations. It also stipulated that once the United States was reimbursed for its administrative costs in Texas, revenues from Texas's public lands and tariffs on imports would be pledged to Texas's public debts up to $10 million, with excess amounts going to U.S. coffers. Section 8 of Douglas's measure especially intrigues, because it specifically extended the Missouri Compromise's 36°30' line to Texas. Later in his career, Douglas would embroil himself in controversy for the very reason that he sponsored legislation, the Kansas-Nebraska Act, specifically repealing the Missouri line. Douglas's Section 8 dedicated Texas to slavery, because only a small fraction of the Texas Republic's territorial claims extended above that latitude.[40]

In a speech on January 6, Douglas used historical precedents to rebut contentions that the outright acquisition of a foreign state was impermissible under the U.S. Constitution and dredged up documents from the 1600s and 1700s to prove that Texas's territory extended southward and westward to the Rio Grande. Once again, he gave a ringing endorsement to the principle of territorial expansion. The *Globe* reported him

[39] John Quincy Adams to Abigail Adams, June 30, 1811, John Quincy Adams to John Adams, August 31, 1811, quoted in Samuel Flagg Bemis, *John Quincy Adams and the Foundations of American Foreign Policy* (1949; rpt., New York, 1973), 182; Merk, *Manifest Destiny and Mission*, 24; Robert W. Johannsen, "The Meaning of Manifest Destiny," in *Manifest Destiny and Empire: American Antebellum Expansionism*, ed. Sam W. Haynes and Christopher Morris (College Station, TX, 1997), 7–9, 15–17; photocopy of "Annexation" editorial in Linda S. Hudson, *Mistress of Manifest Destiny: A Biography of Jane McManus Storm Cazneau, 1807–1878* (Austin, 2001), 61.
[40] *Boston Daily Atlas*, Aug. 15, 1844; Johannsen, *Douglas*, 147–51, CG, 28 Cong., 2 Sess., 64–66; *Washington* (DC) *Daily National Intelligencer*, Dec. 30, 1844.

as arguing that Americans should discard any reservations about gaining new land and saying he hoped "to extend the territory of this republic from the Atlantic to the Pacific, and drive from this continent the last vestige of any foreign power." The only limitation that Douglas imposed upon his country's extension was that it should be done within the constraints of domestic and international law.[41]

On January 25, Douglas tried to author the final wording that would admit Texas to the Union, initially submitting a differently worded resolution as a proposed substitute for one on the floor. He failed to get his version adopted, losing by a close 96–107 vote. However, Douglas did manage by a 109–99 vote to get an amendment linked to the final joint resolution, authored by Tennessee Whig Milton Brown, admitting Texas to the Union. And days later, he made yet another pronouncement of Manifest Destiny's precepts, still months before the term surfaced in the press, in rebutting a Whig congressman's argument that because it would be difficult for the United States to try to govern territory beyond the Rocky Mountain barrier, the United States should encourage Oregon to become a separate republic. Douglas scolded that he did not want to hear the idea of "disunion" promoted again in Congress and claimed the United States needed both Texas and Oregon "like man and wife." Repeating his warnings about Britain's designs on Cuba and Texas, Douglas suggested Britain wanted to turn the North and South against each other over slavery and predicted that steam power would enable U.S. governance of Oregon. In a rhetorical flourish, Douglas called for his nation to control all of North America: "He would blot out the lines on the map which now marked our natural boundaries on this content," the *Globe* recorded, "and make the area of liberty as broad as the continent itself."

Although Douglas's extreme rhetoric solidified his expansionist reputation, in retrospect his unsuccessful resolution on Texas and his successful amendment to Brown's approved Texas resolution seem most memorable for their positions on slavery's part in U.S. territorial growth. Although Douglas's joint resolution in December had applied the Missouri Compromise line to Texas, his unsuccessful resolution of January 25 anticipated his later association with "popular sovereignty," the idea that voters actually living in the states and territories should decide slavery's status for themselves, free of dictation by Washington; it provided that Texas might eventually be subdivided into as many as three U.S. states "with or without the institution of slavery, as the people in each one of

41 CG, 28 Cong., 2 Sess., 85, 95–97.

said States respectively may at the time of their application to Congress for admission [as new states], determine." Given slavery's legality in the Texas Republic, Douglas's amendment probably destined at least two of the possible new states for slavery.

Douglas's friendly amendment to Milton Brown's resolution, however, carried different meanings. Brown's original wording specified that any of possibly five new states carved out of Texas lying south of 36°30' would enter the Union with or without slavery "as the people of each State asking admission may desire"; essentially this phrasing applied the Missouri Compromise principle to Texas, since that sectional deal had allowed rather than mandated slavery in territory below 36°30'. Douglas's amendment, in contrast, made a token gesture toward freedom by emphasizing that slavery would *not* be permitted in any states carved out of Texas *north* of the line, specifically mentioning the Missouri Compromise to validate his amendment. Throughout his later career, Douglas would seek to win acclaim and possibly the presidency by threading a fine needle through the territorial web to satisfy both sections, and possibly this amendment marks the real beginning of his problematic quest. Although the 36°30' line lies north of present-day Amarillo, Texas's Congress in 1836 had claimed for Texas's northwestern boundary land that is not part of the present state on and near the Arkansas River up to the 42° parallel, and Congress had incorporated Texas's claim within its annexation resolution. So there was certainly a genuine chance in 1845 that a free state could eventually emerge in northwestern Texas. A few years later, trying to rebut charges that he and other northern Democrats had been trying in 1845 to expand slavery by annexing Texas, Douglas claimed that only one-quarter of Texas was suitable for cotton or sugar cultivation, and that two or three of the possible five states carved out of Texas would have wound up being free, had the state subsequently subdivided. Whether or not Douglas genuinely believed his claim, he apparently thought in proposing his amendment he might mollify northern critics upset at his recent coddling of slavery south of 36°30'.[42]

The following December, as the Twenty-ninth Congress opened, the reelected Douglas, in his capacity as the new chair of the House's Committee on Territories, made another stab at firming up his northern credentials by opposing any settlement on Oregon that conceded anything

---

[42] CG, 28 Cong., 2 Sess., 225–27, 191–93, 686–87; 31 Cong., 1 Sess., Appendix, 365–66; Pletcher, *Diplomacy of Annexation*, 180–81; A. Ray Stephens and William M. Holmes, *Historical Atlas of Texas* (Norman, 1989), topic 34 (this book lacks page numbers).

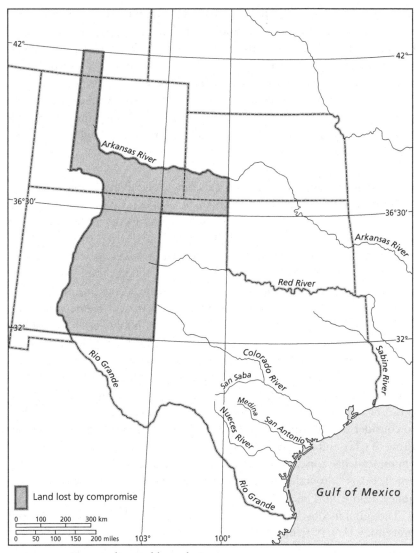

FIGURE 1.2 Texas's disputed boundaries.

Note: This map shows the area of territory (shaded to the north and west of Texas's current borders) claimed by the state of Texas preceding the Compromise of 1850, which awarded it to New Mexico. Douglas was willing during the Mexican War to extend the 36°30' line across Texas to the Pacific Ocean, allowing slavery in territory gained from Mexico in the war and setting a precedent for future acquisitions in Latin America. This map also shows the Nueces and Rio Grande Rivers in south Texas. The U.S.-Mexican War broke out in 1846 because the U.S. government backed Texas's claims, disputed by Mexico, that its limits included the land between the two rivers.

to Britain. He was willing to go to war over Oregon if necessary, he proclaimed, and he introduced a resolution that the 54°40' line was "*not open to compromise*" or arbitration. Meanwhile, he helped steer Texas's admission to the Union through its final steps. Douglas's prestige was growing and he was even talked up for speaker in the Democratic congressional caucus. The *Boston Daily Atlas*, however, was unimpressed. Reflecting on Douglas's role in Texas annexation, the paper dismissed him as "the subservient tool of the slaveholders" for getting a new slave state into the Union.[43]

Like Stephen Douglas, Abraham Lincoln found himself unexpectedly swept up in the sudden Texas excitement of 1844, a year when he was deeply engaged in political activity, campaigning for both the ultimately successful Whig congressional candidate for his district, the Springfield attorney, orator, and "friendly rival" Edward D. Baker, as well as Henry Clay, his party's presidential candidate. While Douglas took his stand in Congress on Texas, Lincoln expressed his own feelings on annexation in a letter to John Hardin on May 21. Glad that rival Democrats were dividing over Texas in the wake of Van Buren's public letter calling for restraint on annexation, Lincoln observed that Democrats in Springfield were "nearly confounded" by Van Buren's statement. Half the Democratic leadership in town favored annexation despite their party leader's discouragement, Lincoln reported. The next night, Lincoln took his own position on Texas at a public meeting at the Illinois State Capitol called to consider recent public letters against immediate annexation, including those of Clay and Van Buren. According to the *Sangamo Journal,* Lincoln announced his concurrence with those letters, called Tyler's tactics to annex Texas "altogether inexpedient," and argued that for the time being annexation would be a mistake.[44]

Though Lincoln later would build his national political career on preventing slavery from expanding anywhere, he seems to have worried more that annexing Texas would bring on a foreign war than that Texas would be a new slave territory or state. In fact, given his reaction to an abolitionist third party that fielded its own candidate for president

[43] CG, 29 Cong., 1 Sess., 86, 126; *Pittsburgh Daily Morning Post,* Dec. 4, 1845; *Boston Daily Atlas,* Dec. 23, 1845.

[44] Donald, *Lincoln,* 107; Watson, *Liberty and Power,* 192–93; AL to John J. Hardin, May 21, 1844, "Speech on Annexation of Texas," May 22, 1844 (from *Sangamo Journal,* June 6, 1844), CWAL, 1: 336–37.

in 1844, he does not seem to have worried much at all about slavery in Texas. Running James G. Birney, a repentant former Alabama slave-holder and lawyer who had freed his own chattels and moved north, the Liberty Party took 65,608 ballots of about 2,700,000 cast, siphoning votes from both major parties in a close election that Polk won by 38,000. The vote was so close in several states that possibly Clay would have won had Birney not been in the race. A mere 8,600 more votes in Michigan, Louisiana, Georgia, and Indiana, if distributed efficaciously, would have won those states and the election for Clay. Alternately, if a mere one-third of the Liberty Party's 15,800 New York votes for Birney had gone to Clay instead, the Kentuckian would have triumphed.[45]

A year later, reflecting in a letter on the narrow outcome, Lincoln reasoned that the Liberty Party cost Clay victory in New York and the election. He also considered the Birney candidacy a self-inflicted wound, given abolitionists' extreme hostility to Texas annexation and Polk's fla-grantly expansionist candidacy. It seemed absurd to Lincoln that abo-litionists would jeopardize Clay's chances with Birney's hopeless quest, partly on the irrelevant logic that Clay owned slaves. In a remarkably clear endorsement of ends over means, Lincoln mused:

What was their [the abolitionists] process of reasoning, I can only judge from what a single one of them told me. It was this: "We are not to do *evil* that *good* may come." This general, proposition is doubtless correct; but did it apply? If by your votes you could have prevented the *extention* [sic], &c. of slavery, would it not have been *good* and not *evil* so to have used your votes, even though it involved the casting of them for a slaveholder?

Lincoln's lament was less that abolitionists might have warded off slav-ery's expansion by withholding their own candidate than that they inter-fered with the election of his Whig hero, Clay. He conceded in the same letter that he actually lacked strong opinions about Texas, since Texans at least practiced the principles of American republican government and he doubted that annexation would make slavery's evils worse than they already were. Whether or not annexation occurred, land-hungry

[45] Richard H. Sewell, *Ballots for Freedom: Antislavery Politics in the United States, 1837–1860* (New York, 1976), 58–79, 109–110; Louis Filler, *The Crusade against Slavery, 1830–1860* (1960; rpt., New York, 1963), 73–74, 77–78; Holt, *American Whig Party*, 194; Woodworth, *Manifest Destinies*, 137; Miller, *Lincoln's Virtues*, 193; Thomas B. Alexander, "The Dimensions of Voter Partisan Constancy in Presidential Elections from 1840 to 1860," in *Essays on American Antebellum Politics, 1840–1860*, ed. Stephen E. Maizlish and John J. Kushma (College Station, TX, 1982), 78.

southern slaveholders would migrate to Texas with their slaves. For every additional slave in Texas, therefore, one fewer would remain in the East. The regrettable point was that abundant planting opportunities in Texas might encourage some slaveholders back east to reconsider freeing slaves they might have liberated. Within that context, Lincoln made an early, if tentative, pronouncement against slavery expansion:

I hold it a paramount duty of us in the free states, due to the Union of the states, and perhaps to liberty itself (paradox though it may seem) to let the slavery of other states alone; while, on the other hand, I hold it to be equally clear, that we should never knowingly lend ourselves directly or indirectly, to prevent that slavery from dying a natural death – to find new places for it to live in, when it can no longer exist in the old.

In various iterations, Lincoln would repeatedly restate these beliefs over the coming years. He feared that a country enabling liberty for whites would disintegrate if northerners dared to attack slavery in states where it already existed. On the other hand, if northerners prevented slavery's spread, they could kill it since slavery required growth to survive.[46]

Douglas and Lincoln arrived at their starkly different positions on America's expansion southward only after the United States and Mexico became embroiled in war, less than a half-year after Congress finalized Texas's annexation. Texas's becoming the twenty-eighth state in the Union, which caused Mexico to break diplomatic relations with the United States, was by no means the only cause of the U.S.-Mexican War, but it was the most important. Among the other irritants were claims disputes and U.S. territorial ambitions. In 1839, the two nations had established a joint claims commission to judge the validity of not only U.S. claims against Mexico but also Mexican claims against the United States, with two members representing each country and provision for a neutral country umpire to arbitrate impasses. The commission met from 1840 to 1842 and reviewed many claims, awarding more than $2 million, mostly to U.S. citizens with complaints about property in Mexico that had been damaged, destroyed, or confiscated in that nation's endemic civil strife. Unfortunately, Mexico was financially strapped and ceased paying interest on the awarded claims after April 1843, leaving more than $3 million in claims still unresolved.

Early in his presidency, James K. Polk tried to parry these unfunded claims into acquisitions of U.S. territory, by appointing a Louisiana

[46] AL to Williamson Durley, Oct. 3, 1845, CWAL, 1: 347–48.

Democratic politician, John Slidell, as "Minister Extraordinary and Plenipotentiary" to Mexico. In November 1845, Polk's secretary of state, James Buchanan, instructed Slidell to offer U.S. settlement of outstanding claims and $5 million for territorial concessions: Mexico would give the United States its territory of New Mexico (then much vaster than the current state) and settle the Texan-Mexican boundary at the Rio Grande River instead of farther north at the Nueces River, which Mexico maintained had been Texas's farthest boundary within Mexico's domain (see Figure 1.2). Hoping to capitalize on Mexico's financial instability, Polk also instructed Slidell to up the ante to $20 million if Mexico would add its California holdings as far as San Francisco, or $25 million if Mexico would cede northern California all the way to Monterey. Slidell, however, got nowhere because Mexican officials never recognized his credentials, which would have implied their acceptance of U.S. annexation of Texas.[47]

Had Mexico acceded to losing Texas permanently, perhaps the dispute over Texas's southern boundary could have been resolved without war. Instead, the boundary argument triggered hostilities. When it was a Spanish province, Texas's southern boundary had been the Nueces, which flows into the Gulf of Mexico at Corpus Christi well north of Texas's modern boundary with Mexico. This limit remained the same after Texas became a Mexican state following independence from Spain. Upon establishing its own independence from Mexico, however, Texas's Congress claimed the Rio Grande as the new republic's southernmost extent, and Santa Anna, in the Treaty of Velasco signed with the Texans after he was captured at San Jacinto, agreed to a provision bolstering the Texans' case. Not surprisingly, Mexico's Congress repudiated Santa Anna's agreement, which had been signed under duress. Hoping to keep the arid lightly populated area extending more than one hundred miles between the two rivers as a buffer against further U.S. expansion southward, Mexican troops occasionally probed the contested region in weak gestures of reclaiming sovereignty. The Texans refused to back down, however, and Polk upheld the Lone Star Republic's boundary claims.

On January 13, 1846, after hearing Slidell's diplomatic mission was a failure, the president ordered U.S. Army Colonel and Brevet Brigadier

---

[47] Pletcher, *Diplomacy of Annexation*, 55–58, 286–90; Lowell L. Blaisdell, "The Santangelo Case: A Controversial Claim," in Odie B. Faulk and Joseph A. Stout, Jr., *The Mexican War: Changing Interpretations* (Chicago, 1973), 57–66; Woodworth, *Manifest Destinies*, 146–47.

General Zachary Taylor, wintering with a troop force in Corpus Christi, to advance southward as a so-called Army of Occupation to a point at Taylor's discretion near or on the Rio Grande's eastern bank. Designed to give the United States de facto possession of the disputed area, this move created a tense situation almost bound to erupt in war. Leaving Corpus Christi in March with some 3,550 men and officers and a considerable baggage train, Taylor moved his troops by land and water to set up a supply base on the Gulf of Mexico a bit north of the Rio Grande's mouth. Taylor's encampment, just up the Rio Grande's eastern bank and almost opposite the Mexican city of Matamoros, virtually invited attack.[48]

Even if Mexican leaders had tolerated the provocation, Polk probably would have gone to war anyway, given his desire for Mexican territory, most especially California – whose ports would be a boon for U.S. trade with Asia – and Mexico's frustrating unwillingness to resolve claims. After receiving new information that Mexico was disinclined to a diplomatic settlement, in the second week of May 1846, Polk raised the issue before his cabinet, which agreed on war if Taylor were attacked. Polk had begun drafting a war message to Congress, when on the night of May 9 a dispatch that the general had written on April 26 arrived, announcing that fighting had already erupted on the border. On April 24, 1,600 Mexican cavalry, light infantry, and sappers had crossed to the Rio Grande's eastern bank and the next day ambushed a patrol of U.S. Army Captain Seth Thornton's dragoons, killing eleven of them, wounding others, and taking twenty-six Americans captive.[49]

Polk convened his cabinet immediately and they agreed unanimously on war. The president devoted Sunday, May 10, to drafting his war message and submitted it to Congress the next day. Although Polk alluded to the claims disputes and persistent extortion of U.S. merchants by Mexican authorities, he justified his decision mainly on the basis of the fighting already in progress. Polk reported he had sent Taylor's troops

[48] Winders, *Crisis in the Southwest*, 91–95; Henderson, *Glorious Defeat*, 98–99, 122, 139; K. Jack Bauer, *The Mexican War, 1846–1848* (New York, 1974), 11; John S. D. Eisenhower, *So Far from God: The U.S. War with Mexico, 1846–1848* (New York, 1989), 32–33, 49–57; introduction and translation from *El Nuevo Bernal Díaz del Castillo o Sea Historia de la Invasión de Los Anglo-Americanos en México* 1949, in *The View from Chapultepec: Mexican Writers on the Mexican-American War*, trans. and ed. Cecil Robinson (Tucson, 1989), xxviii–xxix, 67.
[49] Paul H. Bergeron, *The Presidency of James K. Polk* (Lawrence, 1987), 76; K. Jack Bauer, *Zachary Taylor: Soldier, Planter, Statesman of the Old Southwest* (Baton Rouge, 1985), 148–49; Woodworth, *Manifest Destinies*, 155–57; Winders, *Crisis in the Southwest*, 95–96; Bauer, *Mexican War*, 48

to the border to ward off a Mexican "invasion," noted that the U.S. Congress had upheld Texas's claims to the Rio Grande–Nueces strip by establishing a customs district there and charged that "belligerent" Mexican forces had exhausted America's "cup of forbearance." They had attacked U.S. territory, shedding "American blood upon the American soil." Within two days, the House and Senate approved Polk's call for war, the House by a 174–14 vote and the Senate 40–2, and the president signed the war measure on May 13. In keeping with their party's traditional caution in matters of expansion and war, Whigs supplied all fourteen House votes and both Senate votes against the rush to arms. A majority of voting Whigs in both houses, though, did endorse the war measure, many of them undoubtedly less from conviction than to avoid being cast as unpatriotic.[50]

Stephen Douglas was energized by the outbreak of war. On the day Polk signed the war measure, Douglas gave a stirring address in the House that justified the nation's course and exposed his hope that the hostilities would eventuate in further U.S. territorial growth. Douglas recalled that President Jackson had once nearly gone to war with Mexico over U.S. claims and railed against critics of the war declaration. In bellicose language, Douglas urged that U.S. forces "penetrate" Mexico to its capital, take its government prisoner of war, and "keep them in duress until they shall make a treaty of peace and boundary with us, by which they shall recognize not only the Rio del Norte, but such other line as we shall choose to dictate or accept."[51]

Perhaps Douglas envisioned himself a soldier in this conquering army. Within days, he was considering leaving Washington to fight. Since the United States Army then amounted to a mere 637 officers and 5,925 enlisted personnel, a truly minuscule force outnumbered more than three times by Mexico's regular establishment, Congress recognized that many new troops would be required to prosecute the war successfully, especially since Mexico was defending its own territory. In their war act, the legislators authorized fifty thousand volunteers, who would serve for either one year or the war's duration. After hastily drawing up war plans for campaigns into Mexico's northern states and territories, the president,

---

[50] CG, 29 Cong., 1 Sess., 782–83 (Polk's war message); Nugent, *Habits of Empire*, 199; Bauer, *Mexican War*, 68–69. There were also twenty abstentions in the House and three in the Senate.

[51] CG, 29 Cong., 1 Sess., 906.

his secretary of war William Marcy, and the army's commanding general
Winfield Scott decided to call up immediately 20,000 volunteers from
eleven western and southern states including Illinois (which was allo-
cated four regiments) because they were nearest the theater of war, and
to provide for some 25,000 more men from the Northeast to be enrolled
later on.[52]

Douglas immediately tried to capitalize personally on his state's call-up,
making use of the friendship he had struck up with John J. Hardin during
the militia campaign of 1845 and when they served in the Twenty-eighth
Congress. Though a Whig, Hardin shared Douglas's belligerently expansionist instincts. As tension mounted with Mexico, Hardin had written
to Douglas that the country needed California and that war was the best
solution to his nation's disputes with its southern neighbor. Realizing that
Hardin, on the basis of his prior military record, was poised for an important commission, Douglas wrote to him on May 15, a mere two days
after war was declared. Expecting Hardin to receive a "high command,"
Douglas offered to serve as his booster. When Hardin suggested on June 3
that his friend might actually want to leave Congress and "go along" with
the troops he was raising, Douglas took the bait. While Hardin immersed
himself in raising what became the First Regiment of Illinois Volunteer
Infantry, Douglas met with Marcy and on June 16 reported back to Hardin.
The war secretary had told him Hardin's regiment had been designated for
the administration's planned invasion of Chihuahua. Douglas confided to
Hardin that he wanted to serve with him there "in some capacity," preferably as major, but if need be even as a private. He also lobbied for a
commission through Illinois's congressional delegation. On June 22, eight
days before Hardin's commission as colonel of his regiment, the president
acknowledged in his diary that Illinois's two U.S. senators and a number
of its House members had submitted in writing their formal recommendations for staff and line positions in the Illinois Volunteers, including the
appointment of Douglas as inspector of the Illinois brigade at the rank
of major. Learning that the "fire eating" Douglas would settle for such a
humble slot greatly surprised one Virginia newspaper, which had heard
reports that Douglas aspired to be president some day.[53]

[52] Bauer, *Mexican War*, 71–72, 397; Daniel S. Haworth, "Army, Mexican," in *The United States and Mexico at War: Nineteenth-Century Expansionism and Conflict* (New York, 1998), 21; CG, 29 Cong., 1 Sess., 795; Bauer, *Mexican War*, 71–72, 397.
[53] SAD to John J. Hardin, May 15, June 16, 1846, Hardin to SAD, June 3, 1846 (quoted fragment), in Robert W. Johannsen, ed., *The Letters of Stephen A. Douglas* (Urbana, 1961), 138, 139–40, 140n; (Lacon) *Illinois Gazette*, July 11, 1846, p. 2; James K. Polk

Douglas's appointment depended on Polk, who, according to Congress's war legislation, had selection responsibilities for staff officers in the volunteers. But the president, for both ethical and political reasons, hesitated. He had recent differences with Douglas, most importantly about the Oregon dispute with Britain, which he had discussed with the Little Giant at a White House meeting on June 17. Because they represented the region of the country most likely to provide settlers for Oregon, Douglas and many fellow western Democratic congressmen wanted as much land as possible and contended that Oregon extended through today's British Columbia to the southern boundary of then-Russian Alaska, the 54°40' parallel. This claim had given Democrats their famous campaign slogan in 1844 of "Fifty-four Forty or Fight!" The president, however, considered settling for a more southerly boundary in the months after his election, in contrast to his hawkish stand on protecting Texas's extreme boundary claims. Although his 1845 inaugural address affirmed that U.S. claims to the entire Oregon Territory were "clear and unquestionable," Polk wisely reasoned that the nation, with its relatively weak military establishment, could ill afford a two-front war against both Britain and Mexico. So over the following winter, he began backtracking from his party's aggressive posture on the issue, and this course caused problems with Douglas.[54]

Douglas had demanded all of Oregon in public speeches in Illinois during the late spring and summer of 1845 while Congress was in recess, and he had endorsed preparatory military steps for the eventuality of hostilities over the question. Returning to Congress the next winter, Douglas had offered a resolution endorsing an all-Oregon position. But in January and February 1846, Polk signaled Britain through diplomatic channels that he might accept a settlement roughly at today's boundary separating the state of Washington from Canada, and this became the basis for a treaty that was ratified by the Senate in June.

Still, despite their differences, Douglas conciliated the president by the end of their conversation on June 17, so much so that as Douglas left the room, displaying what Polk interpreted as shame for his assertiveness and promising to support Polk in the future, Polk had responded that Douglas had his blessing to "lead the Democratic party in the House."

Diary, June 22, 1846, in *The Diary of James K. Polk during His Presidency, 1845–1849*, ed. Milo Milton Quaife, 4 vols. (Chicago, 1910), 1: 482–83; *Carrollton* (Illinois) *Gazette* and *Lynchburg Virginian* quoted in *Alexandria* (Va.) *Gazette*, Aug. 4, 1846.

54 Frederick Merk, *The Oregon Question: Essays in Anglo-American Diplomacy and Politics* (Cambridge, Mass., 1967), 366–94; Nugent, *Habits of Empire*, 161, 168; Johannsen, *Douglas*, 169–74.

Possibly because he felt he needed Douglas's support in Congress, Polk told Douglas on June 23, in "a long and friendly conversation," to with-draw his application for a commission, stating he felt it unethical to appoint congressmen to commissions created by those same congress-men's votes. Douglas, being a "sensible man," as Polk put it, complied and withdrew his request later that same day. When explaining to the public, however, why he did not leave for the theater of war, Douglas said he had been influenced by congressional peers who suggested it would be improper for him to leave Washington before Congress adjourned for the summer.[55]

Given his record of service and company command in the Black Hawk War, Abraham Lincoln arguably had as good a claim as Douglas to a commission in the army at the outbreak of fighting with Mexico, but he never sought one. Rather, Lincoln had his eyes on political advancement. During the months before the war, Lincoln angled for a congressional seat, and he was nominated on May 1, 1846, at the Whig convention for the Illinois Seventh Congressional District. Unlike Douglas, who could say he had already been a congressman had he gone off with the army, Lincoln would have had to co-opt his national political career at its very launch-ing moment had he enlisted. Besides, he had two young sons to think about. His second, Edward, was born only two months before the dec-laration of war. Unexcited about Texas and the faddish pronouncements of Manifest Destiny that accompanied annexation, Lincoln stayed home. Fending off charges that he was anti-Christian by his Democratic chal-lenger, the Methodist circuit-riding preacher Peter Cartwright, Lincoln won election in August to the Thirtieth Congress. He would wait, though, to take his seat, since that body was not scheduled to convene for another year and a half.[56]

Lincoln's transformation into an antiexpansionist war critic occurred gradually and was never absolute (Figure 1.3). Possibly Lincoln's turn against the war resulted from a visit he made to Lexington in November 1847 just before taking his congressional seat. His idol Henry Clay was there too, giving a ringing address to a huge audience on the thirteenth, which Lincoln likely attended, lambasting the war declaration, its loss

---

[55] Polk Diary, June 17, 23, 1846, Quaife, ed., *Diary of James K. Polk*, 1: 478–79, 484; SAD to the editors of the *Alton Telegraph*, July 20, 1846, in Johannsen, ed., *Letters of Stephen A. Douglas*, 143; *Carrollton* (Illinois) *Gazette* and *Lynchburg Virginian* quoted in *Alexandria* (Va.) *Gazette*, Aug. 4, 1846.

[56] Donald, *Lincoln*, 107, 113–15; CWAL, 349–80.

FIGURE 1.3 Abraham Lincoln, congressman-elect from Illinois, daguerreotype taken in 1846 or 1847 and attributed by the Library of Congress to Nicholas H. Shepherd.
Courtesy of the Library of Congress (LC-USZ62–5803).

of American lives, slavery's spread, and territorial growth. Clay called on Whigs in the House of Representatives, who had just gained a narrow seven-vote majority in the midterm elections, to exert themselves in the next congressional session by resisting the further expansion of slavery and the swallowing up of any Mexican territory beyond vindicating Texas's claims to the Nueces–Rio Grande borderlands.[57]

---

[57] Baker, *Mary Todd Lincoln*, 136–37; Michael F. Holt, "Lincoln Reconsidered," *Journal of American History* 96 (Sept. 2009): 452–53; Amy S. Greenberg, *A Wicked War: Polk, Clay, Lincoln, and the 1846 U.S. Invasion of Mexico* (New York, 2012), 229–38; Woodworth, *Manifest Destinies*, 213.

Actually, Lincoln had capitulated to the prevailing martial spirit when news of the war first arrived in Illinois. On May 29, 1846, he had asked Hardin to use his influence to guarantee that Illinois Whigs were not excluded from army commissions by ambitious Illinois Democrats exerting influence with a Democratic president, and the next day Lincoln reportedly spoke in a "warm, thrilling and effective way" at a war rally in Springfield that raised some seventy men for the army. Like many western Whigs and some eastern Whigs, Lincoln subsequently took pride in the army's record in Mexico, a nearly unblemished sequence of victorious battles and campaigns; between the start of the war and the time Lincoln arrived in Washington, U.S. land and naval forces pacified California and New Mexico, occupied much of northern Mexico, and penetrated the country's heartland – culminating in General Winfield Scott's conquest of Mexico City, the enemy capital, in September 1847. When news arrived midway through the war that Colonel Hardin had died in action in the American victory at Buena Vista (February 22–23, 1847), Lincoln presided over a public meeting whose resolutions grieved Hardin's death and lauded the "signal triumph of the American arms" in the fray that killed him.[58]

Even after Lincoln began harboring reservations about the war, which bogged down into something of a stalemate after Mexico City fell, he avoided conveying the impression that he would jeopardize the army's prospects by his criticism. Neither he nor fellow Whigs could ignore the lesson of the War of 1812, when New York and New England Federalists had opposed the Madison administration's starting and prosecution of it, leaving them vulnerable to accusations of disloyalty to the nation. The Federalists' seeming obstructionism had helped to sound the death knell of their party, which gradually faded away after the war. Naturally, as soon as Whig congressmen questioned Polk's leading the nation into war with Mexico, savvy Democrats started portraying them as reincarnated Federalists. So Lincoln carefully championed the troops in the field and when he entered Congress supported giving land grants to war veterans. When Herndon questioned his vote on a resolution condemning Polk for starting the war, Lincoln rejoined that his doing so had "nothing to do" with opposing the troops or their being supplied. To a former colleague in the Illinois legislature, Lincoln insisted that his voting for supplies

---

[58] AL to John J. Hardin, May 29, 1846, "Resolutions Adopted at John J. Hardin Meeting," April 5, 1847, CWAL, 1: 381, 392–93; Donald W. Riddle, *Congressman Abraham Lincoln* (Urbana, 1957), 11.

disproved accusations that condemning Polk amounted to opposing the war, calling the whole idea Democratic propaganda.[59]

Still, Lincoln began aggressively attacking the war's genesis soon after Clay's Lexington speech, initiating his verbal assault merely three weeks after he arrived in Washington. On December 2, 1847, with Mary and their children in tow, he reached the capital and took up rooms at a boarding house whose other residents included eight Whig congressmen, including the stridently antislavery Ohioan Joshua R. Giddings, but no Democratic colleagues. Apparently Lincoln challenged the war in part under prodding from his law partner. Answering a letter from Herndon, Lincoln promised that since his partner was "so anxious" he "distinguish" himself, he had "concluded to do so, before long." On December 22, Lincoln introduced a resolution in eight parts, following a preamble, which inquisitorially attacked President Polk's war message of May 11, 1846, as well as his annual messages to Congress of December 6, 1846, and December 7, 1847 (the latter read with Lincoln in his seat). In his messages, Polk had entirely blamed Mexico for the conflict, arguing that it had unreasonably refused to resolve disputes diplomatically while infringing U.S. sovereignty by shedding American blood on American soil. Lincoln's resolutions rhetorically invited the president to confirm or refute evidence that the disputed land between the Nueces and Rio Grande Rivers was legally Mexican under the Transcontinental Treaty with Spain of 1819. Further, he queried whether or not most people living in the strip were really Mexicans who had never (by voting at elections, serving on juries, or fulfilling other duties of citizenship) demonstrated allegiance to the laws of the Texas Republic or the United States prior to Taylor's advance. Lincoln demanded the president prove whether or not the supposed American citizens slaughtered in the Mexican assault that started the war were actually "armed officers and soldiers" who, according to General Taylor's own prior notifications to Washington, were entirely unneeded there for Texas's defense.[60]

Not long afterward, Lincoln went on record against the war two more times. On January 3, 1848, Lincoln joined eighty-four other House Whigs in passing (by four votes) Massachusetts Whig George Ashmun's

---

[59] (Philadelphia) *United States Gazette*, May 16, 1848, p. 1; AL to WHH, Feb. 15, June 22, 1848, AL to Usher F. Linder, Mar. 22, 1848, CWAL, 1: 451–52, 457, 492; Riddle, *Congressman Abraham Lincoln*, 71.

[60] CG, 30 Cong., 1 Sess., 4–12, 66; AL to WHH, CWAL, 1: 420; Donald, *Lincoln*, 119–20.

amendment to an amendment blaming Polk for not only initiating an unnecessary war but also doing it "unconstitutionally." On the eleventh, Lincoln vented his feelings about Polk's handling of the war in a speech assessing the president's annual message to Congress in December and related appropriations requests. Defending the Ashmun amendment, Lincoln intimated he had harbored reservations about the war for some time but had maintained his silence as a "good and patriotic" citizen until Polk's annual message in December with its assertion that congressmen voting for supplies for the army favored the war.

Polk's claim, Lincoln explained, forced him to speak on behalf of congressmen with serious qualms about declaring war on Mexico. Separating the question of going to war from the army's support, Lincoln attacked Polk for deviousness regarding the Rio Grande boundary dispute and again challenged Polk's claim that the disputed area belonged to Texas. True, Texans by the hallowed right of revolution could overthrow Mexican rule and force minorities within their boundaries, much like the minority Tories of the American Revolution, to submit to majority rule. Still, Lincoln reasoned, Polk had been unable to prove that Texans had established their claim to the disputed area by actually ruling the people there. Worse, Polk's annual message had suggested so many and contradictory reasons why he had taken his country to war – including national security, national honor, and territorial expansion – he resembled a man "in the half insane excitement of a fevered dream." Nor did the president know how to prosecute the war; rather, his words suggested "an insane man" so "lost" that he could project neither when the war might stop or with what result. On the one hand, Polk spoke of maintaining Mexico's independence and indicated the United States only coveted Mexico's northern, sparsely settled half, which could easily be populated by Americans once land offices were established and property sold off to U.S. buyers. At the same time, Polk implied that the United States might gain Mexico's less desirable settled southern half. What was the administration really after? Drawing laughter, Lincoln compared Polk to "a man on a hot shovel, finding no place on which he could settle down." Given its double allusion to Polk's insanity, Lincoln's speech was over the top, and one can imagine Lincoln rendering it emotionally. At one point, Lincoln summoned the Old Testament, arguing that Polk's case was so weak he surely had a guilty conscience and "felt the blood of this war, like the blood of Abel, was crying from the ground against him." Several exclamation points punctuate the text of Lincoln's final paragraphs, as his speech builds to its climax.[61]

By now, Lincoln had gone further than Herndon had ever expected when encouraging him to make his mark. When Herndon wrote to him on January 29, asserting, in Lincoln's rephrasing of it, that presidents could constitutionally invade foreign countries without congressional approval in order to prevent invasions of the United States, Lincoln reiterated that the real issue was whether the land Polk supposedly protected was really American. Then Lincoln Whiggisly lectured Herndon that chief executives needed constraint. By Herndon's logic, Polk could preemptively strike British Canada. Yet America's Founding Fathers had known that kings impoverished their peoples by waging wars. Lincoln similarly rebuked an Illinois Baptist minister who defended Polk. Lincoln chastised him for distorting facts by failing to recognize that Polk sent troops into the disputed area while there was still a chance for peace and that the U.S. Army had sparked the war by dispersing Mexican residents near the Rio Grande from their homes and building a fort on a Mexican cotton field, destroying its crops. Lest the minister think the troops' culpability trivial, he should apply the biblical golden rule and consider his reaction had Mexican forces done the same acts to "the humblest" Americans.[62]

So far, Lincoln had not attacked territorial expansion in principle; rather, he disputed the president's dissembling, inconsistencies, and opaqueness in pursuing it. In fact, Lincoln voted against a resolution that would have had the House Committee on Military Affairs consider asking Polk to withdraw east of the Rio Grande all U.S. armies in Mexico and agree to a permanent U.S.-Mexican boundary somewhere between the Rio Grande and the Nueces Rivers rather than farther south. But in June 1848, shortly before the war concluded, Lincoln advocated territorial restraint during a speech in Wilmington, Delaware. From the moment war began, the president had insisted in public, and also in private, that territorial gains had to result from it. The problem, from Lincoln's perspective, was not so much that Polk coveted land, but that his appetite for conquest grew the longer the war dragged on. As recently as his December 1847 message to Congress, Polk had demanded only "indemnity for the past, and security for the future." Yet less than three months later, in February 1848, Polk

[61] CG, 30 Cong., 1 Sess., 95, 154–56.
[62] AL to William H. Herndon, Feb. 15, 1848, AL to John M. Peck, May 21, 1848, CWAL, 1: 451, 472–73.

had submitted to the Senate a peace treaty, then ratified in March (and subsequently approved by Mexico) ending the war by greatly growing U.S.
territory and paying Mexico $15 million to get it. The final U.S.-Mexican
Treaty of Guadalupe Hidalgo of 1848 acknowledged Texas's southern
limits at the Rio Grande and ceded to the United States California down
to San Diego as well as all of Mexico's territory between California and
Texas, with the boundary line left to a future survey. In all, the United
States gained more than 500,000 square miles of land, including the current states of Utah and California, most of New Mexico, and parts of
Wyoming and Colorado, amounting to about 55 percent of Mexico's total
landmass. Why, Lincoln wondered, had the administration so exceeded its
own "stereotyped motto" of only seeking an indemnity?[63]

Had Lincoln thought that Polk intended acquisitions from Mexico to
spread slavery, perhaps he would have opposed territorial expansion
more categorically. But Lincoln was more charitable toward the Tennessee
slaveholding president's motives than were many antislavery northerners
at the time and some historians since. A newspaper account of Lincoln's
Wilmington speech said that he dismissed outright the popular belief
"that this war was originated for the purpose of extending slave territory." He may have been right. Polk believed that slavery was unsuited
for California and New Mexico and never made any statements in public
or in his diary indicating that he looked upon war with Mexico as a way
to open new lands for southern slaveholders.[64]

Still, Lincoln voted against extending slavery into Mexican territory
during the war and possibly began turning against territorial expansion
in principle because it was becoming difficult to differentiate territorial growth southward from the aspirations of slaveholders. On August
8, 1846, early in the war, a Pennsylvania Democratic House member,

[63] CG, 30 Cong., 1 Sess., 93, 7; Mark E. Neely Jr., "Lincoln and the Mexican War: An
     Argument by Analogy," *Lincoln Looks West: From the Mississippi to the Pacific,* ed.
     Richard W. Etulain (Carbondale, 2010), 80; AL speech at Wilmington, Delaware,
     June 10, 1848, CWAL, 1: 475–76; Frederick Moore Binder, *James Buchanan and the
     American Empire* (Selinsgrove, Pa., 1994), 106–107; Richard Griswold del Castillo,
     "Treaty of Guadalupe Hidalgo," in Frazier, ed., *United States and Mexico at War,* 437–
     38; Henderson, *Glorious Defeat,* 177.
[64] AL speech at Wilmington, Delaware, June 10, 1848, CWAL, 1: 476; Morrison, *Slavery
     and the American West,* 41; Merk, *Manifest Destiny,* 168; Sam W. Haynes, *James K. Polk
     and the Expansionist Impulse* (New York, 1997), 148. William Dusinberre argues that
     Polk's own slaveholdings influenced his waging war on Mexico. William Dusinberre,
     Slavemaster President: The Double Career of James Polk (New York, 2003), 130–40.

David Wilmot, had introduced an amendment to an appropriations bill that would make it difficult for Americans ever again to divorce slavery from expansion. Polk had asked Congress for a $2 million appropriation so that he could make an advance payment on any land "concessions" acquired from Mexico in a peace treaty, and Wilmot's amendment, which became known as the "Wilmot Proviso," applied wording adapted from the Northwest Ordinance mandating that slavery and involuntary servitude be prohibited in "any territory" acquired from Mexico. The measure passed 83–64 in the House, never passed the Senate (which proportionately had more members from the slave states), and lurked in American politics for the war's duration. It won wartime endorsements from many northern state legislatures and went before the House in varied iterations so often after Lincoln took his seat that he later claimed he voted for the Wilmot Proviso some forty times.[65]

No matter the presumed exaggeration,[66] as the war continued, Lincoln became sensitized to slavery's claim on U.S. territorial expansion, undoubtedly in part because of the furious southern response to the Wilmot Proviso – including threats of secession – if slaveholders were shut out of the anticipated land grab from Mexico. Opposed to slavery in principle, Lincoln favored the proviso as a way to preclude it where the federal government had constitutional authority to do so, though he stuck with the Whig ticket in 1848 of General Zachary Taylor and Millard Fillmore rather than join the new Free Soil Party, whose platform explicitly opposed slavery extension. Vigorously campaigning for Taylor, Lincoln repeatedly asked voters to support the general – even though he was a slave-owning Louisiana planter – on the presumption that Taylor would refrain from vetoing the Wilmot Proviso if it passed Congress. Taylor had announced he would not veto bills unless he deemed them unconstitutional. Promoting Taylor in Worcester, Massachusetts, Lincoln interrogated territorial expansion in principle, rather than merely the way Polk had pursued it. Conceding that people in Illinois and Massachusetts concurred that however evil slavery was they lacked control over it in

---

[65] CG, 29 Cong., 1 Sess., 1211–17; David Potter, The Impending Crisis, 1848–1861, ed. and completed by Don E. Fehrenbacher (New York: Harper & Row, 1976), 18–24, 54, 64; Jonathan H. Earle, Jacksonian Antislavery and the Politics of Free Soil, 1824–1854 (Chapel Hill, 2004), 123–43; Allan Nevins, Ordeal of the Union: Fruits of Manifest Destiny, 1847–1852 (New York, 1947), 9; Abraham Lincoln to Joshua F. Speed, Aug. 24, 1855, Basler, ed., Collected Works, 1: 323.

[66] It is unknown what votes Lincoln construed as addressing Wilmot's measure. See David Donald, Lincoln (1995; rpt., New York, 1996), 134–35.

states where they did not reside, Lincoln insisted that "the question of the *extension* of slavery to new territories of this country" was different. Given the nation's divisions over slavery, people who truly loved their country "did not believe in enlarging our field, but in keeping our fences where they are and cultivating our present possession, making it a garden, improving the morals and education of the people." Undoubtedly his audience understood the metaphor, however coded. Lincoln was reverting to traditional Whig dogma about developing the nation internally rather than through aggressively acquiring more space as a way of averting a North-South collision over slavery's expansion.[67]

Although Lincoln stayed out of Free Soil Party ranks, he did gently champion an attempt to end slavery in Washington before leaving Congress in March 1849 when his term ended. Alluding to the District of Columbia in their platform, the Free-soilers proclaimed it an obligation of their government "to relieve itself from all responsibility for the existence of slavery wherever that government possesses constitutional power to legislate on that subject and is thus responsible for its existence." In this spirit, Lincoln on January 10, 1849, introduced a measure that originated in boarding house discussions involving Joshua Giddings, who had joined the new party, as well as the Whig mayor of the District of Columbia, seeking slavery's gradual disappearance in the nation's capital. Lincoln moved that the House's Committee on the District of Columbia be instructed to report a bill that would preclude any persons not already being held as slaves in the district from becoming slaves in the future and freeing all children of slave mothers in the district after January 1, 1850, following a stated apprenticeship term that the committee was to stipulate. Further, Lincoln wanted the measure to provide market value compensation for slaves currently in the district freed voluntarily by their owners. Lincoln's proposal was a pipe dream, though he claimed advance approval from fifteen unnamed "leading citizens of the District," since it would only go into effect, according to Lincoln's guidelines, if a majority of the district's free white males approved it by referendum majority vote.

[67] *New York Herald*, Sept. 3, 1848; William J. Cooper, *Liberty and Slavery: Southern Politics to 1860* (New York, 1983), 221–23; John McCardell, *The Idea of a Southern Nation: Southern Nationalists and Southern Nationalism, 1830–1860* (New York, 1979), 283–87; Freehling, *Secessionists at Bay*, 461–62; Donald, *Lincoln*, 129–33; AL Speeches at Taunton, Mass., Sept. 21(?), 1848, Worcester, Massachusetts, Sept. 12, 1848, CWAL, 2: 7, 4; Merk, *Manifest Destiny*, 153–56; Frederick J. Blue, *The Free Soilers: Third Party Politics, 1848–54* (Urbana, 1973), 44–80. Lincoln had supported Taylor for the Whig nomination because he considered Taylor more electable than Henry Clay. AL to "Dear Williams," Apr. 30, 1848 (copy), Herndon-Weik Collection, M406, Reel 1.

They never even had the opportunity to do so, since the committee withheld Lincoln's measure from formal consideration.[68]

As Lincoln moved toward opposing U.S. territorial growth into tropical regions where slavery might flourish, Stephen Douglas was becoming more supportive of expansion southward and Manifest Destiny, perhaps because he was now personally vested in slavery by marriage into the southern aristocracy. Early in his congressional tenure, Douglas had been befriended by David S. Reid, a North Carolinian in the next seat. Their acquaintance led to Douglas's meeting and courting Reid's cousin Martha Martin, the frail daughter of a North Carolina plantation owner who also had some 2,500 acres in a Pearl River cotton plantation in Mississippi. In May 1844, a newspaper correspondent spotted Douglas up in the Senate galleries "*tet a teteing* with a very beautiful young lady in a white veil," very probably Martha Martin. They married in April 1847, during the war, and on the day after they wed Martin's father, Robert, presented Douglas with a deed to the Mississippi plantation with all its improvements and scores of slaves. This made for a considerable dowry, worth about $100,000 at the time, a small fortune in today's money. Apparently sensing that legal status as a slave owner would compromise him politically in Illinois, Douglas declined the gift, arguing that he knew nothing about plantation management. Still, he allowed his father-in-law to will the plantation to his wife and make him executor of the estate, in a document noting Douglas's refusal to possess "this kind of property." Since the will stipulated that for managing the plantation Douglas would earn 20 percent of the net proceeds (upped in a revised will to 33.3 percent), he would profit indirectly from the labor of slaves from the time of the death of his father-in-law.

That was not far off, as Robert Martin died in June 1848. Douglas made his first trip to the Mississippi place immediately afterward, as noted by North Carolina's governor. "You have probably heard of the death of Rob't Martin, of Rockingham," William A. Graham wrote to his brother James on June 9. "He has left his negroes (of whom he has a large number in Miss.) to his daughter, Mrs. Douglass & her children, if she has any,.... Judge Douglas has now gone to Miss. to look after the estate." Although Douglas subsequently fulfilled his legal responsibilities in defending the Martin estate against outstanding claims on it and corresponded with the New Orleans commission house that marketed his

[68] Blue, *Free Soilers*, 69–70, 74–75; CG, 30 Cong., 2 Sess., 212; Miller, *Lincoln's Virtues*, 214–15.

plantation's cotton, he rarely visited the place and left day-to-day operations in the hands of one James Strickland, an overseer. Nonetheless, being
a quasi-slaveholder gave political ammunition to his enemies in Illinois
and elsewhere in the North. One Illinois sheet reasoned he should "resign
immediately" if gaining "a personal interest in the souls and bodies" of
southern slaves made him more anxious to "represent the interests of the
slaveholders" than free workers in his own state. In 1850, insecure and
upset by the appearance in an Illinois newspaper of a reprinted southern article entitled "Hon. S. A. Douglass the Owner of Slaves," Douglas
prepared a defense of his situation for the *Springfield Daily Register*, a
paper edited by his close political ally Charles H. Lanphier. In a cover letter to Lanphier, Douglas admitted that there were "about 150 negroes"
on the place, but he emphasized for the proposed editorial that under
Mississippi law his wife retained "exclusive" title to the slaves and land;
he could neither control them nor apply them to his debts.[69]

Douglas's disavowals ring hollow, since he subsequently investigated
purchasing more plantation land than his wife inherited. In 1852, Douglas
heard from a friend in New Orleans that a plantation Douglas had previously expressed an interest in was now available for sale. Douglas's correspondent announced he had just perfected title on the place, promised it
would absorb a large workforce, and wondered whether Douglas wanted
to act on the opportunity. In 1857, Douglas sold his Pearl River place,
but not to divest himself of human property. Rather Douglas sent his 142
slaves off to a Washington County, Mississippi, cotton plantation that
he had just acquired in partnership with a Louisianan named James A.
McHatton. By this arrangement, Douglas contributed 142 blacks and
wagons, mules, and cattle to work McHatton's approximately two thousand acres of rich land near the Mississippi River. Douglas held his share in
the place in trust for his two underage sons with Martha Martin (she had
died in 1853), Robert M. (b. 1849) and Stephen Jr. (b. 1850). McHatton
remained in control of day-to-day operations on the plantation, thus technically sparing Douglas, as in the past, of the title "slave owner."[70]

[69] Anita Clinton, "Stephen Arnold Douglas – His Mississippi Experience," *Journal of
Mississippi History* 50 (Summer 1988): 56–88; Johannsen, *Douglas*, 207–208, 211;
William A. Graham to James Graham, June 9, 1848, *The Papers of William Alexander
Graham* comp. and ed. J. G. de Roulhac Hamilton (Raleigh, 1960), 3: 230; SAD to David
S. Reid, *The Papers of David Settle Reid*, ed. Lindley S. Butler (2 vols.; Raleigh, 1993–97),
1: 236; *Princeton Bureau Advocate* quoted in *Boston Daily Atlas*, Jan. 23, 1849; SAD to
Charles H. Lanphier, Aug. 3, 1850, enclosure, and editor's comment, in Johannsen, *Letters
of Stephen A. Douglas*, 189–91, 191n.
[70] Sam Butterworth to SAD, Dec. 13, 1852, SAD Papers, UC; Johannsen, *Douglas*, 251, 335,
337–38; Martin H. Quitt, *Stephen A. Douglas and Antebellum Democracy* (New York,
2012).

The issue of Douglas's slaves resurfaced throughout his later political career, but it is unclear how Douglas's feelings about slavery's expansion were influenced by his monetary stake. Although there is no evidence that Douglas's hostile reaction to the Wilmot Proviso originated in his relationship with Martha Martin and gaining plantation interests, Free-soilers suspected as much and his new status probably reinforced a previous disinclination to disapprove of the measure. Throughout the war years, Douglas opposed the proviso becoming American law, taking a stand that disturbed northern antislavery politicians and newspapers while winning friends in the South. He voted against it when it initially came before the House in 1846 – one of only four northern Democratic "Betrayers of Freedom" to do so. When Free-Soilers tried to apply the proviso to territorial governance for Oregon, Douglas as chair of the House's Committee on Territories worked to ensure that Congress base its ban on slavery in the Oregon Territory on the region being above the 36°30' parallel of the Missouri Compromise line (even though the line had never been legislated beyond the Rocky Mountains) rather than on the proviso. In February 1847, Douglas attempted to extend the line by moving that it continue all the way to the Pacific Ocean in respect to any territory acquired from Mexico in the war, a proposal that might have helped prevent the Civil War had it become law but went down to defeat 82–109. Later, while in the Senate, Douglas helped defeat efforts to write the Wilmot Proviso into the Treaty of Guadalupe Hidalgo. Around the time in 1848 that Lincoln was endorsing General Taylor on the logic that he would likely refrain from vetoing a passed Wilmot Proviso if elected president, Douglas, in speeches in Montgomery, Alabama, and New Orleans promoting Democratic presidential candidate Senator Lewis Cass of Michigan, denounced the proviso for violating the right of people in territories and states to decide the slavery question themselves. He would resign his seat in the Senate, he promised, if his constituents in Illinois insisted he support Wilmot's measure.[71]

Seemingly unconcerned in public whether slavery expanded westward or not, Douglas exhibited no reluctance to see it spread southward. To Douglas, the war pointed the nation southward as much as it did westward, and toward its conclusion, he anticipated that the fighting might finish with the United States absorbing the entire Mexican nation. In the months after General Winfield Scott and his army took Mexico City in

---

[71] *Boston Atlas*, Mar. 12, 1847, Dec. 8, 1848; *Montgomery* (Ala.) *Tri-Weekly Flag & Advertiser*, Aug. 10, 1847; Johannsen, *Douglas*, 200–205, 216; CG, 29 Cong., 2 Sess., 425; SAD speech in New Orleans, June 8, 1848, in *New Orleans Delta*, reprinted in Jackson *Mississippian*, June 30, 1848.

September 1847, when it appeared Mexicans might resort to indefinite guerrilla resistance rather than accede to a treaty with significant territorial concessions, Polk and his cabinet briefly considered pressing the war onward until it eventuated in incorporating all of Mexico into the Union. Expansionist Democratic newspapers and some congressional Democrats took up the call for "All Mexico" and showed reluctance to forgo the idea when the president submitted the Treaty of Guadalupe Hidalgo to the Senate, with its far more limited territorial gains. So long as All Mexico seemed an option, Douglas leaned toward endorsing it. A year earlier, Cass had argued in the Senate that it would not be healthy for Americans to amalgamate with Mexico's different racial stock and that it would be best for the United States to settle for "generally uninhabited" or "sparsely" inhabited Mexican territory as a result of the war rather than the entire country. In February 1848, at a time when Cass was a front-runner for the Democratic presidential nomination, Douglas confided to the editor of a St. Louis newspaper his sense that by opposing "the whole of Mexico," Cass might have damaged his chances and hurt the nation. When it came time for Douglas to go on record regarding the Treaty of Guadalupe Hidalgo ending the war, he joined thirteen other senators in the minority against ratification, because he wanted more of Mexico. During Senate consideration of the treaty, he had supported an effort by Mississippi's Jefferson Davis to revise the provisions so that the United States would additionally get a huge swath of today's northern Mexico east of Sonora.[72]

Douglas's proposed extension of the Missouri Compromise line to the Pacific invites consideration in the light of his interest in acquiring all of Mexico. Extension of the line would not only have potentially opened much of Mexico's landmass to slavery's spread; it would also have set a precedent for future U.S. acquisitions in the Tropics. It is hard to imagine free-soil principles and the Wilmot Proviso leapfrogging over all of Mexico to cover acquisitions farther south that might come later. And there would certainly be U.S. growth into the Tropics if Douglas had his way.

---

[72] SAD to Samuel Treat, Feb. 19, 1848, Johannsen, ed., *Letters of Douglas*, 156; Merk, *Manifest Destiny*, 107–43; Hietala, *Manifest Design*, 158–65; Johannsen, *Douglas*, 216–17.

2

Antilles to Isthmus

Stephen Douglas's historical fame before his Kansas-Nebraska Act of 1854 rests largely on his role as chair of the Senate Committee on Territories in navigating through Congress the "Compromise of 1850," a group of separate laws that possibly staved off civil war over slavery for a decade. They included a new fugitive slave measure, a ban on slave trading in the federal district, federal funding of Texan bonds from Texas's days as an independent republic, and a resolution of territorial issues arising from the recent war with Mexico. The compromise set aside *both* the Wilmot Proviso and previous proposals by many national figures, including Douglas, to extend the 36°30' line to the Pacific Ocean, as well as recent southern demands that slavery be legalized in *all* U.S. territories. Instead, the settlement allowed California outright admission to the Union as a free state (bypassing disputes over whether slavery would be permitted during California's territorial phase), resolved Texas's boundary issues, and wrought the territories of New Mexico and Utah from the remainder of Mexico's cession.

The laws about New Mexico and Utah, precedents for Douglas's highly controversial later stance on slavery in Kansas, provided the new territories could eventually become states "with or without slavery, as their constitution may prescribe at the time of their admission." While the Mexican War was in progress, Lewis Cass had championed a formula originated by New York senator Daniel Dickinson to avert congressional disputes over slavery's extension by letting territorial residents "in their respective local governments" decide the question themselves. By applying the Dickinson-Cass solution to New Mexico and Utah, Douglas adopted "popular sovereignty" as a quintessentially American democratic solution (and thus theoretically inoffensive in either North or South) to the dangerous territorial dispute. Virtually all U.S. politicians believed at least theoretically in self-government by the vote of white males.

Given the theory's slippery applicability, however, Douglas championed popular sovereignty at risk to his own career and the Union. Cass's formula left indeterminate and thus disputable just when territorial settlers could ban slavery if they so wanted. Could territorial legislatures do so immediately after coming into existence? This would give initial settlers the ability to chart the future, perhaps permanently, on the slavery issue. Or would territorial residents have to wait for abolition before they submitted a statehood constitution? That interpretation promised slavery a foothold in new territories that even an antislavery majority might later find impossible to eradicate.

Douglas's wizardry at getting these measures through the Senate, after Henry Clay faltered in having them adopted as a package "omnibus" bill, commands extended attention in almost all accounts of the congressional settlement. With Clay off in Newport, Rhode Island, recuperating from the strain of intense brokering with his colleagues, the "sleepless, resilient, and resourceful" Douglas achieved legislative mastery, making 1850 the "annus mirabilis" of the Little Giant's political career.[1]

What is not so well known is that prior to the Kansas controversy, Douglas also became identified with the nation's possible expansion into Latin America. During his first term in the U.S. Senate, Douglas had gained a seat on the prestigious Committee on Foreign Relations – an assignment he claimed to prefer to any other Senate committee – and he remained a member until his death more than a decade later.[2] In that capacity and as a public speaker, Douglas promoted U.S. penetration and eventual annexation of Cuba, Mexico, and Central America as a natural continuation of America's recent territorial grabs. During the three years

---

[1] Holman Hamilton, *Prologue to Conflict: The Crisis and Compromise of 1850* (New York, 1964), 109–11, 114–17, 133–48, 184; Bruce Collins, *The Origins of America's Civil War* (New York, 1981), 81, 89; David Potter, *The Impending Crisis: 1848–1861*, ed. and completed by Don E. Fehrenbacher (New York, 1976), 108–15; Allan Nevins, *Ordeal of the Union,* vol. I: *Fruits of Manifest Destiny, 1847–1852* (New York, 1947), 344; Michael A. Morrison, *Slavery and the American West: The Eclipse of Manifest Destiny and the Coming of the Civil War* (Chapel Hill, 1997), 117, 124–25; Steven E. Woodworth, *Manifest Destinies: America's Westward Expansion and the Road to the Civil War* (New York, 2010), 301, 351–55; Lewis Cass to Alfred O. P. Nicholson, Dec. 24, 1847, in Michael F. Holt, *The Fate of Their Country: Politicians, Slavery Extension, and the Coming of the Civil War* (New York, 2004), 131–32.

[2] CG, 31 Cong., 2 Sess., p. 8; SAD to the *Chicago Tribune,* Jan. 29, 1850, reprinted in *Springfield (IL) Daily Register,* Feb. 13, 1850.

between Texas's annexation and the Mexican War's end, the nation had grown about 64 percent in size. Many Americans expected such growth to continue, and in the wake of the Compromise of 1850 Douglas emerged as a transsectional contender for the Democratic presidential nomination who might reunify northerners and southerners in a mutual quest for empire, if the two regions could surmount their differences about slavery's future in new territory.

Meanwhile, Abraham Lincoln surrendered his House seat in Washington after one term, arguably because his opposition to the Mexican War played poorly with Illinois voters, and focused on his law practice in Illinois. Yet, a strong case can be made that Lincoln's attacks on President Polk had less to do with that decision than once assumed and that his retirement was less absolute than sometimes portrayed. Lincoln remained active in Whig politics and gave his eulogy to Henry Clay during this period. He also briefly addressed U.S. designs on Cuba. Ultimately, Lincoln would take a hard line against letting southern slavery spread anywhere to the south, with consequences not only for Douglas's tropical agenda but also for the Union's very survival.

When Stephen Douglas alleged during the congressional debates on the eve of the Mexican War that the British had designs on Cuba, he reflected a growing interest in the island among Democratic expansionists. In December 1845, not only did a Cuban annexation proposal come briefly before Congress, but a meeting in Douglas's own state, chaired by Illinois's Democratic governor Thomas Ford, endorsed a presidential initiative for Cuba's purchase and promised that Illinoisans were prepared to pay their share of the price. As winter settled over the country, Congressman Joshua Giddings fully expected President Polk to buy the island, and antislavery elements in Massachusetts, alarmed that "the great centre of all slaveholding now remaining out of the limits of the United States" might follow Texas into the Union, issued a warning in the *Liberator* about the possibility of Cuban annexation.[3]

By the time the Mexican War ended, Douglas was personally involved in the Cuba question, courtesy of the same New York newspaperman, John L. O'Sullivan, whose columns had once done so much service in

---

[3] CG, 29 Cong., 1 Sess., 92, 96; report on Springfield's Cuba meeting in *New York Express*, republished in *Alexandria* (VA) *Gazette*, Jan. 2, 1846; R. M. Norman, *Rambles by Land and Water, or Notes of Travel in Cuba and Mexico* (New York, 1845), 59–61; Joshua Giddings to his son, Dec. 27, 1845, Joshua Giddings Papers, Columbus, Ohio Historical Society; (Boston) *Liberator*, Jan. 30, 1846.

kindling public support for Texas's annexation. New York's Cuba consciousness far outstripped that of other northern cities. Empire City merchants, deeply enmeshed in trade with and passenger service to Havana, assumed that commerce with the island would flourish even more once Spanish import tariffs and port regulations in the island were terminated by U.S. control. Although U.S. exports to Cuba in 1848 amounted only to $5 million (in comparison to $67 million in exports to England), Americans imported nearly $13 million worth of Cuban products that year, including about 255 million pounds of sugar (worth some $9 million). Only Great Britain and France exported more to the United States than Cuba, and the United States was Cuba's biggest market, a far larger one than Spain, its mother country. Feeding New York's Cuba ferment was the presence in the city of significant numbers of exiles from the island, including members of the Consejo Cubano (Cuban Council), an annexationist organization founded in 1847. In 1848, *La Verdad* (The Truth), a bilingual newspaper promoting council views, began appearing off the press of *New York Sun* editor Moses Beach, who had recently traveled to Cuba and wanted the island for the Union.[4]

O'Sullivan had honeymooned there starting in late 1846 and continuing into early 1847, taking lodging with his bride at the home of his recently wedded younger sister Mary, who in 1845 had married the well-connected Cristóbal Madan, a planter/merchant in Matanzas. Madan, who traveled to and from the United States on business, belonged to the leading annexation group in Cuba, the Club de la Habana (Havana Club), and he took O'Sullivan to a club meeting and drew him into the Cuba annexation project. In a July 6, 1847, memorandum to the Polk administration, O'Sullivan confided that "intercourse with some of the principal families of the Island" convinced him that Cuban planters would pony up to $150 million to help the United States pay off Spain for annexation, because they believed that continued Spanish misrule would cost them much more. Never again, O'Sullivan contended, might there be

[4] Robert L. Paquette, *Sugar Is Made with Blood: The Conspiracy of La Escalera and the Conflict between Empires over Slavery in Cuba* (Middletown, CT, 1988), 29; U.S. Bureau of the Census, *Historical Statistics of the United States: Colonial Times to 1970*, vol. 2 (Washington, DC, 1975), 902, 904; (New Orleans) *De Bow's Review*, 7 (July 1849): 78–79; Luis Martínez-Fernández, *Torn between Empires: Economy, Society, and Patterns of Political Thought in the Hispanic Caribbean, 1840–1878* (Athens, GA, 1994), 68–73; Philip S. Foner, *A History of Cuba and Its Relations with the United States* (2 vols.; New York, 1962–63), 2: 11; Rodrigo Lazo, *Writing to Cuba: Filibustering and Cuban Exiles in the United States* (Chapel Hill, 2005), 11, 75.

so propitious a moment for Cuba. Spain's current unpopularity there and the likelihood it might be intimidated by America's triumphs in Mexico would surely generate a sale.[5]

O'Sullivan's report accurately represented elite discontent in Cuba with Spanish rule, though island planters differed with each other whether U.S. annexation was the answer. For decades, British officials had pressured Spain to enforce treaties and regulations against the African slave trade to Cuba, partly for humanitarian reasons but also for the preservation of the competitiveness of British sugar-producing island colonies since Britain's Emancipation Act of 1833 abolished slavery throughout the British West Indies. During the early 1840s, an abolitionist British consul in Havana had urged Spanish officials to liberate slaves imported illegally into the island as a step toward emancipation, and Cuba experienced several rumored slave conspiracies and actual revolts that attracted coverage in the American press. Many Cuban planters felt insecure about their future and U.S. slave owners were understandably sympathetic to the planters' plight. Southerners feared that news of abolition in what they labeled the "Queen of the Antilles," ninety or so nautical miles from Florida, might incite their own slaves to rebel. It was further unsettling to Cuban planters and southern slave owners that a revolutionary régime in France in 1848 ended slavery in all of France's overseas possessions – including Guadeloupe and Martinique in the West Indies – and that some antislavery northerners vocally supported emancipation in Cuba. "Spain owns Cuba, and has as perfect a right to abolish Slavery there as the State of Kentucky has to do the same within its territory," the *New York Tribune* pontificated.

Annexationist sentiment on the island ran particularly strongly among the Creoles (resident whites born in Cuba or elsewhere in the Americas). In addition to their insecurities about slavery, Creoles had a litany of complaints about Spain's governance – especially the corruption of colonial officials, restrictions on Cuban foreign trade, and their own virtual disenfranchisement. When it came to administrative appointments, Spain gave great preference to Spanish-born Peninsulares over Creoles. Since the 1820s, moreover, Spain had tightened its colonial grip by abolishing

[5] Robert D. Sampson, *John L. O'Sullivan and His Times* (Kent, OH, 2003), 208; Hugh Thomas, *Cuba, or The Pursuit of Freedom* (London, 1971), 208; Sheldon Howard Harris, "The Public Career of John Louis O'Sullivan" (Ph.D. diss., Columbia University, 1958), 275–76; Lazo, *Writing to Cuba*, 12; Tom Chaffin, *Fatal Glory: Narciso López and the First Clandestine U.S. War against Cuba* (Charlottesville, 1996), 13; John L. O'Sullivan Memorandum, July 6, 1847, Miscellaneous Collections, HSP.

Cuban municipal and colonywide assemblies, stripping Cuba of representation in Spain's legislative body (the Cortes), stationing thousands
of additional occupation troops on the island, censoring the press, and
increasing taxes.[6]

A little less than a year after drafting his Cuba memorandum for Polk,
O'Sullivan drew Douglas into annexation scheming, possibly because
Douglas had an established personal relationship with the president.
Unfortunately, though, all we know about Douglas's role derives from
one laconic entry in President Polk's diary. On May 10, 1848, the president recorded that at noon he had closed his doors to the usual office
seekers, when shortly afterward,

Senator Douglass of Illinois called with John O'Sullivan, Esqr., of New York.
Their business with me was to urge that I would take early measures with a view
to the purchase of the Island of Cuba from Spain. I heard their views, but deemed
it prudent to express no opinion on the subject. Mr. O'Sullivan read to me a paper
embodying his views in favour of the measure.

Clearly Polk's noncommittal response was coy, since he also told his diary
he was already "decidedly in favour of purchasing Cuba & making it one
of the States of [the] Union." On June 17, a week afterward, Secretary of
State James Buchanan authorized America's minister in Spain, Romulus
M. Saunders, to spend up to $100 million to get Spain to turn over the
island. O'Sullivan recommended that the United States could make up the
recommended $100 million purchase price by taxing Cuba while it was
a U.S. territory, then billing Cubans for the balance when they acquired

[6] Pacquette, *Sugar Is Made with Blood*, 131–57, 183–205; David Murray, "The Slave
Trade, Slavery, and Cuban Independence," *Slavery and Abolition* 20 (Dec. 1999): 106;
William Cullen Bryant to the *New York Evening Post*, Havana, Apr. 7, 1849, *The Letters
of William Cullen Bryant* (6 vols.; New York, 1975–92), 6: 42–46; Edward Bartlett
Rugemer, *The Problem of Emancipation: The Caribbean Roots of the American Civil War*
(Baton Rouge, 2008), 1–3; Martínez-Fernández, *Torn between Empires*, 14–17, 59–63;
Arthur F. Corwin, *Spain and the Abolition of Slavery in Cuba* (Austin, 1967), 69–78,
96; Franklin W. Knight, *Slave Society in Cuba during the Nineteenth Century* (Madison,
1970), 23, 88–90, 102, 140, 145; Anton L. Allahar, "Sugar, Slaves, and the Politics of
Annexationism: Cuba, 1840–1855," *Colonial Latin American Historical Review* 47 (Dec.
1994): 282–84; Sam W. Haynes, *Unfinished Revolution: The Early American Republic
in a British World* (Charlottesville, 2010), 216; *Vicksburg* (MS) *Sentinel*, Aug. 25, 1847;
Jackson Mississippian, Mar. 24, 1848; Basil Rauch, *American Interest in Cuba, 1848–
1855* (New York, 1948), 44–46; Heather S. Nathans, "Staging Slavery: Representing Race
and Abolitionism on and off the Philadelphia Stage," in *Antislavery and Abolition Justice
in the City of Brotherly Love*, ed. Richard Newman and James Mueller (Baton Rouge,
2011): 219; Foner, *History of Cuba*, 1: 53–55, 185–86, 201–205, 2: 14; Chaffin, *Fatal
Glory*, 11–12.

statehood, after deducting for net customs proceeds plus Crown lands and other properties accruing to the U.S. government from the takeover.[7]

We know nothing more about Douglas's involvement in Polk's Cuba initiative, which met an unreceptive response from Spanish officials, other than a vote he cast on a related measure shortly before Polk left office. Knowing it would be difficult to pry loose a highly productive colony from a declining foreign power, Buchanan had framed his instructions to Saunders carefully: the minister should "touch delicately" on why Spain would benefit by giving up the island in a "confidential conversation" with Spain's foreign minister, avoiding any written offer that might trigger an immediate and embarrassing Spanish rejection. The less publicity the better, so far as the administration was concerned. But in the fall of 1848 information about Polk's Cuba diplomacy leaked to the press, and in December, a Whig New Jersey senator adverse to getting Cuba "at all times and under all circumstances" balked at the secrecy and moved that Polk inform the Senate if purchase negotiations were in progress and share relevant correspondence consistent with the "public interest." When this resolution came formally before the Senate on January 5, 1849, Douglas joined a 23–19 majority of mostly southern Democrats in favor of tabling it, to preserve Polk's options in pursuing annexation. Only four other northern Democrats joined Douglas in voting to table the resolution, signaling that the Cuban issue, like territorial expansion westward, was at risk of becoming sectionalized.[8]

Already some northerners who wanted Cuba preferred postponing the issue lest it cause the same kind of divisions that the Mexican Cession had generated. In December 1848, the *New York Herald* observed that every "Southern man" ought to realize from the recent proceedings in Congress that if Cuba were annexed it would only be as "a non-slaveholding State." In a letter to former president Martin Van Buren, free-soiler Francis Preston Blair, who favored keeping slavery out of the West despite owning slaves himself, railed against southern designs on the Tropics. Blair

[7] James K. Polk Diary, May 10, 1848, *The Diary of James K. Polk during His Presidency, 1845 to 1849*, ed. Milo Milton Quaife, 4 vols. (Chicago, 1910), 3: 446; James Buchanan to Romulus M. Saunders, June 17, 1848, *The Works of James Buchanan Comprising His Speeches, State Papers, and Private Correspondence*, ed. and comp. John Bassett Moore, 12 vols. (Philadelphia, 1908–11), 8: 90–102; John L. O'Sullivan to James K. Polk, June 17, 1848, James K. Polk Presidential Papers, LC, 2nd Series.

[8] Franklin W. Knight, "Origins of Wealth and the Sugar Revolution in Cuba, 1750–1850," *Hispanic American Historical Review* 57 (May 1977): 231; Thomas, *Cuba*, 212–14; James Buchanan to Romulus Saunders, June 17, 1848, *Works of James Buchanan*, ed. and comp. Moore, 8: 100–101; CG, 30 Cong., 2 Sess., 46, 162–63.

suggested that southerners intended converting the Gulf of Mexico into a modern version of the Greek and Roman empires with the region's "barbarians" subjected to their dominion:

It is against the multiplication of free states & especially along the line of Mexico, that the Southern freebooters fight. They aim to gratify their slave state ambition as well as their personal ambition & avarice by the conquest of Mexico Cuba & the surrounding slave coasts on the Gulf of Mexico.

During congressional debate in 1850, several northerners insisted that they would only welcome Cuba into the Union if the Wilmot Proviso were applied to it. As one New York representative put it, "when Cuba comes into this Union *she must come free.* 'No more slave States, and no more slave territory,' is the decree sent forth by the people." Another representative gave notice that if the United States acquired "Greenland, Nova Zembla, Cuba, Yucatan, the Arctic and Antarctic regions, and to the Torrid Zone," he would prohibit slavery everywhere. An antislavery paper in the nation's capital declared, "Let Cuba come, bringing Freedom, not Slavery, and we shall bid her welcome." Meanwhile, many southern expansionists openly admitted wanting Cuba to benefit their states' special interests. A newspaper in Mississippi's capital believed the island could "restore the equipoise between the sections" with its nearly half-million slaves and "institutions" parallel to the South's.[9]

Any other involvement that Douglas had in Cuba annexation politics prior to the presidential election campaign of 1852 remains a mystery, particularly whether he was connected with attempts by Cuban exiles in the United States to mount a private military expedition to liberate Cuba from Spanish rule. In 1847, Narciso López, a native Venezuelan who had married into a Cuban Creole family and held high rank in the Spanish army and bureaucracy, began a conspiracy to overthrow Spanish control, drawing support from the cities and sugar interests around Cienfuegos, southeast of Havana. Following the collapse of his plot in July 1848,

[9] Francis Preston Blair to Martin Van Buren, July 15, 1850, Martin Van Buren Papers, LC; *New York Herald*, Dec. 23, 1848; CG, 31 Cong., 1 Sess., Appendix, 457, 257; *Washington (DC) National Era*, Aug. 28, 1851; *Springfield (MA) Daily Republican*, Aug. 27, 1849; Lewis Tappan to John Scoble, Sept. 19, 1849, *A Side-Light on Anglo-American Relations, 1839–1858: Furnished by the Correspondence of Lewis Tappan and Others with the British and Foreign Anti-Slavery Society*, ed. Annie Heloise Abel and Frank J. Klingberg (Lancaster, PA, 1927), 234–35; Ralph Waldo Emerson Speech, May 3, 1851, *The Union in Crisis, 1850–1877*, ed. Robert W. Johannsen (New York, 1965), 58; Rauch, *American Interest*, 84–100; *Jackson Mississippian*, Aug. 15, 1851. Nova Zembla is an island in Canada's far north.

López fled to the United States and continued scheming against Spain's control of Cuba.

Brazenly violating the U.S. Neutrality Act of 1818, which criminalized organizing or participating in private armed attacks on foreign countries at peace with the United States, López devoted himself for three years to organizing a private expedition to bring down Spanish rule in Cuba and drew considerable press coverage, much of it inaccurate, of his machinations. One false press report claimed that Springfield's Edward D. Baker, the former Mexican War officer and Whig congressman for whom Abraham and Mary Lincoln named their second son, was using his construction of a railroad across Panama as a cover to enlist López volunteers. Working with Cubans in exile and prominent U.S. collaborators including O'Sullivan (who was arrested by federal authorities in 1851 and tried in 1852 for fitting out a ship for the invasion), López schemed for Cuban freedom, giving mixed signals as to whether he and his associates desired U.S. annexation after liberation.[10]

According to a later account by the plot's second in command (the Cuban exile Ambrosio José Gonzales), López, while raising support in Washington in 1849, met in the Senate's recess room with John C. Calhoun, who had been serving in the Senate since 1845, as well as with four other senators, only one of whom was a Whig. Given Douglas's expansionist inclinations, it would not be surprising if he was among the three unnamed Democrats.[11] Were Douglas in attendance, it might help explain why he became rumored in the press as immersed in Cuban affairs and intending to make getting the island the basis for a presidential bid.

The buzz about Douglas running on a Cuba platform began in 1851, after López's project, increasingly referred to in the press as a "filibuster" expedition, ended in disaster. In the late summer of 1849, the U.S. Navy broke up an assemblage of López's recruits, who were gathered on Round Island (near Pascagoula, Mississippi, in the Gulf of Mexico), before they could even begin their intended descent on the island. In May 1850, however, López and more than five hundred men, mostly American

---

[10] Antonio Rafael de la Cova, *Cuban Confederate Colonel: The Life of Ambrosio José Gonzales* (Columbia, SC, 2003), 5–20; Chaffin, *Fatal Glory*, 36–41, 44–53; Rauch, *American Interest*, 73–79; Foner, *History of Cuba*, 2: 24–25; Robert E. May, *Manifest Destiny's Underworld: Filibustering in Antebellum America* (Chapel Hill, 2002), 7, 29–39, 136, 138; *Springfield* (IL) *Daily Register*, May 7, 1851; David Donald, *Lincoln* (1995; rpt., New York, 1996), 84, 98, 101, 107; http://ehistory.osu.edu/uscw/features/ regimental/pennsylvania/union/71stPennsylvania/eb.cfm.

[11] *Charleston Mercury*, Aug. 25, 1851; Rauch, *American Interest*, 112.

adventurers but also Cuban exiles and other immigrants, evaded U.S. civil and military officers and landed at Cárdenas on the island's northern coast east of Havana, only to be repelled by Spanish forces and forced to flee back to the United States after taking more than thirty casualties. Undeterred, López led some 400 to 450 adventurers to Cuba's coast west of Havana in August 1851. This time there was no escape. Spanish forces killed many of López's men, executed others taken captive, committed still more to imprisonment, and garroted the filibuster chief himself at Havana on September 1. Many Americans reacted furiously to what they regarded as Spanish butchery, most especially Spain's execution by firing squad of Colonel William Crittenden, the nephew of U.S. Attorney General John Crittenden of Kentucky, and his fifty men after they laid down their arms. Riots against Spanish stores and other property erupted in several southern cities when news arrived of the executions, and many American politicians and newspapers had Cuba on their minds going into the 1852 presidential race (Figure 2.1).[12]

In the wake of López's botched invasion, Cuba politics seems to have found Douglas rather than the other way around, though he did work behind the scenes in late 1851 on behalf of an American merchant and journalist resident in Havana, John S. Thrasher, who had been imprisoned by Spanish officials for suspected complicity with the López invaders. Douglas and other supporters of Thrasher's claims of innocence requested the Department of State to exert pressure on Spain on the Maine native's behalf, a campaign that succeeded when Thrasher was released the next year after serving only a tiny fraction of his eight-year sentence.[13]

Douglas seemed perfectly positioned as the 1852 presidential campaign approached to capitalize on mounting public interest in annexing Cuba, given his prior expansionist record. Though López and his organizers had appealed to potential backers in the South with the argument that adding Cuba to the Union would strengthen slavery, the filibuster's cause drew followers throughout much of the nation outside New England, especially among the Democratic masses in mid Atlantic port cities. In New York and Philadelphia, López rallies drew crowds estimated at upward of fifteen thousand people and the Chestnut Theatre in Philadelphia staged a play about the filibuster's first expedition. Clearly, Cuban annexation

---

[12] May, *Manifest Destiny's Underworld*, 1–4, 20–32, 135–38, 229; Charles H. Brown, *Agents of Manifest Destiny: The Lives and Times of the Filibusters* (Chapel Hill, 1980), 47–88; de la Cova, *Cuban Confederate Colonel*, 11–100.
[13] Daniel Webster to SAD, Dec. 17, 1851, SAD Papers, UC.

FIGURE 2.1 Execution of Colonel William Logan Crittenden during López expedition in Cuba, 1851.
Courtesy of Missouri Valley Special Collections, Kansas City Public Library, Kansas City, Missouri.
Note: Although there is no hard evidence that Stephen Douglas was connected with the U.S. adventurers or "filibusters" including Crittenden who invaded Spanish Cuba in 1850 and 1851, he was rumored to be involved in their plots. These reports helped him garner support among territorial expansionists for the Democratic presidential nomination in 1852. Douglas encouraged expansionist backers by denouncing the execution of captured Americans by Spanish authorities in the island.

had potential as a transsectional political issue, and a month after López's death in Cuba, a former Democratic governor of Illinois, John Reynolds, predicted Douglas would campaign for the Democratic presidential nomination in 1852 on the "Cuba invasion question." The next spring, the *Little Rock Democrat* out in Arkansas picked up the refrain. History was repeatable, it argued, if Democrats ran Douglas and Cuba on their party flag the way they had run Polk on a Texas platform in 1844. A Raleigh, North Carolina, newspaper, however, lambasted Douglas and his backers for wanting "more acquisition, another enlargement of the area of plunder or conquest," and cautioned that he was likely to add Canada to his agenda if he got the nomination, so that Cuba and Canada could play the same role as Texas and Oregon did for Polk in 1844. Meanwhile, O'Sullivan kept Douglas abreast of Cuban revolutionary developments.

In April 1852, when Domingo de Goicouría, a Cuban exile connected to the filibusters, visited Washington, he carried a letter of introduction from O'Sullivan to Douglas. O'Sullivan asked Douglas to assist Goicouría in his mission to learn about U.S. democratic institutions.[14]

It was within this context that Douglas, prior to the Democratic nominating convention at Baltimore on June 1, emerged as the candidate of "Young Americans" for the presidential nod. Launched by John L. O'Sullivan and others, Young America had roots in the 1830s and became an identifiable faction in the Democratic Party by the mid-1840s. It began as a cultural bedfellow to Manifest Destiny – a nationalistic reaction against the prior dominance of elitist English standards in American literature and art as well as a celebration of America's relative youthfulness and potential as a country. The term entered common use in its capitalized form following the New England intellectual Ralph Waldo Emerson's speech "The Young American" to the Boston Mercantile Library Association on February 7, 1844, which decried the impact of European "monarchical institutions" on U.S. education and the addiction of American reading audiences to English writers. Emerson lauded the bounty, moral reform impulses, transportation advances, expanse, and freshness of his own country.[15]

Well before 1852, however, Young America's focus shifted to interventionist U.S. foreign policies and territorial growth. Young Americans asserted their bold vision, assertiveness, and willingness to assume risks in comparison to stodgier, more elderly, and less- or anti-expansionist Democratic politicians (whom they derided as "Old Fogies"). They also celebrated America's manly vigor in comparison to old, supposedly decaying European powers – dogmas appealing in a country that had just conquered much of Mexico and whose future seemed boundless. Excited over contemporary developments abroad that appeared inspired by liberal, progressive impulses, Young America expressed brotherhood with

[14] John L. O'Sullivan to SAD, Apr. 13, 1852, SAD Papers, UC; May, *Manifest Destiny's Underworld*, 251–54; Amy S. Greenberg, *Manifest Manhood and the Antebellum American Empire* (New York, 2005), 187–94; Chaffin, *Fatal Glory*, 142–43; *Chillicothe (OH) Daily Scioto Gazette*, Oct. 11, 1851; *Little Rock Democrat* quoted in *Vermont Chronicle*, Apr. 13, 1852; *Philadelphia Public Ledger* quoted in *Fayetteville (NC) Observer*, Apr. 15, 1852; *Raleigh (NC) Register*, Apr. 17, 1852. One Whig paper announced it would absolve Douglas of charges of "sympathy with flibustiering" until he undeceived it. *Washington (DC) Daily National Intelligencer*, Apr. 14, 1852.
[15] Thomas Richardson to SAD, Sept. 16, 1851, SAD Papers, UC; Ralph Waldo Emerson, "The Young American," *Dial*, 4 (Apr. 1844) in *Manifest Destiny*, ed. Norman Graebner (Indianapolis, 1968), 4–15.

republican and nationalist movements in Europe that challenged the established order, such as Young Italy, Young Ireland, Young Poland, and Young Germany. When in 1848 revolutionary turmoil erupted in Sicily, Paris, Berlin, Vienna, and Milan in continental Europe and threatened also to engulf places like Ireland and Poland that escaped full-scale uprisings, many Young Americans embraced the insurrectionary surge – which included the toppling of France's last king and the creation of France's short-lived Second Republic – as a harbinger for the spread of American-like political institutions. Naturally Cuban filibustering commanded Young American support as an anticolonialist challenge to an obviously declining, centuries-old monarchical power. López catered to such sentiments by clothing his soldiers in red outfits modeled on the Carbonari of the Italian states whose secretive societies had been at the center of the republican ferment against Austrian dominion over the last few years.[16]

It made sense ideologically and even physiologically that Douglas should become the darling of the Young Americans. His relatively youthful under forty age played well to the movement; a supporter in California informed him that the only complaints Whigs made against him was his young age, hardly an "objection in this advanced and progressive age." And Douglas projected a vigorous personality despite his short stature. Sara Pryor, the wife of a Virginia journalist, first met Douglas around this time and later remembered that given his "massive head," "resolute face," and "carriage," no one ever would have applied the term "*insignificant*" to Douglas. But it was Douglas's spirited outspokenness for a vigorous U.S. foreign policy, his Anglophobia, his interest in Cuba, and his vocal sympathy in Congress for Louis Kossuth and the 1848 Hungarian uprising in Austria-Hungary against Hapsburg rule that won the hearts of Young Americans. Kossuth's movement was less democratic than many Americans believed, having a lot to do with the discontent of Hungary's Magyar aristocracy over lost class privileges and control over other ethnic groups. But it won great empathy in the United States after armies sent by Russia's czar helped restore Austrian control east of Vienna in 1849. When in late 1851 Kossuth arrived in America and began a fund-raising

---

[16] Edward L. Widmer, *Young America: The Flowering of Democracy in New York City* (New York, 1999), 3, 42–43, 56–59, 101, 103, 125–28, 187, 192–93; Timothy Mason Roberts, *Distant Revolutions: 1848 and the Challenge to American Exceptionalism* (Charlottesville, 2009), 4–7, 46; *Philadelphia Public Ledger*, quoted in Fayetteville (NC) *Observer*, Apr. 15, 1852; *Raleigh* (NC) *Register*, Apr. 17, 1852; "Arkansas" to the (Little Rock) *Arkansas Weekly Gazette*, Apr. 12, 1852, in *Arkansas Weekly Gazette*, May 7, 1852.

tour, Douglas voiced strong sympathy for Kossuth in Congress, spoke at
a banquet for him in Washington, and hinted at eventually backing U.S.
intervention in Hungary.[17]

Douglas's presidential nomination became a project for the Young
American George N. Sanders, a transplanted proslavery Kentuckian from
a slaveholding family who had been living in New York City with his wife,
Anna, and their children since 1845. Sanders had entered politics as a promoter of Texas annexation. In 1851, he purchased O'Sullivan's former
mouthpiece, the *Democratic Review*, and reinstated O'Sullivan (who had
given up the magazine several years earlier) as an editor. Throughout
that year and into 1852, Douglas consulted Sanders about how to promote his own candidacy. Sanders had gone abroad in 1848 in an attempt
to funnel surplus Mexican War arms to European revolutionaries, and
he was a strong backer of Kossuth. Revealingly, one of the officers in
Narciso López's 1850 filibuster to Cuba confided to a fellow officer veteran after that busted affair, "Your enthusiasm in favor of Douglas &
Young America accords entirely with my own views. I am a Douglas
man up to the handle.... I was for him before I ... met George Sanders."
Others in Douglas's camp included George Law, who had been involved
in Sanders's arms schemes, and Pierre Soulé. Law's firm, deeply engaged
in trade with Cuba, benefited from congressional subsidies to carry U.S.
mails from New York to Panama by way of New Orleans and Havana.
Law supported Cuban annexation and gave material support to filibuster operations. The U.S. senator and states' rights lawyer from Louisiana
(and French native) Pierre Soulé was renowned for his fiery oratory and
over the next few years would play a significant role in U.S. diplomatic
machinations to get Cuba.[18]

[17] Fred. A. Snyder to SAD, Oct. 14, 1851, Oliver Shipley to SAD, Jan. 6, 1852, Lewis G.
   Pearce to SAD, Feb. 20, 1852, SAD Papers, UC; Mrs. Roger [Sara Agnes Rice] Pryor,
   My Day: Reminiscences of a Long Life (New York, 1909), 84; Peter N. Stearns, *1848:
   The Revolutionary Tide in Europe* (New York, 1974), 3; David C. Hendrickson, *Union,
   Nation, or Empire: The American Debate over International Relations, 1789–1941*
   (Lawrence, 2009), 187; Donald S. Spencer, *Louis Kossuth and Young America: A Study
   of Sectionalism and Foreign Policy, 1848–1852* (Columbia, MO, 1977), 1–5, 13, 15, 21,
   22, 58, 168; Merle E. Curti, "Young America," *American Historical Review* 32 (Oct.
   1926): 34–55; Roberts, *Distant Revolutions*, 164. Douglas's self-image was of a young
   man. See SAD to a Boston editor in September 1851, quoted in Thomas E. Felt, "The
   Stephen A. Douglas Letters In the State Historical Library," *Journal of the Illinois State
   Historical Society* 56 (Winter 1963): 682.
[18] Yonatan Eyal, "A Romantic Realist: George Nicholas Sanders and the Dilemmas of
   Southern International Engagement," *Journal of Southern History* 78 (Feb. 2012): 109–
   12, 120; Melinda Senters, "Sanders, George N.," *Encyclopedia of Northern Kentucky*, ed.

Later in the year, a report to a Pennsylvania abolitionist meeting observed that as the Democrats convened in Baltimore, Douglas had support among the southern delegations, being "a large slaveholder in the right of his wife, and an earnest advocate to boot for the conquest and annexation of Cuba." Unfortunately, Douglas was handicapped by being identified with Sanders's intemperate columns in the *Review* debunking the Illinoisan's rivals. Douglas's reported links to unsavory entrepreneurs and his reputation for extremism and heavy drinking took a further toll. On the convention's first ballot, his mere twenty votes trailed far behind the "Old Fogy" front-runners, Lewis Cass (116 votes) and James Buchanan (93). Douglas's total surged to 92 on the thirtieth ballot, and he won additional delegates afterward, showing strength in all regions of the country but the mid-Atlantic states. None of the leading candidates, however, could muster the required two-thirds majority for nomination, allowing the nomination instead to fall to Franklin Pierce of New Hampshire, a former U.S senator and relatively unaccomplished volunteer Mexican War general. Youthful enough at forty-seven to appeal to Young Americans, Pierce took the prize on the forty-eighth ballot as one of the few truly dark-horse major-party presidential nominees in U.S. history, on a platform committing his party to "faithful execution" of the Compromise of 1850.[19]

Horace Mann, the antislavery congressman from Massachusetts running for governor on a third-party "Free Democratic" ticket that year, believed that Pierce upstaged Douglas precisely because of the Little Giant's identification with acquiring Cuba to expand slavery. Addressing

Paul A. Tenkotte and James C. Claypool (Lexington, 2009); Roy Morris Jr., *The Long Pursuit: Abraham Lincoln's Thirty-Year Struggle with Stephen Douglas for the Heart and Soul of* America (New York, 2008), 60; SAD to George N. Sanders, Apr. 11, May 18, July 12, Dec. 28, 1851, Jan. 22, 1852, excerpts quoted in *Illustrated Catalogue of the Political Correspondence of the Late Hon. George N. Sanders* (New York, 1914), catalogue nos. 40, 41, 42, 45 (unpaged); Robert W. Johannsen, *Stephen A. Douglas* (1973; rpt., Urbana, 1997), 329–31, 344–65; Widmer, *Young America*, 189–96; "The Nomination – the 'Old Fogies' and Fogy Conspiracies," *United States Democratic Review* 30 (Apr. 1852): 366–84; Theodore O'Hara to John T. Pickett, Dec. 8, 1851, Bonds of "The Hungarian Fund" dated Jan. 1, 1852, John T. Pickett Papers, LC; James Buchanan to Cave Johnson, Dec. 3, 1851, Moore, ed. and comp., *Works of James Buchanan*, 8: 426–27; Chaffin, *Fatal Glory*, 25, 49, 175, 227n; John P. Heiss to SAD, Jan. 11, 1852, SAD Papers, UC.

[19] *Fiftieth Annual Report Presented to the Pennsylvania Anti-Slavery Society, by Its Executive Committee, October 25, 1852. With the Proceedings of the Annual Meeting* (Philadelphia, 1852), 19; Potter, *Impending Crisis*, 142; SAD to George N. Sanders, Feb. 10, Apr. 15, 1852, excerpts, in *Illustrated Catalogue*, nos. 42, 48; *Raleigh Weekly Raleigh Register and North Carolina Gazette*, Mar. 24, 1852.

the House, Mann expressed confidence that the growing fury against the 1850 Fugitive Slave Law was causing a shift in the Democratic Party against slavery. Douglas's "reward for his implied or understood offer of the annexation of Cuba," he suggested, forfeited any chance of earning enough delegate support at the convention from New York, Pennsylvania, Ohio, and Massachusetts to take the prize.[20]

Douglas, however, seems to have drawn a far different lesson than Mann about Democratic Party trends on Cuba, becoming far more a paladin for the annexation movement after the convention of 1852 than before. On June 9, he participated in a nighttime rally sponsored by the Jackson Democratic Association of Washington called to ratify the Democratic ticket of Pierce and William R. King of Alabama. Apparently hoping to push Pierce in a Young American direction at a time when "the public mind" was very conscious of "filibustering and President-making" (as contemporary writer David Hunter Strother put it), Douglas won applause by lambasting Whig president Millard Fillmore for failing to retaliate against Spain for executing López's American recruits in Cuba: "Has the American flag trailed lower in the dust before a foreign power," Douglas railed, "than it has under the present Whig rule? You find, when American citizens were butchered in the island of Cuba, in violation of treaty stipulations, instead of this administration demanding the satisfaction which the outrage and indignity demanded, they content themselves with making apologies for the conduct of American citizens." Douglas probably was alluding to Fillmore's using his annual message to Congress the previous December to censure filibustering and request funds to reimburse Spain's consul in New Orleans for the mob sacking of his office during the post–López expedition rioting. Douglas presumably wished that Fillmore instead had insisted that Spain pay an indemnity for executing American prisoners and threatened war to get it. As limited as his remarks were, they apparently were the inspiration for a Massachusetts paper crowning Douglas "the prince of *Fillubistierism*" later in the month, an identity beginning to stick in the public mind.[21]

---

[20] CG, 32 Cong., 1 Sess., Appendix, 1078, 1076. The Free Soil Party of 1848 gradually became the Free Democratic Party by 1850. Frederick J. Blue, *The Free Soilers: Third Party Politics, 1848–54* (Urbana, 1973), 169n.

[21] *Alexandria* (VA) *Gazette*, June 11, 1852; (David Hunter Strother), "The Virginia Canaan. By a Virginian," *Harper's New Monthly Magazine* 8 (Dec. 1853), 18; *Worcester* (MA) *National Aegis*, June 30, 1852; *Baltimore Argus* quoted in (Springfield) *Illinois State Register*, Jan. 27, 1853; Millard Fillmore, Annual Message, Dec. 2, 1851, CG, 32 Cong., 1 Sess., 16. In August 1852, Congress appropriated $25,000 to fulfill Fillmore's

Exactly one month later, on July 9, Douglas hammered away at the same themes in a speech at Richmond, Virginia. Again he condemned Fillmore for allowing Americans to be butchered in Cuba, arguing that it was irrelevant whether López and his men were in the right or wrong. They deserved a "fair and open trial, with forms distinctly designated." The Fillmore administration had committed the degrading act of apologizing to Spain over the destruction of one building in New Orleans when the "blood of our countrymen" was crying out for Spain to do the apologizing.[22]

By the time the 1852 election ended in Pierce's victory over Scott, one North Carolina Whig could only nervously hope that "the Fillibusters' influence of Douglas and a few others" would somehow not infect an incoming Democratic administration widely expected to attempt a bold initiative for Cuba.[23] No wonder he worried. Douglas had taken to the campaign trail that summer and fall, at a time when the Fillmore administration was considering a British proposal for a "tripartite" convention by which Britain, France, and the United States would guarantee Spain's rule over Cuba indefinitely. They would do this by each disavowing any interest in acquiring the island for themselves and opposing efforts to possess Cuba on the "part of others." Britain's minister to the United States, John F. Crampton, urged the project on Fillmore's resistant secretary of state Daniel Webster, arguing it would not only benefit the European powers but also allow Spain to lessen its costs of military preparedness in Cuba against American attack. With fewer administrative expenses in Cuba, Spain would feel comfortable about reducing its tariffs on U.S. imports into the island. While the administration weighed Britain's initiative, Douglas made it clear he still wanted Cuba. Speaking at New York's Tammany Hall in September, to roars of "Cuba" from the crowd, Douglas recalled that he had supported the island's declaring its independence and then applying for annexation as early as 1845, and that he was willing then "to appropriate from the public treasury any necessary amount of money" to get it. Noting that he had said that the United States should preemptively "seize" Cuba and "hold it at all risks" should any

compensation request. "An Act Making Appropriations for the Civil and Diplomatic Expenses of the Government for the Year Ending the Thirtieth of June, Eighteen Hundred and Fifty-Three," U.S. Statutes, 32 Cong., 1 Sess., vol. 10, p. 89.

22 SAD speech in Richmond, July 9, 1852, in (Springfield) *Illinois State Register*, Aug. 5, 1852.

23 Joseph B. G. Roulhac to Thomas Ruffin, Oct. 5, 1852, *The Papers of Thomas Ruffin*, comp. and ed. J. G. De Roulhac Hamilton (4 vols.; Raleigh, 1918–20), 2: 344.

European country try to get it, Douglas emphasized that his opinions had not changed. The Democratic Party had a mission to accomplish annexation, since the "avowed principles" of the Whigs opposed "progress" of that sort. The audience laughed at Douglas's derision of Whig passivity and loudly cheered when he said he still wanted Cuba.[24]

On November 30, around the time Fillmore's new secretary of state Edward Everett (Webster had died in October) belatedly rejected the tripartite proposal, Douglas again spoke out. Addressing a Democratic evening victory celebration in Washington amid rumors he might serve as Young America's representative in Pierce's cabinet, Douglas attacked Britain's continued rule over Canada, Jamaica, and other Western Hemisphere possessions and reiterated his desire for Cuba. Douglas wanted Cuba as soon as the people there indicated by revolting that they were "worthy of freedom." Making an obvious allusion to the tripartite scheme, Douglas called upon the U.S. military to seize Cuba should Spain try to alienate it to any other power. "If that was filibustering, they would find a good many filibusters in the democratic ranks," the *New York Herald* paraphrased him saying.[25]

Despite that flippant remark and press allusions to Douglas's filibuster proclivities, though, the Little Giant never intended to go on record as advocating such expeditions, possibly because they were blatantly illegal or because López's movement became so identified with slavery that endorsing it risked losing a national constituency for Cuba. From the beginning, antislavery northerners suspected the goal of Narciso López's U.S. affiliates was to add Cuba to the Union as one or more slave states, enhancing the "slave power's" voting strength in Congress. This assumption was hardly unreasonable, since the filibusters and their supporters

[24] Richard Elward to J. F. H. Claiborne, Nov. 14, 1852, Claiborne Papers, Mississippi Department of Archives and History; John Cadwalader to Franklin Pierce, Oct. 28, 1852 (draft), John Cadwalader Papers, HSP; Henry Winter Davis to Samuel Francis Du Pont, Nov. 3, 1852, Samuel Francis Du Pont Papers, Hagley Museum and Library, Wilmington, DE; John F. Crampton to Lord Clarendon, Mar. 7, 1853, in BBPC, 68; Crampton to Daniel Webster, Apr. 23, July 8, 1852, Webster to Crampton, Apr. 29, 1852, WRM, 7: 459–60, 468–71, 75–76; John A. Logan Jr., *No Transfer: An American Security Principle* (New Haven, 1961), 226–28; Sandusky (OH) *Daily Commercial Register*, Sept. 29, 1852; Johannsen, *Douglas*, 370.

[25] *New-York Daily Times*, Nov. 24, Dec. 3, 1852; Edward Everett to John F. Crampton, Dec. 1, 1852, "Correspondence between the United States, Spain, and France Concerning Alleged Projects of Conquest and Annexation of the Island of Cuba," *British Sessional Papers*, House of Commons, vol. 102 (1852–53): 340–46; Lord John Russell to Crampton, Feb. 16, 1853, WRM, 7: 490–93; *New York Weekly Herald*, Dec. 4, 1852; CG, 32 Cong., 2 Sess., 139–46.

often stated publicly that their goal was to ward off emancipation on the island. The *New Orleans Daily Delta*, edited by Laurent J. Sigur, a rabidly profilibuster Democratic expansionist personally involved in the López plots, wanted a *minimum* of two states made out of an Americanized Cuba. Massachusetts U.S. senator John Davis had good cause, during the Compromise debates, to interpret southern military units in López's Cuba landing as evidence of an "eager pursuit of the extension of slavery" to grow "sectional power." Each "additional slave State brings in two Senators" eager to promote policies "adapted to the application of slave labor," he observed. A year later, when López's last invasion of the island had its disastrous conclusion, an antislavery newspaper argued that the expedition subserved "the ends of Slavery."[26]

Davis could have gone further in casting his net, since many of the expedition's northern promoters like O'Sullivan, a self-described "New York Free Soiler," had attitudes similar to those of southern slavery expansionists. In 1850, O'Sullivan encouraged Mississippi governor and multiple plantation owner John Quitman, who had gained fame as a U.S. general in the war with Mexico, to make his own landing in Cuba. O'Sullivan urged Quitman to support López's attempt to help the white islanders preserve "the social tranquility of the country (I refer to the blacks)." A letter O'Sullivan sent to John C. Calhoun calling on him to rally to López's cause rather than let Spain get away with making "a San Domingo of Cuba" by emancipating its slaves further supports the point. Such dangers, O'Sullivan emphasized, should "rouse all the youth and manhood of the Southern States in particular" to join the invading force. Similarly, a New York City mass meeting adopted resolutions of sympathy with Americans executed or imprisoned in Cuba during and after López's fatal 1851 invasion that justified the filibuster in the light of Spain's reported intention of arming slaves to convert Cuba into "a Saint Domingo." Although the motives of most of the adventurers who accompanied López to Cuba in 1850 and 1851 remain unknown, undoubtedly some crusaded for slavery. A Missourian who visited Havana in 1851 inquired in a letter about how to enlist in a filibuster "speculation" to Cuba. Believing that President Fillmore's efforts to prevent Americans

---

[26] *Chillicothe* (OH) *Scioto Gazette*, Dec. 14, 1852; *Ripley* (OH) *Bee*, Jan. 29, 1853; *New-York Daily Times*, Dec. 25, 1852; *Washington* (DC) *National Era*, Sept. 20, 1849; Chaffin, *Fatal Glory*, 80, 106–107, 119, 187, Leonard L. Richards, *The California Gold Rush and the Coming of the Civil War* (New York, 2008), 120; CG, 35 Cong., 1 Sess., Appendix, pt. 2, 884; *Springfield* (MA) *Daily Republican*, Aug. 29, 1851; *Hartford Christian Secretary*, Apr. 18, 1851.

from invading Cuba proved he was an "old abolitionist Cus," this adventurer craved an opportunity to "murder abolitionists" in the near future![27]

Wary of openly endorsing illegal activity associated with slavery's expansion, Douglas never explicitly endorsed filibustering during the campaign or in the interim before Pierce's inauguration. Rather, he would get Cuba by purchasing it or waging national war, and he only wanted hostilities if Spain tried to transfer the island to a stronger European power. On the fourteenth of February 1853, in a lengthy and widely commented-on Senate address a few weeks before Pierce took office, Douglas prolonged his case against the Cuba tripartite proposal, claiming disingenuously that his own country had never resorted to the methods of "seizure, violence, and fraud" that European countries had mastered in creating their own empires. Rather, he baldly asserted, the United States had acquired its North American empire "by honest purchase, and full payment," conveniently ignoring the threats and military steps used in creating preconditions for its successive purchases of much of the continent. Given its upstanding record, America should resist any crippling "disclaimer as to our purposes upon Cuba" as required by the tripartite proposal, since that would imply guilt about America's prior territorial gains. Douglas would pray, instead, that Cubans would rebel for freedom from Spain so that they might be received "into the Union" as the Texans had, as soon as they realized the desirability of annexation for reasons of "interest or safety." To keep options open, he would resist "at all hazards" any pending transfer of the island by Spain to England or another European country.[28]

Douglas was insinuating that it might be necessary to wage war to keep Cuba out of English hands, not that filibusters ought to take it. He was also saying, beneath his aggressive bravado, that unless British rule became an immediate threat, there was no urgency about getting

---

[27] John L. O'Sullivan to John A. Quitman, June 26, 1850, John Quitman Papers, Mississippi Department of Archives and History, Jackson; O'Sullivan to John C. Calhoun, Aug. 24, 1849, in J. Franklin Jameson, ed., *Correspondence of John C. Calhoun*, Annual Report of the American Historical Association for the Year 1899 (Washington, DC, 1900), 2: 1202–03; John Henderson to Quitman, Nov. 6, 1850, in J. F. H. Claiborne, *Life and Correspondence of John A. Quitman* (2 vols.; New York, 1860), 2: 69–71; *New-York Daily Tribune*, Aug. 23, 1851; Lawrence Berry Washington to Henry Bedinger III, July 28, 1851, Bedinger-Dandridge Family Papers, William R. Perkins Library, Duke University, Durham, NC; *New-Orleans Louisiana Courier*, July 28, Aug. 13, 19, 26, Sept. 4, 1851.

[28] *Fayetteville* (NC) *Observer*, Feb. 22, 1853; *Milwaukee Daily Sentinel*, Feb. 2, 1853; CG, 32 Cong., 2 Sess., Appendix, 172–73.

the island. Douglas's position was nuanced enough that when Pierce and George Sanders met together soon afterward at New York's Astor House, they concurred that Douglas "had abandoned everything in relation to Cuba" – or so Sanders's wife jotted in her journal.[29]

Back in Springfield, the rabidly expansionist *Daily Register* saw that Douglas wanted the romantic trappings of the Cuban filibuster label without incurring its criminality. In an editorial entitled "Flybusterism," the paper insinuated that what the term really meant, in Douglas's case, was giving "republicanism, freedom, and democracy" peacefully to other countries – not the piracy and robbery of its original meaning. Confidently, the *Register* predicted that much like words such as "Locofocism" and even "democracy" itself, the latter once consistently denounced by Federalists as anarchy, the term "flybuster" would be "*orthographised*" into an honorable one in the near future.[30]

During the early 1850s, Abraham Lincoln's political career followed a reverse trajectory to Douglas's. While the Little Giant's national fame grew, Lincoln retired from Congress after a single term, without having made a lasting mark in the public eye outside his home state. Some sixteen newspapers from Maine to Georgia took notice of his stand in the House against the Mexican War, in ways ranging from cursory allusions to full reprintings of his words. Only one House colleague, however, mentioned Lincoln's remarks in subsequent debate. If President Polk noticed Lincoln's stand at all, he likely considered it insignificant; he ignored it in his dense diary. Within Illinois, a relatively prowar state, Lincoln's antiwar position gleaned tepid support from Whigs while attracting censure from Democratic newspapers and politicos, some of whom derided him as "spotty Lincoln" for demanding the president name the place where Mexican forces killed Americans on U.S. soil, justifying the war.[31]

---

[29] Anna J. Sanders Journal, Feb. 17, 1853, George N. Sanders Papers, LC.

[30] (Springfield) *Illinois State Register*, Jan. 27, 1853.

[31] Amy S. Greenberg, *A Wicked War: Polk, Clay, Lincoln, and the 1846 U.S. Invasion of Mexico* (New York, 2012), 253; William Lee Miller, *Lincoln's Virtues: An Ethical Biography* (New York, 2002), 168; David Herbert Donald, *Lincoln* (1995; rpt., New York, 1996), 124–25; William C. Harris, *Lincoln's Rise to the Presidency* (Lawrence, 2007), 44; Benjamin P. Thomas, *Abraham Lincoln: A Biography* (1952; rpt., New York, 1973), 120; Gabor S. Boritt, *War Opponent and War President* (Gettysburg, 1987), 14–15. Although most Illinois Whigs agreed with Lincoln on the war (except in southern Illinois, where Whigs were more prowar), they rarely mentioned Lincoln specifically when taking their positions. Richard Lawrence Miller, *Lincoln and His World*, vol. 3: *The Rise to National Prominence, 1843–1853* (Jefferson, NC, 2011), 166–70.

William Herndon contended Lincoln "politically killed himself" in
Illinois by opposing the war and as recently as 2008, a leading Lincoln
scholar bluntly judged Lincoln's criticism of the Mexican War "a colos-
sal political blunder." Lincoln's reactions to the war, however, typified
those of the Whigs of the Old Northwest and may not have been all
that damaging. Mark E. Neely observes that no Whig editor in Illinois
attacked Lincoln's stance on the war and that opposition to Polk's going
to war hardly ruined the simultaneous congressional campaigns of Whigs
in neighboring Indiana and elsewhere in the Old Northwest. Possibly,
Lincoln's decision to retire had most to do with a one-term Whig rota-
tion policy for his congressional district's seat (adopted at the district
convention in 1843), though it may also have been influenced by his
wife's feelings about the nation's capital. Mary Lincoln never took to
the sometimes-crude boardinghouse life in Washington to which she was
exposed. After a mere four months in the district, she had forsaken residence there, going home to Kentucky with the Lincoln children before
returning to Springfield for the balance of her husband's term.[32]

Repudiated or not, Lincoln reunited with his family in Springfield and
returned to his law practice, engrossing himself in debt cases, railroad
company litigation, and other matters far removed from national policy
and earning a decent but by no means spectacular income in comparison
to other attorneys in town. In 1849, Lincoln declined appointment by the
Taylor administration as governor or secretary of the Oregon Territory,
and the next year he rebuffed feelers that he run for Congress again. Yet,
Lincoln was hardly apolitical. He made appointment recommendations
to the Whig administration in Washington, shared his political opinions
with others, and took a stand on the revolutionary turmoil in Europe
similar to Douglas's. In September 1849, he helped draft resolutions for
a meeting in Springfield that embraced the Hungarian revolution against
Austrian rule and called upon Washington to recognize Hungarian

[32] WHH to Jesse Weik, Oct. 28, 1885, *The Hidden Lincoln: From the Letters and Papers of
William H. Herndon* (New York, 1938), 96; Allen C. Guelzo, *Lincoln and Douglas: The
Debates That Defined America* (New York, 2008), 31; Donald, *Lincoln*, 112; Donald
W. Riddle, *Congressman Abraham* Lincoln (Urbana, 1957), 34–40, 53, Miller, *Lincoln's
Virtues*, 171–83; Mark E. Neely Jr., "Lincoln and the Mexican War: An Argument by
Analogy," *Lincoln Looks West: From the Mississippi to the Pacific*, ed. Richard W.
Etulain (Carbondale, 2010), 68–89; Gabor S. Boritt, "A Question of Political Suicide?
Lincoln's Opposition to the Mexican War," *Journal of the Illinois State Historical Society*
67 (Feb. 1974): 79–100; Jean H. Baker, *Mary Todd Lincoln: A Biography* (New York,
1987), 138–43; Greenberg, *Wicked War*, 243–44.

independence quickly if it could be done without provoking Austria. Lincoln's eulogy to Zachary Taylor on July 25, 1850, after the president's death in office, devoted more attention to the general's accomplishments in the fighting in Mexico than any other phase of his career, praising him for his bravery, boldness, and level-headedness in confronting the enemy with inferior forces and weaponry, without condemning the territorial acquisitions his victories facilitated.[33]

Nearly two years afterward, Lincoln gave a different kind of public eulogy, his well-remembered tribute to Henry Clay. This address, in addition to praising the Kentuckian's support of Latin American independence movements after the War of 1812, also exposed Lincoln's developing interest in African colonization, in reaction to Clay's nearly lifelong commitment to the movement.

After presiding over the meeting in Washington in 1816 that organized the American Colonization Society for the Free People of Color (ACS), Clay had worked consistently for colonization legislation at the state and national levels and served as ACS president between 1836 and his death. When the society met in the U.S. House of Representatives chamber in 1827, Clay addressed it, advocating the use of federal funds to send some fifty thousand blacks a year to Liberia, the society's colony in Africa. Clearly, the slaveholding Clay and most colonizationists envisioned the great majority of émigrés, especially initially, as already free blacks rather than slaves. Still, Clay genuinely believed that colonization offered Americans the most promising route to ending their country's curse of human bondage and openly stated in Congress that he favored the gradual elimination of slavery not only in his own state but also in Missouri. To Clay, the most serious obstacle to accomplishing abolition was a worry by southern whites that emancipation would leave a high proportion of free African Americans in their states. He hoped, therefore, that the emigration abroad of free blacks would reduce those percentages to the point of convincing slaveholders that there would be little risk to society's "purity and safety" in a statewide emancipation program.[34]

---

[33] Michael Burlingame, *Abraham Lincoln: A Life*, 2 vols. (Baltimore, 2008), 1: 309–52; Resolutions of Sympathy with the Cause of Hungarian Freedom, Sept. 6, 1849, AL to John M. Clayton, Sept. 16, 27, 1849, AL to Thomas Ewing, Sept. 27, 1849, AL to John Addison, Sept. 27, 1849, AL to the Editors of the *Illinois Journal*, June 5, 1850, AL Eulogy on Zachary Taylor, July 25, 1850, AL to James A. Pearce, Jan. 13, 1851, Call for a Whig Meeting (signed by Lincoln), Apr. 7, 1852, CWAL, 2: 62–65, 86–87, 97, 120.

[34] David S. Heidler and Jeanne T. Heidler, *Henry Clay: The Essential American* (New York, 2010), 131, 217, 447; Harold D. Tallant, *Evil Necessity: Slavery and Political Culture in*

Lincoln's eulogy revealed that he bought into Clay's thinking. After noting approvingly that Clay had taken a gradualist, middle-of-the-road approach to America's slavery dilemma, Lincoln quoted passages from Clay's 1827 address to the Colonization Society and expressed a fervent hope (punctuated with an exclamation mark) that Clay's vision of U.S. blacks' redeeming Africa by introducing American institutions and culture there would be realized. Drawing from biblical stories of Hebrew enslavement in ancient Egypt, Lincoln recalled that the pharaoh's land nearly was destroyed "for striving to retain a captive people who had already served them more than four hundred years." Expressing his hope that similar plagues would never befell his own country (with another exclamation point), Lincoln affirmed it would be a "glorious consummation" if Clay's vision were realized and colonizationists succeeded "in restoring a captive people to their long-lost father-land, with bright prospects for the future." Though Lincoln conceded that Clay's program reassured U.S. slave owners by ridding the country of freed blacks, he emphasized that Clay's ambition was to use colonization as a tool to end slavery itself.[35]

Over the next few years, Lincoln drifted into the colonization movement himself, likely with strong encouragement from his wife. Mary Lincoln's father, Robert Smith Todd, had favored efforts by the Kentucky Colonization Society to send emancipated slaves to Liberia, and in 1827 a slave fathered by Mary's cousin John Todd Russell and the slave's mother had been freed by Russell's grandmother and shipped off there. Several of Mary's relations in Springfield, moreover, became active in the chapter there of the Illinois State Colonization Society. In July 1853, James Mitchell, a Methodist Episcopal Church preacher serving as secretary of the Indiana branch of the ACS, turned up in Springfield, where he published a promotional circular in the local Democratic paper, including a model constitution for the colonization societies he hoped would spring up throughout Illinois. After hearing Mitchell's brief sermon in the local First Presbyterian Church (which Mary had joined recently and where he sometimes attended services), Lincoln paid three dollars for an ACS membership for the church's minister. Lincoln met Mitchell during his visit and became active himself. Although Lincoln cancelled a scheduled

Antebellum Kentucky (Lexington, 2003), 27, 33; Lowell H. Harrison, *The Antislavery Movement in Kentucky* (Lexington, 1978), 32–33; Robert V. Remini, *Henry Clay: Statesman for the Union* (New York, 1991), 179–80, 483–84.

[35] AL Eulogy on Henry Clay, July 6, 1852, CWAL, 2: 130–32.

speech to the Springfield meeting of the Illinois State Colonization Society in January 1854, he did address the organization's annual gathering in 1855 and was elected as one of its eleven managers at the society's January 1857 meeting at the Illinois State House.[36]

Lincoln's colonizing thoughts focused exclusively on Liberia at this time, though he harbored doubts that sending slaves there would really rid his country of bondage since the distance from the United States was so great and the living conditions in the ACS's domain in Africa were too difficult to attract masses of black emigrants. Africa had always been the primary focus of colonization efforts since the British established a colony in Sierra Leone on the continent's western coast in the late 1700s; during Lincoln's childhood and young adulthood, Britain's navy had customarily taken human chattel intercepted on slave ships during its anti-slave trade patrols to Sierra Leone. Starting in 1822, the ACS had commenced sending black colonists to African lands it had purchased from natives in Liberia (adjacent to Sierra Leone). During one of his public addresses in 1854, however, Lincoln admitted not only that he would not know how to end slavery satisfactorily were he assigned that task, but also that colonization in Africa was an unlikely answer, despite its appeal to him. "My first impulse," he explained, "would be to free all the slaves, and send them to Liberia, – to their own native land. But ... its sudden execution is impossible. If they were all landed there in a day, they would all perish in the next ten days; and there are not surplus shipping and surplus money enough in the world to carry them there in many times ten days."[37]

Curiously, Lincoln seems to have been oblivious to Latin America as a nearer and possibly more practicable colonization destination than Africa. At the beginning of his first presidential term, Thomas Jefferson had given thought to sending blacks to Latin American destinations in the wake of panic in Virginia about a reported slave uprising scheme (the 1800 Gabriel Prosser plot). A couple of decades later, Haiti attracted several thousand U.S. black emigrants after its president worked with American

[36] Baker, *Mary Todd Lincoln*, 113, 69; Phillip W. Magness and Sebastian N. Page, *Colonization after Emancipation: Lincoln and the Movement for Black Resettlement* (Columbia, MO, 2011), 14; (Springfield) *Illinois State Register*, July 8, 1853; Paul M. Angle, *Lincoln in the Year 1854, Being the Day-to-Day Activities of Abraham Lincoln during That Year* (Springfield, 1928), 6; Angle, *Lincoln in the Year 1857, Being the Day-by-Day Activities of Abraham Lincoln during That Year* (Springfield, 1930), 9; Eric Foner, "Lincoln and Colonization," in Foner, ed., *Our Lincoln: New Perspectives on Lincoln and His World* (New York, 2008), 145; Michael Lind, *What Lincoln Believed: The Values and Convictions of America's Greatest President* (2004; rpt., New York, 2006), 105–106.
[37] AL Speech at Peoria, Illinois, Oct. 16, 1854, CWAL, 2: 255.

philanthropists to create a fund to pay the passage of black American emigrants. By the time Lincoln eulogized Clay, the idea of colonizing the Caribbean had considerable credibility, partly because escaped blacks in the North and even blacks born free there had to fear being remanded into slavery in the wake of the strict Fugitive Slave Act of 1850. In 1851, a convention attended by U.S. as well as Canadian African American delegates was held at Toronto, and it resolved that Britain's West Indies colonies be considered seriously by blacks desiring to leave the northern U.S. states. That same year, the escaped U.S. slave Henry Bibb advocated Britain's colony of Jamaica as the best second choice for U.S. blacks after Canada, in the *Voice of the Fugitive*, a newspaper he published in Canada. Bibb endorsed Jamaica because it was mostly governed by colored former slaves and the island's colored population was socially and politically equal to whites. Other prominent African Americans promoting resettlement in the West Indies included Henry Highland Garnet and James T. Holly. Garnet moved in December 1852 to Kingston, Jamaica, where he served as pastor in a Presbyterian church. He released a public letter to U.S. blacks the next year, inviting them to become paid sugar laborers on the island. Holly, a onetime Burlington, Vermont, bootmaker who became traveling agent and corresponding editor of Bibb's newspaper, went to Haiti in 1855 and negotiated with Emperor Faustin Soulouque I about resettling U.S. blacks there. This West Indies colonization ferment, however, does not seem to have registered on Lincoln.[38]

Although Lincoln was not speaking, yet, of the Caribbean for colonization, he did give fleeting attention to the region in 1852. Still the loyal Whig, Lincoln threw himself into election-year politics. His name appeared in April on a call for a Whig meeting in town to nominate

---

[38] Lacy K. Ford, *Deliver Us from Evil: The Slavery Question in the Old South* (New York, 2009), 63; Betty Fladeland, *Men and Brothers: Anglo-American Antislavery Cooperation* (Urbana, 1972), 82–84, 89–90; Antonio McDaniel, *Swing Low, Sweet Chariot: The Mortality Cost of Colonizing Liberia in the Nineteenth Century* (Chicago, 1995), 23–32; David Nichols, *From Dessalines to Duvalier: Race, Colour and National Independence in Haiti* (1979; rev. ed., New Brunswick, 1996), 61; Proceedings of the North American Convention Convened at St. Lawrence Hall, Toronto, Canada West, 11–13 September 1851, Henry Bibb editorial in *Voice of the Fugitive*, Dec. 3, 1851, Report of the Committee on Emigration of the Amherstburg Convention ... 17 June 1853, *The Black Abolitionist Papers*, ed. C. Peter Ripley (Chapel Hill, 1986), 2: 156, 200–202, 274; Rugemer, *Problem of Emancipation*, 280–83; David M. Dean, *Defender of the Race: James Theodore Holly, Black Nationalist Bishop* (Boston, 1979), 5–6, 9–10, 12, 17–24. I use the modern spelling "Haiti" throughout this work, which *was* in usage in antebellum and Civil War times. But "Hayti" seems to have then been the preferred spelling in government documents and the press.

candidates for city offices, and he gave campaign speeches in May in Springfield and Peoria for Whig presidential candidate General Winfield Scott. The Springfield address rebutted Stephen Douglas's campaign speech in Richmond, Virginia, for Democratic candidate, Franklin Pierce. Suggesting sarcastically that Douglas's remarks had so many "shirks and quirks" they reminded him of his rival's orations before he became "so much greater man than all the rest of us, as he now is," Lincoln censured Douglas for manipulating language for devious ends and trying to appropriate credit for the Compromise of 1850 from the more deserving Henry Clay. Lincoln rejected Douglas's claim that Scott's candidacy had been forced on southern Whigs by northern delegates to the Whig nominating convention, and he attacked Douglas for misrepresenting the record of Whig president Millard Fillmore (who had taken office upon Zachary Taylor's death in July 1850).

In the portion of his speech upholding Fillmore's presidency, Lincoln spoke out for apparently the first time in his life on anything having to do with Cuba or filibustering, taking a position nearly opposite Douglas's, though he stopped short of attacking Cuban annexation in principle. Probably, Lincoln realized that it would be a losing proposition politically to rule out acquiring the island. After noting that Douglas's public speeches had faulted Fillmore for not demanding redress for Spanish officials in Cuba executing fifty American filibusters without a fair trial, Lincoln expressed doubt not only that any prior treaty with Spain guaranteed trials for Americans within "Spanish dominions" but also that the filibusters merited classification as U.S. citizens. Arguing that the filibusters, in claiming the right to "revolutionize the Spanish government in Cuba," had forfeited their claim to federal protection, Lincoln claimed the Fillmore administration "had no more legal right to demand satisfaction for their treatment than if they had been native born Cubans." Although Lincoln thought Spain's government was one of the world's worst and that its "butchery" of Crittenden's men had been inhumane and needless, he nonetheless criticized Douglas for failing to make a specific policy recommendation of what Fillmore should have done if Spain indeed lacked the right to execute filibusters. All but calling Douglas a hypocrite, Lincoln asserted that logically Douglas's policy should have been to demand war with Spain. There was nothing holding Douglas back from putting a war resolution before the Senate, Lincoln pointed out, and he further observed that Douglas's failure to do so suggested that he was more concerned with stoking his presidential bid by meaningless gestures than with supporting the welfare of Americans abroad. Lincoln's remarks were significant for their lack of empathy for filibusters and filibustering, but also for what they did not say. Lacking was even a perfunctory suggestion that the United States should acquire Cuba either in the immediate future or at some indeterminate point down the road.[39]

Few aspects of Abraham Lincoln's public life leave more unresolved questions than his embrace of the colonization of blacks, given its premise that African Americans did not belong in the United States. Unfortunately, there is little consensus on Abraham Lincoln's racial attitudes, especially his formative ones. Brian Dirck suggests that "as a white child" in Kentucky "surrounded mostly by other white people," the young Abraham would have identified instinctively with the "predominantly white values" of his adults and peers and been naturally "predisposed to view any nonwhite people whom he saw, heard, or read about as marginal, and peculiar." Since Lincoln had limited acquaintance with African Americans prior to being president, he became an easy captive of racial stereotypes. Indeed, in one 1860 letter, Lincoln pointedly told the editor of the *New York Times* he had never participated "in a meeting of negroes in my life." Lincoln scholar Michael Burlingame, who emphasizes that Lincoln ultimately outgrew his own racism, similarly concedes the racism of the youthful Lincoln, highlighting more than two hundred unsigned articles in a Springfield, Illinois, newspaper between the 1830s and 1850s that he *suspects* were written by Lincoln. Some of these pieces took race-baiting positions, like the one arguing against "contamination" of the ballot box by African American voters.[40]

Lincoln scholars also tell us that the adult Lincoln told racist jokes, used the word "nigger," took delight in racially demeaning minstrel shows, and condescended to ribald racial allusions at political gatherings. When campaigning for the U.S. Senate in 1858, Lincoln warned against the danger that America's white laborers might be elbowed from their anvils and plows "by slave niggers" if, as he anticipated at the time, the Supreme Court legalized slavery in the northern states. The *New York Herald* reporter Henry Villard, who followed events in Springfield in the

---

[39] Call for a Whig Meeting in *Illinois Journal*, Apr. 7, 1852, AL Speech to the Springfield Scott Club, Aug. 14, 26, 1852, AL Speech at Peoria, Sept. 17, 1852, CWAL, 2: 120, 135–57.

[40] Brian Dirck, "Lincoln's Kentucky Childhood and Race," *Register of the Kentucky Historical Society* 106 (Summer/Autumn 2008): 320–23, 325, 328; AL to Henry J. Raymond, Dec. 18, 1860, CWAL, 4: 156; Michael Burlingame, *Abraham Lincoln: New Information, Fresh Perspectives*, 48th Annual Robert Fortenbaugh Memorial Lecture (Gettysburg, PA, 2009), 17–18; Burlingame, *Abraham Lincoln*, 1: 108–10.

tense weeks after Lincoln's election as president in 1860, quoted Lincoln as saying the nation's crisis about slavery caused him almost to wish he had lost the election, since "the niggers" would be "the first thing I have to attend to." Lincoln's moral failure to speak out against his own state's proscriptive legislation against free African Americans builds the case for his racist prejudice, as does his refusal in 1858 to sign a petition endorsing the right of African Americans to testify in Illinois courts.[41]

In a savaging of Lincoln's pre–Civil War record on race, Lerone Bennett describes a man with a "color complex" hyperdefensive about his own whiteness who fantasized about blacks' dying out as a race and so obsessively resorted to the words "*n-r, darky* and colored *boy*" that he deserves remembrance "as active as any racist of his time in perpetuating Negro stereotypes." But it is just as easy to suggest Lincoln was relatively enlightened on race for his time and place and that his prejudices were malleable. Phillip Shaw Paludan pointedly observes that Lincoln never used the "N" word in malice, that he lacked the virulently racist attitudes of many political peers, and that much of the evidence for his racism is fragmentary. For all the descriptions of Lincoln as a patron of minstrel shows, there are only two known occasions he attended "minstrel-like" performances. William Lee Miller argues that it is more significant that Lincoln befriended a down-and-out black barber named William de Fleurville ("Billy the Barber") – who showed up in New Salem in 1831 and then, with Lincoln's support, set up a successful business in Springfield and made remunerative property investments – than that Lincoln told jokes involving " 'colored fellows'" and "'darkies'." The barber, who was originally from Haiti, wound up becoming the richest black in Springfield and stayed in contact with Lincoln into the Civil War years.[42]

[41] AL speech at Carlinville, Ill., Aug. 31, 1858, CWAL, 3: 78; Brian R. Dirck, *Lincoln and Davis: Imagining America, 1809–1865* (Lawrence, 2001), 128–29; Lind, *What Lincoln Believed*, 108; Henry Villard report of Nov. 28, 1860, in *Lincoln on the Eve of '61: A Journalist's Story by Henry Villard*, ed. Harold G. and Oswald Garrison Villard (New York, 1941), 29; Robert W. Johannsen, *Lincoln, The South, and Slavery: The Political Dimension* (Baton Rouge, 1991), 33, 33n; George M. Fredrickson, *Big Enough to Be Inconsistent: Abraham Lincoln Confronts Slavery and Race* (Cambridge, MA, 2008), 54; H. Ford Douglas speech to the Western Anti-Slavery Society, Salem, Ohio, Sept. 23, 1860, in *The Black Abolitionist Papers*, vol. 5 (Chapel Hill, 1992), 90; account of Lincoln alluding to "darkey arithmetic" in Francis Fisher Browne, *The Every-Day Life of Abraham Lincoln* (1887; rpt., Lincoln, NE, 1995), 470–71.

[42] Lerone Bennett Jr., *Forced into Glory: Abraham Lincoln's White Dream* (Chicago, 2000), 5, 14, 71, 87, 90, 91, 96; Phillip S. Paludan, "Greely, Colonization, and a 'Deputation of Negroes': Three Considerations on Lincoln and Race," in *Lincoln Emancipated: The President and the Politics of Race*, ed. Brian R. Dirck (DeKalb, IL, 2007), 31; Miller,

Before condemning Lincoln, one must ask whether he could ever
have had a viable career in Illinois politics had he championed black
civil rights, given the values of Illinois's electorate in the 1830s and early
1840s. Although slavery was technically illegal in Illinois by its 1818
Constitution, many Illinois residents, especially in the southern and central parts of the state, hailed from upper slave states like Virginia and
Kentucky. Illinois might have legalized human bondage had not Congress
stipulated that the Illinois Constitution adhere to the Northwest
Ordinance of 1787 regarding the prohibition of slavery as a requirement
for statehood.

Loopholes within Illinois's constitution, such as a provision exempting until 1825 slave workers at the Shawneetown saltworks, even
allowed some blacks to be held in bondage well after statehood, so long
as they were hired out for one-year terms. Furthermore, Illinois's constitution, like Indiana's 1816 document, allowed quasi-slavery in the form
of indentured servitude if the contracts were finalized prior to activation
of the constitution. Contracts, many of them rushed through in the grace
period before the constitution went into effect, bound out blacks to
labor for as much as ninety-nine years! In 1820, 917 African Americans
worked as slaves or indentured servants in Illinois. One can only wonder what the number would have been had there not been the constitutional ban. The climate and terrain of Illinois were suitable for crops
like tobacco and hemp, grown by slaves in the South. After statehood,
Illinois, as was true for all other states, had the right to revise its state
constitution. In 1824, a referendum of the state's voters by 6,822–4,950
turned down calling a new constitutional convention, which might well
have legalized slavery. Over the next two decades, Illinois provided more
court protection of southern slaveholders moving through its boundaries with their human property than any free state other than, possibly,
New Jersey.[43]

Illinois voters and legislators did not want African Americans in the
state at all unless as slaves, and certainly not as equal fellow citizens.
State legislators passed a law in 1829 compelling free blacks (but not
whites) entering Illinois to post bond of $1,000. When drafting a new

Lincoln's Virtues, 40–41; Kenneth J. Winkle, "'Paradox Though It May Seem': Lincoln
on Antislavery, Race, and Union, 1837–1860," Dirck, ed., *Lincoln Emancipated*, 19–20.
[43] Eugene H. Berwanger, *The Frontier against Slavery: Western Anti-Negro Prejudice and
the Slavery Extension Controversy* (Urbana, 1967), 7–8, 11, 14, 15–17; Simon, *Lincoln's
Preparation for Greatness*, 122–25; Paul Finkelman, *An Imperfect Union: Slavery,
Federalism, and Comity* (Chapel Hill, 1981), 96–97, 96n.

state constitution in 1847, exclusionist delegates to the state convention, deeming blacks lazy and unwelcome, provided for a popular referendum on a proposed constitutional article that would deny free blacks the right to enter the state at all. Illinois voters endorsed the prohibition the next year by an overwhelming 60,585–15,903 margin. In 1853, to compensate for the absence of enforcement provisions, the legislature passed a law classified by one authority as the "most severe anti-Negro measure passed by a free state" before the Civil War. This measure imposed a $50 fine, no trivial amount at the time, on free blacks who entered Illinois and remained ten days. It further declared that blacks unable to afford the levy were to be auctioned as labor for payment and then to face new penalties if they did not exit the state within ten days of completing their required labor.[44]

Much of the case for Lincoln's racism depends on incidents from his Illinois political career, at a time when he had to win over a very racist Illinois electorate. Also, much of it is from second- or third-hand stories, derived from published post–Civil War reminiscences by his relatives, friends, and other contemporaries. Memoirs invite skepticism, especially when writers reconstruct conversations held decades previously. Few passages in Lincoln's surviving correspondence actually use the term "nigger," and Lincoln seems to have been far less addicted to the term than his supposedly more liberal law partner, William Herndon. Lincoln did use the term without quotation marks in a note to a newspaper editor in 1859, complaining about manufactured charges that members of his political party were habituated to "stealing niggers and mail-bags." He did so, however, in response to an actual passage in the newspaper calling for his party's next gubernatorial candidate to be someone "who has never been indicted for stealing niggers or mail bags." Clearly in this instance, Lincoln was simply refuting the newspaper's implication that his party interfered with the recapture of runaway slaves, not crafting racist language of his own.[45]

Sadly, Stephen Douglas's early racial attitudes are even more obscure than Lincoln's. Virtually nothing is known about how Douglas developed the hatred of blacks that he eventually embedded in his speech making

---

[44] Berwanger, *Frontier against Slavery*, 32, 44–45, 48–49; Leon F. Litwack, *North of Slavery: The Negro in the Free States, 1790–1860* (Chicago, 1961), 93.

[45] AL to the Editor of the (Clinton) *Central Transcript*, July 3, 1859, CWAL, 3: 390, 390n. Herndon especially used the term in reference to the Democratic Party (e.g. "nigger-driving Democracy"). See WHH to Lyman Trumbull, July 12, 1856, Aug. 4, 1856, Reel 2, Mar. 4, 1857, Reel 3, Lyman Trumbull Papers, LC.

as a nationally prominent politician. One recent student of Douglas, in lamenting the "mystery" of his racism, surmises that possibly he had some kind of an early run-in with African Americans that has remained unrecorded.[46] But this is a case of fumbling in the dark. Because of all the reminiscences about Lincoln that surfaced after his assassination, we simply know far more about his childhood and youth than we do about Douglas's.

The adult Douglas said plenty about race, and most of what he said is repulsive today. As the historian Harry Jaffa critically observes, Douglas was every bit as "convinced of the distinction between superior and inferior" races as were defenders of slavery. A speech maker who seemingly took glee in telling listeners that he lacked moral inhibitions about slavery and hardly cared whether white people decided to practice it or not themselves, Douglas grounded his calls for U.S. territorial expansion southward, Jaffa provocatively argues, on a belief in "racial domination" similar to Hitler's. Intriguingly, Douglas, like Lincoln, seems to have gravitated to African colonization as a potential resolution of his nation's race problem, though apparently with less energy than his rival. James Mitchell claimed during the Civil War that Douglas promised him in the summer of 1854 he would support federal funding of colonization. It might be possible to dismiss Mitchell's recollection were it not that Douglas's name turns up on the annual lists of ACS vice presidents in 1859 and 1860.[47]

When speaking at Tammany Hall in September 1852, Stephen Douglas not only spoke belligerently about annexing Cuba but also insisted that Americans held such a stake in controlling any transit routes across Central America or southern Mexico they could seize them regardless of what the English thought about it. As the crowd cheered, he declared the United States had a "right" to "the Isthmus of Panama, Nicaragua, Tehuantepec [the narrow neck of southern Mexico], and every great route

---

[46] James L. Huston, *Stephen A. Douglas and the Dilemmas of Democratic Equality* (Lanham, MD, 2007), 31.

[47] Harry V. Jaffa, *A New Birth of Freedom: Abraham Lincoln and the Coming of the Civil War* (Lanham, MD, 2000), 310–11; James Mitchell to AL, Apr. 18, 1862, RG48, Roll 8; *Forty-Second Annual Report of the American Colonization Society, with the Proceedings of the Board of Directors and of the Society. January 18, 1859* (Washington, DC, 1859), unpaged; *Forty-Third Annual Report of the American Colonization Society, with the Proceedings of the Board of Directors and of the Society. January 17, 1860* (Washington, DC, 1860), unpaged.

between our two great shores" irrespective of British attempts to control the region indirectly by "her Bulwer and Clayton treaties."[48]

Douglas's remarks expressed Young American Democratic attitudes about one of the most unpopular treaties in U.S. history, the antiterritorial April 19, 1850, Clayton-Bulwer pact with Britain, which Whig secretary of state John M. Clayton had negotiated two months earlier. Clayton made the agreement, which created a kind of Anglo-American partnership for the construction of a Central American canal, to avert a potential war over the isthmus. His concessions, though, jeopardized further U.S. territorial expansion southward and greatly concerned Douglas.

Even before the nation became a Pacific power, Central American canal ideas intrigued Americans, including Douglas's political idols Thomas Jefferson and Andrew Jackson. The latter, when president, had commissioned the Philadelphia financier and newspaperman Charles Biddle to travel to the United Provinces of New Granada (the modern Colombia, which then included Panama) to investigate U.S. canal options in the area.[49] U.S. acquisition of Oregon and California between 1846 and 1848, and the gold rush of 1849, however, gave Central America significance in U.S. foreign policy that it had earlier lacked. This was not only because nearly one hundred thousand Americans lived in California when it applied for statehood in late 1849 and more than thirteen thousand had been enticed out to the Oregon Territory, but also because European governments and entrepreneurs had canal thoughts of their own and the British seemed to be extending their longtime colonial presence in the region. The stakes were high for a U.S. government needing swift and secure communications to defend its new empire on the Pacific, as well as for American merchants trading in the Far East and for thousands of Americans needing reliable mail, freight, and passenger service between the two coasts.[50]

At the outset of the gold bonanza in the winter of 1848–49, easterners mostly went to California by traveling by sea around South America's Cape Horn, a trip that took almost a half-year, though new overrigged

[48] *Sandusky (OH) Daily Commercial Register*, Sept. 29, 1852; Johannsen, *Douglas*, 370.
[49] Thomas Jefferson to William Carmichael, June 3, 1788, *The Works of Thomas Jefferson*, vol. 5 (New York, 1904), 403; John M. Belohlavek, *"Let the Eagle Soar!" The Foreign Policy of Andrew Jackson* (Lincoln, 1985), 238–50; Thomas M. Leonard, *Central America and the United States: The Search for Stability* (Athens, GA, 1991), 7–10.
[50] Thomas M. Leonard, "Central America and the United States: Overlooked Foreign Policy Objectives," *Americas*, 50 (June 1993): 2; Woodworth, *Manifest Destinies*, 329; Walter Nugent, *Habits of Empire: A History of American Expansion* (New York, 2008), 184.

clipper ships sometimes did much better, one of them doing it in just one hundred and eight days. Some Americans crossed the hemisphere more quickly via Central America's isthmus, reducing a trip of about fourteen thousand miles to one of about five thousand nautical miles, but doing so was no easy matter. Paying premium prices, travelers took passage from New York or New Orleans to the dirty and sickly town of Chagres on Panama's eastern coast; then they crossed the isthmus by ascending the Chagres River and making an overland trek to Panama City on the Pacific, before boarding a steamship for the final leg to San Francisco. Thousands of other gold seekers took one of several overland routes to California, risking their lives in crossing mountains, rivers, and deserts in a race to reach the gold fields along a route that was nearly impassable in wintertime because of forage scarcities in the plains and snowstorms in the mountains.[51]

Clearly a canal providing uninterrupted travel and freight through Panama or Nicaragua would be a boon not only to passengers but also to the entrepreneurs who built it and the countries that controlled it. The more northern of the two, Nicaragua, held particular promise for such a project, since it would reduce the New York–to–San Francisco route as compared to a Panama crossing by almost four hundred miles. Moreover, Nicaragua had eastern and interior waterways (the San Juan River and Lake Nicaragua) that could be integrated into a canal project. No water route connected the western shores of Lake Nicaragua to the Pacific Ocean, but the distance between them was less than twenty miles, a shorter gap than the land part of Panama's crossing. Besides, Nicaragua's higher latitudes had a reputation for being healthier than Panama, with travelers reportedly less prone there to contract tropical diseases like malaria.[52]

By the late 1840s, the United States and Britain were so locked into competition for the isthmian crossings that war was remotely possible. In December 1846, the U.S. chargé d'affaires in Bogota, Benjamin Bidlack, negotiated a treaty with New Granada's foreign secretary (ratified by the U.S. Senate in 1848), which granted U.S. freight and citizens the right to travel across the Panamanian isthmus by any present or future route. As a quid pro quo, the Bidlack agreement *required* the United States to pre-serve New Granada's sovereignty over Panama to ensure the isthmus's neutrality against any attempts to interrupt transit there. Whether Britain,

[51] John Haskell Kemble, *The Panama Route, 1848–1869* (Columbia, 1990), 8, 33, 37–38; Richards, *California Gold Rush*, 20–21, 25; Woodworth, *Manifest Destinies*, 321–22.
[52] Kemble, *Panama Route*, 58–59.

already a geopolitical presence in eastern Central America, would accede to such U.S. initiatives remained to be seen. Britain already appointed the superintendents governing Belize, just below Mexico's Yucatán Peninsula, though that settlement would not be formally pronounced a crown colony until 1862. Britain's involvement in Belize dated from the 1600s, when British sugar planters and mahogany and dyewood loggers arrived in the region. Britain also controlled the Bay Islands off Honduras's coast and farther down the isthmus claimed a sizable protectorate dubbed the Mosquito Kingdom (alluding to a British-anointed Mosquito Indian ruler). (See Figure 6.4).

Britain's so-called Mosquito Protectorate included the entire east coast of today's Nicaragua and part of the coastline of Honduras, and it extended well inland from the ocean. Within this area, in 1841, British forces had seized the port of San Juan del Norte at the mouth of the San Juan River, renaming it Greytown for a British colonial official, gaining control over the likely Caribbean outlet for any future canal. Britain retained the port afterward, despite protests from Nicaragua's government, which claimed sovereignty over it. Eight years after this grab, a British agent, fearing a U.S. takeover of Honduras's Tigre Island, off the western Honduran coast and near likely Pacific canal outlets, had it occupied by British forces. The takeover, however, was anticipated by an American agent, who persuaded Honduras to cede the island temporarily to the United States as a precautionary measure. Britain withdrew from Tigre Island rather than risk hostilities, but strained Anglo-American relations persisted in Central America and were exacerbated when U.S. diplomats Elijah Hise and Ephraim Squier negotiated treaties with Nicaragua in 1849. Hise's agreement gave an American company public lands for a transit route as well as the exclusive right to develop railroads, canals, and roads across the Nicaraguan isthmus; Squier's committed the United States to upholding Nicaragua's sovereignty over the transit. Capitalizing on Nicaragua's tilt to the United States, American shipping magnate Cornelius Vanderbilt negotiated a contract from that government to develop a canal and/or alternative transit route through the country.[53]

To defuse an explosive situation, Whig secretary of state John M. Clayton negotiated with Sir William Henry Bulwer, Britain's minister to the United States, the treaty that Douglas so hated. Designed to ensure

[53] Frederick Moore Binder, *James Buchanan and the American Empire* (Selinsgrove, PA, 1994), 144–45; Craig L. Dozier, *Nicaragua's Mosquito Shore: The Years of British and American Presence* (University, AL, 1985), 11, 69–72, 79; Wilbur Devereux Jones, *The American Problem in British Diplomacy: 1841–1861* (Athens, GA, 1974), 65–84.

that a canal would be built and to prevent either nation from dominating it, the treaty's first article provided that neither would assume "any exclusive control" over a ship canal by (1) fortifying such construction; (2) occupying, colonizing, or otherwise ruling "Nicaragua, Costa Rica, the Mosquito coast, or any part of Central America"; or (3) making an alliance or other agreement with a Central American government conferring an advantage to its citizens not equally provided to the other party to the treaty. Other articles provided for the canal's neutrality in the event of an Anglo-American war, required that the U.S. and British governments jointly protect parties engaged in constructing the water passage, endorsed tariff-free ports at both ends of the passageway, guaranteed protection for the canal and its neutrality following its construction, invited other nations to initial similar agreements, gave priority to canal contracts already in effect, and extended Anglo-American protection to anyone effecting isthmian transit by railway.[54]

Well enough. But the treaty suffered from a pernicious imprecision. Did it ban future colonization projects only, or did it also apply to Britain's prior inroads in Central America? Presenting Clayton's work to the Senate for ratification, President Taylor, wishing it ratified, obfuscated masterfully. He observed that Britain already had "nearly half of Central America" in its Mosquito Protectorate, and he invited the Senate to judge for itself how well the treaty preserved "the independence and sovereignty of all the Central American Republics." In fact, the negotiators had agreed to disagree on the treaty's meaning, since it otherwise would almost certainly have failed of ratification in one country or the other. As Bulwer explained to his government, it was "clearly understood" by both negotiators that "her Majesty's Government holds by its own opinions already expressed as to Mosquito, and that the United States does not depart from its opinions ... as to the same subject." Prior to ratifications being exchanged in the summer of 1850, Bulwer announced that Britain did not "understand" the treaty applied to "Her Majesty's settlement at Honduras, or to its dependencies [the Bay Islands]." Upon receiving Bulwer's statement, Clayton then filed his own clarification with the Department of State. He conceded he had written to Bulwer that

---

[54] Zachary Taylor message to the U. S. Senate, Apr. 22, 1850, *Sen. Executive Journal*, 31 Cong., 1 Sess., 166; Clayton-Bulwer Treaty, Apr. 19, 1850, in *The Clayton-Bulwer Treaty and the Monroe Doctrine, a Letter from the Secretary of State to the Minister of the United States at London, Dated May 8, 1882, with Sundry Papers and Documents ...* (Washington, DC, 1882), 82–85.

he understood when signing the treaty that British Honduras "was not embraced" in it, but he also affirmed that when negotiating he had been careful neither "to affirm or deny the British title in their settlement or its alleged dependencies." The "rights of no central American state" had been "compromised by the treaty," the secretary insisted. Later, Clayton suggested his treaty advantaged the United States because it permitted a canal across the British-claimed Mosquito Kingdom and because British Honduras was far from the envisioned canal route and thus not of strategic importance.

Evasion's sum effect, however, was a treaty allowing Britain a continued colonial presence in the isthmus while denying Americans territorial opportunities there, an arrangement Taylor and his commerce-minded party were willing to accept. The Whig president in his submission message criticized expansionists "who would desire to seize and annex any portion of the territories of these weak sister Republics." Clayton and Bulwer's deal inevitably, however, raised the ire of people who believed in America's hemispheric destiny. An appalled Robert J. Walker wrote to Douglas that it would be as easy to stop the Mississippi River's current as to halt U.S. territorial expansion, observing that California and Oregon were farther away than Central America.[55]

For his part, Douglas took an instant dislike to Clayton's treaty. In January 1850, he introduced a resolution requesting Taylor to send the Senate copies of the Hise and Squier draft treaties and official correspondence dealing with Central America, especially documents about Britain's Mosquito Protectorate and the Nicaraguan transit. After hearing from Squier about Britain's naval presence in Central American waters, Douglas joined ten other senators in dissent on May 22 when the Clayton-Bulwer Treaty was ratified 42–11. He especially went on the offensive after Britain's decision in March of 1852 to declare the conversion of its informal control over Roatán, Bonacca, and four islands near Honduras's Caribbean shore into an official "Colony of the Bay Islands." With his Tammany Hall speech in September, Douglas began a sustained

---

[55] H. L. Bulwer to Viscount Palmerston, Apr. 28, 1850, Declaration at the U.S. Department of State, June 29, 1850, John M. Clayton Memorandum, filed July 5, 1850, in *Clayton-Bulwer Treaty and the Monroe Doctrine*, 86–88; Robert J. Walker to SAD, May 4, 1850, SAD Papers, UC; Lewis Cass to James A. Pearce, James A. Pearce Papers, Maryland Historical Society, Baltimore; Jones, *American Problem*, 84–87; Dozier, *Nicaragua's Mosquito Shore*, 80; Elbert B. Smith, *The Presidencies of Zachary Taylor & Millard Fillmore* (Lawrence, 1988), 77; Jay Sexton, *The Monroe Doctrine: Empire and Nation in Nineteenth-Century America* (New York, 2011), 118.

verbal assault on Clayton's work that escalated when Lewis Cass threatened to seize the issue from him a few months later.[56]

On December 30, 1852, shortly after the second session of the Thirty-second Congress convened, Cass introduced a provocative resolution asking President Fillmore to share with the Senate not only what information he had about Britain's declaring the Bay Islands an official colony but also what the administration had done to enforce the Clayton-Bulwer Treaty's anticolonization provisions in the light of Britain's policy. Cass followed up this implicit attack with two more resolutions on January 4, the same day that Fillmore responded to Cass's December 30 request with a report to the Senate from the Department of State. Cass's latest resolutions restated principles announced three decades earlier in President James Monroe's annual message to Congress of December 2, 1823, when Monroe had announced U.S. opposition to any new European colonization projects in the Western Hemisphere. Cass's strong wording, while pledging that U.S. tolerance of "existing" colonial holdings would continue, warned that additional acquisitions – including the takeover of Spanish Cuba by a different power – posed such serious threats to national security that the United States would "adopt such measures as an independent nation may justly adopt in defense of its rights and its honor." Cass obviously intended his resolutions to threaten Britain with war if it persisted in its new colonization venture.[57]

Douglas managed to outflank Cass, however, in his own address of February 14, which was more hawkish than his rival's. In the process, Douglas helped dub the Monroe Doctrine for all time, likely inspired to do so by Squier, who wrote to him that it was time for "a more formal and emphatic affirmation of the Monroe doctrine than has ever yet been made." Observing that U.S. statesmen, orators, and politicians had eulogized Monroe's policy since its announcement in 1823, Douglas emphasized how its terminology had been seeping into the debates, acquiring "the dignified appellation of the '*Monroe doctrine*.'" Rather than praise Cass's ostensibly forceful resolutions, however, Douglas cautioned their recognition of "existing rights" in Central America would logically be taken by Britain as acquiescence in its earlier seizure of the Bay Islands. Besides, the warning clause in Cass's resolutions was redundant since

---

[56] CG, 31 Cong., 1 Sess., pt. I, 159; E. George Squier to SAD, Apr. 9, 1850, SAD Papers, UC; *Sen. Exec. Journal*, 31 Cong., 1 Sess., 186.

[57] E. George Squier to SAD, Dec. 24, 1852, SAD Papers, UC; *Sen. Journal*, 32 Cong., 2 Sess., 57, 199, 204; Paul A. Varg, *United States Foreign Relations, 1820–1860* (East Lansing, 1979), 225.

Monroe had himself given notice thirty years earlier that the nation would not sit by idly if new European colonies arose in the Americas. The Democratic Polk administration's unratified Hise treaty with Nicaragua, Douglas insisted, served national interests better than Clayton's document. The treaty with Bulwer not only invited European intervention in the Western Hemisphere but also pledged the United States to refrain indefinitely from territorial expansion necessitated by future events. Not presently covetous himself of Central America, Douglas hinted that rapidly changing conditions might cause him to decide the country needed Central American land lying "half way between our Atlantic and Pacific possessions" since it embraced "the great water lines of commerce between the two oceans." And there was yet another way the Clayton-Bulwer Treaty jeopardized America's future: in the event of war with England, it stacked the deck against the United States militarily since the British already had strongly fortified Jamaica, "the nearest military and naval station" to the likely canal route. Calling on the president to lodge a formal protest with Britain about its new colony, Douglas predicted Britain would retreat if the United States took a determined stand. Before finishing his remarks, Douglas addressed Cuban issues and derided the fifth article of the treaty ending the Mexican War, which stipulated that the U.S.-Mexican boundary (once surveyed) could only be altered with both nations' consent. Douglas argued that given political disorder below the border, the nation required the ability to take matters into its own hands should it be necessary to take more Mexican territory for national security or humanitarian reasons.[58]

Douglas's fierce attack caused Cass to respond immediately in what became a nearly three-hour debate involving other senators too in which the "Monroe doctrine" was repeatedly invoked. When Cass parried that Douglas's "hypercriticisms" were unwarranted and tried to back him into a corner by asking him whether he really would have the United States deny Britain's "existing rights" in Central America, Douglas again upstaged him by suggesting that all of Britain's possessions in Central

---

[58] *Sen. Journal*, 32 Cong., 2 Sess., 133; CG, 32 Cong., 2 Sess., Appendix, 170–73; Article 5, Treaty of Guadalupe Hidalgo, in *The United States and Mexico at War: Nineteenth-Century Expansionism and Conflict* (New York, 1998), 515–16; Sexton, *Monroe Doctrine*, 127. Lazarus W. Powell, Democratic governor of Kentucky, Hise's state, alerted Douglas to the advantages of Hise's treaty prior to Douglas's remarks, as did Hise. Powell to SAD, Jan. 15, 1853, Elijah Hise to SAD, Feb. 11, 1853, SAD Papers, UC. Much of Douglas's rhetoric on the Clayton-Bulwer Treaty seems derivative from Hise's bitter twelve-page letter.

America had developed after 1823 and constituted violations of the Monroe Doctrine's prohibition against future colonies. When Cass weakly claimed that Douglas's interpretation was indeed implicit within his own resolutions, Douglas asked Cass to reword them so they explicitly discountenanced not only the Bay Islands colony but the Clayton-Bulwer Treaty itself.[59]

Douglas carried his Anglophobic, expansionist crusade into the heated debates on Central America in a special session of the Senate convening on March 4, 1853, the day of Franklin Pierce's inauguration as president. Clayton himself, now sitting in the Senate and representing his state of Delaware, ignited the controversy on March 7 when he introduced resolutions about Central America involving territorial disputes over the San Juan River between Costa Rica and Britain and Honduras's claims to Britain's Bay Islands. The next day Clayton gave a long speech that carried over into the March 9 session, in which he vindicated his handling of the treaty negotiations with Bulwer. Douglas jumped into the fray the very next day, because some of Clayton's remarks attacked his own February speech on the treaty in the Senate, especially his preference for the Hise draft treaty with Nicaragua over Clayton's deal. Douglas defended Guatemalan claims to part of British Honduras and invoked an American duty to uphold "the integrity of every part of Central America" on behalf of states in the region too "weak and feeble" to stand up to the English lion. Douglas punctuated his remarks with Anglophobic allusions to English "aggressions," the "arrogance of British law," and the "haughty Court of St. James." Saying anew that the hemisphere needed liberation from Great Britain, he affirmed that national safety and honor held priority over the benefits of peace.[60]

Douglas's expansionist venom peaked in yet another speech on Central America on March 16, when he not only assailed the British but also asserted he was more antiabolitionist than southerners. Rebutting charges by Clayton that he was manipulating the Clayton-Bulwer Treaty for partisan ends and using extreme language to angle for a Democratic presidential nomination, Douglas asserted his own reasonableness: His refusal to tie U.S. hands in Central America went no further than the Whig Fillmore administration's rejection of the tripartite Cuba pact. Still, in a characteristic burst of Young American rhetoric, Douglas described Clayton's

[59] CG, 32 Cong., 2 Sess., 173–77. See also Gretchen Murphy, *Hemispheric Imaginings: The Monroe Doctrine and Narratives of U.S. Empire* (Durham, 2005), 62–63.

[60] CG, 32 Cong., 3 (Special) Sess., Appendix, 245, 247–56, 257–66.

policies as modeled on European "antiquated" diplomatic norms, which, emanating from a civilization that was little more than a "vast grave-yard" encumbered with the "relics of past centuries," found "no sympathy in the youthful, uprising aspirations of the American heart." Claiming presciently that the Clayton-Bulwer Treaty would do more to inhibit construction of a Central American canal than promote it, Douglas argued that Clayton's agreement failed to eject the British from an inch of their Central American holdings though it asked the United States, "a young nation, with all of her freshness, vigor, and growth," to accept "boundaries to her future growth." And this was a horrible outcome, given that England was an unfriendly power constantly raising fortifications in the Bermudas, the Bahamas, and Jamaica to "point her guns at America." When Senator Andrew Butler defended England as America's "mother" country, the font of its "law, literature, and free institutions," Douglas launched an even more severe diatribe, asserting that British writers universally slandered the American people and their institutions. A "cruel and unnatural mother," Britain had originated the abolition movement, which endangered the American nation by stirring up North-South friction. Britain's missionaries were constantly "perambulating" around the United States dispensing incendiary antislavery publications. When Douglas accused the British of distributing *Uncle Tom's Cabin* throughout the world to make other nations join "a common crusade against the peculiar institutions" of the South, the Senate gallery erupted in such rambunctious applause that the presiding officer warned he might have to clear out visitors (Figure 2.2).[61]

It was quite a performance. One onlooker in the noisy gallery above, the English visitor Henry Murray, thought Douglas was manipulating his topic for advantage in the race for the White House by delivering "Buncombe about England" from the perspective of Manifest Destiny and the "mare's nest called 'Monroe Doctrine.'" Nonetheless, Murray found Douglas's oratorical skills impressive. The senator delivered his "excellent clap-trap" fluently in a clear, loud voice that played to the audience, effectively pulling a hand out of a pocket to shake it in the air when he wished to make a convincing point. Douglas, to Murray, seemed conscious that many in the gallery welcomed his viewpoint and displayed great confidence in the way he delivered his remarks. A Whig paper in Washington was actually more upset than Murray, suggesting that the

[61] CG, 32 Cong., 3 (Special) Sess., 271–76.

FIGURE 2.2 Clayton Bulwer Polka.
Courtesy of the Library of Congress (sm1856 331400).
Note: Largely forgotten today, the Clayton-Bulwer Treaty of 1850, a pact between the United States and Great Britain, sparked heated political debate in the decade preceding the Civil War. Expansionists like Douglas attacked the treaty for curtailing future U.S. territorial growth in Central America while allowing Great Britain to retain colonies it already had in the isthmus. This sheet music, published in Philadelphia in 1856 when Douglas and the Democratic Party were especially concerned with Central American affairs, testifies to Central America's salience in American political discourse.

gallery's outburst was so unseemly as to threaten the Senate's stature as a deliberative institution.[62]

The debate ended ambiguously, with the Senate on March 17 agreeing to Cass's first resolution requesting the president to submit information about the San Juan River dispute and to postpone consideration of the second resolution, about Honduran claims to the Bay Islands, to Monday, March 21. On that day, Douglas briefly spoke again, repeating a self-characterization he made earlier in his speeches on Central America that he was actually peace-loving and never wished to see his country in war (Douglas had suggested a number of times that firmness would be the way to get reasonableness from British leaders). Still, Douglas reiterated that it would be a grave error to bind U.S. leaders forever from pursuing annexations that might prove necessary for the national interest and honor. Immediately after Douglas spoke, the Senate decided to lay on the table Clayton's second resolution and wait for information that President Pierce was bound to assemble during the upcoming congressional break.[63]

By 1853, Stephen A. Douglas had notoriety as one of his nation's leading expansionists and Anglophobes, if not Washington's premier territorial radical. His February 14 outburst caught the attention of the expansionist *New York Herald*, which believed he had laid out a Young American platform for the 1856 presidential race. This was a remarkable prediction, given that Pierce had yet to be inaugurated and the next presidential nominations were more than three years in the future. Back in Springfield, the *Daily Register* reprinted Douglas's various Senate speeches on the Central American treaties along with editorials calling Clayton a British lackey, attacking the Whigs for their caution on expansion, and lauding Douglas's oratory. To the *Register*, the Little Giant's March 10 speech marked the "most brilliant triumph" of his senatorial career.[64]

Naturally, Whigs saw matters differently. The party's mouthpiece in Chicago, the *Tribune*, chastised Douglas for taking "*English* phobia to an extent that borders on insanity" and obsessing about "old disputed claims for little States down in Central America." Rather, he should focus

[62] Henry A. Murray, *Lands of the Slave and the Free: Or, Cuba, the United States, and Canada* (London, 1855), 339–40; *Washington* (DC) *Republic*, quoted in (Springfield) *Illinois State Register*, Mar. 28, 1853.
[63] CG, 32 Cong., 3 (Special) Sess., 280, 290.
[64] *New York Weekly Herald*, Feb. 19, 1853; (Springfield) *Illinois State Register*, Feb. 17, 21, Mar. 25, 28, 29, 1853.

on Chicago's need to beat out rival St. Louis in building a transcontinental railroad to the Pacific. When reports reached the United States that a British warship had attacked and taken a port on the Honduran coast, a Philadelphia paper blamed it on Douglas and allied Democrats for degrading the Clayton-Bulwer Treaty.

Increasingly, too, Douglas was becoming identified with filibustering and the piratical spirit. Almost certainly the antislavery transcendental lecturer Ralph Waldo Emerson used Douglas for his model in a public talk entitled "The Anglo-American." Emerson noted that states on the Mississippi River fostered "low filibusterism" and described the "young American" as understanding the geography of the continent and missing nothing: "He thinks of Cuba, he thinks of Japan, he thinks of annexing South America, in due course! Nothing is impossible."[65]

In England, observers of the American scene saw Douglas as an American villain for his statements on Central America. On New Year's Day, an antislavery British periodical accused Douglas of promoting the idea that America's mission was to extend its domain "through Mexico to Central America, then ocean-ward to embrace East and West, the islands of the Pacific and the Atlantic, including the British possessions and the West Indies." Following his outbursts in the Senate against the Clayton-Bulwer Treaty, one London paper identified him as the "chosen patron" of Young America and asserted that he was pressuring President Pierce into an "impulsive rush against England and her supposed conspiracies." Another London news sheet ridiculed Douglas's "washy outpourings." Calling for English courage in the face of Douglas's "rhodomontade," the *London Daily News* emphasized the senator's charges about British "conduct" in Central America, though it believed England had been duped by "bankrupt English adventurers" into an unbeneficial involvement on the Mosquito Coast that ought to be abandoned as soon as possible.[66]

As it turned out, Douglas, elected by the Illinois legislature in January to a new term as U.S. senator, had less direct influence in the incoming administration than he, his backers, and the press anticipated. Despite Douglas's work for the Democratic ticket during the campaign, Pierce selected former secretary of war Marcy, from the party's Old Fogy faction,

[65] *Chicago Daily Tribune*, Mar. 22, 1853, Apr. 6, 1853; *Philadelphia North American and United States Gazette*, Mar. 15, 1853; *Milwaukee Sentinel*, Jan. 4, 18, 1853; *Raleigh (NC) Daily Register*, Mar. 26, 1853; *New-York Daily Times*, Mar. 24, 1853; Ralph Waldo Emerson, "The Anglo-American," *The Later Lectures of Ralph Waldo Emerson, 1843–1871* (2 vols.; Athens, GA, 2001), 2: 277–95.

[66] (London) *Anti-Slavery Monthly Reporter*, Jan. 1, 1853, p. 14; *London Morning Chronicle*, Apr. 2, 1853; *London Daily News*, Apr. 2, 1853.

as secretary of state. However, the new president did include Cuba annexationists Caleb Cushing of Massachusetts (attorney general) and U.S. Senator Jefferson Davis of Mississippi (secretary of war) within his cabinet family and packed his diplomatic corps in Europe with notorious champions of Manifest Destiny, including Pierre Soulé as minister to Spain. A rakish sort who kept a residual accent from his native France, Soulé was frequently linked with the Little Giant in press columns. Soulé gave a speech in the Senate on January 25 celebrating the manhood of Crittenden and his adventurers as they faced execution in Cuba ("How proudly that boyish chief ... confronts his fate"). Later that year, he signed off on a letter to George Sanders, "a sweet kiss to young America." None other than John L. O'Sullivan was slated as U.S. chargé d'affaires in Portugal.[67]

Even more encouraging to expansionists like Douglas, Pierce's March 4, 1853, inaugural address reaffirmed his country's opposition to European "colonization on this side of the ocean" and proclaimed territorial growth a matter of public policy. Celebrating how the number of stars on America's flag had grown to almost three times their original count, giving the lie to long-standing claims by antiexpansionists that "extended territory" would harm the nation, Pierce proclaimed his independence from "timid forebodings of evil from expansion" and announced that "the acquisition of certain possessions not within our jurisdiction" was necessary to benefit world peace and U.S. commerce, adding the caveat that they ought to be obtained honorably.[68]

Had the president and the Democratic Party caved to the calls of Douglas and other strident party expansionists for Cuba and territorial empire? Some Europeans thought so, as the Little Giant reportedly discovered when traveling abroad. Over the winter, Douglas's wife, Martha, had died of complications from giving birth to their infant daughter, and then the girl herself had died. In May 1853, Douglas sailed for Europe in the hope that a change of scene would revitalize him after the double tragedy. During the extended trip, he spent weeks in London, where he visited Parliament and met with leading politicians and figures prominent in English finance and cultural affairs. Then he sojourned in Turkey, France, Italy, Russia (where, according to one supposed eye-itness account, he

---

[67] Johannsen, *Douglas*, 356, 375–77; John M. Belohlavek, *Broken Glass: Caleb Cushing and the Shattering of the Union* (Kent, OH, 2005), 258; Clement Eaton, *Jefferson Davis* (New York, 1977), 101; *Vicksburg* (MS) *Tri-Weekly Whig*, Feb. 17, 1853; A. Oakey Hall, *The Manhattaner in New Orlean*, ed. Henry A. Kmen (Baton Rouge, 1951); CG, 32 Cong., 2 Sess., Appendix, 119; Pierre Soulé to George N. Sanders, Pierre Soulé Papers, Department of Archives and Manuscripts, Louisiana State University, Baton Rouge.
[68] Franklin Pierce Inaugural, JRMP, 5: 198–200.

had the privilege in St. Petersburg of talking with the czar and observing a review of Russia's army), Sweden, Denmark, and Germany. Possibly on his trip he talked about Cuban matters with Henry Quitman, the son of John Quitman, during his travels. The elder Quitman was just then considering an offer from Cuban exiles that he command a new Cuba filibustering invasion and tried to set up a European encounter of Douglas and Henry, who was planning a European tour of his own. Whether the meeting occurred is unknown.[69]

Douglas got an inkling of his expansionist image abroad, or at least his party's, while sojourning in Paris, after gaining a chance, along with U.S. senator from Tennessee James Jones, to meet with France's recently installed emperor, Napoleon III, and his stunning new wife, Eugénie de Montijo. Elected president of France in December 1848, Napoleon, the nephew of Napoleon Bonaparte, had seized power and overthrown the Republic in 1851 rather than surrender his office according to constitutional mandates and had his coup validated by plebiscite the following year. Apparently Empress Eugénie turned to Douglas during their conversation, saying she had heard he was "a prominent member of a party in the United States, organized for the purpose of wresting Cuba from Spain." When Douglas bantered back that although he indeed belonged to a party, it hardly had been organized "for so small a purpose as the annexation of Cuba," the empress retorted that were she Spain's queen, she would expend "the last drop of Spanish blood" rather than allow a U.S. foothold in Cuba. Again, Douglas tried to parry her assault, this time by bowing and quipping (we can imagine flirtatiously) that were the empress queen of Spain, her Cuban subjects would so love her that they would remain loyal rather than revolt for independence. Was Douglas compromised by his past rhetoric and expansionist stridency? He left the final word to Jones, who immediately reassured the empress that U.S. public opinion did not favor forceful seizure of Cuba from Spain.[70]

Around the same time that Stephen Douglas fended off Empress Eugénie's insinuations, U.S. black leader Frederick Douglass, addressing the

---

[69] Johannsen, *Douglas*, 381–86; John A. Quitman to SAD, May 4, 1853, Quitman Family Papers, Southern Historical Collection, University of North Carolina; Robert E. May, *John A. Quitman: Old South Crusader* (Baton Rouge, 1985), 271–72.

[70] Otto Friedrich, *Olympia: Paris in the Age of Manet* (New York, 1992), 32–33, 45–52; "Senator Douglas Abroad" (originally published in the *Cleveland Plain Dealer*), Paris correspondent of *Cincinnati Enquirer*, respectively, in *Worcester* (MA) *National Aegis*, Dec. 21, 1853, Jan. 11, 1854.

"Colored Men's State Convention" held at Troy, New York, on September 3, alerted his audience to a southern conspiracy afoot to have the nation absorb "Mexico, Southern [Baja] California, Cuba, the Sandwich Islands, all the islands of the Caribbean Sea, and Nicaragua ... placing their black population ... under the banner of the slave power." Douglass's sentiments were indicative of growing northern worries that Cuba's annexation might strengthen slavery in America, as might expansionist schemes for other tropical places including the Sandwich Islands, as Hawaii was commonly known. According to a young southerner allegedly expelled from Yale just that year, college president, Theodore Dwight Woolsey, had exclaimed during a student debate about the island that if slavery were allowed in an annexed Cuba, "I should oppose the measure – even to the dissolution of the Union."

Although annexing Cuba was a longtime U.S. foreign policy goal, it was problematic whether Stephen Douglas could build the cross-sectional coalition necessary to overcome growing antislavery resistance to getting the island or other tropical targets where slavery might flourish. Douglas's urging of expansion southward risked his appearing a tool of the slavocracy, without ensuring he would ever win the South for his presidential ambitions. Already, the *New York Times*'s Washington correspondent labeled Douglas as "beyond comparison, the most suggestive, original, daring, and unscrupulous leader" the Democratic Party had when it came to territorial growth and charged he belonged to a conspiracy of western and southern Democrats to get "St. Domingo, Cuba, and a province of Central America" for slavery. Whether Douglas could overcome such suspicions was problematic.[71]

Back in Washington for the first session of the Thirty-third Congress on December 5, Douglas made an easy target on this score. Taking note of Douglas's reappointment to the Senate's six-man Committee on Foreign Relations, headed by Virginia Democrat James Murray Mason, the antislavery *New York Tribune* prophesied that the United States would avoid waging war for "Liberty" in the near future but might well become belligerent over Cuba.[72]

---

[71] *Proceedings of the Black State Conventions, 1840–1865*, ed. Philip S. Foner and George E. Walker (2 vols.; Philadelphia, 1979, 1: 94; James Hamilton article in *Augusta* (GA) *Constitutionalist*, Mar. 26, 1853; Letter of Washington correspondent, July 1, 1852, in *New-York Daily Times*, July 3, 1852; http://utc.iath.virginia.edu/proslav/prar126mt. html; *Raymond* (MS) *Gazette*, quoted in *Vicksburg Weekly Whig*, May 22, 1850; *Southern Quarterly Review*, 21 (Jan. 1852), 3–4; *Jackson Mississippian*, Feb. 21, 1851.

[72] CG, 33 Cong., 1 Sess., 27; *New-York Daily Tribune*, Dec. 13, 1853.

3

Beyond Kansas

Stephen Douglas was in the friendly surroundings of New York City when he issued his challenge. He was staying at the St. Nicholas Hotel in the strongly Democratic and relatively pro-South metropolis following the passage of his controversial Kansas-Nebraska bill in May 1854 and probably did not yet fully grasp that his legislation made him a pariah in much of the North. After all, his boosters in the city, who threw several events in his honor, seemed untroubled by the vehement objections raised in the northern press and pulpit and on the floors of Congress against his measure. One celebration began around 11:00 p.m. on June 3, when a large gathering congregated outside his hotel, continuing after midnight as a more-than-thirty-piece brass band turned up to celebrate him. As the crowd cried, "Douglas, Douglas," the Little Giant strode to the balcony of the hotel and, after being introduced by a local Democratic leader, defended "the great principle of popular sovereignty" enshrined in his Kansas enactment. Then Douglas threw down the gauntlet. His critics, he warned, should back off in their vituperative attacks because his "Nebraska bill" was gaining popularity as people familiarized themselves with it. In fact, Americans would want the same principles applied in the future whenever *the question of the admission of any new State arises, whether it be Nebraska, Kansas, Oregon, Mexico, Cuba or the Sandwich Islands.*

Douglas's prognostication, picked up by the press, hardly mollified his detractors. The *New York Times* assumed that the very territorial growth for popular sovereignty Douglas optimistically anticipated would make the "extension of Slavery over all the territory which the United States now possess, or may hereafter acquire" into the "great aim and object of the Democratic party." Similarly, the antislavery *Washington National*

Era thought Douglas's remarks confirmation that the senator and his allies intended slavery's extension into future territorial acquisitions and suggested that Douglas's omission in his list of the Dominican Republic, a former Spanish colony on Haiti's eastern boundary that took up roughly two-thirds of the island of Hispaniola both countries occupied, was probably unintended. Before long, the paper predicted, the U.S. government would be secretly prosecuting a "Slave Power" plot for Cuba.[1]

Douglas's remarks at the St. Nicholas and the reaction they sparked suggest that America's sectional crisis in the mid-1850s related to slavery's expansion southward as well as to the west. Most accounts of the Kansas-Nebraska Act and the struggle over slavery in the Kansas Territory in its aftermath, however, treat Douglas's legislation with little thought as to its Caribbean implications. Nor do they sufficiently address linkages between Caribbean issues and the origins of Abraham Lincoln's Republican Party. Republicans rarely regarded Kansas as a cause divorced from other geographies, and it would have been remarkable had they done so since the nation had been growing southward as well as westward since the Louisiana Purchase. Jefferson's main territorial interest in his negotiations with France had been U.S. control of New Orleans and the Mississippi River's outlet to the Gulf of Mexico rather than the absorption of western plains. The Monroe administration's purchase of Florida was southerly growth and the annexation of Texas pointed toward the Tropics as much as it did the Pacific Ocean. As the Republican Party leader William H. Seward of New York emotionally cautioned his U.S. Senate colleagues, principles of governance established in Kansas applied to "all the Territories, present and future," a question with grave stakes since the nation was already embarked "upon a career of territorial aggrandizement."[2] By the time the struggle for Kansas resolved itself, Lincoln was as fully attuned as Douglas and Seward to the Caribbean implications of slavery's option on the West.

It is nearly impossible to imagine Abraham Lincoln ever being president had Congress not enacted Stephen Douglas's Kansas-Nebraska

---

[1] *New York Weekly Herald*, June 10, 1854; (Montpelier) *Vermont Patriot and State Gazette*, June 9, 1854; *New-York Daily Times*, June 6, 1854; *Washington* (DC) *National Era*, June 15, 1854; James A. Rawley, "Stephen A. Douglas and the Kansas-Nebraska Act," John R. Wunder and Joann M. Ross, "'An Eclipse of the Sun': The Nebraska-Kansas Act in Historical Perspective," both in *The Nebraska-Kansas Act of 1854*, ed. Wunder and Ross (Lincoln, NE, 2008), 71–75, 2.
[2] CG, 34 Cong., 1 Sess., Appendix, 1089–1114.

Act of 1854, one of the most divisive pieces of legislation in the nation's history. Douglas's measure, signed into law by President Franklin Pierce on May 30, was highly controversial because in creating the new territories of Kansas and Nebraska it repealed the Missouri Compromise of 1820, which had prohibited slavery in all future territories carved out of the Louisiana Purchase above the parallel of 36°30'. Since Kansas and Nebraska lay above that line, they should have become territories without slavery. But Douglas's measure substituted popular sovereignty for the 1820 ban, allowing the two territories' settlers to decide whether to allow human bondage. To Douglas, chair of the Senate's Committee on Territories, the measure sensibly renewed principles of local democratic rule already applied by Congress in the Utah and New Mexico popular sovereignty language of the Compromise of 1850. Countless northerners, though, considered Douglas's decision a sellout to the Slave Power, the arbitrary overturning of a sectional contract that had preserved the Union for decades, and worried that slavery might thrive in Kansas, given its location directly west of the slave state of Missouri (Nebraska, lying directly west of the free state of Illinois, seemed less endangered). One critic questioned whether Douglas had been self-interested in pushing his legislation, given his Mississippi slaveholdings, where whippings took a daily toll on "woman's shrinking flesh." Now he could dispose of slaves at a premium to southerners bound for Kansas who needed laborers there (Figure 3.1).[3]

Douglas intended his measure to facilitate the construction of a northern transcontinental railroad originating possibly in Chicago to the Pacific Ocean, since western lands could not be surveyed prior to territorial organization. He integrated the Missouri Compromise repeal into his bill not to spread slavery, but because southerners in Congress informed him that territorial organization would fail without it. Convincing himself that the climate of Nebraska and Kansas was inhospitable anyway to slavery, Douglas apparently expected that free-soil would win out in any sectional competition. But he had trouble convincing northern public opinion, even in his own party. When the House of Representatives recorded its narrowly positive tally for the Kansas legislation on May 22 (113–100), as many free-state Democrats voted for rejection as passage (they split 44–44). Most northern Democrats who voted positively

---

[3] *Detroit Democrat* quoted in *Chicago Daily Tribune*, Jan. 27, 1854; "A Southron" in the *St. Louis Intelligencer*, quoted in *Chicago Daily Tribune*, Sept. 29, 1854.

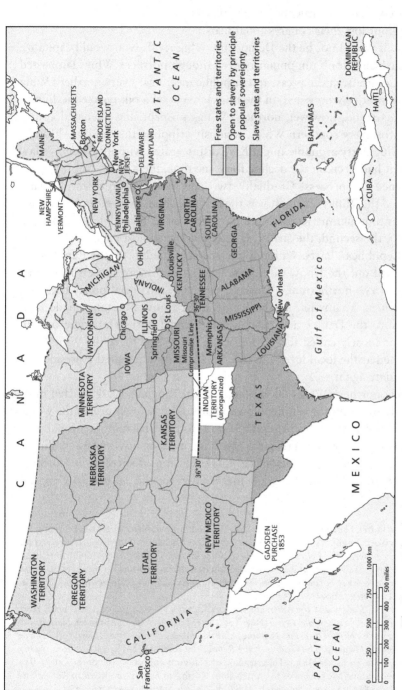

FIGURE 3.1 The Kansas-Nebraska Act.

Note: Stephen Douglas's Kansas-Nebraska Act of 1854 was hated in much of the North because it allowed slavery in two new territories located in what was previously unorganized territory north of the 36°30' parallel (the southern boundary of the state of Missouri). The Missouri Compromise of 1820 had prohibited slavery in this region.

angered their constituents. In the fall 1854 election, all but seven of the forty-four lost their congressional seats.[4]

Yet it would not be the Democrats' Whig rivals who would capitalize on the legislation's unpopularity even though northern Whigs lambasted it in Congress, in the press, and at public meetings. Every northern Whig representative who voted on the Kansas-Nebraska bill rejected it. In taking this stand, however, northern Whigs unsurprising alienated countless proslavery southern Whigs, seriously crippling their party. Although the Whig Party arguably might have disintegrated without Douglas's law since it had been on the decline for some time, the Kansas-Nebraska Act hastened the process. Gradually, two new political organizations supplanted the Whigs. The first was the transsectional, anti–Roman Catholic and antiimmigrant Know Nothing Party (more formally the American Party); the second, the stridently free-soil and almost exclusively northern Republican Party. Within a few years, in the North, the Republicans squeezed out the Know Nothings, who had no more success at uniting their party's northern and southern wings on territorial policy than had the Whigs. Meanwhile in the South, most Know Nothings made their way into the Democracy, though some joined anti-Democratic organizations loosely called the "Opposition." Here and there the Whig Party survived at the local level, but the Whigs never nominated a presidential candidate again.[5]

Few northern Whigs taking umbrage at Douglas's work reacted more angrily than Abraham Lincoln, who harnessed the measure, in the words of one historian, as his personal "vehicle to ride" back into national politics. Beginning with his remarks at a Whig meeting in Winchester, Illinois, in late August 1854, Lincoln gave a succession of speeches in northern and central Illinois towns and cities, calling for the election to Congress

[4] David Potter, *The Impending Crisis, 1848–1861*, ed. and completed by Don E. Fehrenbacher (New York, 1976), 145–62, 165–67, 169–72, 175; Michael A. Morrison, *Slavery and the American West: The Eclipse of Manifest Destiny and the Coming of the Civil War* (Chapel Hill, 1997), 142–47, 154; Robert W. Johannsen, *Stephen A. Douglas* (1973; rpt., Urbana, 1997), 390–418; Nicole Etcheson, *Bleeding Kansas: Contested Liberty in the Civil War Era* (Lawrence, 2004), 11–15.

[5] Morrison, *Slavery and the American West*, 126, 131, 138–39, 152, 154; Michael F. Holt, *The Political Crisis of the 1850s* (New York, 1978), 101–38; Tyler Anbinder, *Nativism & Slavery: The Northern Know Nothings and the Politics of the 1850s* (New York, 1992); William E. Gienapp, *The Origins of the Republican Party, 1852–1856* (New York, 1987), 16–67; Steven E. Maizlish, "The Meaning of Nativism and the Crisis of the Union: The Know-Nothing Movement in the Antebellum North," in *Essays on American Antebellum Politics, 1840–1860*, ed. Stephen E. Maizlish (College Station, 1982), 166–98.

of men who would have the Kansas measure repealed and the Missouri line restored. With his political ambitions rekindled by Douglas's measure, Lincoln also attempted an aggressive but ultimately unsuccessful letter-writing campaign during the fall and winter hoping to round up sufficient support so the Illinois legislature would choose him as the state's next U.S. senator. Though he tried to remain a Whig as long as possible, Lincoln ultimately joined the migration to Republican ranks and in May 1856 played a prominent role at the state Republican convention in Bloomington. Later that year, he also campaigned for the famous western explorer and former U.S. senator from California, John C. Frémont, the Republicans' first presidential candidate.[6]

Lincoln's initial attacks on the Kansas-Nebraska Act were western-centered, yet he also seems to have been concerned about slavery's course southward. In the Senate, Douglas had charged northern congressional free-soilers with hypocrisy for professing devotion to the Missouri Compromise, since at the end of the Mexican War they had unanimously opposed proposals to extend the 36°30' line farther westward to lands that Mexico ceded. Lincoln rejoined that just because he and similarly inclined Whigs wanted to keep the 1820 sectional bargain for the land (including Kansas and Nebraska) encompassed by the Louisiana Purchase to the east, they were not compelled for consistency's sake to apply the Missouri line "to any future territory acquired by the United States." At Springfield on October 4, Lincoln clarified his argument by analogy: "If a man comes to me ... and advises me to build an addition to my house and I decline to do so, shall that man burn my house down, and say I have decided against any house at all, because I am unwilling to spread it out and extend it?" Twelve days later, at Peoria, Lincoln not only denounced Douglas's law for permitting slavery into Kansas and Nebraska but also for foreshadowing the principle that it could "spread to every other part of the wide world, where men can be found inclined to take it." As if he feared his audience might miss his point, Lincoln repeated that "the authors of Nebraska" intended their "principle" for "future use"

---

[6] Gienapp, *Origins of the Republican Party*, 122–23, 286–95; George B. Forgie, *Patricide in the House Divided: A Psychological Interpretation of Lincoln and His Age* (New York, 1979), 251; AL to Thomas J. Henderson, Nov. 27, 1854, AL to Elihu N. Powell, Nov. 27, 1854, AL to Hugh Lemaster, Nov. 29, 1854, AL to Joseph Gillespie, Dec. 1, 1854, AL to Elihu B. Washburne, Dec. 19, 1854, Jan. 6, Feb. 9, 1855, AL to Ichabod Codding, Nov. 27, 1854 (copy), CWAL, 2: 288–306; David Herbert Donald, *Lincoln* (1995; rpt., New York, 1995), 178–85, 187–94; Richard J. Carwardine, *Lincoln: Profiles in Power* (London, 2003), 59.

in "the planting of slavery wherever in the wide world, local and unorganized opposition can not prevent it." To Lincoln, such a construction would make slavery last forever, and he warned that the Declaration of Independence itself was now jeopardized; instead of liberty, slavery would become "the chief jewel of the nation – the very figure-head of the ship of State." Already, he reported, "the liberal party throughout the world" worried that slavery was "undermining" republican institutions in "the noblest political system the world ever saw."[7]

Though Lincoln did not specify where U.S. slavery might head under Douglas's script, he surely envisioned the Gulf-Caribbean, given Douglas's public identity as apostle for Manifest Destiny and the annexation of Cuba. Plenty of other politicians of all persuasions measured the Kansas legislation by its Caribbean implications. A former Whig congressman from Virginia, John Minor Botts, for instance, accurately predicted that repealing the Missouri Compromise would ultimately do more to cripple the South's pursuit of empire in the Tropics than to abet it, because it would harden northern resistance to the acquisition of Mexico and Cuba as slave states. More typically, commentators predicted that passage of the Kansas legislation would foster slave expansion southward. A Washington correspondent for a Philadelphia paper, taking note of political turmoil occurring in Spain, interpreted Douglas's bill as a trap to upstage Pierce for the 1856 Democratic presidential nomination, observing that "the South" was "bent upon acquiring all the territory it can in that direction." Similarly, the Democratic *Washington Union* suggested the bill applied "to all future acquisition" and would draw Cuba into the Union for slavery. A Democratic meeting called at Aurora, Illinois, to endorse the Kansas-Nebraska Act, resolved that the Democratic Party should now champion popular sovereignty "in any future legislation upon territories now or hereafter to be acquired."[8]

Antislavery northerners, in fact, began bracing themselves for Caribbean slavery projects originating in Douglas's measure. An Ohio Presbyterian minister sermonized about his concern about whether, if the "insatiable" and ruthless "slave power" could impose "this great fraud upon freedom," anything could stop it "from demanding Cuba

[7] CG, 33 Cong., 1 Sess., 277; CWAL, 2: 226–27, 229, 230–33, 234–40, 240–84, 285.

[8] John Minor Botts to the *National Intelligencer*, Washington (DC) *Daily National Intelligencer*, Feb. 16, 1854; Washington correspondent's report, Jan. 26, 1854, in *Philadelphia Inquirer*, Jan. 28, 1854; *Washington Union*, quoted in *New York Tribune* and republished in (Dedham, MA) *Norfolk Democrat*, May 26, 1854; Aurora resolutions of October 5, 1854, quoted in *Chicago Daily Tribune*, Jan. 29, 1855.

or Hayti, or the Sandwich Islands?" The *Chicago Tribune* wondered whether now "Slavery" imagined it could "push Uncle Sam into quarrels with his neighbors to acquire territory and slave states out of it." Abolitionist minister Theodore Parker argued privately that the time had arrived to "defeat our great enemy" in its planned grab of Cuba and its intentions to legalize the African slave trade, a program antislavery types frequently lumped together with slavery's Caribbean projects. An upset Senator Charles Sumner of Massachusetts predicted in turn to Parker that the South would strike for Cuba, Mexico, and Haiti. Black abolitionist William Wells Brown expected "our Southern masters" to follow up their triumph in Kansas and Nebraska by taking Cuba but told a Boston audience he hoped they could be staved off in Haiti. The *National Era* warned northern congressmen that if Douglas got away with repealing the Missouri Compromise, southern ambitions would "be satisfied with nothing short of the seizure of Cuba" and "the absorption of all portions of Mexico fit for slave tillage."[9]

On June 20, free-soil northern congressmen convened a bipartisan gathering in Washington chaired by Whig U.S. senator Solomon Foot of Vermont, which unanimously adopted an address to the American people warning about the Kansas law's implications for territory "which hereafter may be acquired." Painting an alarming picture, the document anticipated that President Pierce would seek Cuba and half a dozen Mexican states for slavery, even if such programs meant war with Spain, England, and France. Further, the slave states and their lackey president wanted the Dominican Republic and Haiti for "the dominion of slavery." Once those objectives were secured, the congressmen predicted, the government would seek a Brazilian alliance giving U.S. slavery entrée into the Amazon River valley. Foot carried the message home when Congress adjourned. Addressing a Whig and free-soil gathering in Montpelier, Foot claimed that Pierce's "pliant administration" and associated northern "dough-faces" were bent on handing the South two slave states in Cuba, worth four senators and twelve representatives in Congress, plus

[9] Rev. J. B. Bittinger, *A Plea for Humanity. A Sermon Preached in the Euclid Street Presbyterian Church, Cleveland, Ohio* (Cleveland, 1854), 22; *Chicago Daily Tribune*, Feb. 10, 1854; *Washington* (DC) *National Era*, Feb. 9, 1854; Theodore Parker to Charles Francis Adams, May 19, 1854, Adams Family Papers, Reel 542, Massachusetts Historical Society; Charles Sumner to Theodore Parker, June 7, 1854, in Life and Correspondence of Theodore Parker, ed. John Weiss, 2 vols. (New York, 1864), 2: 140; (Boston) *Liberator*, Oct. 20, 1854; *Wooster* (OH) *Republican*, Sept. 7, 1854; Gienapp, *Origins of the Republican Party*, 76.

Mexico, Central America, and the Dominican Republic. The senator's concern about the latter was shared by the *New York Evening Post*, which speculated that the United States would extract land grants from the Dominican Republic for buttressing up its weak government; in a country thinly inhabited by an "enervated and inferior race," a mere one hundred to two hundred Americans could seize control, give slavery constitutional protection, and "open a new slave market" prior to the logical step of complete annexation. Likewise, the *National Era* convinced itself that Douglas intended to give "slavery an opportunity of insinuating itself" in the Dominican Republic, until it enfolded "the whole island in its crushing coils."[10]

Later in the year, Lincoln heard from an Illinois politico appalled by the Caribbean implications of Douglas's law. A self-identified "Anti-Nebraska" Illinois state legislator inclined to favor Lincoln's candidacy for a U.S. Senate seat told him the time had arrived to settle "forever whether slavery shall be restricted to its present limits, or whether by the annexation of Cuba, by appropriating our own territory once consecrated to freedom, & by the conquest of Mexico or other territory extend the terra of slavery indefinitely." The slave states, he argued, had to be forestalled in their quest for political dominance in Washington.[11]

Given what was actually happening at the time, antislavery jeremiads of a Kansas-Caribbean nexus amounted to more than fear-mongering. In October 1853, a scrawny Tennessee-born adventurer named William Walker led a band of filibusters, many of them gold rush dropouts, from California to Mexican Baja California and stayed for months before being chased out by Mexican irregulars. During his occupation, Walker declared the founding of an independent Republic of Lower California with him as president. In May 1854, around the time Walker retreated to U.S. territory, Douglas moved in the Senate that the Committee on Foreign Relations investigate the "expediency" of official U.S. recognition of the Dominican Republic. In June, the Pierce administration instructed a commissioner sent there to seek a lease on part of one of the country's bays for an American naval coaling station. More significantly, that same spring the Pierce administration acquired a new slice of Mexico.

[10] Report from Washington, DC, June 21, 1854, in *New-York Daily Times,* June 22, 1854; *St. Albans* (VT) *Messenger,* Nov. 11, 1854; *New York Evening Post,* May 24, 1854; *Washington* (DC) *National Era,* June 1, 1854.
[11] Augustus Adams to AL, Dec. 17, 1854, AL Papers, Series 1, LC.

The Gadsden Treaty – negotiated in 1853 and ratified by the Senate on April 25, 1854 – for $10 million gained some forty-five thousand square miles in today's southern New Mexico and Arizona to support a potential southern transcontinental railroad line to the Pacific Ocean. The agreement also gave the United States transit rights in Mexico's narrow Isthmus of Tehuantepec. Meanwhile, Pierce's administration committed military aggression in Central America. In July 1854, an American naval captain bombarded and literally leveled the port of Greytown in Britain's Mosquito Protectorate over port fees imposed by local authorities.[12]

Free-soilers especially feared southern intentions to make Cuba into a slave state in reaction to rumors reaching the United States that Spain was on the verge of capitulating to long-standing British pressure to emancipate Cuba's slaves and "Africanize" the island. Southerners took alarm even at talk of emancipation in Cuba, which would preclude them from ever making it an American slave state. Besides, southerners naturally worried that "Africanization" might inspire their own slaves to rebellion given Cuba's proximity to southern shores. Some southern expansionists wanted the United States to get Cuba by war or purchase before their doomsday scenario began. Others preferred filibustering, since filibusters presumably could strike more quickly than the government, doing so before Spanish officials even got emancipation under way. In May 1854, Georgia congressman Alexander H. Stephens predicted privately that by August Spanish authorities in Cuba would declare free about half the island's slaves. Stephens wondered when aid would leave American shores to help Cuba's besieged planters avert the catastrophe.[13]

[12] Joseph A. Stout, Jr., *Filibustering in Mexico, 1848–1921* (Fort Worth, 2002), 33–37; *Senate Journal*, 33 Cong., 1 Sess., 406–407; Donathon C. Olliff, *Reforma Mexico and the United States: A Search for Alternatives to Annexation, 1854–1861* (University, AL, 1981), 39–43; *Senate Journal*, 33 Cong., 1 Sess., 406–407; Robert E. May, "Lobbyists for Commercial Empire: Jane Cazneau, William Cazneau, and U.S. Caribbean Policy," *Pacific Historical Review* 48 (Aug. 1979): 392–94; Larry Gara, *The Presidency of Franklin Pierce* (Lawrence, 1991), 130–32; David F. Long, *Gold Braid and Foreign Relations: Diplomatic Activities of U.S. Naval Officers, 1798–1883* (Annapolis, 1988), 124–28. Douglas's resolution called the Dominican Republic the "republic of Dominica," a common appellation at the time.
[13] Alexander H. Stephens to J. W. Duncan, May 26, 1854, *The Correspondence of Robert Toombs, Alexander H. Stephens, and Howell Cobb*, Annual Report of the American Historical Association for 1911, ed. Ulrich Bonnell Phillips (Washington, DC, 1913), 2: 345; Stephens to ?, May 9, 1854, *Life of Alexander H. Stephens*, ed. Richard Malcom Johnston and William Hand Browne (1878; rev. ed., Philadelphia, 1884), 276. For long-standing southern fears of military threats to U.S. slavery from the British West Indies or British forces using Haiti and Cuba see Matthew J. Karp, "Slavery and American Sea

Africanization rumors were the main reason John Quitman accepted a commission from Cuban exiles in the United States to head an expedition to Cuba "at as early a time as possible." By the time the Kansas-Nebraska bill passed, Quitman was deeply mired in filibuster plans, recruiting a mostly southern officer corps, stockpiling supplies, scouring for ships to charter, and even marketing bonds for the supposed Republic of Cuba he would found across the Gulf of Mexico. In the Senate, John Slidell of Louisiana attempted to legalize Quitman's scheme by promoting legislation that would temporarily suspend the Neutrality Act of 1818. Although Quitman went to great lengths to maintain secrecy, his plot became so infamous that a theater in New Orleans ran a farce based on it entitled *Those Fifteen Thousand Filibusters!* Press reports and speculations about Quitman's doings appeared so frequently that it is no exaggeration to call his conspiracy one of the worst kept secrets of the day. A Charleston, South Carolina, newspaper reported on the day before the president signed the Kansas legislation, "Gen. QUITMAN is the reputed chief of the filibusters, and boasts that ten thousand men are awaiting a signal at New Orleans to sail for Cuba." A Cincinnati sheet posted a story stating that $600,000 had been deposited in Louisiana's state bank to fund an invasion of Cuba and members of a local club had invested in $10,000 expedition shares. "Gen. Quitman of Mississippi," the report noted, was "at its head, and, is to take the command." Quitman's invasion plot continued churning the news even after a federal judge in June 1854 forced him to post $3,000 bond to curb his invasion for the next nine months. As Lincoln started speaking out on Kansas, a press story originating in Washington asserted that "agents of the Cuban expedition now fitting out under the command of Gen. Quitman" had been in the capital sounding out Pierce and cabinet members as to whether or not they would allow the filibuster to occur.[14]

Power: The Navalist Impulse in the Antebellum South," *Journal of Southern History* 77 (May 2011): 283–324.

[14] Robert E. May, *John A. Quitman: Old South Crusader* (Baton Rouge, 1985), 270–92; *New Orleans Daily Picayune*, June 14, 1854; *Charleston (SC) Daily Courier*, May 29, 1854; *Cincinnati Daily Enquirer*, June 27, 1854; *New Orleans Bulletin* report in (Natchez) *Mississippi Free Trader*, June 17, 1854; New York *Evening Post* account summarized in *New York Herald*, June 19, 1854; Q.E.D. to the *New York Herald*, June 20, 1854, in *New York Herald*, July 2, 1854; report dated Washington, Sept. 11, in the *New York Tribune*, reprinted in *Natchez Courier*, Oct. 25, 1854; *Richmond Whig*, June 21, 1854; *Washington (DC) Daily National Intelligencer*, June 19, July 22, 1854; (Rochester, NY) *Frederick Douglass' Paper*, June 23, 1854.

Although Pierce came out strongly against Quitman's plot, a major factor (along with the waning of the emancipation scare) in Quitman's cancelling the enterprise in April 1855, the president was nearly as worried as southerners about Cuban Africanization. Pierce could hardly afford politically to alienate the Democratic Party's strong southern base with inaction. No sooner did he take office in March 1853 than he appointed a special agent to travel to Havana and check on conditions there; when the agent reported finding no evidence of Africanization plans, the administration sent a second investigator. Secretary of State William L. Marcy instructed James Buchanan, now U.S. minister to Great Britain, to warn the English to relax their pressure on Spain to free Cuba's slaves if they wished to preserve good relations with the United States. Additionally, the administration launched brazen initiatives to acquire the island, well aware that their timing was auspicious; neither Britain nor France was likely to intervene to preserve Spain's rule over Cuba since in 1854 they became bogged down militarily in the Crimea.[15]

Initially, the administration tried to take advantage of a February 1854 naval incident at Havana when Spanish authorities seized the New York and Atlantic Steamship Company's vessel *Black Warrior* for alleged violations of Spanish port regulations. Amid jingoistic calls for war, the president announced that if no settlement with Spain were reached, he would employ all the means Congress put at his disposal to gain redress for U.S. grievances and uphold the American flag. Although Spanish authorities released the vessel on March 16, Pierce still hoped that Spain's precarious national finances would play to the administration's advantage in getting the island. Marcy told the U.S. minister in Madrid, Pierre Soulé, to offer Spain up to $130 million for Cuba, adding that if it resisted, Soulé should investigate other ways "to detach that island from the Spanish dominion and from all dependence on any European power." That summer, Pierce requested a $10 million congressional appropriation for a three-man commission to negotiate a purchase in Madrid, hoping that a strategy promoted by Buchanan and the banker August Belmont (U.S. chargé d'affaires to The Hague) would work. The scheme sought to pry Cuba from reluctant Spanish officials by bribes and pressure from European bondholders of Spain's defaulted national debt. Buchanan and Belmont

---

[15] Joshua R. Giddings to "My Dear Sir," Aug. 20, 1853, quoted in *New York Herald*, Sept. 1, 1853; Robert E. May, *The Southern Dream of a Caribbean Empire, 1854–1861* (Baton Rouge, 1973), 35–36, 54; Allan Nevins, *Ordeal of the Union*. vol. 2: *A House Dividing, 1852–1857* (New York, 1947), 42, 49, 58–59, 62.

believed that the bondholders would welcome U.S. annexation as a step toward having their loans repaid. When Congress denied the appropriation, Marcy asked the U.S. ministers to Spain, Britain, and France to meet at Ostend, Belgium, counting on them to mature the plan.

The gathering that followed, initially at Ostend and continuing in Prussia at Aix-la-Chapelle, mustered considerable diplomatic brain power, since it included several lesser Democratic officials, such as Buchanan's secretary of legation, the New Yorker Daniel Sickles. Instead of implementing the intended financial strategy, however, the trio at Aix-la-Chapelle on October 18 signed the misleadingly dubbed "Ostend Manifesto." This disgracefully expansionist diplomatic brief warned that Cuba was on the verge of being "Africanized" into a "second St. Domingo, with all its attendant horrors to the white race" and justified U.S. ownership under the national security logic of "self-preservation." Not intervening, the ministers argued, was tantamount to "base treason against our posterity." Restraint might even break up the Union, since the nation's "internal peace" (meaning the security of the slave states) would be endangered. The ministers implied that the nation should go to war for Cuba if necessary, stipulating that if Spain refused its sale, "then, by every law, human and divine, we shall be justified in wresting it from Spain." Although they sent the document by courier to Washington and did not release it publicly, the conference itself drew negative press attention abroad, and soon summaries of the manifesto circulated in American papers, causing a number of prominent northern Democrats including Lewis Cass to denounce it rather than become identified with a document widely perceived as proslavery.[16]

Given Stephen Douglas's notoriety as a Cuba acquisition activist, it is surprising how rarely his name is mentioned in the Cuba schemes of Pierce and Quitman. Daniel Sickles wrote to Douglas from London in April 1854 mulling over diplomatic strategies for the island. Whether Douglas did anything with Sickles's information, however, is unknown. Douglas did attend a White House conference on Cuban policy with the

---

[16] May, *Southern Dream*, 41–44, 67–71; Nevins, *Ordeal of the Union: A House Dividing,* 354–63; Irving Katz, *August Belmont: A Political Biography* (New York, 1968), 31; Frederick Moore Binder, *James Buchanan and the American Empire* (Selinsgrove, PA, 1994), 200–16; James Buchanan, Pierre Soulé, and John Y. Mason, "The Ostend Manifesto," in *Manifest Destiny and American Territorial Expansion: A Brief History with Documents,* ed. Amy S. Greenberg (Boston, 2012), 126–27; Richards, *Slave Power,* 199.

Senate Committee on Foreign Relations' other Democratic senators and the chair of the House Committee on Foreign Affairs, but what he said or advised also remains unrecorded. According to one newspaper, President Pierce used that occasion to announce that he intended to follow a diplomatic strategy for Cuba and issue a presidential proclamation against filibustering, which Slidell unsuccessfully opposed. The most suggestive document about Douglas's involvement in the 1854 Cuba machinations is a May 1854 letter to Quitman from New York congressman Mike Walsh. Walsh claimed that Douglas had reassured him that Pierce would allow Quitman to sail for Cuba unimpeded by federal authorities, so long as Quitman's preparations avoided the kind of public attention that would necessitate Pierce's enforcing the Neutrality Act.[17]

At the same time, Douglas remained attentive to U.S. interests in Central America, especially when news arrived that American filibusters had seized control of Nicaragua, then in the middle of a civil war. In mid-1855, William Walker took an "American Phalanx" of fifty-six adventurers from California to Nicaragua's western coast and, with the help of allied Nicaraguans, emerged the republic's dominant figure. After a hard military campaign, Walker in late October negotiated a treaty that created a provisional coalition government with the native Nicaraguan Patricio Rivas as president, but with himself holding the real power as commander in chief of the army. Since Nicaragua had never recognized Britain's protectorate on the Mosquito Coast, Walker's success had the potential to advance Douglas's longtime goal of U.S. strategic and commercial supremacy in the region, but much depended upon the filibuster's objectives and British reactions.

Would the U.S. government regard Walker as a potential ally? On November 10, the American minister to Nicaragua, a North Carolina slaveholder named John H. Wheeler, recognized the Rivas-Walker régime without prior clearance from Washington. Secretary of State Marcy, however, feared that Walker's intrusion would exacerbate American territorial disputes in the isthmus with Great Britain and reprimanded Wheeler, ordering him to cease relations with Walker's régime. When Walker's appointee as minister to the United States, a disreputable adventurer and promoter named Parker French, turned up in Washington in December,

[17] Daniel Sickles to SAD, Apr. 26. 1854, quoted in Amos Aschbach Ettinger, *The Mission to Spain of Pierre Soulé, 1853–1855* (New Haven, 1932), 295–86; John Slidell to James Buchanan, June 17, 1854, James Buchanan Papers, HSP; *New York Herald* quoted in (Concord) *New Hampshire Statesman*, June 17, 1854; Mike Walsh to John A. Quitman, May 25, 1854, John A. Quitman Papers, Houghton Library, Harvard University.

Marcy rejected his credentials. Further, President Pierce issued an executive proclamation reminding Americans that filibustering was unlawful and cautioning that U.S. citizens should neither participate in Nicaraguan military operations nor recruit for them. Over the following months, the administration attempted to enforce this policy by preventing men and supplies for Walker from leaving U.S. ports.[18]

Defying the administration, Walker's agents signed up volunteers for Nicaraguan military service anyway, raising men and funds in port cities like San Francisco, New York, New Orleans, Mobile, and Philadelphia, as well as interior locales, especially in the South, California, and the Old Northwest. Many filibuster recruits managed to elude the federal dragnet against them, by pretending to be emigrants bound for the California gold fields via the Nicaraguan crossing. Meanwhile, many U.S. families and individuals eager to start anew abroad or pursue business schemes on the isthmus investigated Nicaraguan opportunities, and some traveled there. Douglas was approached in March 1856 by former Illinois Democratic senator Sidney Breese, who thought that the Little Giant might help his "enterprising" son Henry's prospects with a letter of recommendation to Walker. A lawyer in the town of Carlyle, Illinois, Henry was contemplating "trying his fortune in Nicaragua where … a fine field is open."

Although many Americans disparaged the pint-size Tennessean as a pirate, large numbers worshipped the charismatic Walker (popularly the "gray-eyed man of destiny") as an exemplar of American manliness and honor who would beneficially engraft on the benighted natives of Central America the democratic and progressive tendencies of his own country. According to the *New York Times*, such a throng crowded into a meeting for Walker at the city's National Hall on May 9 that it overflowed the site, causing a second meeting to be organized outside the building. Down in New Orleans, Douglas's Young America accomplice Pierre Soulé, who had returned from Spain, braved late April temperatures of more than 100° to tell a crowd at the St. Louis Hotel they should rally to Walker's support. Even observers inclined to disparage filibusters as lawless, such

[18] Arturo J. Cruz, Jr., *Nicaragua's Conservative Republic, 1858–93* (Cambridge, UK, 2002), 29–42, 44; Charles H. Brown, *Agents of Manifest Destiny: The Lives and Times of the Filibusters* (Chapel Hill, 1980), 257–313, 324–25, 387; May, *Southern Dream*, 98; Robert E. May, *Manifest Destiny's Underworld: Filibustering in Antebellum America* (Chapel Hill, 2002), 45–46, 140–41; Franklin Pierce Proclamation, Dec. 8, 1855, JRMP, 5: 388–89; William Perry to Thomas Sturchy, Mar. 25, 1856, PRO, General Correspondence Colombia and New Granada, F 55/124; Richard W. Van Alstyne, "American Filibustering and the British Navy: A Caribbean Analogue of Mediterranean Piracy," *American Journal of International Law* 30 (Jan. 1938): 141.

FIGURE 3.2 William Walker.
Source: From Sara Agnes Rice Pryor, *My Day: Reminiscences of a Long Life* (New York: Macmillan Company, 1909), p. 120.

as the editors of the *Chicago Tribune*, conceded that Walker and his soldiers were men of "muscle and activity." With their "feats of daring," they would surely conquer all of Central America (Figure 3.2).[19]

Anxious to reverse the Pierce administration's nonrecognition policy and to increase the flow of men and materiel from the United States, Walker approached Douglas for help, an unsurprising decision given the

---

[19] Amy S. Greenberg, *Manifest Manhood and the Antebellum American Empire* (New York, 2005), 135–69; May, *Manifest Destiny's Underworld*, 156–57; Ivor D. Spencer, *The Victor and the Spoils: A Life of William L. Marcy* (Providence, 1959), 370–71; Sidney Breese to SAD, Mar. 29, 1856, SAD Papers, UC; *New-York Daily Times*, May 10, 1856; *New Orleans Daily Delta*, Apr. 29, 1856; *Chicago Daily Tribune*, Apr. 7, 1856; *New York Herald*, May 17, 1856.

Little Giant's record of favoring American hegemony in Central America. During February and March 1856, Walker and his accomplices lobbied Douglas to exert his influence on behalf of Walker's claims to official U.S. recognition. On February 14, after rumors appeared in the press that Douglas favored a U.S. alliance with Walker "against John Bull," Parker French beseeched Douglas to back Walker and suggested the way to get the Pierce administration to help Walker yet save face on its non-recognition policy would be for Congress to modify the Neutrality Act of 1818, which upheld English interests in the isthmus. A month later, the Democratic newspaperman and editor John P. Heiss, serving as a U.S. State Department agent on a mission to Nicaragua to investigate conditions there, contacted Douglas from Walker's capital in Granada. Heiss asserted that the filibuster was so solidly entrenched he could resist military opposition from all the other Central American states. Thus he merited U.S. recognition under the nation's standard practice of recognizing governments secure in their tenure. Douglas's "valuable services" were needed to help a movement "tending to Americanize" the entire isthmus. Then, on March 30, Walker personally wrote to Douglas from Granada, massaging Douglas's Anglophobia. Walker told Douglas his government had intercepted mails proving that England was supplying Costa Rica with two thousand muskets to expel him. By that date, too, the Cuba filibuster plotter John Quitman had upped the pressure on the Little Giant. Quitman had issued a public letter endorsing Douglas for the 1856 Democratic presidential nomination partly because, as a "man of progress," he had the right "Central American principles." Clearly, Walker and his allies expected a lot of Douglas.[20]

Through April 1856, however, Douglas refrained from endorsing filibustering in a public statement, even though there was pro-Walker feeling in his own state's Democratic Party. Former governor John Reynolds considered Walker an improvement on Nicaragua's former government despite being a "philabuster" and believed his expedition, with support from Pierce, might succeed in conferring freedom on all of Central

[20] *New York Herald*, Feb. 12, 1856; Parker French to SAD, Feb. 14, 1856, John P. Heiss to SAD, Mar. 14, 1856, William Walker to SAD, Mar. 30, 1856, SAD Papers, UC; Roy F. Nichols, *Franklin Pierce: Young Hickory of the Granite Hills* (1931; rev. ed., Philadelphia, 1958), 460–61; John A. Quitman to "My Dear Sir," Mar. 24, 1856 in *Natchez Free Trader* (no date provided) and Quitman to a friend, Mar. 24, 1856 (different version of same letter), in *Cincinnati Enquirer* (no date provided), extracts republished in *Washington* (DC) *Constitution*, Feb. 9, 1860. Walker had intercepted a British dispatch dated February 4, which Wheeler forwarded to the Department of State, promising two thousand shoulder arms for Costa Rica. Brown, *Agents of Manifest Destiny*, 340.

America. Douglas's tongue, though, remained silent. As the flagrantly expansionist *New Orleans Delta* – which favored the Little Giant for president as "safer and sounder" on Cuba than Pierce and stronger "in all questions of international difficulty involving the 'manifest destiny' of the United States" – noted, Douglas remained "uncommitted towards Central America." Douglas's laggardness likely had something to do with his being preoccupied by health problems that began in the fall of 1855. In late October, Douglas developed severe hoarseness that morphed into such a horrific case of bronchitis that death was feared, and he underwent a series of throat operations in Cleveland, starting in late December. He did not return to Washington until early February, and he could not resume his congressional duties for some time more. But Douglas's delay in taking a public stance on Walker also reflected his understanding that filibustering was a criminal activity, which he had avoided explicitly endorsing in the past.[21]

Finally, in the Senate on May 1, Douglas took his stand, perhaps with his eye on the upcoming Democratic nominating convention scheduled for Cincinnati on June 2. Douglas applauded Walker's movement after California senator John B. Weller moved that the president submit to the Senate correspondence between Nicaragua and the U.S. government and announced that he disliked the administration's nonrecognition policy regarding Walker's régime. Saying that his California constituents were pressuring him on the issue, Weller defended Walker as a man of character whose purpose was "to aid in establishing free institutions in Nicaragua" and contended it was particularly important to stabilize U.S.-Nicaraguan relations given that country's importance for communication with the Pacific coast. He contended Costa Rican forces had been waging "a war of extermination against these countrymen of ours." Douglas entered the fray after William Seward cautioned that recognizing Walker would incite further Costa Rica depredations against Americans on the isthmus and that the United States should depend on overland communication to the Pacific via a transcontinental railroad through its own territory rather than on transit through an unstable foreign territory. Seward predicted that the "interposition" of a "large North American element" in Central America would lead inevitably to demands that the isthmus be annexed, which would greatly complicate U.S. relations with Great Britain (Figure 3.3).

[21] John Reynolds to Lyman Trumbull, March 31, 1856, Reel 1, Lyman Trumbull Papers, LC; *New Orleans Daily Delta*, Apr. 4, May 2, 1856; Johannsen, *Douglas*, 484–85.

FIGURE 3.3 William H. Seward.
Courtesy of the National Archives and Records Service (111-B-4559).

Apparently provoked by Seward's implicit disavowal of Manifest Destiny in Central America, Douglas retorted that he had no intentions of rehashing his well-known opposition to the Clayton-Bulwer Treaty, but he wanted it understood that Britain's construction of that document threatened all U.S. interests in Central America. Further, though he respected Pierce's conduct of U.S. diplomacy, he considered Walker's government "as legitimate as any which ever existed in Central America" and believed it merited recognition under the nation's traditional policy of accepting the legitimacy of governments in control of their domain. Arguing that Walker's régime was more stable than any Central American government since the overthrow of Spanish rule, Douglas said he had no qualms about "an American by birth" commanding Nicaragua's army since all American citizens had a "sacred" right to expatriate themselves if they so desired. Nicaragua might "become an asylum" for American emigrants, just as the United States had been for Europeans. Nicaragua was as justified in giving Walker a military command as American revolutionaries had been when they commissioned men like Lafayette. Although Douglas did not want Americans to violate international law, the nation had "great interests which should lead us to sympathize deeply with the movement now going on in Central America." Not only should the United States never discourage attempts to "consolidate and perpetuate" forms of government in Central America similar to its own institutions, it should consider annexing the entire region once it was sufficiently "Americanized." Contending that he did not want to tie the president's hand by demanding official correspondence, Douglas announced his opposition to Weller's resolution. Pierce should be given a free hand in giving the Senate information when he deemed it expedient, not upon demand. After additional discussion, Weller withdrew the resolution as Douglas requested.[22]

Four days after Douglas went public for Walker, Britain's minister to the United States John F. Crampton (who earlier in his Washington tenure had derided Douglas as an "arch-Filibustero" in a dispatch home) used Douglas's speech as proof that Great Britain should now anticipate "Yankee supremacy" in all the transit routes across Central America to California, possibly through the agency of "some piratical 'Branch American Government'" (an obvious allusion to Walker's régime). Around the same time, U.S. newspapers took note of the arrival in New York City and then Washington of a new envoy to the United States from Walker's government. Reportedly, Pierce and his cabinet were holding heated debates on Walker and Douglas was bringing to bear all the pressure he could so that Pierce would reverse course on recognition. Walker's replacement for Parker French, Granada's curate Padre Augustin Vijil (sometimes spelled Vigil), was a native Nicaraguan with an unblemished reputation, obviating the objections that had complicated the administration's reaction to Parker French. Douglas's name became further associated with Walker's after he telegraphed the organizers of the Walker meeting in New York City on May 9, promising to attend unless his work in Congress made it impossible for him to leave Washington. On May 14, Pierce, likely with an eye on his renomination chances at the upcoming Democratic convention, bowed to the pressure from Douglas and other Democratic expansionists and officially received Vijil as minister. Secretary Marcy confided in a missive to Buchanan's replacement

[22] CG, 34 Cong., 1 Sess., 1069–72.

as U.S. minister in London, George M. Dallas, that the decision, which he considered premature, was driven by reports that Britain was providing military aid to Walker's enemies in Costa Rica and elsewhere on the isthmus.[23]

Amid speculation that the Democratic national convention would endorse Walker's cause in Nicaragua and that Douglas's presidential candidacy would be the beneficiary, the party's delegates gathered at Smith and Nixon's Concert Hall in Cincinnati on June 2 and gave Douglas half a loaf. Their platform is best remembered for its ringing, unanimous endorsement of the Douglas-Cass territorial dogma of popular sovereignty. Defining the "organic laws establishing the Territories of Kansas and Nebraska" as the sole way to resolve the sectional dispute over slavery and preserve the Union, the convention spelled out the Kansas-Nebraska principle, using capital letters to drive home its point: "NON-INTERFERENCE BY CONGRESS WITH SLAVERY IN STATE AND TERRITORY, OR IN THE DISTRICT OF COLUMBIA." But the platform also reflected mounting pro-Walker ferment in northern cities at the time; in fact, Parker H. French was in Cincinnati while the convention met, lecturing one night at the local Masonic Hall. Reflecting this rising profilibuster spirit, especially in their own party, the delegates adopted a set of foreign policy planks separate from their domestic statements, whose first sentence bluntly asserted that foreign policy positions were every bit as important as domestic ones.

The endorsements that followed spelled out Douglas's line on Latin America. The second foreign policy plank, adopted by a 239–21 vote, called for the upholding of the Monroe Doctrine "with unbending rigidity." The third, passing 180–56, backed the U.S. right to maintain "free communication" across the isthmus of Central America and U.S. claims to "preponderance in the adjustment of all questions" of isthmian transit. The fourth, voted through by a 221–38 margin, gave William Walker's régime an indirect but ringing endorsement, saying that the party

[23] John F. Crampton to Lord Clarendon, July 31, 1854, May 5, 1856, BBPC, 105, 151; report from Washington, May 3, 1856, *Charleston Daily Courier*, May 7, 1856; report from Washington, May 5, 1856, *New York Herald*, May 6, 1856; *New-York Daily Times*, May 5, 1856; report from Washington, May 15, 1856, *New Orleans Daily Delta*, May 22, 1856; Franklin Pierce to the Senate and the House of Representatives, May 15, 1856, JRMP, 5: 373–74; Alejandro Bolaños-Geyer, *William Walker: The Gray-Eyed Man of Destiny*, Book 4: *War for Liberation* (Lake Saint Louis, MO, 1990), 21; *Chicago Daily Tribune*, May 8, 1856; *Worcester* (MA) *National Aegis*, May 21, 1856; William L. Marcy to George M. Dallas, June 16, 1856, WRM, 7: 138–41. Douglas wound up passing on the New York event. *Alexandria* (VA) *Gazette*, May 13, 1856.

approved "the efforts which are being made by the people of Central America to regenerate" the isthmian crossing. The fifth resolution summoned America's next president to make "every proper effort" to ensure U.S. "ascendancy in the Gulf of Mexico." In fact, the party was pushing such an exclusively expansionist, hemispheric program that only one of the category's planks – a call for freedom of the seas and free trade – was not specifically oriented to the Gulf-Caribbean. Appalled, the Whiggish Philadelphia diarist Sidney George Fisher lambasted the platform for enshrining "the principles of filibusterism & universal rapacity & arrogant dictation to other nations & southern aggression."[24]

But the convention withheld its nomination from the candidate most identified with the Kansas-Nebraska Act, the Monroe Doctrine, and America's southward expansion. Douglas remained in Washington as his candidacy fell short, just as it had in 1852. Starting with 63 votes on the first ballot, he nearly doubled that total on the sixteenth, with 122. However, James Buchanan, recalled from his diplomatic post in England at his own request, arrived back on U.S. soil toward the end of April and won the nomination, as a result of the work of his adept set of managers in Cincinnati. The Pennsylvanian edged out Douglas and Pierce, with Lewis Cass also receiving a handful of votes. Buchanan had the advantage of being out of the country when the Kansas-Nebraska bill was debated and enacted, saving himself from being identified with legislation that was becoming increasingly unpopular in the North, as the competition between free state and proslavery settlers for control of the Kansas Territory deteriorated into bloody civil strife. Besides, Buchanan's candidacy meshed with the party's Caribbean beat. As one of the authors of the Ostend Manifesto, Buchanan gained appreciation as a Cuba annexationist, especially in the South. Slidell of Louisiana wrote to him in April 1855 that the wording of the manifesto reflected Buchanan's "sound judgment and practiced pen." At Cincinnati, Slidell emerged a key wire puller for Buchanan, lining up votes for his candidate (Figure 3.4).[25]

---

[24] Report from Washington, *Charleston Daily Courier*, May 7, 1856; *Jackson* (MI) *Citizen*, May 8, 1856; *Official Proceedings of the National Democratic Convention Held in Cincinnati, June 2–6, 1856* (Cincinnati, 1856), 23, 26, 30–31; *Cincinnati Daily Enquirer*, June 3, 4, 5, 1856; Sidney George Fisher Diary, June 7, 1856, *A Philadelphia Perspective: The Diary of Sidney George Fisher Covering the Years 1834–1871*, ed. Nicholas B. Wainwright (Philadelphia, 1967), 257.

[25] *Official Proceedings ... 1856*, pp. 38–60; Johannsen, *Douglas*, 505–20; Nevins, *Ordeal of the Union: A House Dividing*, 434–37, 452–60; Roy Franklin Nichols, *The Disruption of American Democracy* (1948; rpt., New York, 1962), 22–32; John Slidell to James Buchanan, Apr. 3, 1855, James Buchanan Papers, HSP; May, *Southern Dream*, 72.

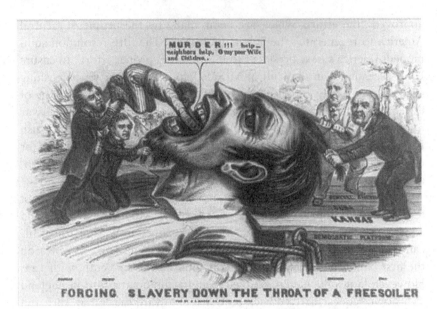

FIGURE 3.4 *Forcing slavery down the throat of a freesoiler*, 1856 lithograph by
J. L. Magee.
Courtesy of the Library of Congress (USZ62–92043).
Note: This anti-Democratic cartoon shows Democrats using force to impose slav-
ery on Free-Soilers. At the cartoon's left, Douglas (far left) is joining President
Franklin Pierce in gagging the Free-Soiler with slavery. At the far right, it is made
evident that James Buchanan, the Democratic presidential nominee, and Lewis
Cass stand on a proslavery platform linking Cuba with Kansas.

Though disappointed, Douglas was hardly crushed by his defeat,
partly because the convention's message seemed an indication that he
was on the right track politically with his recent position statement on
Walker's government. Even before the convention finished its work, a
reporter in Cincinnati surmised that the Democratic platform's Latin
American planks were designed "to set up in business for the next four
years, Stephen A. Douglas." Still in his early forties, the Little Giant could
look ahead to 1860 and was told to do so by his friends. By no means
embittered, Douglas rushed west to Indiana and Illinois after Congress
adjourned in late August and stumped for the Democrats' bachelor
candidate, who wound up victorious in November.[26]

---

[26] Cincinnati correspondent's report, June 4, 1856, *Louisville Daily Journal*, June 6, 1856;
Johannsen, *Douglas*, 521; Nevins, *Ordeal of the Union: A House Dividing*, 452.

Though a latecomer to Republican ranks and relatively inexperienced in national politics, Abraham Lincoln received the second highest total of votes for the vice-presidential nomination at the first Republican national nominating convention, convening at Philadelphia on June 17. That gathering is mostly remembered for nominating Frémont and adopting a free-soil platform with attacks on popular sovereignty. Its preamble disparaged the Missouri Compromise's repeal and slavery's penetration of the Kansas Territory; its policy pronouncements demanded that the "twin relics of barbarism – Polygamy and Slavery" be kept out of the territories, the allusion to polygamy being an attempt to tap into anti-Mormon prejudice at a time of tension between Washington and Mormon church authorities in the Utah Territory. Slavery's prospects southward, however, also received attention, with Republicans inverting what had occurred at the Democratic gathering in Cincinnati. Speakers repeatedly denounced the "Slave Power," a term generally understood as incorporating southern designs on the Tropics. Owen Lovejoy of Illinois, the martyred abolitionist Elijah's brother and a former Liberty Party and abolitionist activist, took the Democracy to task, asking whether the "manifest destiny of the American nation" was "to go fillibustering over the continent" and "plant slavery" in conquered territory, a question that aroused the delegates to loud cheering. Unlike the Democracy's platform, which implicitly endorsed the Ostend Manifesto, the Republicans' document denigrated its logic:

That the highwayman's plea, that "might makes right," embodied in the Ostend Circular, was in every respect unworthy of American diplomacy, and would bring shame and dishonor upon any Government or people that gave it their sanction.[27]

From its organizational moments, the Republican Party reflected free-soil concerns about Latin America as well as Kansas. In fact, tropical worries surfaced even at the meeting that summoned the Philadelphia nominating convention. When delegates gathered at Pittsburgh in February 1856 to formalize a national Republican organization and plan for the party's nominating meeting, they adopted an address to the American people, complaining that the Pierce administration was trying

---

[27] *Proceedings of the First Three Republican National Conventions of 1856, 1860, and 1864, Including Proceedings of the Antecedent National Convention Held at Pittsburg, in February, 1856, as Reported by Horace Greeley* (Minneapolis, 1893), 66, 31, 33, 34, 43–45; Richard H. Sewell, *Ballots for Freedom: Antislavery Politics in the United States, 1837–1860* (New York, 1976), 112, 159–60, 277n.

to spend $200 million to get Cuba and threatening war against every nation in Europe to service the Slave Power by preventing the emancipation of Cuba's slaves. Certainly Republicans expressed more concern with the Tropics than the third national party competing in the 1856 election, the American Party, which gave its own presidential nod to former chief executive Millard Fillmore. That party's platform entirely ignored Caribbean affairs, dwelling mostly upon supposed threats to America's political system from immigrants. Still, even the Know Nothings worried somewhat about tropical expansion. A Fillmore campaign song alluded to Buchanan as a man whose "coat has turned at least once a year, / From the Hartford to the Ostend Convention," and American Party members frowned on the idea of making the Catholic peoples of Latin America U.S. citizens. Resolutions for Fillmore at a Philadelphia mass meeting denounced the Ostend Manifesto as piracy and predicted that Buchanan, if elected, could be expected to support filibustering.[28]

Following their Philadelphia convention, Republican concerns about the Tropics deepened because of new developments in Central America. By 1856, the isthmus's other states were beginning to see the growing number of American filibusters in Nicaragua as seriously threatening their own security. In March 1856, Costa Rica's president, Juan Rafael Mora, had declared war on the filibusters and sent an army under the command of his brother to invade Nicaraguan territory. Mora hoped to topple the Walker-Rivas régime but was frustrated when a horrific outbreak of cholera among Costa Rican troops forced abandonment of the campaign. Nicaragua's neighbors became even more alarmed by developments after the Costa Ricans' withdrawal. After a long period of deteriorating relations with President Rivas, Walker declared him a traitor on June 20, causing Rivas to take up arms against him. Undaunted, Walker claimed the presidency for himself and took office on July 12, following a tainted election held only in the parts of the country remaining under his control. According to Walker's statistics, his 15,835 votes approximately doubled the combined vote of three Nicaraguan candidates. In his inaugural address at Granada, Walker pushed all the buttons of Manifest Destiny. He lambasted Central America's "imbecile rulers" and promised

[28] Thomas Hudson McKee, *The National Conventions and Platforms of All Political Parties, 1789 to 1904* (1901; 5th ed., rev., 1904), 100–102; *Official Proceedings of the Republican Convention Convened in the City of Pittsburgh, Pennsylvania, on the Twenty-Second of February, 1856* (New York, 1856), 23; *Fillmore & Donelson Songs for the Campaign* (New York, 1856), 26–27; *Philadelphia Public Ledger*, July 3, 1856; (Wilmington) *Delaware Weekly Republican*, Oct. 30, 1856.

his own administration would encourage the arts, civilization, education, and "the utmost liberty of speech and action compatible with order and good government." He also announced his intention to make Nicaragua a "highway" for interoceanic commerce by allowing "the greatest possible freedom of trade" within its borders. Perhaps more significantly, Walker, soon after taking office, initiated land expropriations from his Nicaraguan enemies that were designed to solidify the filibusters' control over the country and entice a new wave of land-seeking immigrants from the United States.

Walker's usurpations had repercussions both in Washington and throughout the isthmus. Even before news arrived in Washington that Walker had claimed Nicaragua's presidency, Padre Vijil abandoned his ministerial post on June 23 (debarking for Nicaragua two days later), leaving John P. Heiss temporarily in charge; Heiss had returned to the United States in April from his mission to Nicaragua, where he had acquired mining interests. On August 12, Heiss solicited Douglas's opinions on Nicaraguan matters, predicting that Pierce would disapprove of Walker's assuming Nicaragua's presidency, a prophecy that was fulfilled when Vijil's replacement as minister plenipotentiary arrived a few days later. Walker had unwisely chosen for the mission one of his régime's arms suppliers and recruiters, the New York City shipping firm executive and Tammany Hall operative Appleton Oaksmith, who had attended the Granada inauguration. When Oaksmith arrived in Washington, Pierce and Marcy refused to receive him, though they also refrained from recognizing Walker's enemies in Nicaragua as the country's legitimate government. Making matters worse for the filibuster, Guatemala, Honduras, and El Salvador formed an alliance against him and launched an offensive into Nicaragua that conquered ground from the filibuster army and initiated what would be remembered as Central America's "National War."[29]

[29] Michel Gobat, *Confronting the American Dream: Nicaragua under U.S. Imperial Rule* (Durham, NC, 2005), 38; E. Bradford Burns, *Patriarch and Folk: The Emergence of Nicaragua, 1798–1858* (Cambridge, MA, 1991), 207; Brown, *Agents*, 304–305, 325–36, 343–50; Ralph Lee Woodward Jr., *Rafael Carrera and the Emergence of the Republic of Guatemala, 1821–1871* (Athens, GA, 1993), 287–89; William O. Scroggs, *Filibusters and Financiers* (New York, 1916), 173, 175–76, 201–203; Bolaños-Geyer, *William Walker*, Book 4, pp. 62, 65; text of Walker's inaugural, from *El Nicaraguense*, enclosed with John H. Wheeler to William L. Marcy, July 15, 1856, WRM, 4: 544n–545n; William O. Scroggs, ed., "Walker-Heiss Papers: Some Diplomatic Correspondence of the Walker Regime in Nicaragua," *Tennessee Historical Magazine* 1 (Dec. 1915), 334; Documents about the North American Chontales Company, John P. Heiss Papers, Tennessee Historical Society, Nashville; John P. Heiss to SAD, Aug. 12, 1856, SAD Papers, UC; John

Desperate for reinforcements from the United States, Walker tried to offset Pierce's nonrecognition policy by enlisting southern aid. Hoping to preserve his rule by attracting more men, funds, weapons, and supplies than he had been so far receiving from the South, Walker issued a decree on September 22 that repealed prior legislation outlawing slavery in Nicaragua, effectually legalizing human bondage in the isthmus. The initiative energized many southern expansionists for his cause as intended, particularly in the Gulf states, but it had the secondary effect of appalling antislavery northerners.

Even before Walker embraced slave labor, many Republicans and northern abolitionists anticipated he would do something of the sort. They already identified filibustering with the Democratic Party and proslavery aggressions in Kansas, and they knew Walker hailed from a slave state. "Freedom shrieks in Kansas, and rabid democracy ... yells for Walker, Nicaragua, injustice, strife, and piracy generally," complained one Republican correspondent from New York in May 1856. Horace Greeley's *New York Tribune* dubbed Walker "the agent and pioneer of the Slavery Extension leaders," an "advanced guard" in a plot to make all of Central America into not only slave states but a base for a military campaign to take the "great prize" of Cuba. Once word arrived in mid-October that Walker had legalized slavery, antislavery northerners considered their worst fears realized. After hearing the news, the *New York Times* reported a prevailing impression that Walker was "the tool of Southern Slaveholders – pledged to carry out their programme of restoring Slavery in Central America, wresting Cuba from Spain," and legalizing the African slave trade. The *Liberator* bemoaned the filibuster opening Nicaragua to the "'peculiar institution'" and pronounced him "agent of the Slave Power."[30]

Over the summer and early fall, Republican orators and editorialists capitalized on the Ostend Manifesto and Walker's filibuster to convey urgency to Frémont's candidacy. A Republican sheet in Indiana took

J. TePaske, "Appleton Oaksmith, Filibuster Agent," *North Carolina Historical Review* 35 (Oct. 1958): 427–29, 433–38; Nichols, *Franklin Pierce*, 460–61; Hersch Lauterpacht, *Recognition in International Law* (Cambridge, UK, 1947), 352.

[30] "VIOLA" letter of May 26, in *Milwaukee Daily Sentinel*, May 30, 1856; *New York Tribune*, May 5, 1856, quoted in Bolaños-Geyer, *Gray-Eyed Man*, Book 4, p. 23; *New-York Evangelist*, May 22, 1856; (Washington, DC) *National Era*, June 19, Oct. 23, 1856; *New York Herald*, Oct. 19, 1856; *Daily Cleveland* (OH) *Herald*, Oct. 22, 1856; New-York Daily Times, Nov. 18, 24, 25, 1856; (Boston) *Liberator*, Oct. 24, 1856; *Milwaukee Daily Sentinel*, Oct. 27, 1856; *Boston Daily Advertiser*, Oct. 30, 1856; May, *Manifest Destiny's Underworld*, 262–64.

note of Buchanan's Cuba credentials, for instance, as evidence of his "devotion to the interests of Slavery and Fillibusterism." The *New York Tribune* alerted voters that the logic used in "the attempt to steal from the Free States the Territory of Kansas" mirrored the doctrine "enunciated by Mr. Buchanan at Ostend," and that both initiatives amounted to a Slave Power plot to increase the security of slaveholders by preserving southern dominance of the U.S. Senate. In Rhode Island, textile manufacturer Rowland Gibson Hazard regularly referenced Buchanan's Ostend Manifesto assistance to the Slave Power in his stock campaign speech for Frémont. Similarly, Founding Father Alexander Hamilton's son James A. Hamilton weighed in with a lengthy public letter, emphasizing southern Caribbean plots as cause enough for northern voters to reject Buchanan's candidacy. Hamilton asserted that southerners sought to obtain Cuba through Buchanan's agency as groundwork for a planned empire outside the Union, one including Central America, Mexico, and all of the United States above Kansas's border with Nebraska in addition to Cuba.[31]

Republican songwriters and cartoonists mocked Buchanan's expansionist record and Walker's aggressions in Central America. One Republican songster printed a number of pieces with Caribbean themes and allusions. A tune in it alluded to the Democracy's candidate, saying, "Let Buchaneers [meaning Buchanan] quarrel for Cuba and slaves – Fremont's the man for the Free." Another cynically traced Buchanan's Cuba machinations in Europe:

> To Ostend once went this very old man,
> And this honest scheme did reveal –
> We'll buy Spain's daughter, Cuba if we can,
> And what we can't buy we'll steal

Still another songster tune announced that Republicans refused "Buck's Ostend brags, brags, brags." "John Fremont's Coming," in the same publication, adapted the familiar tune of "Old Dan Tucker" to promise that "Border ruffians, filibusters, Will be swept by strong nor'westers," with border ruffians applying to armed Missourians who entered Kansas to give proslavery types control over the territory. A song to the same tune

[31] *Richmond* (IN) *Palladium*, Oct. 2, 1856; *New-York Daily Tribune*, June 30, 1856; Shearer Davis Bowman, *At the Precipice: Americans North and South during the Secession Crisis* (Chapel Hill, 2010), 56; James A. Hamilton to Hamilton Fish, Oct. 4, 1856, *Fremont, The Conservative Candidate: Correspondence between Hon. Hamilton Fish, U.S. Senator from New York, and Hon. James A. Hamilton, Son of Alexander Hamilton* (n.p., 1856), 13–18.

entitled "Get out of the way, old Buchanan" reported Buchanan's intentions to spend the nation's treasure for Cuba or seize it and highlighted
his presumed plans for Walker and Central America:

> Says, it is no more than justice,
> To sustain the filibusters
> In the slave regeneration
> Of the Nicaraguan nation!

An Englishman who passed the last part of the election campaign in
Chicago, St. Paul, and other parts of the Midwest stereotyped Republicans
as hating filibustering even more than the English did because they felt it
tarnished America's image overseas and strengthened slavery.[32]

Such attitudes hardly receded after the election, when Buchanan
defeated Frémont by a sixty electoral vote margin (Fillmore only won
eight electoral votes). Writing to a southern correspondent early in
December 1857, the Bostonian railroad developer and executive John
Murray Forbes observed that the significance of the territorial question
transcended the outcome in Kansas, because whatever happened there
would determine whether the United States would conquer or buy "all
the territory and islands north of Panama for the mere extension of
your institution." Forbes noted that some of the South's "bold and ultra
men" were calling for slavery in Mexico, Central America, and Cuba
and observed that the Democrats' Cincinnati platform gave northerners
plenty to worry about. He warned that the North was becoming so outraged that only a presidential candidate "sharply opposed to the extension of slavery at home and abroad" could win northern electoral votes
in 1860. Similarly, a Republican who favored giving Frémont a second
shot at the White House in 1860 told Illinois Republican U.S. senator
Lyman Trumbull that southerners planned to "keep the balance of power
in the Senate for many years to come" by swallowing up Cuba, Central
America, and Mexico.[33]

Southerners processed the Republicans' 1856 campaign message that
their opposition to slavery's expansion was two-directional. A month
after the election, the *New Orleans Delta*'s correspondent in Washington

---

[32] Thomas Drew, comp., *The Campaign of 1856: Fremont Songs for the People, Original
   and Selected* (Boston, 1856), 7, 8–9, 17, 56–58; James Stirling letter, Jan. 11, 1857, *Letters
   from the Slave States* (London, 1857), 1–35, 108.
[33] John Murray Forbes to J. Hamilton Cowper, Dec. 4, 1856, *Letters and Recollections of
   John Murray Forbes*, ed. Sarah Forbes Hughes (2 vols.; Boston, 1899): 1: 152–55; Samuel
   Hoard to Lyman Trumbull, Mar. 14, 1858, Lyman Trumbull Papers, Reel 4, LC.

observed that Republican policy amounted to a belief "that one section has the right to indefinite expansion, while the other is to be restricted to its present confined limits." Only Cuba's acquisition, the paper argued, would restore enough southern voting power in the U.S. Senate to ensure "an effectual check" on Republican attacks (an allusion, probably, to the requirement than any alteration to the U.S. Constitution abolishing slavery would require among other things a two-thirds Senate vote). Without explicitly alluding to Douglas, the *Delta* registered its appreciation of northern Democrats willing to help the slave states achieve that territorial goal.[34]

About two weeks after Buchanan's victory, in a Catholic ceremony in his bride's home, Douglas married for the second time. His new wife, Adele Cutts, the stunning daughter of a federal government clerk resident in the capital and younger than Douglas by twenty-two years, was politically attuned and seemingly quite a catch for the lately disheveled Douglas. Cutts had been schooled at a Catholic academy, was fluent in French, and circulated comfortably in Washington society. After the ceremony, the newlyweds traveled to upstate New York to visit Douglas's mother and then to Philadelphia, New York City, and Chicago, making it back to Washington in time for Christmas and taking up residence in Douglas's house. Everywhere they went, the couple attracted public notice, and it became apparent that feminine influence was quickly changing Douglas's lifestyle and appearance. He shaved off whiskers he had grown before his marriage, dressed more finely, and began hosting sizable entertainments.[35]

It was during these first months of Douglas's second marriage that William Walker's project of Americanizing Nicaragua disintegrated, with consequences for Douglas's political career. By the time of Douglas's wedding, the filibuster régime was on the ropes with its territorial sway drastically circumscribed after many military setbacks. Not only did Costa Rica in November join the raging war against him, subjecting the

---

[34] *New Orleans Daily Delta*, Dec. 13, 1856; John Ashworth, *Slavery, Capitalism, and Politics in the Antebellum Republic*. vol. 2: *The Coming of the Civil War, 1850–1861* (New York, 2007), 23–24.

[35] Johannsen, *Douglas*, 542–44; Orville Hickman Browning Diary, June 12, 1857, *The Diary of Orville Hickman Browning*, ed. Theodore Calvin Pease and James G. Randall. Vol. 1: 1850–1864 (Springfield, IL, 1925), 289; letter dated Willard's Hotel, Washington, Jan. 14, 1858, (Hiram Fuller), *Belle Brittan on a Tour at Newport, and Here and There* (New York, 1858), 29; William Allen Butler, *A Retrospect of Forty Years, 1825–1865*, ed. Harriet Allen Butler (New York, 1911), 304.

filibusters to hostilities on multiple fronts, but the ruthless U.S. shipping magnate Cornelius Vanderbilt backed the Costa Rican campaign. Walker had earned Vanderbilt's enmity by cooperating in a plot involving rival U.S. entrepreneurs to squeeze Vanderbilt's Accessory Transit Company out of its extremely remunerative contract with Nicaragua's government for travel and shipping rights on Nicaragua's isthmian crossing. In late November 1856, Walker ordered Granada's abandonment and destruction; and over the next few weeks he lost control of the transit route and thus the possibility of receiving significant reinforcements. In the last days of March 1857, enemy forces besieged Walker at Rivas, near Nicaragua's Pacific coast. A month later, U.S. naval commander Charles H. Davis negotiated a deal with Costa Rica's commanding general that mercifully allowed Walker to surrender to Davis and provided for the evacuation of the filibusters from Nicaragua. Walker laid down his arms on May 1 and returned to the United States, arriving in New Orleans to a hero's welcome on May 27, 1857.[36]

Despite his prior endorsement of Walker's cause, Douglas refrained from private or public activities on Walker's behalf as the filibuster's defeat played out, but he remained committed to his longtime goal of putting the entire Central American isthmus under U.S. dominance. These feelings caused him to take issue with a treaty that George Dallas signed in London with British foreign minister Lord Clarendon on October 17, 1856, which included provisions that ended Britain's Mosquito protectorate and incorporated an August 1856 Anglo-Honduran convention that terminated British colonial control of the Bay Islands off Honduras.

No sooner did lame-duck President Pierce submit the Dallas-Clarendon Convention to the Senate in December for ratification than Douglas and other critics raised objections. Provisions giving the Bay Islands special status as a self-governing entity within Honduras and exempting its inhabitants from Honduran military service smacked of continuing British colonialism. Further, the convention depended upon ratification of a previous British agreement with Honduras, meaning those islands would remain British if the Anglo-Honduran treaty failed. The convention encountered resistance as soon as it went before the Senate, partly from southerners upset that the incorporated Anglo-Honduran convention banned slavery. Marcy confided to Dallas on January 4, 1857, that the "whole filibuster interest" was working against the pact. With pro-

[36] T. J. Stiles, *The First Tycoon: The Epic Life of Cornelius Vanderbilt* (New York, 2009), 204–206, 218–19, 222, 268–84, 288–99; Brown, *Agents of Manifest Destiny*, 359–408.

Walker elements, including the Nicaraguan attorney and judge Fermin
Ferrer, Walker's newest appointee to be minister to the United States,
lobbying against the convention, the Senate requested additional documents from the president. Then it debated the Dallas treaty in executive
session throughout early February, deciding on February 16 to postpone its determination until after Buchanan's inauguration. When the
Senate finally approved the convention by a 32–15 margin on March
12, it added many amendments, including blunt wording putting the Bay
Islands under Honduran sovereignty. Predictably, the British found the
amendments unacceptable and the agreement was never implemented.[37]

Douglas, who preferred outright repeal of the Clayton-Bulwer Treaty
as a better way to open up Central America to U.S. penetration, apparently spearheaded the opposition to the Dallas-Clarendon pact. On
January 27, the *New York Herald*'s Washington reporter asserted that
"'Young America,' headed by Senator Douglas" had favored "war"
against the treaty "from first to last." He did so even though Democratic
senator James Mason of Virginia, who headed the Committee on Foreign
Relations (which Douglas sat on), favored it and the committee endorsed
ratification. In February, noting that Douglas had eschewed speech
making on the convention, the protreaty *New York Times* claimed that
Douglas had been "the most silently efficient" of the treaty's opponents,
far more effective than senators such as Lewis Cass who had been nois-
ily speech-making against it, confirming the axiom that he "who refrains
from words only to abound in activity, is a very dangerous councilor in
the affairs of a great nation." When in March the Senate tacked on the
amendments that killed the treaty, the *Times* attributed it to a realization
from "the opposition manifested by Judge DOUGLAS and the Southern
propagandists of Slavery" that the treaty would never be approved in its
negotiated form. Unsatisfied even with the concessions, Douglas cast one
of the twelve votes against the amended treaty.[38]

[37] *Sen. Exec. Journal,* 34 Cong., 3 Sess., 163, 173, 184–85, 189–90, 193–94, 242–48; Craig
L. Dozier, *Nicaragua's Mosquito Shore: The Years of British and American Presence*
(University, AL, 1985), 104–105; Binder, *Buchanan and the American Empire,* 229–30;
Spencer, *Marcy,* 378–80; Gara, *Presidency of Franklin Pierce,* 144–45; Fermin Ferrer to
John J. Crittenden, Feb. 1, 1857, in *Charleston* (SC) *Courier,* Feb. 10, 1857 and report of
Washington correspondent in *Courier,* Feb. 7, 1857; Scroggs, *Filibusters and Financiers,*
217; Wilbur Devereux Jones, *The American Problem in British Diplomacy, 1841–1861*
(Athens, 1974), 155–58.
[38] Report from Washington, Jan. 27, in *New York Weekly Herald,* Jan. 31, 1857; *New-York
Daily Times,* Feb. 18, Mar. 14 (report from Washington correspondent dated Mar. 12).
In 1859, Douglas claimed he was "deposed" from his seat on the Committee on Foreign

Douglas mostly turned his attention away from Central American matters for the remainder of the year, though the isthmus remained on his mind. Giving a major address in Springfield in May upon his return to Illinois from Congress, Douglas, according to Lincoln's fellow Republican and friend Orville Browning, who was in the audience, claimed that "Negroes were an inferior race" and that effort "to recognize the equality of the human race was the cause of the degradation and imbecility of Mexico & Central America."[39] At year's end, however, William Walker gave Douglas new cause to think about the Tropics.

A filibustering addict by the time he returned to the United States in the spring of 1857, Walker wasted little time in organizing a reprise expedition to Nicaragua, claiming he remained its legitimate president and making much out of his legalization of slavery to attract stronger southern backing. In well-publicized recruiting and fund-raising orations at places like New Orleans, Mobile, and Nashville, Walker assumed the persona of sectional knight, attacking abolitionism, championing slaveholding as morally worthwhile, and asserting that he was a surrogate for southern expansionists. Slipping out of Mobile, Alabama, aboard the steamship *Fashion* on November 14 with nearly two hundred men, Walker landed with his main force on November 25 near Greytown, sending a smaller group farther down the coast for a second landing. This time, however, the U.S. Navy stopped him preemptively. On December 8, Commodore Hiram Paulding, under vague orders to prevent any filibuster invasion of Central America or Mexico, aimed his warship's artillery on Walker's encampment and landed sailors and marines in order to prevent Walker's escape into the interior and force the filibuster's surrender. Later in the month, a naval captain finished off the invasion by taking Walker's accomplices down the coast into custody. For a second time Walker returned to the United States from Central America in defeat, this time arriving initially in New York, where he was briefly taken into federal custody.[40]

Controversy erupted in Washington and throughout the nation over the legality of Paulding's arresting Walker on foreign soil, leading

Affairs in 1857 because of his opinions on Central America. He seems to have meant his misunderstanding with the committee chair, Mason, the year before, which led to his resigning from the committee for a five-day period before he was reinstated on his own request. *Cleveland* (OH) *Plain Dealer*, Jan. 3, 1859; CG, 34 Cong., 1 Sess., 465, 495.

[39] Orville H. Browning Diary, June 12, 1857, in Pease and Randall, eds., *Diary of Orville Hickman Browning*, 289.

[40] May, *Southern Dream*, 111–14, 127; May, *Manifest Destiny's Underworld*, 49–50, 159, 266.

Douglas to side with Walker, possibly as much for political expediency as because of his continuing expansionism. Douglas's gospel of popular sovereignty and his viability as a future presidential candidate had taken a beating throughout 1857, undermined by the U.S. Supreme Court and developments in Kansas. In March, Chief Justice Roger B. Taney's decision in *Dred Scott v. Sandford* emasculated popular sovereignty, declaring that territorial governments lacked power under the U.S. Constitution to prohibit slavery. Later in 1857, though free-soilers greatly outnumbered them in their territory, proslavery Kansans controlled a constitutional convention at Lecompton and drafted a statehood document that, if approved by Congress, would have made slavery legal in Kansas. Only some twenty-two hundred of about nine thousand registered voters in the Kansas Territory had voted in the elections for delegates to the Lecompton meeting, which were boycotted by many free-soil settlers because they considered the selection process weighted to proslavery interests. Obviously, the Lecompton Constitution misrepresented the popular will in Kansas, and its critics were unappeased by a subsequent territorial referendum on its passage since voters were only given the option of accepting the constitution with or without slavery, not the right to reject it in its entirety. Even if they rejected slavery, they would be unable to cleanse Kansas of human bondage since slaveholders were exempted from having to divest themselves of the two hundred or so slaves they had already taken there.[41]

Popular sovereignty's embarrassment in Kansas hurt Douglas considerably in the North, where plenty of residual anger remained over his earlier overturning the Missouri Compromise. On June 12, 1857, making an attempt at damage control, Douglas gave an extemporaneous speech that suggested majority opinion could still govern slavery in the territories, even if legislatures were now prohibited from banning it. Douglas reasoned that territorial masters' legal rights to slaves depended upon protection from local authorities and regulations, which would not be forthcoming if a majority of the settlers disfavored slavery, an argument he would elaborate the next year during his campaign for reelection to the Senate. Douglas contended that unless territorial populations enacted slave codes and established patrols to protect

[41] Kenneth M. Stampp, *America in 1857: A Nation on the Brink* (New York, 1990), 93–96, 266–67, 270–74; Potter, *Impending Crisis*, 299–300, 307–11; James A. Rawley, *Race and Politics: "Bleeding Kansas" and the Coming of the Civil War* (Philadelphia, 1969), 215; Eric H. Walther, *The Shattering of the Union: America in the 1850s* (Wilmington, DE, 2004), 124, 134.

slave owners' property, slavery would wind up "as dead as if it was prohibited by a constitutional prohibition," all but saying that slaves would run away en masse without local support of masters' rights. In his debates with Lincoln in 1858, Douglas predicted the inevitable eroding of human bondage in areas lacking proslavery "local police regulations." Yet again, in a twenty-page *Harper's Magazine* article in September 1859, Douglas theorized that local will would ultimately control slavery in territories.[42]

Douglas not only insinuated that free-soil territorial settlers might defy the nation's highest court, he also fought Kansas becoming a state under the Lecompton document. On December 9, 1857, Douglas told the Senate not only that the Lecompton gathering was unauthorized by Congress and thus lacked legitimacy, but also that its constitution negated principles of popular government by denying Kansans the right to reject the entire document. Douglas continued his attacks through the following winter, especially after the territory's referendum on December 21, 1857, marred by fraudulent voting, approved the Lecompton Constitution with unlimited slavery by a 6,226–569 margin. Defying President Buchanan, who on February 2, 1858, asked Congress to approve Kansas's admission as the nation's sixteenth slave state, Douglas helped spearhead the opposition, often voting with antislavery colleagues like Ohio's senator Salmon P. Chase. His moral hand was strengthened because free-soilers in Kansas on January 4 rejected Lecompton by an overwhelming margin in their own, separate balloting. Though Kansas's admission under Lecompton eventually passed the Senate despite Douglas's efforts, it was defeated in the House by a 120–112 margin on April 1. Later in the month, Douglas completed his apostasy in some southern eyes by working with Republican senators against the "English bill," a compromise measure that passed both houses of Congress and allowed southern congressmen to save face on the Kansas dispute. It gave Kansas's settlers another shot at statehood under the Lecompton document, but only *if* they would accept a drastically reduced federal land grant as compared to what they would get if Kansas remained a territory until its population increased to 93,000, the number required for a congressional representative. In their plebiscite on August 2, 1858, Kansas voters decisively turned down statehood with the reduced land grant, 11,300 to 1,788, ending the

[42] Johannsen, *Douglas*, 569–70, 669–70, 707–10; Allen Nevins, *The Emergence of Lincoln*, vol. 2: *Prologue to Civil War, 1859–1861* (New York, 1950), 48.

territory's prospects of becoming a slave state, as more northerners than southerners were migrating there all the time.[43]

Douglas's evolving territorial policies pleased many northerners who had written him off as a proslavery tool. His break with President Buchanan commanded so much respect in antislavery circles, in fact, that some prominent eastern Republicans began praising his courage and integrity in the hope he would switch parties. Antislavery New York City editor Horace Greeley even rallied Republicans to back the Little Giant for reelection as U.S. senator, to the disgust of Lincoln, who already had his sights set on challenging Douglas for the seat. By the same token, however, Douglas boxed himself into a corner with many former southern supporters, so much so that to remain a viable candidate for the Democratic presidential nomination in 1860 he badly needed to make a southward expansionist gesture to slaveholders. He all but admitted as much when a couple of Republican congressmen paid his Washington residence a visit on December 14. According to a memorandum about the meeting kept by Indiana representative Schuyler Colfax, Douglas promised that the only proslavery measure he intended to pursue was Cuba's annexation by honorable means.[44]

Paulding's arrest of Walker offered Douglas the perfect opportunity to cater to southern tropical expansionists, who increasingly coveted Central American territory to compensate for their pending defeat in Kansas. As early as December 1857, Spain's minister to the United States, Gabriel García Tassara, considered it obvious that "the proslavery faction" intended "annexation and filibustering to obtain compensation for the major and inevitable reverse" facing it in Kansas, with Walker its "instrument." As protests over Walker's apprehension erupted throughout much of the South, the *New York Herald* chastised "Southern fire-eaters" for

[43] Johannsen, *Douglas*, 569–70, 587–613; James M. McPherson, *Battle Cry of Freedom: The Civil War Era* (1988; rpt., New York, 1989), 167–69; Allan Nevins, *The Emergence of Lincoln*, vol. 1: *Douglas, Buchanan, and Party Chaos, 1857–1859* (New York, 1950), 296–300; Potter, *Impending Crisis*, 320–25; Walther, *Shattering of the Union*, 124, 134; Eric Foner, *The Fiery Trial: Abraham Lincoln and American Slavery* (New York, 2010), 98–99; Avery O. Craven, *The Growth of Southern Nationalism, 1848–1861* (Baton Rouge, 1953), 295–96, 302–303; Christopher Childers, *The Failure of Popular Sovereignty: Slavery, Manifest Destiny, and the Radicalization of Southern Politics* (Lawrence, 2012), 266–67.
[44] Johannsen, *Douglas*, 632–33; Potter, *Impending Crisis*, 320–22; Donald, *Lincoln*, 204–205; Colfax memorandum cited and summarized in James L. Huston, *Stephen A. Douglas and the Dilemmas of Democratic Equality* (Lanham, MD, 2007), 138.

being silent on Kansas and expending their wrath and indignation on "Nicaragua filibusters" rather than the West. To the *Herald*, southerners were engaged in a quixotic quest, since now it was obviously "all up with the 'little gray-eyed man of destiny.'"[45]

Douglas was well aware of the rising southern filibuster tide, especially in the Deep South, where his support was eroding because of his Kansas stand. On December 16, a Walker operative in Alabama, the merchant Julius Hessee, reported to Douglas that Central America was becoming a subject of increasing interest to "our people," who realized that great commercial advantages would accrue to them after the isthmus's "Americanization." Hessee enclosed a copy of proceedings from a mass Walker meeting at Mobile's Ampitheatre that involved Alabama public figures, including a former governor. Speakers condemned U.S. naval interference with Walker and insisted that the filibuster's success in Nicaragua was vital to southern interests; one of them bluntly endorsed "the extension of slavery into that beautiful and productive country" as a means of accruing strength and commercial benefits for the South. The meeting's resolutions included an attack on the Clayton-Bulwer Treaty, a defense of the right of Walker's followers to "emigrate" to Nicaragua, and a justification of American domination of Nicaragua. That document alone might have drawn Douglas to Walker's defense. But during Congress's Christmas recess, one of Douglas's supporters sent him explicit advice from Washington about how to capitalize on the Paulding-Walker incident. This backer had just chatted with Douglas's Democratic colleague from Georgia, Senator Robert Toombs, one of the most powerful southern politicians in the country, and learned that Toombs was "indignant at the action of Old Buck [Buchanan] against Walker." Douglas needed to seize the moment by visiting Toombs and joining forces "against the administration for interfering illegally with Walker." Such a course, especially if combined with a stand for U.S. annexation of Cuba, would "excite in the South" sympathy for Douglas's political ambitions while embarrassing "the old fossil" Buchanan, ruining the president as a competitor when Democrats chose their next candidate in 1860. Douglas possibly listened. His longtime ally, Illinois Democratic congressman Thomas L. Harris, a fellow Caribbean expansionist, confided privately

45 Extract from Gabriel García Tassara to the Prime Minister, Dec. 27, 1857, in "Bleeding Kansas and Spanish Cuba in 1857, a Postscript," ed. and trans. Thomas Schoonover and Ebba Schoonover, *Kansas History* 11 (Winter, 1988–89), 241–42; *New York Herald*, Jan. 15, 1858; May, *Southern Dream*, 114–15.

to newsman Charles H. Lanphier on January 1, 1858, that southerners were outraged by Paulding's arrest of Walker and that it was common knowledge in Washington that "Douglas will have Toombs on his side." The Paulding incident, he implied, had significantly compromised the Buchanan administration.[46]

Douglas made his expected gesture to southern expansionists after both houses of Congress erupted in January in heated, highly sectionalized debates on the Walker-Paulding affair that stretched into February. Republicans rallied to the support of a president they mostly despised, some of them attacking slavery's expansion southward in the course of defending the legality of Paulding's action. Deep South Democrats, conversely, championed slavery's right to expand southward and the legitimacy of Walker's movement on Central America. Douglas stated his position after the Senate on January 7 received a set of documents from Buchanan concerning Walker's apprehension with an accompanying message from the president explaining administration policy. Buchanan's message conceded that technically Paulding had committed a "grave error," having infringed the territory of a foreign country without permission from its government, but nonetheless portrayed Paulding's behavior as moral and "gallant." The commodore had rescued Nicaragua from a dreaded filibustering invasion, a crime meriting the most drastic punishment possible under U.S. law because it violated the law of nations and Christian principles while usurping Congress's war-making powers. Filibustering retarded American commercial penetration of the isthmus and delayed the inevitable U.S. dominance of Central America, the president believed, because it besmirched the nation's image there. After the message was read, Senator Mason moved its referral to his Foreign Relations Committee, but the motion triggered sustained debate (and reference was deferred until the next Senate meeting on January 11).

Douglas spoke after William Seward, in the debate on the seventh, praised Buchanan not only for sustaining Paulding's arrest of Walker but also for legitimizing the arrest by Seward's own doctrine (meant to justify northern antislavery) that there was a superior doctrine of morality, or "higher law," that sometimes trumped statutes. Douglas began his

---

[46] Julius Hessee to SAD, Dec. 16, 1857 (with enclosed printed proceedings of "Nicaragua Meeting in Mobile," Dec. 13, 1857), James B. Steedman to SAD, Dec. 28, 1857, SAD Papers, UC; Thomas L. Harris to Charles H. Lanphier, Jan. 1 (1858), Charles H. Lanphier Papers, AL Presidential Library, Springfield, IL. Toombs, in fact, boldly denounced Paulding and defended the filibusters at a White House dinner party. See William Gore Ouseley to Lord Clarendon, Jan. 9, 1858, BBPC, 187–88.

remarks by agreeing with Buchanan that Paulding had violated U.S. law in arresting Walker. Under the U.S. Neutrality Act of 1818, Douglas contended, the U.S. Navy lacked statutory authority to make arrests more than one marine mile from America's coastline. Further, Douglas said he opposed filibustering because it was more likely to obstruct the "extension of the area of freedom and the American flag" than to speed it up. Rehashing ideas he had articulated for years, he announced a preference that America's expansion proceed gradually rather than through violence, with annexations of foreign territory occurring once foreign peoples were so Americanized they would become reliable citizens. This belief in inevitable expansion, but not its immediacy, Douglas noted, governed his well-known opposition to the Clayton-Bulwer Treaty. Douglas balanced those seeming concessions to Buchanan, however, with an attack on federal authorities for presuming that every three armed men leaving the country intended to attack foreign nations. Further, Douglas would grant Walker immunity from U.S. law enforcement after leaving U.S. territorial limits since he had been granted Nicaraguan citizenship during his initial intervention in Nicaragua, sacrificing, Douglas believed, his U.S. citizenship. If U.S. naval authorities could take Walker into custody on Nicaraguan soil, Great Britain would be justified in seizing an emigrant from Ireland who became naturalized in the United States.[47]

Douglas's speech struck the *New-York Christian Observer* as a blatant attempt to legitimize his recent defiance of the president over Lecompton in the eyes of "extreme Southern defenders of Walker." If so, the Little Giant succeeded with one of Buchanan's former southern expansionist supporters, Georgia Democratic congressman Augustus R. Wright, who only weeks earlier had privately judged the president "the soundest man in all the North." Disgusted by Buchanan's standing behind Paulding's intervention in Nicaragua, Wright condemned the president for striking a *"vital blow"* against southern interests, adding he had "more *confidence* today in the *Douglas Democrats"* than in "administration men." At a time when southerners needed to strike for their important interests "in Central America, which was literally ours," the administration was trying to seduce them with the *"moonshine"* of Kansas.[48]

[47] CG, 35 Cong., 1 Sess., 216–25.
[48] *New-York Christian Inquirer*, Jan. 16, 1858; Augustus R. Wright to Frank [Francis Calaway Shropshire], Dec. 18, 1857, undated (but almost certainly some time in January 1858), and Mar. 5, 1858, transcribed copies in manuscript biography of A. R. Wright, Beulah Shropshire Moseley Family Papers, LC.

Aided by his stand on Walker, Douglas now seemed poised for a political comeback, assisted considerably by his vivacious new wife and the social opportunities afforded by his spectacular new home in Washington. After his marriage to Adele Cutts, Douglas had a new residence constructed at the intersection of New Jersey Avenue and I Street, and on the night of January 19, 1858, the Douglases threw a ball, which one newspaper correspondent deemed the "most successful and brilliant *fete* ever attempted" in the nation's capital. According to the correspondent's account, Douglas and his wife sent out more than fourteen hundred invitations, and incredibly some two thousand persons attended. Among the attendees were congressional leaders, foreign diplomats, important army and navy officers, Secretary of the Navy Isaac Toucey, the president's private secretary, and the postmaster general's wife and daughter. One attending Republican congressman marveled, "There was a great deal of display.... Two parlors and a dancing Hall all opened into each other making one grand and magnificent room one hundred feet in length – with splendid mirrors from the floor to the ceiling hanging in all parts of it." Surely this extravaganza earned Douglas goodwill across party lines.[49]

Of course, the challenge for Douglas was retaining the newfound respect he earned in the North by challenging slavery in Kansas while reaching out to slavery expansionists on Walker's filibuster to Nicaragua. On April 20, the Democratic state convention in Springfield did overwhelmingly renominate him for a new Senate term and endorsed the national party's Cincinnati platform of 1856, an indication that most Illinois Democrats remained comfortable with a platform that not only endorsed popular sovereignty but also promoted the notion of the country spreading southward. Still, Douglas's reelection was hardly ensured, given the rising strength of Republicans in Illinois and anger among proadministration Democrats over his breaking with Buchanan on Kansas. Despite all the praise of Douglas back east, Illinois Republicans never fell in line behind the Little Giant, who consistently expressed a willingness to tolerate Kansas's admission as a slave state if that was what its settlers genuinely wanted. Part of the Republican dislike of Douglas related to his willingness to support filibustering in Central America. As one of Lyman

---

[49] Correspondent of the *Cincinnati Gazette* report dated Jan. 20, 1858, in *Chicago Daily Tribune*, Jan. 25, 1858; David S. Reid to Henrietta S. Reid, Dec. 11, 1857, *The Papers of David Settle Reid*, ed. Lindley S. Butler (2 vols.; Raleigh, NC, 1993–97), 2: 210; Henry L. Dawes to his wife, Jan. 20, 1858, Henry L. Dawes Papers, LC; Nichols, *Disruption of American Democracy*, 136.

Trumbull's correspondents put it, taking the "Southern *chute*" on the Paulding question might or might not help Douglas in the slave states but would surely lose him northern ground. The president recognized Douglas's predicament. Writing to a Pennsylvania politician days after Douglas's Senate speech on the Walker-Paulding affair, Buchanan bemusedly observed, "Douglas has alienated the South on the Kansas question & the North upon the Filibuster question."

Since U.S. senators were chosen by votes of state legislatures, Douglas's political prospects hinged on how the Illinois fall state elections turned out; if his supporters controlled the next state legislature, he would retain his seat, boosting his credibility for a presidential bid in 1860 in what we would call today a crucial "swing" state (Pennsylvania and Indiana were other key lower North states the Republicans lost in 1856 and needed to take). Douglas commanded the support of almost all the Democratic newspapers in Illinois, but he hardly led a unified state party. Not only did some forty to fifty backers of Buchanan (in the lingo of the times "Buchaneers" or "Danites") bolt from the April 20 convention, but Buchanan's supporters subsequently fielded a full ticket for statewide offices and legislative candidates of their own in a minority of the state's election districts. Belatedly, in September, the Buchaneers persuaded state supreme court justice and former congressman Sidney Breese to enter the Senate contest against Douglas and Lincoln.[50]

As President Buchanan anticipated, Douglas's credibility in the North on filibustering would indeed be tested, with Lincoln throwing down the gauntlet. On June 16, 1858, some twelve hundred delegates came together for the Republican state convention at Springfield and nominated Lincoln as their candidate against Douglas's reelection. That night, in his famous "House Divided" address to the delegates in the stifling heat of the hall of the House of Representatives, Lincoln made possibly the most radical-sounding pronouncement of his entire pre–Civil War career, suggesting that the nation could not continue indefinitely with both free and slave

[50] Allen C. Guelzo, *Lincoln and Douglas: The Debates That Defined America* (New York, 2008), 67–68, 134–38; Nevins, *Emergence of Lincoln*, 1: 349–50; David Zarefsky, *Lincoln, Douglas, and Slavery: In the Crucible of Public Debate* (Chicago, 1990), 40; Harry V. Jaffa, *A New Birth of Freedom: Abraham Lincoln and the Coming of the Civil War* (Lanham, MD, 2000), 84, 312; William H. Bissell to Lyman Trumbull, Jan. 9, 1858, Lyman Trumbull Papers, Reel 3, LC; James Buchanan to Joseph B. Baker, Jan. 11, 1858, *The Works of James Buchanan*, comp. and ed. John Bassett Moore, 12 vols. (New York, 1908–11), 10: 177.

states. Inevitably, he affirmed, it would become either "*all* one thing, or *all* the other." Lincoln was no abolitionist, and he hardly intended to signal his conversion to a radical antislavery position. Still, his biblically grounded wording afforded ammunition for the profoundly negative image southerners developed of him over the next couple of years, as he emerged a contender for the Republican presidential nomination and as the party's candidate in 1860. From the perspective of many slave state politicians and voters, Lincoln and his party intended war against southern institutions.

During his speech, Lincoln predicted that either slavery's opponents would succeed in stopping its further spread or slavery's "*advocates*" would "push it forward, till it shall become alike lawful in *all* the States, *old* as well as *new* – *North* as well as *South*." Presumably, when Lincoln alluded to future "new" states he had in mind western territories like Kansas that were already on a path to eventual statehood. Throughout the 1850s, however, many expansionists had spoken of annexing Cuba as a new state rather than as a territory, and it might well be that Lincoln's allusion to "*new*" states was broader than it first appears. Perhaps some of the new states would be tropical, and Lincoln meant the term "South" as much in a directional, compass-driven sense, as in a U.S. regional sense.[51]

Such a hypothesis becomes plausible in light of Lincoln's exchanges with Douglas during their ensuing debates – a series of encounters on Lincoln's challenge that the front-runner Douglas reluctantly accepted because of the effectiveness of the underdog Lincoln's electioneering to that point. In July, Lincoln started speaking at the same Illinois towns as Douglas, arriving on Douglas's heels to take advantage of the crowds drawn by his rival and to leave a later impression on them. Realizing that debates would neutralize this tactic and allow him to rebut Lincoln's assertions, Douglas agreed to participate in debates, though only seven, each in a different congressional district, rather than the fifty his opponent wanted. Amid banners, picnicking, parading, and other fanfare, varying

[51] AL speech at Springfield, June 16, 1858, CWAL, 2: 461–69; William C. Harris, *Lincoln's Rise to the Presidency* (Lawrence, 2007), 91; Steven A. Channing, *Crisis of Fear: Secession in South Carolina* (1970; rpt., New York, 1974), 231; Robert W. Johannsen, *Lincoln, the South, and Slavery: The Political Dimension* (Baton Rouge, 1991), 104–105; Harold Holzer, *Lincoln President-Elect: Abraham Lincoln and the Great Secession Winter, 1860–1861* (New York, 2008), 139–40; Gabor S. Boritt, "'And the War Came'? Abraham Lincoln and the Question of Individual Responsibility," *Why the Civil War Came*, ed. Gabor S. Boritt (New York, 1996), 9, 10.

audiences that ranged from four thousand to twenty thousand listeners (the exception being the debate before about fourteen hundred at the southern Illinois village of Jonesboro), including an astonishing press representation, attended the three-hour encounters. What they heard was remarkable oratory with the tall Lincoln in his rather shrill voice and the squat Douglas in a contrastingly low voice defining often in profoundly eloquent ways the issues that divided them. Their exchanges, moreover, found an audience way beyond Illinois's borders, since major newspapers in other states reprinted transcripts of the debates from Illinois papers.[52]

Speaking extemporaneously, the two candidates gave slavery extension southward far more attention than historians acknowledge, the only time during their rivalry that they directly engaged each other on the issue. Just before Lincoln's nomination, a friend in Washington had promised to send him occasional issues of the *Washington States*, describing it as obsessed with U.S. foreign affairs "and fillibustering generally," an unsurprising description of a paper established in the capital the year before by Walker operative John P. Heiss. Perhaps Lincoln's reading of the *States* before the debates influenced his remarks about slavery heading southward, though he would have found it difficult to avoid the issue since Douglas goaded him about it in the early debates.[53]

On August 21, in their initial encounter at the northern Illinois town of Ottawa, Douglas, speaking first, asked Lincoln a rapid-fire series of questions, hoping to pin unpopular positions on his opponent and the Republican Party (which he denigrated as the "Black Republicans"). Douglas wanted to lead Lincoln into liberal statements that would damage him when the campaign reached southern parts of the state, where public opinion was more racist and less disturbed by slavery than in northern Illinois. At the end of his interrogation, Douglas queried, "I desire him to answer whether he is opposed to the acquisition of any more territory unless slavery is first prohibited therein," obviously alluding to the Tropics since no one expected the fugitive slave haven of Canada to allow slavery. When Lincoln responded with a vague restatement of his House Divided position that the opponents of slavery needed to stop its spread, Douglas demanded more specificity: "I want to know ... whether he will ... resist the acquirement of any more territory unless slavery therein shall

---

[52] Harris, *Lincoln's Rise to the Presidency*, 85, 106–107, 112, 113, 126, 130, 134, 138, 140; Zarefsky, *Lincoln, Douglas, and Slavery*, 49–51, 53–54.

[53] Josiah M. Lucas to AL, June 15, 1858, AL Papers, Series 1, LC; *Washington* (DC) *States*, April 17, 1857.

be forever prohibited." Saying that he had based this and all his other questions on "the fundamental principles of the Black Republican party," Douglas persisted: "I want him to answer this last question." The Little Giant was hardly willing to let up on an issue that might give him an edge in a state where Manifest Destiny remained popular.

In the second debate, at Freeport, Lincoln got the first word and immediately answered Douglas's "interrogatories" from Ottawa. Lincoln's speech is more remembered for countering Douglas's questions with four questions of his own than for Lincoln's answers to Douglas; it was here, not far from the Wisconsin boundary, that Lincoln famously provoked Douglas's controversial "Freeport Doctrine" by asking the Little Giant, with the Dred Scott case in mind, whether residents in any federal territory still could keep out slavery prior to statehood. Often overlooked, however, is the last of Lincoln's answers to Douglas, which amounted to a between-the-lines denial of Manifest Destiny. Rather than attack territorial expansion outright, Lincoln unenthusiastically conceded that "honest" acquisitions of territory were acceptable, so long as they did not aggravate "the slavery question among ourselves." His answer ruled out the nation getting Cuba in the foreseeable future since Republicans opposed obtaining the island with its slavery system intact; they would certainly scotch if they could any schemes to annex it. And since Lincoln only wished new territory by "honest acquisition," he implicitly negated filibuster attempts to annex Mexico or Central America by conquest. Undoubtedly aware of his own evasiveness, Lincoln tried to turn the issue back on Douglas, asking in his own fourth question whether Douglas favored acquiring new territory even if it harmed the nation by agitating the slavery dispute.

Ever ready to voice his vision of the Tropics becoming Americanized, Douglas readily took Lincoln's bait. Just the month before, at Chicago on his return from Washington, Douglas had given a speech from the balcony of the Tremont House to a wildly enthusiastic audience that contended that Mexico, Central America, and South America were so weakened from the mixing of whites, blacks, and Indians (whom he designated "superior and inferior races") that the entire region suffered from "deterioration, demoralization and degradation below the capacity for self-government." Now, at Freeport, though he mocked Lincoln for the "yankee-fashion" trick of bouncing back a question rather than answering it, Douglas reaffirmed that whenever it was necessary for U.S. "growth and progress" to add more land, the nation should do so, leaving the inhabitants by principles of the "Nebraska bill" to decide slavery for themselves. Americans swarmed like hives of bees, and needed new hives to "make their honey." To "increase, and multiply, and expand" was "the law of this nation's existence," Douglas asserted. Great nations died if they failed to grow. The country should follow its destiny north-ward, southward, and to the "islands of the ocean." Apparently Douglas judged his audience well, because transcripts of his speech have these particular remarks being interrupted by exclamations of "Good" and "Good, good, hurra for Douglas" from the audience. For good measure, Douglas rehashed Lincoln's opposition to the Mexican War, as he did on a number of occasions throughout the debates. He also alluded to an Illinois Republican meeting's statement in August 1854 that the new party opposed any new territorial acquisitions unless slavery was already prohibited in them.[54]

Douglas continued hammering away on these themes, drawing Lincoln into a dialogue that became increasingly explicit about the Tropics and filibustering. In a nondebate speech at Joliet on August 31, Douglas charged that Lincoln had sided with Mexico "against his own country" in the 1846–48 war and ridiculed antiexpansionists who thought the country had all the territory it would ever need. Emphasizing America's youth, he said that once American settlers reached the Pacific, they would "diffuse" northward and southward to cover "the entire conti-nent of America." Presumably, given what Douglas said on other occa-sions, he meant the whole hemisphere, but he might have simply meant North America including Mexico and Canada. Then he went on a racist tirade regarding Cuba that exposed his own tolerance of tropical slav-ery in acquired lands. Professing curiosity as to Lincoln's willingness to annex Cuba, Douglas implied Lincoln would never be so foolish as to follow his principles and abolish slavery in the island as a precondition of annexation:

Will he set loose a million of slaves and then annex the Island with a million and a half of negroes and less than half a million of white men? Will he go for annexing

[54] Debate at Ottawa, Aug. 27, 1858, Debate at Freeport, Aug. 27, 1858, *The Lincoln-Douglas Debates*, ed. Rodney O. Davis and Douglas L. Wilson (Urbana, 2008), 2–82 (quotations on pp. 9, 37, 47); SAD speech, July 9, 1858, in *Chicago Daily Tribune*, July 10, 1858; Mrs. John A. Logan, *Reminiscences of a Soldier's Wife: An Autobiography* (1913; rpt., Carbondale, 1957), 60–61. Harry Jaffa uses Douglas's remarks on territorial expansion at Freeport to argue that had Republicans absorbed Douglas into their party after his Lecompton stand and nominated him for president in 1860, the South would not have seceded from knowledge that under popular sovereignty tropical areas would have become slave states. Jaffa, *New Birth of Freedom*, 309–10.

it as a free negro colony, and making out of it a free negro State with two Negro Senators and as many negro Representatives as it may be entitled to?

"Great laughter" ensued, after which Douglas continued in the same vein, talking about a "Divine decree" mandating America's spread over the "entire continent" and "adjacent islands." Unless the Union kept growing and using popular sovereignty to decide on slavery's status in new areas, "the mission of the white race on this continent," it would die.[55]

Still on the expansionist offensive in the third debate on September 15 at Jonesboro, Douglas alluded to the determination of Lincoln's "sectional party" to prevent slavery in any territory the nation "might hereafter acquire." Repeating his standard slogan that the nation could remain healthy with both free and slave states, as the Founding Fathers created it, Douglas (to reported applause) envisioned Americans soon advancing their national interests by acquiring Cuba and eventually taking "any portion of Mexico or Canada, or of this continent or the adjoining islands" it wanted, letting "the people" decide slavery for themselves. Presumably, by "people," he meant the U.S. citizens settling in and dominating the annexed areas, given his loathing for the actual inhabitants in the Tropics.

That last argument gave Lincoln an opening that Douglas surely did not anticipate in the fifth debate, held at Knox College in Galesburg on October 7. Here Lincoln finally embraced the definitively antiexpansion stand his rival had tried to pin him to since the debates started, but with a twist. Returning to the question that Douglas had posed to him at Freeport about future acquisitions, Lincoln lambasted Douglas's entire doctrine about slavery's spreading southward on popular sovereignty's wings. Then Lincoln laid out an apocalyptic vision of what northern voters should expect if Douglas got his way, turning Douglas's own racism into an antiexpansionist weapon. Alluding to Douglas's insistence that popular sovereignty decide slavery's fate in the tropics, Lincoln wondered whether Douglas really meant what he was saying:

If Judge Douglas' policy upon this question succeeds ... until all opposition is crushed out, the next thing will be a grab for the territory of poor Mexico, an invasion of the rich lands of South America, then the adjoining islands will follow, each one of which promises additional slave fields. And this question is to be left to the people of those countries for settlement. When we shall get Mexico, I don't know whether the Judge will be in favor of the Mexican people that we get with it settling that question for themselves and all others; because we know

---

[55] Douglas speech on Aug. 31, 1858, in (St. Louis) *Missouri Republican*, Aug. 31, 1858.

the Judge has a great horror for mongrels, [*Laughter*,] and I understand that the people of Mexico are most decidedly a race of mongrels. [*Laughter*] I understand that there is not more than one person there out of eight who is pure white, and I suppose from the Judge's previous declaration, that when we get Mexico or any considerable portion of it, that he will be in favor of these mongrels settling the question, which would bring him somewhat into collision with his horror of an inferior race.

Lincoln then predicted that any new acquisitions would inevitably exacerbate the slavery question as they did during the Mexican War and urged Americans to rethink the virtues of acquisitions that would endanger the Union. Lincoln had no doubt, moreover, that when Douglas talked of America's growth, he really meant slavery's spread southward. Under Douglas's prescription, Lincoln explained, "Whoever wants to go out filibustering ... thinks that more territory is needed. Whoever wants wider slave fields feels sure that some additional territory is needed as slave territory." Lincoln concluded his speech with assertions that the nation's very "liberties and national greatness" were at stake in the policy of territorial extension Douglas favored, and it was "extremely important" that Americans consider the risks of endangering the Union before embarking on Douglas's acquisitive agenda (Figure 3.5).[56]

Douglas would never cede the last word on territorial expansion to anyone. In their sixth meeting, at Quincy, Douglas reiterated that the nation's health depended on its remaining a house divided. With both free and slave states minding their own business when it came to slavery, the nation could take advantage of its multiplying population by growing geographically, fulfilling the "destiny" that "Providence" had "marked out for us," making the continent an "ocean-bound republic." He left unmentioned that the only way the United States of America could be truly ocean-bound would be to incorporate all of Central and South America. Just adding Canada and Mexico would leave the nation with landed boundaries.[57]

The close election, on a very rainy day in much of Illinois on November 2, was encouraging, in a way, to *both* Douglas and Lincoln. On the one

---

[56] SAD speech at Jonesboro, Sept. 15, 1858, AL speech at Galesburg, Oct. 7, 1858, Davis and Wilson, eds., *Lincoln-Douglas Debates*, 86–99, 183–203.

[57] Douglas speech at Quincy, Oct. 13, 1858, Davis and Wilson, eds., *Lincoln-Douglas Debates*, 225–42.

FIGURE 3.5 Mural painted by Ralph F. Seymour in 1958 to commemorate the Lincoln–Douglas debate one hundred years earlier at Knox College, Galesburg, Illinois.
Courtesy of Special Collections and Archives, Knox College Library, Galesburg, Illinois.

hand, voters gave Democrats control of the state legislature, by a margin of forty to thirty-five in the House of Representatives and fourteen to eleven in the state Senate, sewing up Douglas's reelection. When the legislature convened in January, Democratic members unified behind Douglas, Republicans rallied for Lincoln, and Douglas triumphed by fifty-four votes to Lincoln's forty-six. But the overall popular vote for legislative candidates had actually favored Republicans, and some of the districts Douglas candidates took were only narrowly carried, one of them by a mere seventy-eight votes. Conditions looked auspicious for Lincoln and the Republicans in the future since the northern and more Republican part of the state had been growing more rapidly than southern Illinois in recent years. Republicans might well take the state in the next presidential contest, given that voting in presidential elections was statewide rather than by individual legislative districts. Moreover, reapportionment of state legislative districts following the 1860 census would likely put that body in the Republican column, helping Republicans in future Senate races.[58]

Still, for the time being, Stephen Douglas could bask in victory congratulations pouring in from supporters all over the country and use his reelection triumph as a springboard to the Democracy's 1860 presidential nomination, *if* he could persuade southern supporters of the Buchanan administration to look beyond his recent dalliance with Republicans on Kansas affairs. Throughout the summer and early fall of 1858, newspapers published reports of his campaign for reelection and stories of William Walker's efforts to organize a third expedition to Nicaragua in the same issues, usually on the same page.[59] Would Douglas now try to recover his southern popularity by newly championing Walker's filibuster or schemes to annex Cuba and Mexico?

During the campaign, upon learning that Douglas in his Chicago speech had reendorsed the Democracy's Cincinnati platform, the Republican *New York Commercial Advertiser* cautioned party members to "consider the foreign as well as the domestic policy of the country" in taking the measure of the Little Giant, given the Cincinnati document's embrace of aggressive U.S. dominance of the Tropics and covert support for William Walker. The endorsement proved Douglas remained a pure Democrat, the paper argued, despite joining Republicans against the Lecompton Constitution; Republicans, therefore, should disabuse themselves of thoughts that he had undergone a political conversion. Clearly, Douglas intended to play to Democratic expansionists and seek the presidency with aggressive Caribbean policies Republicans could never accept. The *Advertiser* represented a common wisdom in Republican circles that would become more pronounced as the months passed. When, after the election, Douglas headed to New Orleans instead of rushing to Washington for the opening of the next Congress, some observers, according to the Republican *Chicago Tribune*, believed they were already witnessing the initial stages of this Caribbeanized election

[58] Guelzo, *Lincoln and Douglas*, 281–87; Jaffa, *New Birth of Freedom*, 312; Harris, *Lincoln's Rise to the Presidency*, 96; Johannsen, *Douglas*, 678.

[59] Johannsen, *Douglas*, 679–82; Chicago *Daily Press and Tribune*, Aug. 27, 1858, Nov. 30, 1858; (Boston) *Liberator*, July 30, 1858; *Washington* (PA) *Reporter*, Aug. 11, 1858; *New-York Times*, Aug. 27, 1858; *Savannah Daily Morning News*, Sept. 11, 1858; (NC) *Weekly Raleigh Register*, Sept. 29, 1858.

strategy. By their logic, Douglas journeyed to the Crescent City hoping to show southern "fire-eaters" that "he is all right on fillibustering" – a more important cause to them anyway, the *Tribune* believed, than the Dred Scott decision.[60]

[60] *New York Commercial Advertiser,* July 12, 1858; *Chicago Daily Press and Tribune,* Nov. 30, 1858. "Fire-eaters" was a term commonly used to connote radical southerners who favored secession from the Union.

4

Caribbeanizing the House Divided

In the early fall of 1859, about a half-year before the Democratic Party was scheduled to hold its national nominating convention in Charleston, South Carolina, three schooners sat at anchor in Cleveland harbor, each one with a flag on its mast bearing the words: "Douglas and Cuba, 1860!"[1] The flags reflected a hope that Stephen Douglas might harness his identification with Manifest Destiny in yet another bid for the American presidency, and they challenge the traditional narrative about the coming of the American Civil War.

According to most accounts, America's final showdown over slavery's expansion occurred in the two years after Douglas helped prevent Kansas statehood under the proslavery Lecompton Constitution. Feeling betrayed by the Little Giant, southern Democrats demanded insurance against Douglas's Freeport Doctrine in the form of a federal "slave code" for the territories, by which Congress would guarantee slave property within a territory should its legislature prove unwilling or unable to do so. Meanwhile, Lincoln and the Republicans made political hay in the North by claiming that *Dred Scott* and Lecompton demonstrated that a Slave Power plot was afoot to foist slavery on all the western territories. The next step, they predicted, would be to impose slavery on the North itself. In 1860, the Democratic Party fractured from an inability to resolve the territorial dispute. Northern Democrats (or the "National Democrats" as they dubbed themselves) chose Douglas as their presidential candidate; southern Democrats selected Vice President John Breckinridge of Kentucky. The Democrats' bitter division helped Lincoln get elected

[1] *Cleveland Plain Dealer*, Aug. 27, Oct. 1, 1859.

president on a Republican platform denouncing popular sovereignty as fraudulent and denying the authority of *either* territorial legislatures or Congress to legalize slavery in a territory. Reacting angrily to Lincoln's victory, seven southern states seceded from the Union over the next three months, setting the stage for the Civil War.

Unfortunately, this narrative obscures how much Caribbean issues were woven into the electioneering of 1858–60,[2] when even John Brown's raid on Harpers Ferry, Virginia, had a Caribbean dimension. To Americans worried that the October 1859 attack so enraged southerners as to imperil the Union, Brown was the North's William Walker, applying filibustering ruthlessness to a southern locale. Addressing Iowa's state's legislature, conservative Republican governor, Samuel J. Kirkwood, described the abolitionist's "mad" offense as a greater crime "than the invaders of Cuba and Nicaragua were guilty of," though northerners might be excused from sympathizing with Brown's disinterested motives in the same way many Yankee citizens earlier had empathized with "the gallant Crittenden, who died so bravely in Cuba." Similarly, Republican U.S. senator James Doolittle of Wisconsin asserted that hostile campaigns in Nicaragua had been succeeded by similar attacks on Virginia and reassured southerners that Republicans would "join with you and go with you to put down this fillibustering." The solution, according to *New York Times* editor Henry J. Raymond, was for the federal government to extend the protection of the same Neutrality Act that interfered with invasions of Nicaragua to the slave states themselves. Contrarily, though, Massachusetts antislavery transcendentalist Henry David Thoreau referenced Walker to justify Brown: "If Walker may be considered the representative of the South, I wish I could say that Brown was the representative of the North.... No man in America has ever stood up so persistently or

---

[2] The most penetrating integration of Caribbean issues in the 1860 election is James L. Huston," The Unrecognized Revolution: The Election of 1860 and the Upheaval in American Foreign Policy" (http://www.by.edu/historic/conferenceo8/jhuston.pdf). See also William L. Barney, *The Road to Secession: A New Perspective on the Old South* (New York, 1972), 123–46; Bruce Collins, *The Origins of America's Civil War* (New York, 1981), 139, 143; William W. Freehling, *Road to Disunion*. vol. 2: *Secessionists Triumphant* (New York, 2007), 327–28; Allan Nevins, *The Emergence of Lincoln*, vol. 2: *Prologue to Civil War* (New York, 1950), 293; Avery O. Craven, *The Growth of Southern Nationalism, 1848–1861* (Baton Rouge, 1953), 329–31; Roy Franklin Nichols, *The Disruption of American Democracy* (1948; rpt., New York, 1962), 348; Douglas R. Egerton, *Year of Meteors: Stephen Douglas, Abraham Lincoln, and the Election That Brought on the Civil War* (New York, 2010), 57–58, 72–73, 190.

effectively for the dignity of human nature." Thoreau wished there were more filibustering Browns![3]

Meanwhile, southerners ramped up their own Caribbean imagery, comparing Brown's plot to the hemisphere's bloodiest slave revolt – the uprising beginning in the French colony of Saint-Domingue in 1791 and ending on January 1, 1804, with Haitian independence as a black republic. That fighting had caused the deaths of an estimated 60,000 blacks and 100,000 whites, though gruesome massacres and other atrocities committed against whites were possibly far fewer than asserted by the revolution's critics. Before warfare and insurrection erupted in Saint-Domingue, with its vast destruction to property, the colony had a hugely profitable plantation economy based on harsh slave labor, especially in sugar and coffee. With the flight of capital and subdivision of the former colony's plantations into small farms after the revolution, Haiti went into economic decline, with staple production faltering and the nation saddled with indemnity payments to France to compensate dispossessed planters.[4]

In stark contrast to northern abolitionists, who often remembered the uprising and its leader Toussaint Louverture in a celebratory way, southern whites almost universally harbored horrific images of the racial and economic turmoil in Saint-Domingue, which they generally called Santo Domingo or St. Domingo. To southerners, Haiti's economic decline after independence (as well as commercial setbacks in British West Indies colonies like Jamaica after emancipation) represented a convenient rationale for clinging to their own slave labor system. Saint-Domingue's insurrection, however, particularly threatened southern security. Located southeast of Cuba about fifty miles across the Windward Passage, Haiti is

[3] Dan Elbert Clark, *Samuel Jordan Kirkwood* (Iowa City, 1917), 148–49; CG, 36 Cong., 1 Sess., 36; New-*York Times*, Jan. 17, 1860; Henry David Thoreau, "A Plea for Captain John Brown" (speech at Concord, Mass.), Oct. 30, 1859, in *John Brown's Raid on Harpers Ferry: A Brief History with Documents*, ed. Jonathan Earle (Boston, 2008), 117; "Editor's Table," *Harper's New Monthly Magazine*, Apr. 20, 1860, p. 698; Orestes A. Brownson, "Politics at Home," *Brownson's Quarterly Review*, July 1860, in *The Works of Orestes A. Brownson*, ed. Henry F. Brownson (1882–1907; rpt., 20 vols.; New York, 1966), 17: 116.

[4] Alfred N. Hunt, *Haiti's Influence on Antebellum America: Slumbering Volcano in the Caribbean* (Baton Rouge, 1988), 9–10, 16–20, 22–24, 39–40; Matthew J. Clavin, *Toussaint Louverture and the American Civil War: The Promise and Peril of a Second Haitian Revolution* (Philadelphia, 2010), 9, 13; David Brion Davis, *The Problem of Slavery in the Age of Revolution, 1770–1823* (Ithaca, 1975), 73–74; James Graham Leyburn, *The Haitian People* (New Haven, 1941), 14–15, 33, 94–95; Harold Palmer Davis, *Black Democracy: The Story of Haiti* (New York, 1936), 89–95, 115–17.

only about six hundred miles from America's coastline, and thousands of white survivors of its carnage went into exile in the United States after making their escape, often arriving at southern ports and establishing residence in southern Louisiana or elsewhere on the Gulf Coast. Long before 1859, southern whites fell into the habit of citing the Haitian Revolution in making their case for maintaining slavery by tight control over their black laborers and stifling abolitionist agitation, selectively remembering murderous killings of whites in the French colony and entirely ignoring atrocities committed by whites against blacks during the turmoil.[5]

Instinctively, then, white southerners drew upon Saint-Domingue for a frame of reference following the hostilities at Harpers Ferry. Brown intended on a grand scale what blacks had "done in St. Domingo in 1791," argued one southern commentator. A newspaper in Natchez, Mississippi, asserted that had Brown succeeded, "out of the ashes of our fair Republic would have risen another Saint Domingo." Lincoln tried to discredit such notions in his Cooper Union address in New York City in February 1860, when he repudiated assertions that Republicans would meddle with slavery in states where it was already established, denied Brown was a Republican, and suggested secession would increase rather than decrease the likelihood of future Browns. Implying the uniqueness rather than applicability of the Saint-Domingue example, Lincoln contended that "the slave revolution in Hayti" was an exception to the rule that servile rebellions foundered because informants usually tipped off authorities in advance. Still, southern politicians regularly referenced the insurrection to justify withdrawing from the nation over Lincoln's election, arguing that it would be absurd for southern whites to risk the fate of Saint-Domingue by staying in a country governed by an antislavery president and party. Let the abolitionism unleashed by Lincoln's election lap up its first blood, sermonized minister Benjamin M. Palmer to a huge Thanksgiving Day 1860 crowd at New Orleans's First Presbyterian Church, and southern "institutions" would be overturned, so that "within

[5] Mitch Kachun, "Antebellum African Americans, Public Commemoration, and the Haitian Revolution: A Problem of Historical Mythmaking," *Journal of the Early Republic* 26 (Summer 2006): 249–73; Stephanie McCurry, *Confederate Reckoning: Power and Politics in the Civil War South* (Cambridge, MA, 2010), 12–13; Edward B. Rugemer, "The Southern Response to British Abolitionism: The Maturation of Proslavery Apologetics," *Journal of Southern History* 70 (May 2004): 246–47; Clavin, *Toussaint Louverture*, 1–3, 14–23; Lacy K. Ford, *Deliver Us from Evil: The Slavery Question in the Old South* (New York, 2009), 26–27, 84–86, 129; Elizabeth R. Varon, *Disunion!: The Coming of the American Civil War* (Chapel Hill, 45–46, 211; Ludwell Lee Montague, *Haiti and the United States 1714–1938* (Durham, NC, 1940), 3; Hunt, *Haiti's Influence*, 10, 21, 37–40, 123–39.

five and twenty years the history of St. Domingo will be the record of Louisiana."[6]

Rhetorically, then, the disunion crisis of 1859–60 fed off Caribbean allusions. More importantly, new Caribbean expansion initiatives in Washington, William Walker's filibustering finale in Central America, and the activities of a new proslavery filibustering group called the Knights of the Golden Circle affected electioneering in 1860. These "breaking" events infected U.S. domestic politics at a critical moment, because the election hinged upon territorial issues inseparable from tropical expansion agendas. Ever since being founded a half-decade earlier, the Republican Party had been dedicated to stopping slavery's extension southward as well as to the west, and some Republican partisans worried as much about the former as the latter. One Chicago Republican categorically defined Cuba as "more important" than Kansas. Since their party's founding, Republicans harbored fears of slave state intentions toward the Tropics, and developments in 1859–60 confirmed their apprehensions. As *New York Tribune* editor Horace Greeley emphasized, it was the "demand of the Republican party" that "Territories already won from Mexico, and those which may be won hereafter from her, and those which shall come to us on the North and South, shall be the homes of free labor and freemen ONLY and FOREVER." Yet southern expansionists desired the opposite. Slaveholders' very exclusion by "interdictive laws" from the western territories, a Texas newspaper declared, mandated "new fields of enterprise" to restore the Union's "lost balance of power," such as "cotton and sugar lands in Mexico." A Georgia newspaper agreed, declaring in March 1860 that "Anglo-Americans" deserved all of Mexico. Texas governor, Sam Houston, should take it over and "enslave the negroes and mixed breeds" so that southerners could "try their hand at developing

---

[6] Southerner quoted in Hunt, *Haiti's Influence*, 140; (Natchez) *Mississippi Free Trader* quoted in Charles Joyner, "'Guilty of Holiest Crime': The Passion of John Brown," in *His Soul Goes Marching On: Responses to John Brown and the Harpers Ferry Raid*, ed. Paul Finkelman (Charlottesville, 1995), 313; text of Lincoln's Cooper Union speech in Harold Holzer, *Lincoln at Cooper Union: The Speech That Made Abraham Lincoln President* (New York, 2005), 270–72; William L. Barney, *The Secessionist Impulse: Alabama and Mississippi in 1860* (Princeton, NJ, 1974), 232–33; Mitchell Snay, *Gospel of Disunion: Religion and Separatism in the Antebellum South* (1993; rpt., Chapel Hill, 1997), 175–79; Charles B. Dew, *Apostles of Disunion: Southern Secessionist Commissioners and the Causes of the Civil War* (2001; rpt., Charlottesville, 2002), 30–41, 57, 70, 71; William W. Freehling and Craig M. Simpson, ed., *Secession Debated: Georgia's Showdown in 1860* (New York, 1992), 120; Clavin, *Toussaint Louverture*, 47–73; Palmer's sermon in *Washington* (DC) *Constitution*, Dec. 22, 1860.

the country."⁷ Caribbean matters significantly impacted both the Douglas and Lincoln candidacies in 1860.

When schooner captains unfurled "Douglas and Cuba, 1860" banners on their masts in 1859, they testified to one of Stephen Douglas's best remaining credentials to lead a united Democratic Party into the 1860 election – his transsectional stature as champion of the Monroe Doctrine and Manifest Destiny. To some southerners, especially those who believed the climate and soil in Latin America more promising for future slave societies than America's West, Douglas's reliability as a Caribbean expansionist offset his apostasy over Kansas. As Georgia congressman-elect Augustus R. Wright put it in a public letter in late 1857, Douglas already had "done more than any living man to roll back Northern fanaticism." Wise southern Democrats would "forget the dead, defunct and wholly useless controversy about Lecompton" and attend instead to Central America, Mexico, and Cuba. A year later, Democratic U.S. senator Albert Gallatin Brown of Mississippi defended William Walker's attempt to plant a "slave-holding state in Nicaragua" to his constituents and explained that he would never allow his disagreement with Douglas over the "Kansas-Lecompton question" to drive him politically from "a great man." Slavery, Brown maintained, "must go South if it goes at all." A Virginia newspaper reporting Douglas's comments about America's inevitable acquisition of Cuba praised him as a man who would better expand "southern institutions" than "any man" in Virginia or South Carolina.⁸

Such thinking persisted to the eve of the 1860 Democratic nominating convention. An unidentified southern woman announced in a letter to a Louisville newspaper a few months beforehand, "I am for ... Douglas, Cuba and peaceful annexation." Just prior to the Charleston meeting, Alabama Democrat John W. Womack, after a trip through eastern Mississippi, asked a contact in the Illinois Democracy to alert "such of the Democratic Delegates from the West and the North, as you may

---

⁷ "Skinner" to Lyman Trumbull (marked "confidential"), Mar. 8, 1858, Lyman Trumbull Papers, Reel 3, LC; Horace Greeley speech on Aug. 6, 1859, *New-York Daily Tribune*, Sept. 14, 1859; *Austin (TX) State Gazette*, Oct. 9, 1858; *Augusta (GA) Daily Chronicle and Sentinel*, Mar. 10, 1860.

⁸ Augustus R. Wright letter in *Cleveland Plain Dealer*, Oct. 25, 1858; letter in *Richmond South*, Sept. 20, 1858; A. G. Brown speech of Sept. 17, 1858, both in *New York Evening Post*, Sept. 21, 1858; *Macon (GA) Daily Telegraph*, Aug. 16, 1859, quoted in Egerton, *Year of Meteors*, 57–58.

happen to meet on their way to Charleston" that Douglas was regarded in both Alabama and Mississippi as "the ablest statesman of the present day" and the party's best hope against "the black Republicans." Womack explained that people in his parts especially revered Douglas as an advocate for "Young America" who remained free of the "old fogyism" preventing the nation from achieving "its bright destiny."[9]

Leading up to the Charleston convention, Douglas built on his prior record of support for southward expansionism, and he did so more than historians recognize. Immediately after his Senate campaign against Lincoln, Douglas heard from southern backers that he could line up slave state support for a presidential run in 1860 if he vigorously championed slavery's expansion into the Caribbean. On November 8, 1858, a Louisianan told him to stand up for "Southern territorial acquisition" when he returned to his Senate seat from Illinois and listed the annexations that would do the trick: "We would have Cuba, Central America and northern Mexico." Southerners, he added, considered getting them a "question of right" and insisted that such acquisitions be "slave-territory." Douglas had everything to gain politically by endorsing such a program, including upstaging President Buchanan; the chief executive had proved by his proclamations against Nicaraguan filibustering that he opposed the country *"acquiring* that territory." A Caribbean strategy would achieve a South-West political alliance and isolate New England, which Douglas's correspondent hardly needed to mention was generally considered the most antislavery part of the country. Days later, an Arkansan promoted a five-point program that he declared would let Douglas take slave states in "the presidential canvas," the first three parts of it requesting, respectively, (1) Cuba's acquisition, by force if necessary; (2) the repeal of those sections of the U.S. Neutrality Law of 1818 requiring the navy to interdict filibusters bound with arms for Central America, Mexico, or South America; (3) U.S. intervention to establish "good order and government in Mexico." "You have the game in your own hands" for 1860, the Arkansan ended triumphantly.[10]

Did Douglas listen? After his Senate campaign closed, he took a Caribbeanized message to southern and northern voters alike. Late in the fall of 1858, the Little Giant began his return to Washington for the

[9] Anon. to the editor of the *Louisville Democrat* in *Cleveland Plain Dealer*, Jan. 13, 1860; John W. Womack to P. B. Foulke, Apr. 10, 1860, John A. McClernand Collection, AL Presidential Library, Springfield, IL.
[10] Edward Delaney to SAD, Nov. 8, 1858, Thomas S. Drew to SAD, Nov. 12, 1858, John T. Reid to SAD, Nov. 13, 1858, David Hubbard to SAD, Dec. 26, 1858, SAD Papers, UC.

next session of Congress, but he did so in a roundabout, unhurried way. Douglas went down the Mississippi River accompanied by his wife, two children, and a maid[11] before journeying by sea from New Orleans to New York City via a stop in Havana, Cuba, and then on to Washington by way of Philadelphia and Baltimore. His pace was so leisurely that he arrived in the capital after the Thirty-fifth Congress's second session was already a month under way (Figure 4.1).

As Douglas progressed downriver, he made speeches in the major cities where he stopped, as if he was so much in the habit now of addressing public audiences that he found it hard to stop. It is evident, though, that something else was driving him. He seems to have been consciously testing the waters in the South for an 1860 run for the White House, to see how much his recent stand on Kansas affairs diminished his popularity in the slave states and whether he could compensate for lost support with an agenda of U.S. expansion to the Tropics.

In each city, Douglas's orations included strong endorsements of American territorial expansion southward. Answering a serenade at the Planters' House hotel in St. Louis, Douglas affirmed that northern and southern Democrats still adhered to common principles, suggested his reelection thwarted Lincoln's "heresy" that the nation could no longer survive half-slave and half-free, and predicted that mutual sectional agreement on the principles of popular sovereignty would enable the nation to grow steadily into "Mexico, Cuba, and all the adjoining country and adjacent islands." Mounting a chair so that the crowd could see him at Memphis's Exchange Building, he claimed he was testing whether Tennesseans still could reach common ground with Illinoisans on national policy. After attacking Lincoln and the Republicans over their territorial principles and arguing that soil conditions and climate were the true determinants of slavery's viability in the national domain, he reiterated his axiom that there was no practical way to prevent local opinion on the issue from prevailing. Turning to foreign affairs, he asserted that the nation modeled "constitutional liberty" for the entire world and could never fulfill its destiny without further territorial growth. True, America's "hive" was large enough for its current "swarm of bees, but a new swarm comes next year, and a new hive is wanted." Douglas boasted of his own farsightedness in opposing the limiting treaty ending the Mexican War, since "the time would come when we would be compelled to take more." Alluding to a discussion he had with Lewis Cass, he claimed that when

[11] *New York Herald*, Dec. 30, 1858.

FIGURE 4.1 Stephen A. Douglas, carte de visite portrait, circa 1858 (photographer unknown).
Courtesy of Chicago History Museum.

Cass questioned his interest in Central America on the logic of its distance from Washington, he had destroyed Cass's premise by retorting that Central America was less than halfway to California. As with Mexico, he told the Exchange crowd, the day would arrive when "the time will come when our destiny, our institutions, our safety will compel us to have it."

Likewise, Americans did not need Cuba yet, but Spain's government was disintegrating. Ultimately, the United States would have to seize it given the island's commanding position at the entrance to the Mississippi River, lest it fall to England, France, or another stronger European country than Spain. Apparently Douglas's call for expansion southward earned a welcome reception, as the crowd reportedly laughed at his account of conversing with Cass and rendered "immense applause" when he said about Cuba, "we are compelled to take it, and we can't help it." Douglas's remarks at the Odd Fellows Hall in New Orleans, invited by a committee headed by Pierre Soulé, pushed a similar line: "It's our destiny to have Cuba, and you can't prevent it if you try!" he exclaimed, reportedly to sustained "thunderous" applause, so loud it "seemed as if it would raise the roof off the building." As America's population grew, it would need Central America and Mexico too. Yet, in ending his rant, Douglas reportedly "disclaimed being a filibuster." The crowd in the most profilibustering city in America did not seem to care, and a "rousing huzza honored him as he closed," just before cannons roared, fireworks exploded, and music began in his honor.[12]

One wonders whether Spanish officials in Cuba knew about Douglas's militantly expansionist speeches when he turned up in Havana aboard the steamship *Black Warrior* on December 16; U.S. newspaper correspondents there noted that word had arrived in port that President Buchanan had just asked permission of Congress to purchase Cuba and that Douglas carried with him a copy of Buchanan's speech. Reportedly, Douglas jested while on the island about Uncle Sam "putting the key of the Gulf in his breeches pocket," refraining otherwise from mentioning political subjects. Though Captain-General José de la Concha, Spain's leading administrator there, gave Douglas a warm half-hour reception, he failed to provide him with the dinner invitation he customarily extended to arriving notables. The Douglases spent their week in Cuba taking in local attractions in the company of the U.S. consul general in Havana, Charles Helm, and his spouse, including sites with meaning to U.S. filibuster history. The party traveled by railroad to Matanzas, the coastal

---

[12] *St. Louis Daily Missouri Republican*, Nov. 25, 1858; extracts from report on Douglas's Nov. 29 remarks in the *Memphis Eagle and Enquirer*, Nov. 30, 1858, in *New York Herald*, Dec. 6, 1858; SAD to Pierre Soulé and others, in Robert W. Johannsen, ed., *The Letters of Stephen A. Douglas* (Urbana, 1961), 430, 431n; report on Douglas's speech in New Orleans from *New Orleans Crescent*, in *Cleveland Plain Dealer*, Dec. 17, 1858. The antislavery *Washington National Era*, Dec. 9, 1858 argued Douglas had "proclaimed himself a *filibuster*" by his Memphis speech.

city that had been a key unrealized military objective during the landing of Narciso López's expedition in 1850. Douglas also made an inspection of fortifications in Havana harbor before boarding the *Empire City* for New York on December 23. Apparently his health benefited from his time in the place he had long been coveting for his country, as he was reported as looking exceptionally rested on his arrival in New York.[13]

Douglas embarked from Cuba with his beliefs intact that U.S. destiny included acquiring the island, even though newspaper reports said that the Cuban people reacted angrily and publicly when news arrived of Buchanan's annexation initiative and Douglas probably witnessed some of the demonstrations in Havana. Helm alluded to this hostility in a subsequent letter to Douglas, along with an alert that Douglas would receive some Havana cigars he was sending. "Nothing has occurred since you left us," Helm reported, "to change my opinion as to the feelings of the people of Cuba on the subject of a sale of the Island. They are opposed to any transfer to the United States." One wonders, moreover, whether Douglas had any inkling of a renewed determination in Madrid against alienating Spain's treasured colony. General Leopoldo O'Donnell, Spain's prime minister, was thoroughly committed to his nation's continued rule. An enhanced Spanish military presence on the island, some thirty thousand troops by 1859, ensured the island could resist anything short of an all-out foreign attack. Nonetheless, Douglas continued to express bombastic imperialism in his public speeches, just as he had during his Mississippi River voyage.[14]

While in New York, Douglas spoke in a pounding rain to a crowd outside his hotel, repeating his standard fare condemning the Clayton-Bulwer Treaty and anticipating an "American destiny" in Latin America, though not necessarily through military conquest. When someone in the crowd queried whether Douglas wanted war for Cuba, Douglas emphasized that for the time being his country should serve as the protector of weak Latin American countries against covetous European powers. The proper policy was "Americanization" of the Tropics first, "annexing

---

[13] *New York Herald,* Dec. 22, 29, 31, 1858; *Cincinnati Daily Enquirer,* Jan. 9, 1859; *Harper's Weekly,* Jan. 1, 1859, p. 7; Walter B. Smith II, *America's Diplomats and Consuls of 1776–1865* (Washington, D. C., 1986), 173. Damon Wells noted that the *Habana Crónica de la Marina* only gave a single sentence to Douglas's arrival. Damon Wells, *Stephen Douglas: The Last Years, 1857–1861* (Austin, 1971), 154.

[14] Charles J. Helm to SAD, Jan. 21, 1859, SAD Papers, UC; *Cleveland Plain Dealer,* Dec. 24, 1858; Wells, *Douglas,* 155; Wayne H. Bowen, *Spain and the American Civil War* (Columbia, MO, 2011), 28.

afterwards." "Americanization" conveyed a code that Democratic politicians frequently employed to connote a gradual and natural U.S. cultural infiltration of Hispanic countries. One commentator explained regarding the Cuban people that Americanization entailed getting them "somewhat ... assimilated to our customs, sentiments and institutions, through contact with Americans emigrating to Cuba and settling among them." Stopping at Baltimore, his last stop on the way to Washington, Douglas reiterated his standard call for America to fulfill "the destiny which the Almighty has marked out for us," predicting the nation's likely absorption of "Province after Province of Mexico" and "Cuba too" and expounding the expansionist trope that America required territorial growth for survival. He again denounced the Clayton-Bulwer Treaty as an impediment to U.S. extension into Central America and argued that to ensure their nation survived indefinitely, Americans would have to fulfill "the constitutional law of our existence" by growing their domain.[15]

By the time Douglas arrived in Washington, Congress was a month into its session, and Douglas almost immediately caught up on Buchanan's Cuba machinations and enhanced his own Caribbean résumé. During the previous year, the administration had received reports from U.S. diplomats abroad and other informants and political allies that Spain's economy was so precarious as to jeopardize its government's stability. Spain's rulers, the administration learned, so sorely needed funds to retain power that they might sell their treasured colony if the United States would provide an instant down payment the moment an agreement was reached. Acting on these assurances, Buchanan called for Cuba's acquisition through diplomacy in his December 6, 1858, annual message, which asked Congress for the power to authorize an immediate transfer of funds to Spain even before a treaty gained Senate ratification. Douglas was pulled into the project when Buchanan's ally, Slidell of Louisiana, after consulting the Senate Democratic caucus, introduced a bill to the Senate on January 10, 1859, appropriating $30 million as a down payment in a Cuba purchase treaty. The bill dominated Senate debate between February 9 and 26, igniting an outpouring of support throughout the slave states and enthusiasm from northern Democrats anticipating a boom in U.S.-Cuban trade from annexation. Incorporating the island would end American tariffs on

[15] *Cincinnati Daily Enquirer*, Jan. 9, 1859; "Pontiac" to the Editor of the *New-York Times*, Jan. 8, 1859, in *New-York Times*, Jan. 15, 1859; *New York Herald*, Dec. 29, 31, 1858; *New York Times*, Jan. 1, 1859; *Speeches of Senator S. A. Douglas, on the Occasion of his Public Receptions by the Citizens of New Orleans, Philadelphia, and Baltimore* (Washington, DC, 1859), 15–16, 11–12.

Cuban sugar and eliminate Spanish import barriers against U.S. manufactured and agricultural goods. Seeing the scheme as evidence of new
Slave Power designs on the Tropics, however, Republicans used delaying stratagems to prevent a formal vote prior to Senate adjournment
on March 3. Meanwhile, House resolutions for Cuba's acquisition also
failed of action.

Douglas on February 25 cast two votes against tabling the measure
but was remarkably silent during the extended debate other than fleeting remarks urging that the bill should be voted up or down. Still, an
Associated Press account of Douglas's bellicose remarks on Cuba in
the Democratic caucus on January 15 circulated widely throughout the
country, embellishing his credentials as a radical regarding southward
Manifest Destiny while alienating Republicans, Whiggish southerners, and even more cautious expansionists in his own party. Reportedly,
Douglas told his Democratic colleagues he would support Slidell's legislation, reasoning that Buchanan would never have promoted it "without
sufficient data to justify" the assumption that the down payment would
work. But Douglas added portentously that the only truly promising tactic for Cuba would be *"to seize the island by way of reclamation, and
negotiate afterward."* Reacting disgustedly to what he read of the caucus, former Kentucky congressman and governor Robert Perkins Letcher
judged Douglas's stand a forfeiture of whatever claim he had as a "man
of dignity, firmness, and proper self-respect." An antislavery newspaper
concluded that Douglas had "planted himself upon the extreme Southern
plank of the platform," noting that even Senator Jefferson Davis of
Mississippi was unprepared to take such a radical step as war for Cuba
and had said so in the caucus.[16]

Likely, Douglas's awareness of widespread opposition in Havana to
U.S. annexation influenced his unenthusiastic embrace of Slidell's bill.
Additionally, Douglas's building personal ire against Slidell may have
restrained him from playing a prominent role in animated Cuba debates
on the Senate floor. Perhaps he lacked interest in facilitating legislation for

---

[16] Robert E. May, *The Southern Dream of a Caribbean Empire, 1854–1861* (Baton Rouge,
1973), 163–86; CG, 35 Cong., 2 Sess., 1352, 1363; Huston, "Unrecognized Revolution,"
10; *New York Herald*, Jan. 17, 1859; *New-York Times*, Jan. 17, 1859; *Baltimore
Daily Exchange*, Jan. 18, 1859; *Weekly Raleigh* (NC) *Register*, Jan. 26, 1859; *Weekly
Vincennes* (IN) *Western Sun*, Jan. 22, 1859; *Washington* (DC) *National Era*, Jan. 20,
1859; *Charleston* (SC) *Daily Courier*, Jan. 22, 1859; *Fremont* (OH) *Journal*, Jan. 28,
1859; Robert Perkins Letcher to John J. Crittenden, Jan. 20, 1859, John J. Crittenden
Papers, LC; *Long Island Farmer and Advertiser*, Feb. 1, 1859.

which his rival could take credit. "Junius," the anonymous Washington, D.C., reporter for the Republican organ in Chicago, the *Daily Press and Tribune*, observed that several northern and southern newspapers generally affiliated with Douglas opposed Slidell's measure. Later, the abolitionist Henry B. Stanton recalled (without clarifying whether he was then in the Senate gallery) that at the moment the Senate rejected Slidell's bill, Douglas was observed "rubbing his hands in great glee at the discomfiture of his sly, sour enemy." The previous fall, a press report had surfaced of slave runaways from the Douglas family's Mississippi plantation, and a number of newspapers subsequently printed accounts, rumored as leaked by Slidell, of cruel treatment of slaves on the Douglas holdings. Although Slidell denied being the original source of what Douglas not surprisingly labeled a falsehood, and though Douglas publicly accepted Slidell's denial, the dispute simmered in the press while the Cuba bill was before the Senate and may have influenced Douglas's lack of enthusiasm for the Louisianan's annexation measure.[17]

It turned out, though, that Douglas's bellicose remarks on war for Cuba in caucus and in his recent public speeches overshadowed his lackluster support for Slidell's legislation in the public mind, electrifying many of his supporters. A northern backer reassured Douglas that exceptions "to your participation in the Senatorial caucus on the Cuba question" were misguided and that the Little Giant had taken the correct position and had the "Democratic masses" on his side. A Vermont acquaintance was even more explicit, saying the Buchanan-Slidell talk of buying Cuba was "Childish" and that the best way to get it would be to capitalize on an incident in Cuban waters and "seize the Island," negotiating afterwards. Going into the 1860 presidential contest, it seemed possible that if Douglas continued championing American expansion southward he might divert voters' attention from slavery in the West, recover his credibility with southerners, and win the Democratic presidential nomination, saving the Union at least for the time being. Intriguing in this light is a letter from fire-eating South Carolina congressman Laurence M. Keitt's wife Susanna

---

[17] *Chicago Daily Press and Tribune*, Feb. 3, 7, 18, 1859, Sept. 13, 1858; Henry B. Stanton, *Random Recollections* (New York, 1887), 202; SAD to the editor of the *Washington* (DC) *States*, published in *Washington States*, Jan. 11, 1859; Johannsen, ed., *Letters of Stephen A. Douglas*, 433–34, 434n; *Weekly Vincennes* (IN) *Gazette*, Jan. 15, 1859; *Memphis Daily Appeal*, Jan. 18, 19, 1859. The controversy led Douglas to revise his partnership contract for the plantation, which he visited in May 1859. After a possibly cursory investigation, Douglas proclaimed himself satisfied with its laborers' condition. Martin H. Quitt, *Stephen A. Douglas and Antebellum Democracy* (New York, 2012), 190–91.

to her father two months before the 1860 Democratic convention: "I am in favor of Douglas," she explained, "because Southern men can rule him and get what they want; – and then he is in favor of taking Cuba.... The only way the South can save herself is to spread South, Get new territory, enlarge herself, and spread her institutions and cut loose from the north." Susanna Keitt's husband probably shared her views, since later that year he endorsed disunion in the event of a Republican victory, but seemed to be willing to remain in the Union if the Democrats won.[18]

Douglas could not have been insensitive to this possible road to the White House. During the 1859 Cuba debates, a Kentuckian, writing at the behest of "some of the most sagacious politicians of our state," announced that ninety percent "of all parties here are for acquiring Cuba at the cannon's mouth" and believed Douglas their best bet to champion such policy. "*Yes* or *no*, on that subject," he added, would make or ruin "at a single breath" a candidate's "prospects for the Presidency." Similarly, a Georgian booster of Douglas's presidential aspirations explained the necessity of proving to southerners that "you antiLecompton democrats are not traitors to the great democratic party" and told the Little Giant how to do it: "Strike a giant blow for *Cuba, Porto Rica* [sic], *Sonora* and *Chihuahua*. Ignore the slavery issue and point the south to the West Indies Mexico and Central America, and at the same time give the *Clayton-Bulwer treaty* and *Hiram Paulding* a deadly blow." Douglas also heard from a California Democrat who reported, "We go for Cuba. It takes well." The Californian elaborated that people expected to buy twice as much sugar for the same price once the island was in the Union. Closer to the convention, a moderate Arkansas booster who opposed territorial slave codes, urged Douglas to capitalize on his support in 1856 for recognition of William Walker's régime in Nicaragua, which had established Douglas's "character as the man for the times." Now Douglas should turn his attention to the "disorganization of government in Mexico" and "outrages" committed against U.S. citizens on the border, as well as U.S. relations with Great Britain and Spain, "to draw public attention from fanaticism & sectionalism which now threatens civil war among

---

[18] William H. Ludlow to SAD, Jan. 22, 1859, D. A. Smalley to SAD, Feb. 1, 1859, Albert L. Collins to SAD, Feb. 18, 1859, A. L. Grinn to SAD, Feb. 19, 1859, A. L. Grinn to SAD, Feb. 19, 1859, SAD Papers, UC; Susanna Keitt to her father, Feb. 25, 1860, Laurence Keitt Papers, William R. Perkins Library, Duke University, Durham, NC; Eric H. Walther, *The Fire-Eaters* (Baton Rouge, 1992), 184–85. Some correspondents wanted restraint on Cuba. George W. Thompson to SAD, Feb. 11, 1859, Benjamin Balch to SAD, Feb. 22, 1859, E. Smith to SAD, Mar. 2, 1859, SAD Papers.

ourselves and which is not likely to be averted unless by a bold stroke of foreign policy."[19]

When Douglas's supporter told him to manipulate Mexican affairs to political advantage, he had good reason to do so. Mexican instability at that particular time was gobbling up U.S. newsprint and U.S. or European intervention there seemed increasingly possible. A poem in an American magazine's January 7, 1860 issue wanted the former:

> Regretting Mexico's distracted state,
>   A helping hand I think we ought to render,
> By raising forts, and, ere it be too late,
>   Upon her frontier armed assistance tender;
> To link with us would be a better fate,
>   Than torn to pieces by each new pretender.[20]

Mexican politics were rarely stable following independence from Spain, but the country entered a period of particularly bad turmoil after Mexico's incumbent president in 1857 suspended the nation's constitution and dismissed its congress. This decision triggered a civil conflict known as the war of the Reforma, with conservatives under General Félix Zuloaga in Mexico City and liberals under Benito Juárez at Veracruz on the Gulf of Mexico both claiming legitimacy as Mexico's government. Compounding the disorder, strongmen or "caudillos" independent of both factions called the shots in some regions. In January 1858, the U.S. minister in Mexico established official relations with the conservatives, but in April 1859 a new U.S. minister reversed course and tilted to the liberals.

U.S. observers worried about European intervention, since both sides in Mexico's internecine warfare confiscated property of foreign nationals, including large silver shipments. The situation seemed more fraught once General Miguel Miramón ousted Zuloaga as the conservatives' president in January 1859 and his régime cut financial deals making Mexico dependent on European lenders, including an arrangement with Swiss financier Jean-Baptiste Jecker (partner of French emperor Napoleon III's half

---

[19] T. N. Hornsby to SAD, Feb. 1, 1859, Barton Pringle to SAD, Feb. 22, 1859, Isaac T. Pratt to SAD, Feb. 15, 1859, Thomas L. Drew to SAD, Jan. 7, 1860, SAD Papers, UC. One southerner told Douglas he needed to convince delegates to the Democratic nominating convention in a handbill that climate and soil would determine slavery's place in the western territories and southerners should realize slavery would "extend Southwardly Never Northwardly." John J. Flournoy to SAD, June 8, 1860, SAD Papers.

[20] "The Message Made Easy," *Vanity Fair*, Jan. 7, 1860, p. 24.

brother, the Duke de Morny). Jecker supplied Miramón with $600,000 in instant credit in return for $15 million in bonds. Spain considered dispatching troops to collect on debts and retaliate against murderers of Spanish nationals on several occasions. In January 1860, French and British warships threatened to shell the liberals' stronghold at Veracruz, demanding payments on loans and compensation for forced assessments on foreign residents there.

All the while, U.S. leaders pressed their own grievances against Mexico, raising the spectre of a clash with the European powers south of the border. On January 19, 1859, President Buchanan provided the Senate with a list of some $10 million in U.S. claims against Mexico, covering alleged crimes of extortion and property seizures against U. S. nationals in Mexico and reparation demands for detentions, imprisonments, and executions of American citizens. A month earlier, in his second annual message to Congress, Buchanan had declared that since "anarchy and violence" existed on America's southwestern frontier, Congress should authorize him to deploy military forces "to assume a temporary protectorate over the northern portions of Chihuahua and Sonora." Additionally, he wanted authority to use American naval and land forces in protecting the Tehuantepec transit route across Mexico's southern neck and the isthmian crossings across Nicaragua and Panama. Buchanan renewed this proposal in his third annual message of December 1859, which devoted twelve paragraphs to Mexican relations. Though Congress withheld its permission, American naval forces on March 6, 1860, under Commander Thomas Turner, took into custody two vessels at Antón Lizardo, south of Veracruz, which the conservatives had leased in Cuba. To the displeasure of a Spanish commander in Mexican waters, Turner had them taken to New Orleans for judgment by a U.S. admiralty court (which two months later ruled the seizures illegal). Two agreements with Mexico's liberals negotiated by Buchanan's new minister to Mexico, Robert M. McLane also seemed to foreshadow greater U.S. involvement. The treaties, which included a U.S. payment of $4 million to Juárez's government for tariff concessions, granted the United States perpetual transit concessions across Mexico's northern frontier and powers to intervene within the Tehuantepec transit area to protect lives and property. A clause clearly designed to enable American intervention (while allowing Juárez to save face) made it obligatory on both governments to seek the assistance of the other when they were incapable of protecting each other's citizens. McLane's treaties were rejected by the Senate on May 31, 1860, however, by a vote of eighteen for and twenty-seven against.[21]

Nowhere were U.S.-Mexican relations more precarious than along the lower Rio Grande boundary. American filibuster attacks and rumored plots, Mexican reprisals and cattle raids into Texas, and smuggling controversies roiled the area. So alarmed were Texans at escaped slaves finding refuge across the Rio Grande that the state legislature passed a law richly rewarding slave hunters for going into Mexico and seizing them. In September and October 1859, the lower Rio Grande exploded in the "Cortina War," named for Juan Nepomuceno Cortina, a native of Camargo in the north Mexican state of Tamaulipas. The bearded local folk hero who had served in irregular Mexican cavalry forces in the U.S.-Mexican War led a mounted party of some fifty to seventy-five men on September 28 from his mother's ranch north of the Rio Grande to nearby Brownsville, Texas, retaliating for instances when Tejanos had been cheated out of their land by Anglo frontier lawyers and local courts. Cortina's men rode through the streets killing a few men; after occupying the city overnight, they evacuated it and returned to his mother's property.

Despite his retreat, Cortina remained a threat in the borderlands. Two days afterwards, he released a proclamation justifying the sortie. On October 24, he repulsed a counterattack by a combined force of Anglos from Brownsville and Mexican militia from Matamoros, capturing two pieces of their artillery. Women and children fled Brownsville and hysteria erupted throughout Anglo communities in the lower Rio Grande,

[21] The previous paragraphs are based on: Donathon C. Olliff, *Reforma Mexico and the United States: A Search for Alternatives to Annexation, 1854–1861* (University, AL, 1981), 5, 65, 84–108, 111, 115, 117, 125, 138–39, 141–47; Thomas David Schoonover, *Dollars over Dominion: The Triumph of Liberalism in Mexican-United States Relations, 1861–1867* (Baton Rouge, 1978), 22; Alfred Jackson Hanna and Kathryn Abbey Hanna, *Napoleon III and Mexico: American Triumph over Monarchy* (Chapel Hill, 1971), 28, 36; Ronnie C. Tyler, *Santiago Vidaurri and the Southern Confederacy* (Austin, 1973), 16, 26–27, 32–33; Ralph Roeder, *Juarez and His Mexico: A Biographical History* (2 vols.; New York, 1947), 1: 188, 221–22; Walter V. Scholes, *Mexican Politics during the Juárez Regime, 1855–1872* (Columbia, MO, 1957), 29; (Washington, DC) *National Democratic Quarterly Review* 1 (Mar. 1860): 223; *Sen. Ex. Doc.* 18, 35 Cong., 2 Sess., pp. 1–2, 85–90; J. Fred Rippy, *The United States and Mexico* (New York, 189; JRMP, 5: 512–17, 561, 563–69; David F. Long, *Gold Braid and Foreign Relations: Diplomatic Activities of U.S. Naval Officers, 1798–1883* (Annapolis, 1988), 109–10. All twenty-one Senate Republicans voting on the McLane-Ocampo treaty voted against it, mostly from protectionist fears that the treaty's trade reciprocity provisions would undercut U.S. tariffs against European goods under prior American most-favored nation agreements with European countries. Pearl T. Ponce, "'As Dead as Julius Caesar': The Rejection of the McLane-Ocampo Treaty," *Civil War History* 53 (Dec. 2007), 350–51, 357.

with grossly fabricated reports circulating far and wide that Cortina had sacked Brownsville. Rumor had it his men had killed one hundred residents and that he would exterminate Anglo inhabitants as part of a Mexican re-conquest of southern Texas all the way to the Nueces or Colorado River. In December, U.S. army troops under Major Samuel P. Heintzelman, reinforced by Texas Rangers, secured Brownsville and in the weeks following Heintzelman drove Cortina into northern Mexico. Still, small military engagements persisted, and Texas Governor Sam Houston considered taking matters into his own hands. Two years earlier, as U.S. senator, Houston had promoted his own protectorate scheme, introducing a resolution that the Senate's Committee on Foreign Relations investigate the "expediency" of a U.S. protectorate over Mexico and the independent Central American states to uphold "republican government." Now with Cortina on the loose, Houston threatened the War Department he would attack across the river unless the U.S. army itself seized the Mexican side of the Rio Grande. Taking Houston's threat seriously, a U.S. State Department special agent in Austin assumed the governor intended making his intervention plan "the controlling issue" in the 1860 presidential race and to get elected on it. Finally, the War Department sent reinforcements, dispatching Colonel Robert E. Lee to command the Department of Texas with authority to conduct operations if necessary in Mexican territory. By late March, 1860, conditions on the border stabilized considerably.[22]

Yet, even as the Cortina crisis died down, a new U.S. filibustering organization seemed poised to invade Mexico and further inflame the

[22] Juan Mora-Torres, *The Making of the Mexican Border* (Austin, 2001), 22–35; Samuel Truett, *Fugitive Landscapes: The Forgotten History of the U.S.-Mexican Borderlands* (New Haven, 2006), 45–47; William D. Carrigan, *The Making of a Lynching Culture: Violence and Vigilantism in Central Texas, 1836–1916* (Urbana, 2004), 72–73; Ronnie C. Tyler, "Fugitive Slaves in Mexico," *Journal of Negro History* 57 (Jan. 1972): 10; Charles W. Goldfinch, "Juan N. Cortina, 1824–1892: A Re-Appraisal" (Ph.D. diss., University of Chicago, 1949), 14, 17,25, 27; Robert J. Rosenbaum, *Mexicano Resistance in the Southwest: "The Right of Self-Preservation"* (Austin, 1981), 42–45; Arnoldo De León, *They Called Them Greasers: Anglo Attitudes toward Mexicans in Texas, 1821–1900* (Austin, 1983), 53–54, 83–85; Thomas W. Cutrer, *Ben McCulloch and the Frontier Military Tradition* (Chapel Hill, 1993), 169–70; Durwood Ball, *Army Regulars on the Western Frontier, 1848–1861* (Norman, 2001), 131–37; John T. Eldridge to H. R. Runnels, Nov. 3, 1859, *The Indian Papers of Texas and the Southwest, 1825–1916*, ed. Dorman H. Winfrey and James M. Day, vol. 4 (Austin, 1995), 342; Jerry D. Thompson, ed., *Fifty Miles and a Fight: Major Samuel Peter Heintzelman's Journal of Texas and the Cortina War* (Austin, 1998), 17–34; CG, 35 Cong., 1 Sess., 716, 735–37; Duff Green to "Dear Sir," (Feb.) 10, 1860, Green to Lewis Cass, Feb. 20, 1860, Despatches from Special Agents of the Department of State, M37, Roll 13, National Archives, Washington, DC; Oscar J. Martínez, *Troublesome Border* (Tucson, 1988), 66.

slavery expansion question. Sometime in the mid- or late-1850s, George Washington Lafayette Bickley, a native Virginian and charlatan, founded the Knights of the Golden Circle, a secret order dedicated to filibustering and spreading slavery southward. The group's name signaled its program of achieving a circular slavery empire extending outward from Cuba and embracing not only the U.S. southern states but everything within a 1200-mile radius, including Mexico, Central America, and part of South America, with Mexico the first stop. As Bickley reportedly put it in early 1860 to a meeting of followers in Montgomery, Alabama, "*the work of Americanizing Mexico belonged of right and of necessity to the people of the South.*" Much about the membership size, leadership, and activities of the KGC remains murky, and its leaders gave mixed signals as to whether their purpose was to enhance southern strength within the Union or only after secession. What is certain is that the KGC numbered somewhere between a thousand men and the fifty thousand members Bickley claimed, that its leaders disseminated propaganda, gave speeches and held conventions and other meetings in southern locales in 1859–60, and that the organization appeared frequently in the news in the months before the Charleston convention.

Between February and April 1860, KGC leaders mobilized men in the Lone Star State and elsewhere for a Mexican filibuster, even contacting Governor Houston in the hope of coordinating operations (they were rebuffed). A Montgomery, Alabama paper authoritatively announced in February 1860, "Large numbers of persons belonging to the order of the Knights of the Golden Circle are passing through this city every day en route for Mexico. About five hundred have left Charleston and larger numbers from Baltimore, Philadelphia, and other cities." In March, a Democratic U.S. congressman warned his colleagues that if they did not rally to the president's Mexican policies, three thousand Knights would take things into their own hands. The KGC, riven by factionalism, never activated their invasion. Nevertheless, newspaper stories on the Knights peppered U.S. newspapers that winter and spring, infiltrating election-year discourse, along with reports of the order's proslavery purpose. Summarizing his conversation with a Knights recruiter, a *New York Herald* correspondent in Montgomery, Alabama explained that the organization was exclusively southern and sought "an outlet for the expansion of slave institutions" to compensate for being entirely shut out of Western territories.[23]

---

[23] Mark A. Lause, *A Secret Society History of the Civil War* (Urbana, 2011), 107–12; David C. Keehn, *Knights of the Golden Circle: Secret Empire, Southern Secession, Civil War* (Baton Rouge, 2013); Joseph A. Stout, Jr., *Schemers & Dreamers: Filibustering in Mexico,*

By the time the *Herald* report went to press in April 1860, U.S. urban booksellers were carrying William Walker's *The War in Nicaragua*, an autobiographical account of his filibuster campaigns in Central America between 1855 and 1857. Walker's *War* endorsed new tropical plots for slavery and fed the Caribbean ferment heading into the 1860 election campaign. Defending filibustering as harmonious with God's natural laws, Walker proclaimed America's "pure white American race" as destined to overwhelm the "Hispano-Indian race" inhabiting Central America and Mexico. Reassuring "former comrades" that their toils would inevitably triumph, he proclaimed that honor would recall the filibusters to "pursue the path we have entered." If doubt remained about Walker's intentions to fasten slavery on conquered peoples, *The War in Nicaragua* dispelled them. Walker claimed that former Spanish colonies in Latin America, since ridding themselves of slavery following independence, had become dens of "disorder and public crime." Nicaragua would thrive with the "introduction of negro-slavery" and the additional enslavement of the isthmus's pure native population, as well as what he expected to be an accompanying destruction of Nicaragua's mixed races (which he called its "half-castes"), upon whom he blamed the country's deterioration. Arguing that the U.S. slave states lacked the surplus black labor Nicaragua needed, Walker suggested a revived, legalized, and regulated African slave trade to make up the difference. Explicitly telling southern men to neutralize the Republicans' containment strategy, Walker said that the slave states' true destiny was in the tropics

1848–1921 (Fort Worth, 2002), 53–55; C. A. Bridges, "The Knights of the Golden Circle: A Filibustering Fantasy," *Southwestern Historical Quarterly* 44 (Jan. 1941): 287–302; *Montgomery* (AL) *Daily Confederation*, Feb. 25, 1860; George Bickley to Lewis Cass, Apr. 13, 1860, Records of the Department of State, Miscellaneous Letters, National Archives; reporter "*Southern Confederacy*" in *Chicago Daily Press and Tribune*, Mar. 27, 1860; Roy Sylvan Dunn, "The KGC in Texas, 1860–1861," *Southwestern Historical Quarterly* 70 (Apr. 1967): 552–53; Adrienne Caughfield, *True Women and Westward Expansion* (College Station, 2005), 124; Elkanah Greer to Sam Houston, Mar. 22, 1860, Governors Letters, Sam Houston, Texas State Library and Archives, Austin, TX; *Scout and Ranger, Being the Personal Adventures of James Pike of the Texas Rangers in 1859–60*, ed. Carl L. Cannon (1865; rpt., Princeton, 1932), 124–26; CG, 36 Cong., 1 Sess., 1242; *New York Herald*, Mar. 21, Apr. 4, 5, 1860; *Boston Daily Advertiser*, Mar. 28, 1860; *Milwaukee Daily Sentinel* Apr. 4, 1860; *Daily Cleveland Herald*, Jan. 7, 1860; *Jackson Semi-Weekly Mississippian*, Jan. 10, 1860; *Charleston* (SC) *Tri-Weekly Courier*, Jan. 31, 1860; Greenville (AL) *Southern Messenger*, Apr. 4, 1860; *Macon* (GA) *Daily Telegraph*, Apr. 2, 7, 10, 1860; Philadelphia *Public Ledger*, Apr. 4, 1860; *New York Times*, Apr. 20, 1860; Samuel P. Heintzelman Journal, Apr. 12, 13, 20, 21, 30, May 10, 1860, Thompson, ed., *Fifty Miles and a Fight*, 230, 231, 235, 237, 240, 245–46.

rather than the West. Inevitably they would realize he was fighting their cause and help him.[24]

No wonder, then, that Republicans vexed themselves about slave plots in the tropics as the 1860 presidential race heated up. In April 1860 – the same month as the Charleston Democratic convention – Wisconsin Republican James R. Doolittle sternly cautioned his Senate colleagues that "Walker and his fillibusters," "slave propagandists," and the Knights might overrun "Cuba, Mexico, Central America, all tropical America ... planting slavery throughout the whole of that region, until, extending across all Central America and tropical America, it shakes hands with the empire of Brazil." The next month, Maine Republican John J. Perry elaborated this theme in the House, opposing new U.S. acquisitions on a variety of grounds, but emphasizing that William Walker's expeditions into both Mexico and Nicaragua were for slavery and future U.S. territorial gains in Mexico, Central America, and Cuba would strengthen its hold on his nation. Cuba would add three hundred thousand victims to America's slave population and, by inevitably becoming a slave state, enhance southern power in both congressional houses, reinforcing "the proslavery interests of the country."[25]

Republicans fretted as much about the political implications of tropical schemes as their practical outcomes. Would Democratic expansionist projects gain enough traction with the electorate to divert voters' attention from the party's divisions over Kansas and deny Republicans the presidency just when that high office seemed to be within their grasp for the first time? While Slidell's Cuba bill was under consideration in early 1859, Illinois U.S. senator Lyman Trumbull alerted Lincoln that Democrats in Washington were "attempting to get up a new issue in the Cuba question" to compensate for being "a declining party." Although Republicans would never allocate the requested $30 million to presidential discretion, Trumbull admitted being disinclined to put himself squarely "against the acquisition of Cuba under any and all circumstances," conceding the issue's public appeal. As Trumbull put it to a different addressee, Republicans needed to be wary of being positioned as invariably opposed "to the expansion of the Republic when a fair

---

[24] William Walker, *The War in Nicaragua* (1860; rpt., Tucson, 1985), 429–31, 256–80; *Washington* (DC) *Constitution*, Mar. 29, 30, 1860; *New York Herald*, Mar. 28, 1860; *Milwaukee Daily Sentinel*, Apr. 25, 1860; *Mobile Daily Register*, Apr. 3, 1860.
[25] CG, 36 Cong., 1 Sess., pt. 2: 1629–32, Appendix, 380–84.

opportunity offers." Later in the year, Republican U.S. Senator Henry Wilson of Massachusetts reportedly told a political meeting in Brooklyn, New York that the "Slave Power" controlled the nation's government, ruining U.S. commerce with "people south of us" by alienating them with filibustering attacks. The election of an antifilibustering president would gain the nation $200,000,000 in commerce with Latin America. When the first session of the Thirty-sixth Congress convened in December 1859, the *New York Tribune*'s Washington correspondent addressed the political implications of tropical issues, reporting that Slidell intended to bring his failed Cuba bill before Congress again, though he knew it would never pass, as a means of "making it an issue before the Charleston Convention." Slidell would do so for "mere partisan purposes," seeking "advantage in the coming Presidential election." Similarly, in March 1860 the *Chicago Tribune* cautioned that the "Douglasites" would "stir up a feeling in favor of a war with Mexico" as a diversion beneficial to their party's northern wing. It was telling, in the partisan sense, that Maine representative Perry formally entitled his address to the House in May 1860 "The Fillibustering Policy of the Sham Democracy" and that he emphasized the importance of educating free state voters to understand that "to vote with the Democratic party is to vote for the policy and schemes of pro-slavery extensionists" coveting the tropics.[26]

Republicans realized that of all the possible Democratic candidates in 1860, no one was better positioned to capitalize on the Caribbean ferment than Douglas, since he was identified with war for Cuba, Walker's cause in Nicaragua, and Buchanan's Mexican protectorate request. In congressional debate in February 1859, Douglas urged Congress to grant the president discretionary authority to intervene immediately and *anywhere* abroad, without prior authorization, once "sudden injuries upon our citizens, or outrages upon our flag" occurred. Douglas wrapped his futile proposal in Anglophobia, stating categorically that the troubles in Latin America could be attributed to British consuls and agents who, in their anxiety to drive out U.S. bankers and merchants told "revolutionary chiefs in Mexico" and elsewhere to seize the property of Americans rather than Europeans. Douglas's identification with southern expansion was further strengthened by the republication of John Quitman's 1856

---

[26] Lyman Trumbull to AL, Jan. 29, Feb. 15, 1859, AL Papers, Series 1, LC; Trumbull to B. C. Cook, Jan. 20, 1859, Lyman Trumbull Papers, Reel 4, LC; *New-York Daily Tribune*, Oct. 27, Dec. 10, 20, 22, 1859; I. B. Turner to an unnamed addressee, from Jacksonville, IL., Sept. 10, 1858, in the *Chicago Press and Tribune*, Oct. 4, 1858, Mar. 28, 1860; CG, 36 Cong., 1 Sess., 382.

public letter endorsing Douglas for that year's Democratic nomination because he would be uninfluenced by "old fogies" and stood with the South on Central American and Cuban matters.[27]

Although one of Lincoln's correspondents dismissed the possibility that northern voters would endorse Douglas's "Cuba and other Fillibustering schemes," other Republicans, especially in Illinois where partisans best knew Douglas, believed otherwise and thought he might recoup his tarnished stature among slave state Democrats over Lecompton and emerge a formidable presidential threat. The influential Illinois Republican John M. Palmer thought not only that Douglas might win the office in 1860 on the basis of his southward expansion policies but also that he could destroy the Illinois Republican Party in the process. Naturally southerners would rally to Douglas, since "territories proposed to be acquired" were closer to their homes than Kansas and had climates and soils adaptable "to the profitable application of Slave Labor." Unfortunately, sufficient numbers of northerners to elect Douglas would join them, including "professing Anti Slavery men" who naïvely thought Douglas a free-soiler for his recent Kansas stand. So would Illinois party members who were Manifest Destiny devotees themselves ("our people are aggressive and acquisitive") and found Douglas's expansionism appealing in its own right. The way to head off Douglas's presumed strategy, from Palmer's perspective, was for Republicans to challenge him for leadership of the Mexican annexation movement, while insisting that Mexico be free-soil once acquired so as to benefit the small farmers and "greasy" mechanics of the North rather than slaveowners. Another Illinoisan argued Republicans not only should go for Mexico with the Wilmot Proviso applied to it, but should follow up by taking Central America, Cuba, Canada, and possibly Europe if she wished "to come in"![28]

Many Republicans concurred that Douglas's expansionist record made him a serious contender for 1860, with one party paper explaining that the "secret" of Douglas's stand on the Slidell Cuba bill in committee was his sensitivity that southern Democrats in 1860 would make Cuba the price of supporting a northern nominee from their party as they once had insisted on Texas. Disgusted that Douglas even attended that Democratic caucus, signifying a disinclination to cooperate with Republicans beyond

---

[27] CG, 35 Cong., 2 Sess., 1118, 1222–23; *Washington* (DC) *Constitution*, Feb. 9, 1860.
[28] Hawkins Taylor to AL, Nov. 8, 1859, Series 1, LC; John M. Palmer to Lyman Trumbull, Dec. 9, 1858, J. P. Cooper to Trumbull, Dec. 14, 1858, Lyman Trumbull Papers, LC, Reel 4.

the Lecompton dispute, the Republican *Chicago Tribune*'s correspondent Junius railed that Douglas's buccaneering speeches on Cuba signaled his renewed "communion" with the Buchanan wing of his own party. The *Tribune*'s editor and co-owner Joseph Medill agreed, observing privately that the Cuban issue posed a serious threat to Republican victory in the next presidential election:

> The Democratic party, of all shades and factions, go in for the Annexation of Cuba and the payment of $200,000,000 ..., or if that fails to seize her by force.... Now, it is dangerous for the Republicans to take unqualified ground against the annexation of Cuba. Nor is it safe to take qualified ground for annexation (The Whigs tried that on Texas)[.] If we go half way we gain no credit for the concession, while we help on a wrong. The Democracy are a unit also, on bringing Cuba as a slave state, into the Union, when we obtain her from Spain. The *negative* of that position is not altogether safe for us to take openly and prominently in closely balanced districts and states. Nor can we ignore the issue.... The Democrats will bring it forward conspicuously and constantly next campaign.

Medill proposed that Republicans promote reciprocal free trade with Cuba as an alternative to annexation, subverting the appeal of Democratic expansionism by suggesting Americans could gain access to Cuban markets without incorporating the island's Catholic population into its body politic. This would save the U.S. treasury a major expenditure and cater to nativist voters. In February 1860, the *Tribune*'s Washington correspondent "Chicago" interpreted a Cuba acquisition resolution submitted to the U.S. House by known Douglas ally and Illinois congressman John A. McClernand as "a bid for Douglas at Charleston." In March 1860, even closer to the Democratic conclave, the *Tribune* charged that "Douglasites" in Congress were trying to stir up war feeling against Mexico to divert the party from its southern wing's agenda.[29]

Throughout the country, Democratic state conventions passed Cuba annexation and tropical expansion resolutions in 1859 and 1860, further suggesting the issue's potential to reunite the party. Much of the Cuba ferment was southern. In 1859, for example, Louisiana Democrats declared

---

[29] *Long Island Farmer and Advertiser*, Feb. 1, 1859; Carl Schurz to James R. Doolittle, Feb. 11, 1860, "Letters of Carl Schurz, B. Gratz Brown, James S. Rollins, G. G. Vest et al., Missourians, from the Private Papers and Correspondence of Senator James Rood Doolittle of Wisconsin," *Missouri Historical Review* 11 (Oct. 1916): 10–11; Junius letter, Jan. 18, 1859, in *Chicago Press and Tribune*, Jan. 22, 1859; Joseph Medill to "Friend Gurley," Aug. 15, 1859 (draft), Joseph Medill Papers, Chicago Historical Society, Chicago, Ill.; *Chicago Press and Tribune*, Feb. 23, Mar. 28, 1860; CG, 36 Cong., 1 Sess., 812. In contradistinction to Medill's position, Republicans in 1860 were more likely to promote protectionism as an alternative to geographical expansionism than to endorse reciprocal free trade as a means of averting it. Huston, "Unrecognized Revolution," 1, 12, 14–16.

Buchanan's Cuba acquisition policies as "essential" to American prosperity. Texas's party convention demanded Cuba as a matter of imperative self-protection, also calling on the President to cut a deal with Mexico for the recovery of fugitive slaves. In April 1860, just before the Charleston gathering, Missouri Democrats endorsed Cuban annexation at their state convention. Northern Democratic gatherings, however, made similar pronouncements. In February 1859, the Connecticut state Democratic convention deemed Cuba essential not only for commercial and strategic reasons but also for cutting off a key supply point for the illicit trade in foreign slaves. That June, the state Democratic gathering at Bangor, Maine endorsed the annexation of Cuba as beneficial to humanity. In Illinois, the party resolved that "manifest destiny points to the acquisition of Cuba, and portions of Mexico essential to our prosperity and security." In neighboring Indiana, the party instructed its Charleston delegates to vote as a unit for Douglas's nomination and endorsed "the honorable and peaceful acquisition of Cuba." Vermont, Michigan, and Ohio Democrats chimed in also on Cuba.[30]

Understanding the trans-sectional appeal of Douglas's Caribbean policies restores contingency to Douglas's role in the breakup of the Democracy at Charleston in 1860 and the ensuing presidential campaign, a four-way race including the candidate of a new Constitutional Union party, former Whig John Bell of Tennessee, in addition to Lincoln, Douglas and Breckinridge. Bell was so moderate for a southern slaveholding politician that he had opposed *both* the Kansas-Nebraska Act and the Lecompton Constitution. To avoid offending anyone, the Constitutional Unionists, whose main goal was to ward off disunion, adopted a skeleton one-resolution platform affirming the Constitution, laws, and unity of the nation and pledging to defend "public liberty and national safety" against homegrown and foreign enemies. During the campaign, U.S. senator John J. Crittenden of Kentucky, who spoke in the border states as Bell's surrogate, portrayed slavery's expansion as a bogus issue on the logic that the territories were unsuited for plantation husbandry.[31]

---

[30] *Washington* (DC) *Constitution*, Oct. 18, 1859, Apr. 13, 1860; Ernest William Winkler, ed., *Platforms of Political Parties in Texas* (Austin, 1916), 79; Cleveland *Plain Dealer*, Feb. 15, July 2, 1859; *Memphis Daily Appeal*, June 4, 1859; *Washington*(DC) *Daily National Intelligencer*, Jan. 14, 1860; *Richmond* (VA) *Enquirer*, Jan. 24, 1860; Robert E. May, "A 'Southern Strategy' for the 1850s: Northern Democrats, The Tropics, and the Expansion of the National Domain," *Louisiana Studies* 14 (Winter 1975): 350.

[31] Thomas Hudson McKee, *The National Conventions and Platforms of All Political Parties, 1789 to 1904* (1901; 5th ed., rev.: Baltimore, 1904), 117; Potter, *Impending Crisis*, 417.

Hindsight portrays Douglas's hopes going into Charleston as forlorn, yet Douglas throughout 1859 and right up to the convention received requests for copies of his speeches and elaborations of his positions, and often outright endorsements, from southerners. Once again, correspondents prodded him on ways Caribbean matters might help him to get the Democratic nomination or win the presidency. In February 1860, for instance, a booster recommended he induce Texan governor Sam Houston, *"half crazy"* anyway with his Mexican Protectorate scheme, to actually carry out his threatened invasion of Mexico and thus remove him physically as a possible presidential competitor. The same month, a moderate Arkansas supporter who opposed territorial slave codes urged Douglas to capitalize on his support in 1856 for recognition of William Walker's régime in Nicaragua, which established Douglas's "character as the man for the times." Douglas should now turn his attention to the "disorganization of government in Mexico" and "outrages" committed against U.S. citizens on the border, as well as U.S. relations with Great Britain and Spain, "to draw public attention from fanaticism & sectionalism which now threatens civil war among ourselves and which is not likely to be averted unless by a bold stroke of foreign policy."[32]

Charles F. Henningsen was among the correspondents making overtures to the Douglas camp with Caribbean projects in mind. A European exile, Henningsen had served in Walker's officer corps in Nicaragua, married a Georgian, and was widely rumored in 1859 as engaged in a Sonora filibuster plot. He also had been recently quoted in the press for justifying the African slave trade. Henningsen informed Douglas through a third party that he was prepared to muster his "humble pen" for Douglas's cause among southerners prior to the "approaching" nominating convention, if Douglas sent him private assurance that if president he would interpret the Neutrality Law the same way Daniel Webster did in official correspondence with Mexico's secretary of foreign relations in 1842. Facing Mexican protests about U.S. emigration to the then independent Republic of Texas, when Mexico still claimed sovereignty over Texas, Webster had insisted U.S. citizens had every right under international law to forswear their allegiance to their own country and move elsewhere. If Douglas pledged to interpret the law in Webster's spirit, Henningsen would return the favor by promoting

---

[32] Unsigned letter to SAD, Feb. 18, 1860, Thomas L. Drew to SAD, Jan. 7, 1860, SAD Papers, UC; Egerton, *Year of Meteors*, 190.

Douglas's candidacy in public letters to the southern press while keeping confidential Douglas's promise.[33]

Republican worries in 1859 and early 1860 about Douglas and new southern designs on the tropics were actually double-edged. Many moderate and conservative Republicans contested slavery expanding southward not only because of their dislike of the institution as a labor system but also because they wanted to reserve the tropics as an outlet for U.S. freed blacks. Republicans like Wisconsin's Doolittle saw Latin America as a possible colonization haven capable of resolving the nation's race and slavery problems simultaneously. When Doolittle warned the Senate of southern plots to spread slavery to Brazil, he did so in the context of endorsing a colonization alternative to what he called "questions of empire" determinative of "the destiny of this great Government." Doolittle argued that Caucasians were created by God to inhabit temperate zones like the American West and could never survive in the tropics over the long haul. The Haitian rebellion proved his case: there, "laws of climate, of disease, of health, overcame the white man." But white Americans could follow the advice of many of their nation's early leaders by "colonization and deportation" of emancipated slaves, sending blacks to places *they* were suited to occupy by God's plan. Republicans believed, he announced, that "if the colored population could be colonized in some place in a tropical climate congenial to their constitution, by the voluntary action of States and individuals, without being in a state of slavery, they can maintain themselves in a state of very considerable advancement." When James Mason of Virginia interjected that sending four million slaves southward posed a significant financing problem, Doolittle in a muddled response insinuated blacks would emigrate on their own hook since "tropical States" would offer them the "social and political equality" in an area "where color is no degradation." Further, the U.S. government could negotiate treaties by

[33] C. F. Henningsen to "My Dear Farnham," Dec. 24, 1859, in *New-York Times*, Jan. 5, 1860; H. M. B. Hartley to SAD, Feb. 11, 1860 (with enclosed letter Charles F. Henningsen to Hartley, Feb. 8, 1860), Joseph H. Smith to SAD, Feb. 27, 1860, SAD Papers, UC; M. de Bocanegra to Daniel Webster, May 12, 1842 (translated), Webster to Waddy Thompson, July 8, 1842, *The Writings and Speeches of Daniel Webster*, 18 vols. (Boston, 1903), 12: 116–31; biographical sketches of Henningsen in *Frank Leslie's Illustrated Newspaper*, Apr. 18, 1857, *New York Herald*, Feb. 16, 1862. For Henningsen's 1859 plot, see *Port Gibson* (Miss.) *Daily Southern Reveille*, May 4, 1859; letter from an anonymous U.S. Army dragoon, Apr. 10, 1859, from Gila Mines, California, in *To Utah With the Dragoons and Glimpses of Life in Arizona and California 1858–1859*, ed. Harold D. Langley (Salt Lake City, 1974), 160; *Natchez* (MS) *Courier*, Feb. 19, 1859.

which recipient states would provide emigrating former slaves and already freed blacks living in the border South with free homesteads and houses as incentives. Doolittle suggested, in fact, an inverse relationship between southern and Republican plans for the tropics. Latin American peoples, in his schema, would welcome U.S. blacks at the very moment they realized Americans had ceased filibustering against them for slavery.[34]

Doolittle was hardly the only conservative Republican politico pitching tropical colonization. During the debates over the Walker-Paulding affair in early 1858, Congressman Eli Thayer of Massachusetts, one of the country's most notorious promoters of free-soil emigration to the Kansas Territory, reportedly incited some southern colleagues to outrage and caused dread in others with Latin American colonization ideas, though his target population was European newcomers rather than African Americans. To Thayer, it was "astonishing" that northern congressmen were in the habit of passively conceding the tropical "Americanization" question to representatives from the Gulf states, when the free states had a more than sufficient surplus white immigrant population to trounce the southern masters in a race to dominate the region. By the time Thayer delivered this inflammatory challenge to southerners, moreover, the border state and conservative Republican Blair family had been converted to colonization as the answer to America's dilemma over slavery, possibly after Francis Preston Blair Sr. read the prospectus of E. George Squier's Honduran Inter-Oceanic Railway company. Throughout the 1850s, the former U.S. diplomat to Central America and ethnographer carried on a crusade in lectures and publications for Central American colonization projects. Squier wanted black laborers for a trans-Isthmian railroad project across Honduras that he was promoting with financial support from Robert J. Walker, the former U.S. treasury secretary of Texas annexation fame. Blair underlined descriptions in the prospectus of Honduras's rich natural resources and of land concessions by Honduras's government to the company.[35]

It is hard to overstate how well-connected the Blairs were. Blair Sr. had been induced early in Andrew Jackson's presidency to leave his plantation

[34] CG, 36 Cong., 1 Sess., pt. 2: 1629–32.
[35] Sharon Hartman Strom, "Labor, Race, and Colonization: Imagining a Post-Slavery World in the Americas," *The Problem of Evil: Slavery, Freedom, and the Ambiguities of American Reform*, ed. Steven Mintz and John Stauffer (Amherst, 2007), 264–67; CG, 35 Cong., 1 Sess., 227–29; Washington reporter of the *Albany* (NY) *Journal*, quoted in (Boston) *The Liberator*, Jan. 22, 1858; Nicole Etcheson, *Bleeding Kansas: Contested Liberty in the Civil War Era* (Lawrence, 2004), 35–38, 77.

and modest slave holdings in Kentucky and edit Jackson's newspaper organ in the capital, the *Washington Globe*. Since then, Blair Sr. had become wealthy, and by the late 1850s spent most of his time at his Silver Spring estate near Washington. Blair's son Francis (Frank) Blair Jr. of St. Louis entered the U.S. House of Representatives in 1857. Blair Jr.'s brother Montgomery, a onetime Judge of the Court of Common Pleas at St. Louis, had moved to Washington in 1853, where he carried on a successful legal practice and represented Dred Scott in his Supreme Court case. As prominent figures from an iconic border state family, the Blairs represented a slaveholding region where the "peculiar institution" was far less economically and numerically entrenched than in the cotton states of the Deep South. Despite having slaves themselves, the Blairs joined the free-soil movement in the late 1840s and later became Republicans because they wanted the West reserved for white settlers. In 1856, Blair Sr. had chaired the very first Republican national nominating convention. Two years later, Frank Blair Jr. began freeing his own slaves.[36]

By 1857, the Blairs were promoting Central American colonization schemes to state legislatures, governors, and Congress for already free and newly emancipated blacks as a means of encouraging masters to free their slaves since resettlement would remove blacks from the country. Colonization abroad would assuage slaveholders' racial anxieties over intermingling and competing with their onetime laborers once freed and also, as Montgomery Blair put it privately, "disabuse" southerners of their worries that Republicans wished to give blacks equality in the South and the right to rule whites in those places where they were the numerical majority. In early 1857, Francis Blair Sr. and Frank Blair Jr. exchanged letters on the topic, with Blair Sr. encouraging his son to make a case in Congress for sending U.S. blacks to the isthmus. Blair Sr. wanted the federal government to protect emigrants and predicted that colonizing blacks in the tropics would not only lead to prosperity for the onetime chattels but also enrich the United States by fostering trade with Central America comparable to England's commerce with Australia.

[36] William Ernest Smith, *The Francis Preston Blair Family in Politics* (2 vols.; New York, 1933), 1: 96, 97, 101, 102, 177 182, 183–87, 189, 210, 216, 223; Frederick J. Blue, *The Free Soilers: Third Party Politics, 1848–54* (Urbana, 1973), 110; Francis P. Blair Sr. to Frank Blair Jr., Mar. 22, 1857, Frank Blair Jr. to Blair Sr., Blair Family Papers, Rolls 1 and 2, respectively, LC; Louis Gerteis, "Slaves, Servants, and Soldiers: Uneven Paths to Freedom in the Border States, 1861–1865," in *Lincoln's Proclamation: Emancipation Reconsidered*, ed. William A. Blair and Karen Fisher Younger (Chapel Hill, 2009), 172–74.

Blair Jr. took the scheme to Congress in a major address on January 14, 1858. He also went public, giving speeches in northern cities promoting black emigration southward. In his congressional speech, Blair announced his intention to formally propose a resolution calling on the federal government to acquire territory in South or Central America as a U.S. "dependency" for colonizing "colored persons from the United States who are now free, or who may hereafter become free," with federal guarantees for the colonists' political and "personal" rights. Addressing the Mercantile Library Association of Boston in remarks that were later published, Blair suggested that all four million American slaves could be gradually assisted by the U.S. government in resettling in Central America. The slaves, he contended, had already acquired "intelligence," "industry," and a "progressive" nature by learning to till America's soil; as liberated emigrants they would muster those skills to improve Central America's vacant lands and mahogany forests, take republican institutions southward, and convert Central America into a "dependency of the United States." All "the nations and islands of the Gulf would fall under the emigrants' influence – making the region "our India, but under happier auspices."

Like Doolittle, with whom they collaborated in a network of Republican colonizationists including Iowa's newly elected governor Samuel Jordan Kirkwood and Missouri former congressman Edward Bates, the Blairs conceptualized black emigration as an alternative to southern designs on the tropics as an empire for slavery and exerted their influence against William Walker's filibustering plots and other Caribbean initiatives advancing the slavocracy. The Blairs, in fact, believed Latin American nations would welcome black colonists precisely because they would serve as a hedge against conquering white southerners. As Senior put it to Junior, Central Americans would realize the alternative to colonization was falling under "Walker's plan under military rule supplied by Slaves by importation from Africa," making the isthmus and likely Mexico too into a "nucleus" for an eventual independent southern confederation.[37]

---

[37] Francis P. Blair Sr. to Frank P. Blair, Jr., Feb. 14, Mar. 19, Aug. 27, Sept. 8, 1857, Montgomery Blair to Francis P. Blair Sr., Aug. 6, 1858, Blair Family Papers, LC; Clark, *Kirkwood*, 143–45; Frank P. Blair, Jr. to James R. Doolittle, Oct. 15, Nov. 3, 1859, Montgomery Blair to Doolittle, Nov. 11, 1859, Duane Mowry, contributor, "Letters of Edward Bates and the Blairs – Frank P. Sr. and Jr. – and Montgomery, from the Private Papers and Correspondence of Senator James Rood Doolittle of Wisconsin," *Missouri Historical Review* 11 (Jan. 1917), 133–37; CG, 35 Cong., 1 Sess., 203–14, 35 Cong., 2 Sess., 318; Frank Blair Jr., *The Destiny of the Races of this Continent: An Address*

At least two Republicans who caught the Caribbean colonization fever shared their thoughts with Lincoln in private letters. Writing Lincoln in June 1858, just before the convening of the Illinois Republican state convention in Springfield that nominated Lincoln for U.S. senator, the Hillsboro Republican lawyer and former state attorney general Wickliffe Kitchell shared worries about the increasing blending of the races in America through interracial sex and implied Lincoln should use his influence to get the convention to resolve itself for colonization under federal "patronage." Kitchell explained he especially liked the idea of sending willing blacks, with the permission of their masters, "to Central or South America or both." Lincoln also heard from Chicagoan Norman B. Judd, a former Democrat who was now chair of the Illinois Republicans' state central committee and member of the Republican national committee. In a startlingly expansionist letter to Lincoln, Judd laid out some foreign policy ideas for a Lincoln presidency. Predicting eventual U.S. initiatives to carve new free states out of Mexico's unoccupied territory, Judd sounded more like Douglas than Lincoln in affirming that America's "national destiny is expansion" and that anyone who got in the way would be run over since Americans were naturally "free booters" and "filibusters." Additionally, he insisted that only racial separation would save America from ultimate fragmentation or slave rebellion and asked Lincoln to consider the need for furnishing "the servile race" with "a peaceful exodus" from the country.[38]

Not all Republicans on board the colonization cause, however, hailed from the party's conservative wing. Since the movement's proponents posited it as a humanitarian alternative to the discrimination in the United States and since the vast majority of colonizationists insisted black emigration should be voluntary rather than forced, the excitement about the tropics infected some northern antislavery radicals. Gerrit Smith, a fervent abolitionist deeply involved in the planning for John Brown's raid on Harpers Ferry, wrote Blair that he concurred with southward colonization. Southern whites, Smith argued, would be more likely to emancipate slaves if they were assured blacks would leave the country afterwards, and the best way to accomplish this would be to establish "a well-protected black State in Mexico or Central America" for former

---

Delivered before the Mercantile Library Association of Boston, Massachusetts. On the 26th of January, 1859 (Washington, DC, 1859); *Chicago Daily Press and Tribune,* Dec. 2, 1859, Mar. 23, 1860.

[38] Wickliffe Kitchell to AL, June 14, 1858, Norman B. Judd to AL, June 6, 1860, AL Papers, Series 1, General Correspondence, LC.

slaves. Blacks would be cooperative, Smith believed, so long as the plan was promoted in language protective of blacks' self-respect. The *National Era*, an abolitionist paper in Washington, D.C., endorsed Smith's thinking, saying that "Manifest Destiny" was pointing to the inevitable day when the "tropical zone" of South and Central America would join the American Union, the issue being whether slavery or freedom would control the new acquisitions. U.S. senator Ben Wade of Ohio, generally considered one of the most radically antislavery Republicans in Congress despite his visceral racism against blacks, envisioned a time when his government would "make inducements for every free black among us to find his home in a more congenial climate in Central America or in lower Mexico" so that the nation might be entirely divested of them.[39]

Doolittle and company's embrace of tropical colonization schemes hardly occurred in a vacuum. Rather, the upsurge of interest in colonization projects southward both reflected and triggered a growing focus on the tropics among America's free black community. In 1859, the mulatto Haitian general Fabre Nicholas Geffrard had gained power in his country after leading a successful rebellion. Attempting to return Haiti to republican forms of government after a decade of rule by an emperor, he envisioned attracting 100,000 black emigrant laborers from the United States and growing his nation's economy through cotton production. Early in 1859, Geffrard invited America's free blacks to Haiti; by spring, a debate roiled northern free black communities and the press whether African Americans could better their condition by accepting the invitation. After learning about Frank Blair, Jr.'s colonization ideas, James T. Holly, already one of Haiti's proponents among free black Americans, wrote Blair and assured him that "thousands" of blacks could be "readily enrolled as emigrants to the intertropical regions of our continent with the slightest effort." Given the proper inducements for emigrants, Holly promised he could personally muster approximately a thousand free blacks a year (and eventually far more) from Canada and the United States to seek

[39] "Tropical Colonization" and letter from Frank Blair, Jr., Apr. 24, 1858, in *Washington (DC) National Era*, Feb. 24, 1859; CG, 36 Cong., 2 Sess., 104; Richard H. Sewell, *Ballots for Freedom: Antislavery Politics in the United States, 1837–1860* (New York, 1976), 324–26; Louis Filler, *The Crusade against Slavery* (New York, 1960), 87; Bertram Wyatt-Brown, "'A Volcano beneath a Mountain of Snow': John Brown and the Problem of Interpretation," in Finkelman, ed., *His Soul Goes Marching On*, 14, 20; David Herbert Donald, *Lincoln* (1995; rpt., New York, 1996), 231, 244. Eric Foner argues it is simplistic to reduce Republican support for colonization to racism in *Free Soil, Free Labor, Free Men: The Ideology of the Republican Party before the Civil War* (1970; New York, 1971), 279–80.

"homes in our American tropics." Subsequently, Holly published several brief articles promoting Haiti in the *Anglo-African Magazine*. Black emigration eyes strayed beyond Haiti, too. In June 1859, J. Dennis Harris, a black plasterer living in Cleveland, formed the Central American Land Company to promote black settlement in Central America, and then shifted his focus to black resettlement in Jamaica.

Emigration followed. A vanguard of some two hundred free blacks left New Orleans in June 1859 for Port-au-Prince, and by early 1860, several hundred blacks from Louisiana had settled in Haiti's Artibonite Valley. Hoping for more takers, Geffrard's government issued proclamations in September 1860 promising colonists financial incentives and guarantees of civil equality, religious freedom and other enticements including three years of draft-exempt status. Most important, the government offered emigrants who stayed a full year and harvested their first crop a homestead of five *carreau*, the equivalent of approximately sixteen acres. To make sure U.S. blacks heard about these offers, Haiti's government appointed the radical antislavery *New York Tribune* reporter James Redpath as salaried General Agent of Emigration to Haiti from the United States and Canada. An accomplice and booster of John Brown who had traveled extensively in Haiti and published his impressions of it, Redpath left Haiti in the fall of 1860 to set up his main office in Boston. He also established branches in other cities and published and distributed circulars boosting settlement in Haiti. He appointed James Holly, who passed up the chance to be rector of a New York City church because of his commitment to Haitian colonization, as paid agent of the cause. J. Dennis Harris, who traveled to the Caribbean in mid-1860 and published *A Summer on the Borders of the Caribbean Sea* to promote emigration, also signed on with Redpath, lecturing and recruiting for his Emigration Bureau.[40]

How much Republican ferment for tropical colonization infected Lincoln remains an open question, since Africa seems to have remained the focus of his thought on resettling blacks. According to historian Eric Foner, Lincoln met with Blair Jr. at least once in 1857, possibly twice, and

[40] *Chicago Daily Press and Tribune*, Apr. 23, June 18, June 30 (report reprinted from *New Orleans Daily Picayune*, June 22, 1859); David M. Dean, *Defender of the Race: James Theodore Holly, Black Nationalist Bishop* (Boston, 1979), 323–34; John McKivigan, *Forgotten Firebrand: James Redpath and the Making of Nineteenth-Century America* (Ithaca, 2008), 1–20, 44, 61–64, 67–68; C. Peter Ripley, ed., *The Black Abolitionist Papers* (5 vols.; Chapel Hill, 1985–92), 2: 439n–40n; David Nicholls, *From Dessalines to Duvalier: Race, Colour and National Independence in Haiti* (1979; rev. ed., New Brunswick, NJ, 1996), 82–84.

it is hard to believe that they would not have conversed over the Blairs' project. Nonetheless, when Lincoln asserted in a Springfield speech in June 1857 that "a very large proportion" of Republicans favored separation of the races as the best way to avert racial "amalgamation" and that colonizing blacks was the only way to achieve it, he also reflected on the need to convert sufficient numbers of people to the moral propriety of transferring "the African to his native clime." On the other hand, at Cooper Union in New York City on February 27, 1860, in the most important speech that he gave immediately prior to his nomination, Lincoln referenced Jefferson's belief in colonization as a means to gradually eradicate slavery in the country without mentioning Africa at all.[41] Perhaps he was changing.

The 1860 presidential nominating season, therefore, occurred in a time of considerable colonization flux. Republican responses to Douglas's candidacy and southern Caribbean plots in part reflected the party's growing interest in black resettlement abroad.

In the end, Republican worries about Douglas manipulating Caribbean expansion programs to take the presidency proved unfounded, though his operatives at the Democrats' 1860 convention reportedly sought the support of southern delegates by pledging that Douglas, if elected, would work for annexing some or all of Mexico as well as Cuba. Long before the Charleston gathering, Douglas announced that he was unwilling to relax his opposition to a congressional slave code for the western territories and this stance ruined any remaining possibility of his leading a united party into the presidential campaign. The Democratic convention at Charleston's Institute Hall between April 23 and May 1 failed to nominate a candidate at all, following the withdrawal on April 30 of fifty of 120 southern delegates after Douglas's supporters and the convention's majority refused to embed a territorial slave code plank in the party's platform. The other delegates remained to see if a nomination could be made anyway; but a ruling that nomination had to be by two-thirds the number of original delegates to the meeting (rather than two-thirds of those remaining) prevented supporters for any of the six men proposed, including Douglas who beat his nearest rival on the first ballot 145½-36½, from mustering sufficient totals. After fifty-seven votes failed to

[41] Eric Foner, *The Fiery Trial: Abraham Lincoln and American Slavery* (New York, 2010), 128; AL speech at Springfield, June 26, 1857, CWAL, 2: 409; text of Lincoln's Cooper Union speech in Holzer, *Lincoln at Cooper Union*, 273.

produce a nominee, the Institute Hall group scheduled June 18 as a date to try again, this time in Baltimore, with a request to state parties to fill the convention seats that had been vacated. The bolters similarly delayed nominating anyone in Charleston and arranged their re-assemblage for Richmond, Virginia on June 11. Although the dual postponements left weeks for party operatives to compromise and reunify, they failed to do so and ultimately the arguing factions put up Douglas and Vice President Breckinridge on separate Democratic tickets.[42]

Caribbean expansion issues lurked behind the ensuing campaign. As William Freehling observes, Douglas's popular sovereignty doctrine forfeited southern trust not only because slave state politicians and opinion makers considered it a backdoors way of banning slavery from the West, but also because it might keep slavery out of the tropics. To one Virginia newspaper, getting Mexico or Cuba "under the unfriendly legislation and Squatter Sovereignty theories of the Illinois Senator" would likely eventuate in new free states for the Union. One month before the Charleston conclave, the pro-Douglas *Cleveland Plain Dealer* tried to get southern Democrats to rally behind popular sovereignty as a tool for southward expansion. Republicans in the House of Representatives, the paper argued, would never appropriate funds for Mexican annexation if the slave states insisted on congressional protection of slavery in all U.S. territories, but they had fewer objections to popular sovereignty. Many southerners in 1860, however, found such logic dubious, since rather than championing slavery's extension southward, Douglas had at best only hinted at it in recent years. At Belleville, Illinois (near the slave state/Missouri border), Douglas during a non-debate speech in his recent Senate canvass had suggested that although popular sovereignty should decide Cuba's fate after the United States acquired it, he had "no doubt" what the inhabitants' verdict would be "since they will never turn loose a million free negroes to desolate that beautiful island."[43] To gain for himself the largest possible

---

[42] (Little Rock) *Arkansas State Gazette*, May 5, 1860; *Chicago Daily Press and Tribune*, June 24, 1859; *Washington* (DC) *Constitution*, June 25, July 2, 1859; Nevins, *Emergence of Lincoln*, 2: 212–23; Freehling, *Road to Disunion*, 2: 307, 311, 314, 321–22.

[43] Freehling, *Road to Disunion*, 2: 273; *Cleveland Plain Dealer*, Mar. 27, 1860; *Lynchburg Virginian* quoted in *Weekly Vincennes* (IN) *Gazette*, Dec. 25, 1858; Douglas at Belleville quoted by reporter for *Richmond South* in *New York Evening Post*, Sept. 21, 1858. James Huston contends that since Douglas's speeches during the campaign banished Caribbean extension themes in deference to repeated justifications of popular sovereignty and the integrity of the Union, "Manifest Destiny had been wiped completely off the agenda of live public issues." Huston, "Unrecognized Revolution," 14. My argument is that Huston overstates Manifest Destiny as a non-issue.

national constituency, Douglas's championing of popular sovereignty for all present and future U.S. territories purposely left slavery's future southward indeterminate, a position that by 1860 fell short for slave state expansionists demanding certainties, not probabilities.

Unless tropical areas were annexed as fully-formed slave states, a strong possibility remained under popular sovereignty that almost all Latin American acquisitions would have free labor systems if annexed because slavery was illegal in them at the time and freedom had a head start. Moreover, recent trends in Kansas, with free-soilers gradually getting the upper hand in the territory, suggested slavery might not win even if it started on a level playing field. During Senate debates on the Lecompton Constitution, Republican stalwart William Seward of New York taunted southerners by predicting that in any competition between free and slave labor systems, even in Cuba and Central America, the former would win out sooner or later given its progressive, enlightened nature, and that federal government backing for slavery would make little difference in the long run: "You may, indeed, get a start under or near the tropics, and seem safe for a time," he threatened slave state senators, "but it will be only a short time." Sooner or later, white laborers would demand freedom for slaves, because it was in their own interest to live in a free, prosperous, strong country.[44]

Many southerners hardly needed Seward to convince them. Louisiana Attorney General Thomas J. Semmes told a large public meeting in New Orleans at the time of the Charleston convention that without a congressional slave code guaranteeing slavery in territories, Yankee emigrants would flood into Mexico and Central America as soon as they were annexed and convince the local "mongrel half breeds to exclude slaves." In a striking editorial half a year earlier, the *New York Tribune* had predicted danger for a Douglas Caribbean candidacy for this very reason. Douglas could not win the slave states, it observed, even though he approved the Ostend Manifesto, counted William Walker and Cuba filibuster plotter John Quitman among his friends, and was "a political buccaneer" who "would annex Cuba, Nicaragua, and the Tropic of Cancer to this country." Observing that radically-inclined southern Democrats like senators John Slidell, Jefferson Davis, Robert Toombs of Georgia and Albert Gallatin Brown of Mississippi longed for "annexation, for expansion, in the direction of the tropics" as well as control of the West and legalization of the African slave trade, the editorial insisted

44 CG, 35 Cong., 1 Sess., 944; Varon, *Disunion*, 309.

they would never entrust such an agenda to Douglas. He had forfeited their trust by his "Anti-Lecompton contest, and his Popular Sovereignty doctrines." Further, Douglas's identification with popular sovereignty would deny him enthusiastic backing from more conservative and cautious southern Democrats. The latter would go "stark mad" were the quarrels "over the negro question" already roiling the nation to engulf "all Central America" and Mexico. Southern Democrats, in other words, wanted the slavery question settled in advance of annexation, something popular sovereignty precluded.[45]

So the southern repudiation of Douglas at Charleston by no means represented a rejection by slave state Democrats of a tropical agenda; it suggested the opposite, as one slave state delegate made explicit just before the meeting fractured. During the fateful debate over the platform's territorial plank, North Carolinian William W. Avery (the convention's resolutions committee chair) emphasized that the "principle of popular sovereignty … would exclude every southern man with his slaves from all the Territories of Mexico and Central America" if they were acquired by the United States. To Avery, this would be an unmitigated disaster, as "in the future" there would be "no opening of a country for us which should develop and increase southern labor." Ultimately, Avery prophesied, containing slavery where it was would either trigger race war in the South or southerners would have to accept emancipation and black equality, a change as repulsive to the region's nonslaveholders as to its master class.[46]

Caribbean expansion, in other words, remained on the table at Charleston, but not necessarily to Douglas's advantage. *Both* Democratic factions wanted Cuba planks in the platform. When the convention voted on Cuba, all 272 delegates voting, including eighty slave states delegates, expressed their approval of annexation, provoking a proslavery member of the European Rothschild banking family then in the country to declare that the plank "smells of a filibuster." Following the breakup

[45] Semmes quoted in Freehling, *Road to Disunion*, 2: 273; *New-York Daily Tribune*, Sept. 2, 1859. Related to this point is Walker's *War in Nicaragua* (p. 265), which critically noted that "the free labor democracy of the North" had raised "scarcely a voice" endorsing slavery in Nicaragua, even though the Democracy "relied on the slave States for its success … and … should have looked with favor on a measure which tended to strengthen slavery in the Southern States."
[46] Avery's speech in *Chicago Daily Press and Tribune*, May 2, 1860; Egerton, *Year of Meteor*, 72–73; Freehling, *Road to Disunion*, 2: 298–99. Though Avery did not walk out of the Institute Hall gathering in Charleston, he joined the withdrawal in Baltimore and participated in Breckinridge's nomination. "Avery, William Waightstill," *Dictionary of North Carolina Biography*. vol. 1: A–C (Chapel Hill, 1979), 71–72.

of the Charleston gathering, talk continued among a few of the Little Giant's supporters of Douglas's playing the Cuba card, but there was confusion about how to use it. A Douglas booster in Missouri drafted an editorial for the press specifically mentioning the Cuba plank and calling on southerners to rally to the "gifted, true and indomitable statesman" who had "spent more time and money for the South than any other man in America." On the other hand, another Douglas supporter advised him to convert Cuban annexation into a northern scheme: Democrats should emphasize how the illicit African slave trade to Cuba would cease with the island under U.S. control. The advice addressed a serious issue: according to a count by one British official, at least 170 slaving ships, 117 of them owned by Americans, brought human cargoes from Africa to Cuba between 1859 and 1861. Douglas's greatest need, though, was recapturing his southern support, not winning over northern expansionists. In the end, both final platforms adopted in Baltimore included Cuba annexation statements, eliminating Douglas's remaining chance of making the issue his own. The pro-Douglas document ignored the slave trade to Cuba and instead included a plank in its final popular sovereignty-endorsing platform resolving that Democrats favored getting the island "on such terms as shall be honorable to ourselves and just to Spain." The Breckinridge Democrats in their territorial slave code-endorsing platform at Baltimore inserted the same phrasing, adding that the country should get the island "at the earliest practical moment." Rather than repress Cuban annexation, Breckinridge Democrats favored highlighting its urgency.[47]

Unlike Stephen Douglas, Abraham Lincoln mostly avoided Caribbean affairs in his speechmaking immediately following their debates in Illinois in 1858. Further, the Republican Party convention in Chicago in mid-May 1860 that nominated him for president failed to mention Cuba, or even colonization, in its platform. Such silences, however, hardly implied disinterest in the Caribbean on either the party's or Lincoln's part. The Republican national platform in 1860 did condemn the African slave trade as "execrable" and demand its total eradication, which had Cuban

47 McKee, *National Conventions*, 109, 110–11; Salomon de Rothschild letter to unidentified recipient, Jan. 3, 1860, *A Casual View of America: The Home Letters of Salomon de Rothschild, 1859–1861*, trans. and ed. Sigmund Diamond (Stanford, 1961), 42; clipping signed "A National Democrat," enclosed in James H. Birch to unnamed addressee (presumably SAD), May 3, 1860, R. B. Davis to SAD, June 14, 1860, SAD Papers, UC; Long, *Gold Braid*, 319; *Official Proceedings of the Democratic National Convention, Held in 1860, at Charleston and Baltimore* (Cleveland, 1860), 55.

implications because much of the illegal international trade in Africans found its way to ports on that island. The platform's affirmation that "the normal condition of all the territory of the United States is that of freedom" and its denial to Congress and territorial legislatures of power to legalize slavery in a U.S. territory applied to tropical lands acquired in the future, even if left unspecified.[48] Moreover, in his "Second Lecture on Discoveries and Inventions" given to the Phil Alpha Society at Illinois College in Jacksonville in February 1859, Lincoln seems to have satirized Douglas's expansionism just when Douglas was getting a lot of press attention for his Caribbean pronouncements.

In his first speech on inventions, given some ten months earlier, Lincoln said nothing explicit about Young America and territorial expansion. But his 1859 version gave Young America its first words: "We have all heard of Young America. He is the most *current* youth of the age. Some think him conceited, and arrogant; but has he not reason to entertain a rather extensive opinion of himself? Is he not the inventor and owner of the *present*, and sole hope of the *future?*" Then, after suggesting that Young America was thriving in a bounty of imports from abroad, including cigars from Havana, Lincoln launched into an elaborate satirical commentary on Young America's territorial aspirations:

He [the Young American] owns a large part of the world, by right of possessing it; and all the rest by right of *wanting* it, and *intending* to have it. As Plato had for the immortality of the soul, so Young America has "a pleasing hope – a fond desire – a longing after" teritory [*sic*].... He is a great friend of humanity; and his desire for land is not selfish, but merely an impulse to extend the area of freedom. He is very anxious to fight for the liberation of enslaved nations and colonies, provided, always, they *have* land, and have not any liking for his interference.

What really gives away Lincoln's mocking of Douglas is what comes next – an insinuation that the generic Young American was greedy, conceited, insincere in his humanitarianism, and liked to drink and smoke:

As to those who have no land, and would be glad of help from any quarter, he considers *they* can afford to wait a few hundred years longer. In knowledge he is particularly rich. He knows all that can possibly be known ... and is the unquestioned inventor of '*Manifest Destiny*.' His horror is for all that is old, particularly "Old Fogy"; and if there be any thing old which he can endure, it is only old whiskey and old tobacco.[49]

---

[48] McKee, *National Conventions*, 113–14.
[49] AL, "First Lecture on Discoveries and Inventions," Apr. 6, 1858, "Second Lecture on Discoveries and Inventions," Feb. 11, 1859, CWAL, 2: 437–42, 3:356–63.

Just as Lincoln's remarks at Illinois College implied Caribbean themes without specifically mentioning the tropics, so did an address Lincoln gave on September 16, 1859 intended as a rebuttal to Douglas's article in the September 1859 *Harper's Magazine* which attempted to reinvigorate popular sovereignty. Addressing an audience in Columbus, Ohio, Lincoln asserted that Douglas's doctrine played into southerners' hands and should not be trusted. If "those who are for slavery" could just keep Congress from taking action against slavery until a territory was ready for statehood, they would be able to plant their labor system "in all the territories that we now have, or hereafter may have." After making this allusion, which surely concerned future tropical accessions, Lincoln predicted that Douglas's doctrine "that there is no wrong in slavery, and whoever wants it has a right to have it" would lead to a revival of the African slave trade and the imposition of the South's labor system on the northern states, themes he would revisit in his speeches over the coming weeks.[50]

How much Stephen Douglas's losing presidential candidacy in 1860 benefited or suffered from his record on Manifest Destiny and tropical expansionism remains hard to measure. During the campaign, Democrats dredged up Lincoln's record on the U.S.-Mexican War yet again, in an effort to paint an implicitly negative image on the Republican regarding U.S. extension, reminding their own base that the two candidates had taken far different positions on territorial growth over the years. One accusatory Douglas campaign song painted Lincoln as virtually treasonous in his opposition to the war effort:

> "Old Abe" from Kentuck did go,
> To settle further west,
> And while our troops were in Mexico,
> *Refused them food or rest!*

During a mid-summer campaign speech at a Democratic mass meeting at Springfield, former congressman and longtime Douglas operative William A. Richardson of Illinois apparently worried that voters might not instinctively grasp how much Lincoln's opposition to the war threatened the nation's empire. So he brought up Lincoln's wartime vote in favor of a resolution withdrawing U.S. troops to American territory and queried, "Suppose that policy had prevailed, would you have had the

[50] AL, Speech at Columbus, Ohio, Sept. 16, 1859, CWAL, 3: 401–25 (quotations on 412 and 423); Donald, *Lincoln*, 233.

vast territory lying upon the Pacific? Would you have brought into your midst sixty millions of dollars annually from California?" Republicans, in turn, mustered evidence that Lincoln had supported the troops while the war was in progress, hoping to neutralize the issue. In the absence of voter opinion and exit polls, it is impossible to tell which line of argument was more compelling. When a veteran who had lost an arm in the wartime fighting turned up at a Douglas meeting and got the audience to roar "no" in response to his question whether they would vote for a man who had opposed the war as immoral and unnecessary, he was likely preaching to the choir.[51]

What is certain is that Douglas's spread eagle expansionism remained essential to his political identity during the campaign throughout the country, as Britain's minister to the United States, Lord (Richard B.) Lyons emphasized in a dispatch providing thumbnail sketches of the several U.S. presidential candidates for the benefit of his government. Labeling Douglas "the Representative of the Northern Democratic or milder Pro-Slavery Party," Lyons summarized his western territorial policies and reported he was "suspected of Filibustering tendencies." A one-page biography in *Harper's Weekly* published just before the Charleston convention (and republished and quoted in the press during the campaign) took a similar tack. The unsigned piece described Douglas as "a strict supporter of the 'Monroe Doctrine'" who had opposed the Clayton-Bulwer Treaty, tripartite proposal on Cuba, and McLane agreements with Mexico because of their constraints on U.S. territorial prospects. It claimed he had staked out a position on filibustering distinctive from most contemporaries. By denying the power of U.S. authorities to arrest filibusters beyond America's coastal waters, Douglas had defended the right of "General Walker, or any other American, the privilege of ... going to other lands and there taking himself a new allegiance." Voters picked up on the same cues. A U.S. naval engineer who wrote Douglas from Buffalo mentioned spending several evenings in Douglas's company following the senator's return from Europe in 1853 and remembered being so impressed by Douglas's "views of what our foreign policy ought to be" that he was convinced that Douglas would bring the United States to a "high position among the nations of the earth" if he gained the presidency. Close to the balloting, a Douglas picnic in Warrensville Ohio had a pageant of sorts

---

[51] *Weekly Vincennes* (IN) *Western Sun*, Sept. 1, Oct. 13, Aug. 4, 1860; *Chicago Daily Press and Tribune*, May 26, Aug. 30, Sept. 10, 1860; John J. McKinnon to SAD, June 4, 1860, SAD Papers, UC.

with groups of women holding flags from different states and territories to symbolize their candidate's broad support. One of the women, however, stood just off from the others, and was described as "looking wishfully towards the Union" while holding a Cuban flag. The symbolism was clear. Douglas was the candidate for Cuban annexationists.[52]

Whether Douglas's southward expansionism paid dividends in the slave states in 1860 is another matter. Undoubtedly, much of the southern filibuster community held Douglas in high regard. One booster in Mississippi identified himself in a letter to Douglas as a Mexican War veteran who had been "with Genl= William Walker in his campaine [*sic*] in Nicaragua" and supported Douglas's nomination for president. Around the same time, William Walker's father, James Walker of Nashville, Tennessee, planned a Washington trip that may have had political purposes connected to Douglas's expansionism, since his son was then planning his next invasion of Central America. In a letter of introduction to Douglas from one of Walker's neighbors, the writer explained his delight that the filibuster Walker was "enrolled" among Douglas's "devoted political friends," and explained that Walker's father would give Douglas "items of political intelligence." Indeed, just before the Baltimore convention, the press reported that Walker favored Douglas for president and was working for his nomination. The Caribbean activist Pierre Soulé joined Douglas's Louisiana cohort, to the disgust of a pro-Breckinridge newspaper in Nashville, Tennessee, which sneered, without any evidence, that Douglas like Soulé must have made investments in Central American land that would benefit from a filibuster re-conquest of Nicaragua. Also joining the Douglas camp was Congressman Miles Taylor, who introduced a Cuba annexation resolution in the House in February 1860. Alexander H. Stephens of Georgia, another key supporter of Caribbean initiatives in the 1850s, backed Douglas's claims on the presidency. Still, though Douglas got letters of support from most corners of the South as the campaign progressed, his backers focused mostly on his Unionism, his position on popular sovereignty, his actual and potential local support, and his chances for victory in the election.[53]

---

[52] Lord Lyons to Lord Russell, July 23, 1860, BBPC, 234; "Hon. Stephen A. Douglas," *Harper's Weekly*, Apr. 21, 1860, p. 242; "Mr. Douglas and the Presidency," *New-York Daily Tribune*, May 5, 1860, *Cleveland Plain Dealer*, June 26, 1860; Allen C. Stimers to SAD, June 30, 1860, SAD Papers, UC; *Cleveland* (Ohio) *Plain Dealer*, Sept. 19, 1860.

[53] James A. Smith to SAD, June 16, 1860, H. T. Foote to SAD, May 14, 1860, J. George Harris to SAD, May 15, 1860, Pierre Soulé to SAD, July 27, 1860, Miles Taylor to SAD, July 29, 1860, SAD Papers, UC; Dispatch dated May 5, 1860 to *Cincinnati Enquirer* in

Though Douglas did prodigious speechmaking throughout much of the country during his presidential campaign, he erased Caribbean themes from his rhetoric until just before the election, when he brought up Cuba at Montgomery, Alabama on November 2. The night before, following his arrival in town, some locals had thrown tomatoes and eggs at him during a torchlight procession, expressing their displeasure with his presence. But Douglas shrugged off the hostile behavior and spoke the following afternoon anyway, lambasting both antislavery northerners and southern secessionists for endangering the Union by eschewing moderate and reasonable compromises on the slavery question, especially its expansion. Trying one last time to make the case that climate should and must determine slavery's territorial status, he hypothesized in a flight of ridiculous, speculative fancy that antislavery Republicans like Lincoln, if they moved to an annexed Cuba, would themselves naturally accept slavery there because it was natural in the tropics:

... suppose we should acquire the Island of Cuba, and I trust we will very soon, (cheers,) and after we acquired it, it should be colonized by Sumner, Seward, Chase, Giddings, Lincoln and men of that class, nobody but Abolitionists going there, do you think they would free the negroes in Cuba? ("No," and laughter.) How long would it be before they would each have a plantation? They might make some few excuses, saying that it made a great difference whether the slaves had Christian masters or not, and whether they had kind, prudent men to take care of them. (Cheers and laughter.) Any man of brains who will go to Cuba and stay a week will find that that Island with slave labor to secure tropical productions, is the choicest country on the face of the earth; but if their negroes were set free, with no power over them to direct them, they would be a curse to any country.

Douglas then emphasized that Cuba because of slavery was prosperous compared to Haiti, even though Haiti's land was of far better quality, and followed that up with the prediction that if "we should take San Domingo" and let whites govern it, they would "establish slavery by the first act of their Legislature." Apparently pleased with his argument, Douglas drummed it in a second time towards the end of his speech, by hypothesizing absurdly that if a pestilence swept every person off the island of Cuba and Seward, Giddings, and "their Emigrant Aid Societies" replaced them, those antislavery northerners would quickly not only

Memphis Daily Appeal, May 9, 1860; *Washington* (DC) *Constitution*, Mar. 7, 1860; *Nashville Union and American*, July 6, 1860; *House Journal*, 36 Cong., 1 Sess., 220–21; Robert W. Johannsen, *Stephen A. Douglas* (1973; rpt., Urbana, 1997), 250–51.

establish slavery in the island but even legalize the slave trade from Africa to stock it![54]

In many ways, the Caribbean issue had played out for Douglas despite his decade of agitating it. Many leading southern politicians by 1860 considered slavery's further southward expansion an urgent matter, but not according to any scenario Douglas had in mind. Rather than con-template the future role of Caribbean gains within the American Union, many Breckinridge Democrats in 1860 envisioned tropical accruals to an already independent slave nation, an idea that had been circulating in southern radical circles for decades. Virginia's Nathaniel Beverley Tucker, one of the very first southern nationalists, predicted years before the 1860 election that once a "Southern Confederacy" originated, slavery's extension into South America, Jamaica and Cuba would follow. Though Breckinridge denied that his was a secessionist candidacy and used his party's Cuba annexation plank as evidence Unionists could safely sup-port him, many of his Caribbean expansionist backers saw his campaign as a step to empire beyond the Union. Jefferson Davis, who served on Breckinridge's National Executive Committee in Washington during the 1860 campaign, is a good example. In a speech to the Mississippi Democratic State Convention the year before, Davis had alluded to the impending day "when, by the acquisition of tropical territory, we shall complete the circle of our products" and praised the convention's plat-form for endorsing Cuba's acquisition. But he also emphasized that the Republican Party intended the destruction of the South's labor system and that Cuba "would be indispensable" should the slave states be com-pelled to leave the Union and form a "separate confederacy." James D. B. De Bow, New Orleans editor of one of the South's most influential journals and longtime champion of southern Caribbean causes, revealed Douglas's eroding popularity in the slave states despite his advanced position on U.S. growth southward. Addressing the Jackson Democratic Association of the District of Columbia a week before the presidential balloting on November 6, De Bow envisioned the "not too distant future" when the "tottering dynasties of Mexico and of Central America, and the anomalous relations of Cuba" would allow "an extension southward of our institutions to the Caribbean seas." But he hardly thought a Douglas presidential administration would do it. Rather, he thanked Douglas

[54] David R. Barbee and Milledge L. Bonham, Jr., ed., "The Montgomery Address of Stephen A. Douglas," *Journal of Southern History* 5 (Nov. 1939): 527–28, 543–44, 550–51.

for his past services to the slave states, assailed him for his recent "fatal heresy," and said the inauguration of an "ABOLITION PRESIDENT" (meaning Lincoln) would necessitate secession.[55]

By 1860, Douglas, who had never explicitly endorsed slavery's extension southward into the empire he coveted, could hardly garner the support of such men as Davis and De Bow with a southward expansion program, given how he construed his own popular sovereignty dogma. The table had been turned on Douglas when it came to Manifest Destiny. This may help explain why during the campaign Douglas did so little speechmaking on Caribbean matters. He had lost the issue long before his last-ditch effort to revive it in Montgomery.

Douglas, the Caribbean expansionist, wound up running a non-Caribbean campaign, but not so the Republicans. Instead, Douglas's Caribbean record and the Democracy's and slave states' prior filibustering history became fodder for Republican discourse reminding freesoil-inclined northern voters that tropical issues were among the important reasons they should reject the Little Giant for Lincoln's candidacy. As soon as Lincoln was nominated, Edward Bates released a public letter endorsing him and condemning the rival Democracy's "lusts of foreign domain, as manifested in its persistent efforts to seize upon tropical regions ... for the mere purpose of making slave States." Throughout the campaign, Republican promoters emphasized that Caribbean policies helped to distinguish their cause from their rivals. As a party sheet in Ohio put it, the Republican creed was "eternal hostility" to taking slavery "into territories that are free" as compared to the Democrats, who "propose purchasing Cuba ... for no other purpose than to extend the boundaries of slavery." When a New York City paper suggested Republicans cared little about foreign policy because their platform ignored it, the Republican *New York Commercial Advertiser* rebutted that the Caribbean region held considerable importance in the party's worldview. Bitterly denouncing filibustering and Democratic administrations' efforts over the last

---

[55] John Breckinridge to Caleb Cushing, July 6, 1860, *Chicago Daily Press and Tribune*, July 12, 1860; *Washington* (DC) *Constitution*, Sept. 19, Nov. 1, 1859, Sept. 15, 1860; Walther, *Fire-Eaters*, 38, 220–21; William J. Cooper, *Jefferson Davis: American* (New York, 2000), 313; Robert F. Durden, "J. D. B. De Bow: Convolutions of a Slavery Expansionist," *Journal of Southern History* 17 (Nov. 1951): 441–61; Memphis *Daily Appeal*, Mar. 27, 1861; Barney, *Secessionist Impulse*, 111; Prospectus for *The Southern Confederacy* in *Washington* (DC) *Constitution*, July 10, 1860.

fifteen years to use violence to grow the nation southward, the *Advertiser* promised a Lincoln administration would be starkly different:

We shall have no Mexican wars under his administration, no fillibustering raids upon Nicaragua or Costa Rica, no Ostend manifestos, no recommendations to appropriate thirty millions of dollars for the purpose (apparently) of exciting an insurrection in Cuba. On the other hand, we look forward to the acquisition of fresh influence among our Southern neighbors – influence obtained by acting towards them in a spirit of justice and kindness. Our country's flag will be respected abroad.... [56]

The closer the fall elections approached, the more Republicans warned voters to anticipate new initiatives for spreading slavery southward if they allowed the Democrats to prevail. The *Sandusky* (Ohio) *Daily Commercial Register*, for instance, cautioned that Douglas and his party would do anything they could "for the benefit of Slave labor," and to that end were pledged to getting Cuba and "to plunder Mexico of additional territory, over which slavery is to be extended." Similarly, Carl Schurz of Wisconsin, a German immigrant and lawyer who had become a prominent figure in Republican state politics, hammered at slavery's designs on the tropics in his campaign-year speechmaking. At St. Louis's Verandah Hotel, he emphasized that "the wildest fillibusters" could "always count upon" Douglas's "tenderest sympathies." At New York City's Cooper Union, alluding to Douglas's support for President Buchanan's Mexican protectorate proposal, Schurz offered his "suspicion that Mr. Douglas tried to effect that centralization of power in the hands of the President, expecting to be President himself, and that then he would use if for ... the conquering of Cuba and a part of Mexico," in turn restoring to him his forfeited "lost favor of the Slavery propagandists." Even a Republican campaign songster referenced tropical affairs as it reminded voters of proslavery filibusters' connections with the Ostend Manifesto and implicitly the incumbent Democratic president Buchanan, who was one of the attendees in Belgium:

> In the days of our first President,
>   A long time ago,
> When Slavery was condemned to die,
>   And Freedom bid to grow,
> We coveted no other lands,
>   Nor islands in the sea;

[56] Edward Bates to O. H. Browning, June 11, 1860, *Chicago Daily Press and Tribune*, June 21, 1860; *Wooster* (Ohio) *Republican*, Sept. 20, 1860; *New York Commercial Advertiser*, Aug. 15, 1860.

> No Filibuster diplomats
> Did represent the Free;
> No "Conference" of Buchaneers
> To all the world did show
> Democracy an empty name,
> A long time ago.[57]

How much Douglas's decade of expansionist rhetoric helped or limited his totals in the final presidential count is impossible to determine. Second in the popular voting to Lincoln, Douglas fared horribly in electoral votes, winning only one state (Missouri, by a narrow margin over John Bell), and taking three of New Jersey's electoral votes to Lincoln's four. Possibly Douglas's longtime identification with Manifest Destiny helps explain his lingering support in the South. In this spirit, just before the voting an "ardent supporter of the Little Giant" addressed an audience in Savannah, emphasizing how "American Liberty" was prepared to plant one of its feet upon Central America. It is more likely, however, that Douglas's expansionist record did him more good with northern Democrats than southern Democrats, since northern expansionists like George N. Sanders and National Democratic Committee Chairman August Belmont were still laboring for his campaign and only 163,568 of his total 979,425 popular votes came from the slave states. John Breckinridge outpolled Douglas about 3–1 in the South.[58]

Although it is tempting to cast 1860 Republican Caribbean campaign jeremiads as mere propaganda to prod the faithful to the polls, they also reflected genuine fears that gained credibility as the campaign wore on. Throughout the electioneering, new reports of KGC activity circulated through the northern press. On October 13, less than a month before the election, a Philadelphia paper published reports that two thousand

[57] *Sandusky* (Ohio) *Daily Commercial Register*, June 26, Aug. 27, 1860. Carl Schurz, "Slavery at War with the Moral Sentiment of the World," Aug. 1, 1860 speech, Schurz, "Douglasism Exposed and Republicanism Vindicated," Sept. 13, 1860 speech, *The Campaign of 1860: Comprising the Speeches of Abraham Lincoln, William H. Seward, Henry Wilson, Benjamin F. Wade, Carl Schurz, Charles Sumner, William M. Evarts* (Albany, 1860), 6–7, 7–8 (both speeches independently paged); *Chicago Daily Press and Tribune*, Aug. 8, 1860; *The Republican Campaign Songster, for 1860*, ed. William H. Burleigh (New York, 1860), 223–24.

[58] *Chicago Daily Press and Tribune*, Nov. 5, 1860; Potter, *Impending Crisis*, 442; Montgomery Blair to Francis P. Blair Sr., Aug. 14, 1860, Blair Family Papers, Reel 5, LC; August Belmont to SAD, May 18, July 28, 1860, SAD Papers, UC; McCurry, *Confederate Reckoning*, 56.

Knights were posted on the U.S. side of the Rio Grande, "prepared at any moment to pour into Mexico" and go all the way to Mexico City, with hundreds of other KGCs at Memphis ready to join them. Although the KGC plans never actualized, William Walker did spend the campaign season invading Central America, validating Republican warnings of continued slave power plots on the tropics. Around the time he finished proofing his *War in Nicaragua*, Walker shifted his intended base of operations from the Panamanian isthmus to the Bay Islands off Honduras, hoping to stage his attempt to reconquer Nicaragua (which he still claimed to rule as its elected president) from the British colony. In November 1859, Britain had ceded its claims over the islands to Honduras, and reports reached the United States that English settlers on Roatán – the largest of the islands – were discontented over the prospects of losing the Crown's protection and would be receptive to filibuster aid against the retrocession. Walker saw clear advantages to mobilizing his men there prior to landing on the Central American isthmus, where he naively expected to be welcomed. Ever the unrealistic optimist, Walker boasted of receiving a letter from Granada, reporting "the people in Nicaragua are ripe for our return." During the spring of 1860, he and his associates forwarded as many as 150 recruits towards the islands, cleverly dispatching them in separate, small parties on different schooners to avoid attracting the attention of the U.S. press and the federal legal and military officers who had the responsibility of enforcing the Neutrality Act. By June, Walker was on site at Roatán.[59]

Unfortunately for Walker, little went right following his arrival. Tipped off to his plot, Britain sent reinforcements to the Bay Islands and delayed transferring the colony to Honduras, undercutting local sympathy for Walker. In danger of having his supplies preemptively seized and perhaps his force imprisoned by British officials, Walker abandoned Roatán on June 21 and spent weeks in nearby waters, passing part of the time ashore at Cozumel Island, close to Mexico's Yucatán peninsula, and otherwise navigating around the Bay of Honduras, hoping additional men and supplies would arrive prior to launching his military campaign. Finally, after returning briefly to Roatán's vicinity in late July, Walker mustered some 110 men and collected them on a schooner. Before dawn on August 5,

[59] *Philadelphia Saturday Evening Post*, Oct. 13, 1860; William Walker to Callender I. Fayssoux, Mar. 14, 26 (quotation), Apr. 28, May 7, 1860, Callender I. Fayssoux Collection of William Walker Papers, Latin American Collection, Howard Tilton Memorial Library, Tulane University, New Orleans; Robert E. May, *Manifest Destiny's Underworld: Filibustering in Antebellum America* (Chapel Hill, 2002), 51–52, 246.

he landed his men on Honduras's coast near Trujillo and overwhelmed an inadequately-manned fort; then he took the town itself. A couple of weeks later, a British warship arrived and its commander, Norvell Salmon, demanded that Walker surrender his weapons to Honduran officials and agree to evacuate the area. Instead, the filibuster slipped out of the fort with some eighty men under nighttime cover and left behind the ill and wounded filibusters who had followed him. Walker's force followed an eastward coastal course after leaving Trujillo, but he was pursued by British naval and Honduran ground forces and surrendered to Salmon on September 3. Although Salmon gave protection to Walker's recruits, he delivered Walker and his second-in-command, Colonel A. Francis Rudler, to Honduran authorities. The Hondurans held Rudler for months, releasing him the next year, but they executed Walker on September 12.[60]

During the 1860 presidential election, Walker's last filibustering foray was constantly in the news, with the first reports of Walker's execution arriving a little over a month before the balloting. To Republicans and abolitionists, the expedition seemed absolute proof of the slave power's aggressive appetite. The *Chicago Tribune*, which closely covered Walker's last operations, stated authoritatively that "slave propagandists of the Gulf States" were behind the movement, which might be aimed at Cuba as much as at Central America; Walker's arrival in the Bay Islands proved "the conquest of the Central American States is not abandoned by the fillibustering party of the South." A San Francisco paper carried a report that Walker had told the editor of a Montgomery newspaper he had reached an understanding with France's government "that if he would establish ... slavery, by law, in Nicaragua," French merchant ships would take to his domain "as many slaves from Africa as could be profitably carried there."[61]

To some northern expansionists, Walker's death was a lamentable tragedy. The Cairo, Illinois chapter of the Sons of Malta, an expansion-inclined fraternal group, described Britain's turning Walker over to the Hondurans as an infringement of the Monroe Doctrine and "American rights in the Gulf of Mexico." Conversely, Republicans celebrated his execution. Angrily contradicting suggestions in the New Orleans press that

---

[60] May, *Manifest Destiny's Underworld*, 247; Charles H. Brown, *Agents of Manifest Destiny: The Lives and Times of the Filibusters* (Chapel Hill, 1980), 449–55.

[61] *Chicago Daily Press and Tribune*, June 1, 16, Aug. 9, 21, 23, 24, 25, 29, Sept. 1, 4, 11, 25, 1860, Oct. 1, 3, 1860; *Philadelphia Saturday Evening Post*, Sept. 29, 1860; *McKinney (TX) Messenger*, Sept. 21, 1860; *Greenville South Alabamian*, Oct. 6, 1860; *San Francisco Daily Alta California*, Oct. 19, 1860; (Boston) *The Liberator*, Sept. 7, 1860.

Walker was a liberator like Lafayette, the *Chicago Tribune* lambasted him as a murderer and pirate whose sole aim was "the extension and perpetuation of Slavery." He deserved to be hung, the *Tribune* declared, as did his compatriots.[62]

Walker's last expedition influenced Republican responses to the southern secession movement, which began in earnest following Lincoln's election. Outraged at the doings of South Carolina's Robert Barnwell Rhett, owner of the *Charleston Mercury* and arguably the most important secessionist fanatic in the country, Francis P. Blair Sr. exploded to son Frank Jr., "You see Rhett has at last avowed the Scheme over which Calhoun's mind brooded for 30 years. You see the vision that beckons his followers is '*Empire across this continent to the Pacific, and down through Mexico to the other side of the great Gulph* [sic] *and over the Isles of the sea &c &c.*'"[63] The Republican response to secession over the coming winter in no small sense was guided by feelings similar to Blair's. Lincoln could have spoken for that political veteran, their thoughts on this matter so overlapped.

---

[62] *Cincinnati Daily Enquirer*, Oct. 19, 1860; *Chicago Daily Press and Tribune*, Oct. 1, 1860.

[63] [Francis P. Blair Sr.] to Frank Blair Jr., Nov. 22, 1860 (draft), Blair Family Papers, Reel 2, LC.

5

A Matter of Inches

On February 1, 1861, three days before delegates from six slave states gathered in Montgomery, Alabama, to create the Confederate States of America, an angry Republican newspaper up north engaged its readers with a cynical editorial. In a flight of fancy entitled "Died too Soon," the *Chicago Tribune* imagined the late William Walker taking measure of America's sectional crisis "from the spirit land." How frustrated the filibuster would be, the paper mused sarcastically, having forfeited his life commanding a "ragged handful" of men, when he could be still on earth serving the new nation. Were he alive, he might even become "Military Dictator of the Southern Republic." It was such a disturbing thought, the *Tribune* editors confessed, that they would hesitate to attend a séance, lest Walker's spirit appear to "rap" out "his vehement sympathies with Secession." Surely Walker must feel cheated, "taking off" for the spirit world when he could have had "a scrimmage" under his own flag had he stuck around.[1]

The *Tribune*'s back-to-the-future moment seems bizarre, but the paper had cause to link William Walker's invasions of Central America with the formation of the Confederacy. In 1858, the filibuster had attracted press attention by appearing with Alabama's leading secessionist, William L. Yancey, at the Bethel Church in Montgomery for a rally that initiated a constitution for a Montgomery chapter of the so-called League of United Southerners, a never fully launched organization dedicated to the formation of an independent slave state republic.[2] Certainly, the *Tribune*'s

---

[1] *Chicago Daily Tribune*, Feb. 1, 1861.
[2] *Montgomery Mail*, quoted in *New-York Times*, June 22, 1858; *Montgomery Confederation* quoted in *New York Herald*, July 21, 1858; *Tuskegee* (AL) *Republican*, July 15, 1858; Eric

Republican readers would have grasped the message since their party from its founding had dedicated itself not only against southerners' spreading slavery westward but also acquiring slave plantation lands in the Caribbean.

Memories of Walker's appearance with Yancey, however, probably less explained the *Tribune*'s outburst than recent developments in Washington, with Congress debating a new sectional compromise that made slavery's southward growth a focus of political discourse. As the slave states began withdrawing from the Union in December 1860 and January 1861 in protest of Lincoln's election, lawmakers groped for a legislative resolution of southern discontent, and their most promising proposition virtually guaranteed the future admission of new Caribbean slave states to the Union. While Douglas sacrificed his beloved popular sovereignty to seal a sectional deal that would have allowed slavery's extension southward, Lincoln grew appalled that compromise proposals might give the South's "peculiar institution" a new lease on life in the Tropics. By reaffirming his party's commitment to preventing slavery's spread westward *or* southward, Lincoln ensured that his rival would be unable to repeat his nation-saving miracle of 1850.

No sooner did telegraphic reports in early November announce Abraham Lincoln's triumph than the states of the Deep South gave early indications of their unwillingness to remain in the Union to test the incoming administration's intentions on slavery. Within a week of Lincoln's election as president, South Carolina's legislature voted unanimously to convene a state convention on December 17 to consider withdrawal, and other states took steps to follow. On November 14, Alabama's governor announced that on December 6 he would call for delegates to be elected to a state secession convention; also on November 14, Mississippi's chief executive summoned his state's legislature for a special session to take action. Georgia, Louisiana, and Florida similarly took procedural steps toward secession before November ended. As Stephen Douglas headed to Washington for what might be the final congressional session of a united nation, he heard discouraging news from his own recent vice-presidential candidate, former Georgia governor Herschel V. Johnson. "I think the Union is gone. S. Carolina will

H. Walther, *The Fire-Eaters* (Baton Rouge, 1992), 70–72, 255; David S. Heidler, *Pulling the Temple Down: The Fire-Eaters and the Destruction of the Union* (Mechanicsburg, PA, 1994), 130–32, 134.

secede and ... will drag the Cotton States with her very soon," Johnson wrote on November 25.[3]

There seemed little hope as Douglas arrived in the capital that the outgoing president James Buchanan could stem the secession tide. On December 3, Buchanan's annual message to Congress displayed his inadequacy for a crisis of this magnitude. To rekindle southern Unionism, Buchanan urged antislavery northerners to cease agitating the slavery issue – a presidential pipe dream if there ever was one – and he asked northern states to recover southern goodwill by repealing their "personal liberty" laws interfering with the recovery of escaped slaves. However, he neither proposed national legislation to address southern concerns nor prepared for military action to thwart secession, even though he maintained the South lacked constitutional grounds for leaving the Union. Weakly suggesting that it lay beyond presidential powers "to restore peace and harmony," Buchanan left everything in Congress's hands. Either Congress or the state legislatures, he felt, should initiate a constitutional amendment to resolve disputes over fugitive slaves and slavery's status in all states where slavery might "hereafter exist" as well as in the nation's current states and territories.[4]

The next day, the House of Representatives established a committee of one member from each of the thirty-three states to address "the present perilous condition of the country," but thirty-eight Republican congressmen cast the sole votes against creating it, an ominous indication their party might be unwilling to bend, and the committee waited a full week before meeting. Unfortunately, this group lacked a high-profile national figure with the influence to drag reluctant colleagues to unpopular positions and it violated principles of inclusivity. The Republican speaker did not appoint a single Democrat from a nonslave state east of the Pacific Coast.[5]

---

[3] William W. Freehling, *The Road to Disunion*, vol. 2: *Secessionists Triumphant* (New York, 2007), 385–415, 422; William L. Barney, *The Secessionist Impulse: Alabama and Mississippi in 1860* (Princeton, 1974), 194, 198; David Potter, *The Impending Crisis, 1848–1861*, ed. and completed by Don E. Fehrenbacher (New York, 1976), 490–91; Heidler, *Pulling the Temple Down*, 165; Robert W. Johannsen, *Stephen A. Douglas* (1973; rpt., Urbana, 1997), 809; Herschel V. Johnson to SAD, Nov. 25, 1860, William M. Johnston to SAD, Dec. 15, 1860, SAD Papers, UC.

[4] James Buchanan Annual Message, JRMP, 5: 627–38.

[5] Potter, *Impending Crisis*, 492–93; Roy F. Nichols, *The Disruption of American Democracy* (1948; rpt., New York, 1962), 394–95; Russell McClintock, *Lincoln and the Decision for War: The Northern Response to Secession* (Chapel Hill, 2008), 97; Johannsen, *Douglas*, 812–14.

Douglas found himself in the center of the secession maelstrom because he served on the more promising parallel committee in the Senate. The upper house's "Committee of Thirteen" had more prestigious members than its House counterpart but the disadvantage of starting its work later. It was not authorized until December 18, and another two days passed before vice president and recent presidential candidate John Breckinridge, who presided over Senate deliberations, appointed its membership. Along with Douglas, Breckinridge placed several powerhouses in national politics, including leading Republican William Seward, Deep South Democratic stalwarts Jefferson Davis of Mississippi and Robert Toombs of Georgia, and the influential John J. Crittenden of Kentucky. A longtime Whig who like Lincoln gave up on the party grudgingly, Crittenden had flirted with Know-Nothingism in the mid-1850s before helping to found the Constitutional Union Party. Like Douglas, Crittenden had a reputation of risking opprobrium in his own section with unpopular stands he believed in the country's best interests. Despite owning slaves, Crittenden had opposed the annexation of Texas, the Kansas-Nebraska Act, *and* the Lecompton Constitution. The Committee of Thirteen had several onetime contenders for the 1860 presidential nominations and was roughly balanced by region, subregion, and party. Altogether, there were three northern Democrats, five Republicans, two Deep South Democrats, and three Upper South/Border slave state members on the committee.[6] Still, South Carolina seceded on the day the committee was constituted, and signs were hardly auspicious for meaningful results from its deliberations.

Meanwhile, Lincoln remained in Springfield (famously growing his beard during this interval), worrying more that lawmakers in Washington might cut a deal with the South, sacrificing principles he believed in, than that the slave states would carry through on their secession threats. Lincoln had reentered national politics in 1854 to stop slavery's spread, and fears of its future expansion governed his response to the secession crisis. On December 10, he urged Illinois senator Lyman Trumbull to remember what Republicans stood for, beginning his letter, "Let there be no compromise on the question of *extending* slavery. If there be, all our labor is lost." The very next day, responding to a request for guidance

[6] Allen Nevins, *The Emergence of Lincoln.* Vol. 2: *Prologue to Civil War, 1859–1861* (New York, 1950), 390; Albert D. Kirwan, *John J. Crittenden: The Struggle for the Union* (Lexington, 1962), 13, 183–84, 248, 268, 300–307, 314, 325, 344, 348–50; Douglas R. Egerton, *Year of Meteors: Stephen Douglas, Abraham Lincoln, and the Election That Brought on the Civil War* (New York, 2010), 190; McClintock, *Lincoln and the Decision for War*, 97.

from Republican Illinois congressman William Kellogg, a member of the House Committee of Thirty-Three, Lincoln reiterated: "Entertain no proposition for a compromise in regard to the *extension* of slavery. The instant you do, they have us under again; all our labor is lost."[7]

Lincoln had cause for concern. Some Republican congressmen and opinion makers, including Seward's collaborator and *Albany* (New York) *Evening Journal* editor Thurlow Weed, were amenable to territorial deals. On the twenty-fourth of November and again in December, Weed floated compromise proposals including an extension of the old Missouri Compromise line of 36°30' to the Pacific, which would have allowed slavery in territory south of the parallel. In a similar spirit, Republican national chairman and governor of New York and merchant Edwin D. Morgan, who had a stake in the Cuban sugar trade, suggested to Lincoln that perhaps the time had come to consider buying Cuba. Such talk of compromise upset and confused Henry Adams, then serving as a private secretary to his father, Republican representative from Massachusetts (and John Quincy Adams's son) Charles Francis Adams. Over the late fall and winter, Henry Adams assumed a second responsibility as unpaid correspondent for the *Boston Advertiser*, sending it unsigned letters about the unfolding situation in Washington. In the first letter, dated December 4, Adams dismissed rumors that Republicans were bending as "clap-trap," but cautiously added, "as far as anyone can know."[8]

Lincoln, however, disfavored all territorial concessions and refrained even from issuing public statements to mitigate southern concerns about his presidential plans. Lincoln hoped secessionists were bluffing and counted on southern Unionists stopping them in their tracks if they were not. Fearing statements on his part might be taken as weakness, Lincoln told Senator Truman Smith of Connecticut that although he realized instability was bad for the economy, nothing good would come of "fawning around" the very secessionist "*scoundrels*" who caused the

---

[7] AL to Lyman Trumbull, Dec. 10, 1860, AL to William Kellogg, Dec. 11, 1860, CWAL, 3: 149, 150; Harold Holzer, *Lincoln President-Elect: Abraham Lincoln and the Great Secession Winter, 1860–1861* (New York, 2008), 85–90; McClintock, *Lincoln and the Decision for War*, 73–74.

[8] Edwin D. Morgan to AL, Dec. 16, 1860, AL Papers, Series 1, LC; James A. Rawley, "Lincoln and Governor Morgan," *Abraham Lincoln Quarterly* 6 (Mar. 1951), 272, 279–80; Henry Adams to the *Boston Daily Advertiser*, Dec. 7, 1860, and editor's notes, *Henry Adams in the Secession Crisis: Dispatches to the Boston Daily Advertiser, December 1860–March 1861*, ed. Mark J. Stegmaier (Baton Rouge, 2012), xi, xiv, 3.

crisis. Rather, the burden lay on the southern disunionists to rectify the situation.[9]

As it turned out, Lincoln's position represented his party's thinking more than Weed's did, especially regarding territorial concessions. In an editorial deriding reported plans of "compromise-makers" in Washington to offset Lincoln's "glorious" election victory by extending olive branches to the South, the *Chicago Tribune* headlined, "NO, NOT AN INCH!" A Republican Marylander fortified Lincoln's stoicism saying, "If we are not to assert the Wilmot Proviso in all new organized governments of free territory, then we have gained nothing." Republicans worried with good cause that if their untried party offered concessions before Lincoln even took office, it would sacrifice its credibility with the northern electorate. Many Republican politicians and newspapers even threatened southern- ers with war if they persisted in secession, an unpromising negotiating tactic given the obsession that southern leaders had with personal and regional honor. No wonder that on the evening of December 13, a group of twenty-three representatives and seven senators from nine slave states released a public statement that the Union was beyond repair and the South should secure its "honor" and "safety" in a new nation.[10]

Even so, Douglas and his colleagues on the Committee of Thirteen labored on, though hampered by internal committee rules that, given Republican attitudes at the time, almost guaranteed failure. Unwilling to abort secession without ironclad evidence that that they were wrong about the antislavery intentions of Lincoln and Republicans and skepti- cal that such proof would be forthcoming, the two Deep South senators on the committee insisted on a mechanism that would ensure Republican backing for any proposal that they risked endorsing. On December 22, Davis insisted that any "proposition" emerging with the committee's endorsement to the full Senate would have to have majorities of *both* the Republicans and non-Republicans ("other parties" in Davis's language),

[9] AL to WHS, Dec. 8, 1860, AL to Truman Smith, Nov. 10, 1860, CWAL, 3: 148, 138; William C. Harris, *Lincoln's Rise to the Presidency* (Lawrence, 2007), 279–80; Holzer, *Lincoln President-Elect*, 69–76, 124–27; McClintock, *Lincoln and the Decision for War*, 48–53.

[10] *Chicago Daily Tribune*, Dec. 5, 1860; Worthington G. Snethen to AL, Nov. 3, 1860, William Cullen Bryant to AL, November 1, 1860, Benjamin Welch Jr. to AL, Nov. 3, 1860, James A. Hamilton and other New York Republicans to AL, Jan. 29, 1861, AL Papers, Series 1, LC; Lyman Trumbull to David Davis, Dec. 24, 1860, Davis and Family Papers, AL Presidential Library, Springfield, IL; Potter, *Impending Crisis*, 492–93, 525; McClintock, *Lincoln and the Decision for War*, 53–58; Carl Schurz, *The Reminiscences of Carl Schurz*, vol. 2: 1852–1863 (New York, 1909), 211–12.

and his committee colleagues had little choice but to agree if they wished to keep Davis and Toombs, and by extension the Deep South states, negotiating.[11]

Davis's rule almost immediately came into play regarding a package deal proposed by Crittenden, now Douglas's firm ally despite their different party roots. Douglas told a group of callers serenading him at his Washington residence on December 1 that the time had come for American "patriots" to save the Union by eschewing partisanship and forgetting past disagreements.[12] Though Crittenden's plan addressed a number of southern grievances, its most important provision thrust slavery in the Tropics to the center of U.S. political discourse at a time when many observers believed southern aspirations for expanding slavery southward influenced their bolt from the Union. In public letters addressed to Alabama's most famous secessionist, *New York Times* editor Henry Raymond dressed down William L. Yancey by charging, "Part of your scheme is to extend your conquests into Mexico and Central America, – to add control of the Caribbean Sea to your supremacy over the Gulf, – to bring Cuba into your Southern Union." A stalwart Whig, Crittenden had opposed President Buchanan's schemes for acquiring Cuba and making Mexico into a U.S. protectorate, but he recognized that if southerners were reassured prospects in the Caribbean basin would compensate for their setbacks in the West, he might undermine the momentum toward secession. He believed it was a sacrifice worth making.[13]

The Kentuckian's scheme (presented to the full Senate on December 18) included six proposed irreversible amendments to the Constitution buttressed by four proposed congressional resolutions that mostly addressed domestic issues, such as southern grievances about northern resistance to the Fugitive Slave Act and apprehensions Republicans would end slavery in Washington, D.C. The first of Crittenden's amendments, however, had glaring Caribbean implications. It assuaged southern resentment of the North's successes at barring slavery from the West by extending the

---

[11] *Sen. Reports*, 36 Cong., 2 Sess., No. 288, p. 2; Dispatch from Washington dated Dec. 24 in *New Orleans Daily Delta*, Dec. 30, 1860.
[12] Johannsen, *Douglas*, 812–13; Damon Wells, *Stephen Douglas: The Last Years, 1857–1861* (Austin, 1971), 261.
[13] Johannsen, *Douglas*, 812–13; Henry J. Raymond to William L. Yancey, Dec. 19, 1860, Henry J. Raymond, *Disunion and Slavery: A Series of Letters to Hon. W. L. Yancey of Alabama* (New York[?], 1861–[?]), 15; John Dovan to SAD, Dec. 13, 1860, SAD Papers, UC; Freehling, *Road to Disunion*, 2: 456; John J. Crittenden to Samuel Smith Nicholas, May 19, 1858, John J. Crittenden Papers, LC; CG, 35 Cong., 2 Sess., Appendix, 155–60.

old Missouri Compromise line across America's remaining territories to the Pacific Ocean – north of the line, slavery would be banned, while it would gain federal protection to the south. By giving Congress the responsibility of ensuring slavery in territory below 36°30', Crittenden's amendment partially validated southern demands for a federal territorial slave code in all the territories and was more pro-South than the original 36°30' provision in 1820, which had only allowed the *possibility* of territorial slavery below the line. But it was the amendment's words applying the line to territory "hereafter acquired" as well as the nation's current domain that brought the Caribbean into play and gave the package its gravitas. As Breckinridge observed in a public letter to Kentucky's governor, that assurance represented the package's "vital" component since three-quarters of the nation's current territory would fall to the north, given where the 36°30' parallel intersected America's remaining territorial domain. "The Southern States cannot afford to be shut off from all possibility of tropical expansion towards the tropics by the hostile action of the Federal Government," he insisted.[14]

Lurking behind Breckinridge's assertion was the balance of voting power in Congress, though southerners sought tropical acquisitions for many economic, political, and demographic reasons. Southerners had little real hope for slavery in any current western territories, including New Mexico and Utah, where a handful of slaves were held under the popular sovereignty provisions of the Compromise of 1850. By Lincoln's election, southerners had clearly lost the battle for Kansas; that territory would become the nation's newest free state before the Confederacy was even formed when Buchanan signed its statehood bill on January 29. Protecting U.S. slavery in any tropical countries or colonies the government might acquire, though, presented another case entirely: the addition of senators and representatives from new slave territories and states to the south might easily offset Republican and antislavery voting power in Congress. In the House especially, the slave states had been losing ground gradually for decades, because that branch of Congress was

[14] CG, 36 Cong., 2 Sess., 112–24; "CHICAGO" to the *Chicago Tribune*, Dec. 19, 1860, in *Chicago Daily Tribune*, Dec. 19, 1860; Freehling, *Road to Disunion*, 470; John Breckinridge to Beriah Magoffin in *Macon* (GA) *Daily Telegraph*, Jan. 16, 1861; Kenneth M. Stampp, *And the War Came* (Baton Rouge, 1950), 168. Anything but a territorial expansionist, Crittenden apparently believed his hereafter clause would preclude future annexations rather than encourage them because neither northerners nor southerners would concur in gains guaranteed to the other section. John J. Crittenden to Larz Anderson, copy in his daughter's handwriting, Mar. 26, 1861, John J. Crittenden Papers, William R. Perkins Library, Duke University.

based on population and immigrants greatly preferred the free states, where they did not have to compete with slave labor. In 1850, at a time when 21 percent of New York's population had been born abroad, South Carolina's foreign-born total was a measly 1 percent. Between 1800 and 1860, the southern hold on House seats fell from 46 to 38 percent, and it was bound to decline further once the 1860 census was taken into account. Breckinridge asserted in his letter that southerners would be exposed to "incessant anti-slavery agitation" without annexations from the Tropics. With such considerations in mind, the historian Kenneth Stampp judged the hereafter clause the "nub of the whole matter," the sole provision promising "ultimate advantage to the South" over the long haul.[15] Paradoxically, though, Crittenden's hereafter wording not only gave the package its great promise; it also sealed its doom.

Douglas was so anxious to preserve the Union that he backed Crittenden's scheme though it meant repudiating popular sovereignty, the very principle he had championed since the 1850 debates. Crittenden's plan turned Douglas's principles on their head by *predetermining* slavery's status in all territories whatever their locale, essentially restoring U.S. policy to the very Missouri Compromise that Douglas's Kansas-Nebraska Act had upended. In his recent presidential race, however, Douglas had shown a tendency to put country before ambition. He did so again. As he confided to Charles Lanphier, publisher of the *Illinois State Register*, Crittenden's scheme had the overriding virtue of banishing *"the slavery question from Congress forever."* Later in the congressional session, Douglas told his colleagues that although Crittenden's scheme contradicted his own beliefs, he had been willing to support it to save the Union and still would. "No man," Douglas insisted, "labored harder than I have to get it passed," a stand that undoubtedly surprised many of his longtime supporters.[16]

Much – perhaps the Union itself – hinged on whether President-elect Lincoln and Republicans in Congress would concur on a proposition that starkly violated the party's founding and most unifying principle, opposition to slavery's expansion. Would Republicans render irrelevant their hard-fought free-soil victories in Kansas with an irreversible

[15] Leonard L. Richards, *The Slave Power: The Free North and Southern Domination, 1780–1860* (Baton Rouge, 2000), 48–49, 102; Stampp, *And the War Came*, 167; *Macon Daily Telegraph*, Jan. 16, 1861; Nichols, *Disruption of American Democracy*, 467.
[16] SAD to Charles H. Lanphier, Dec. 25, 1860, C. H. Lanphier Collection; CG, 36 Cong., 2 Sess., 1391, Appendix, 41; John D. Bail to Lyman Trumbull, Jan. 3, 1861, Lyman Trumbull Papers, LC; CWAL, 2: 424n.

constitutional amendment opening the Tropics to slaveholders, one of the very possibilities they thought they forestalled by electing Lincoln? A Republican paper in Ohio editorialized shortly before the election that with Lincoln inaugurated, Republicans could rest assured that for at least a score of years the "annexation of Cuba, filibuster schemes in Central America and the dismemberment of Mexico, for the extension of slavery and the increase of its power" would "be forgotten." Propositions to restore the 36°30' division put such presumptions into jeopardy. As a "CONSERVATIVE REPUBLICAN" put it in a public letter, northern voters like him had with their ballots authorized Lincoln to "forever destroy" the projects of politicians who intended to tempt "the cupidity of the South" with "the acquisition of Cuba, the renewal of the slave trade, the annexation of Southern Republics." If they acceded to Crittenden's scheme, Lincoln and Republican congressmen would risk alienating the very constituency that put them in office. One voter threatened Senator Trumbull that a "storm of indignation" would greet all northwestern congressmen voting for or sanctioning Crittenden's plan once they made their way home. Indeed, a Philadelphian bluntly told Crittenden that the whole problem with having his program accepted by Republican northerners was its "protection of slavery in any territory that may be acquired hereafter" below the Missouri Compromise parallel.[17]

They need not have worried. Remaining in Springfield until mid-February, the president-elect kept posted on the evolving negotiations in Congress through the newspapers, letters from confidants in the capital, and visitors who traveled out to consult him, among them Thurlow Weed. Weed arrived in Springfield on December 20 intending to advocate Crittenden's plan. Had he desired, Lincoln could have sent word by mail and through Weed and others to Washington that Republicans should sacrifice principle to save the Union. Perhaps members of his party's conservative wing could have been brought on board, giving Crittenden's amendments and resolutions a fighting chance. As president-elect, Lincoln had ample patronage to promise congressmen as bait for carrying out his wishes. Over the coming months he would be choosing a cabinet and appointing federal officials to jobs all across the nation.[18]

[17] *Sandusky* (OH) *Daily Commercial Register*, Oct. 20, 1860; *Washington* (DC) *Daily National Intelligencer*, Dec. 17, 1860; A. W. Metcalf to Lyman Trumbull, Feb. 6, 1861, Lyman Trumbull Papers; J. Fisher Leaming to John J. Crittenden, Feb. 6, 1861, John J. Crittenden Papers, LC.
[18] Holzer, *Lincoln President-Elect*, 165; *Chicago Daily Tribune*, Dec. 22, 1860. Lincoln's silence was not absolute. For exceptions, see Holzer, *Lincoln President-Elect*, 92–95.

Instead, although Lincoln demonstrated flexibility regarding concessions on enforcement of the Fugitive Slave Law, he demanded that Republicans nix compromise on the territories, emphasizing that slaveholders would immediately capitalize on such deals by penetrating the Tropics. As early as December 13, responding to reports that the Missouri Compromise line might be restored, Lincoln instructed Republican Illinois congressman Elihu B. Washburne that such propositions would unleash "filibustering and extending slavery." When Thurlow Weed wrote to Lincoln about plans to convene a governors' conference to deal with the crisis, Lincoln responded sternly, just before the New Yorker's Springfield jaunt, that "the Missouri line extended" "would lose us every thing we gained by the election; that filibustering for all South of us, and making slave states of it, would follow." Weed should inform the governors he remained "inflexible on the territorial issue." It is striking how consistently Caribbeanized Lincoln's message was, as he similarly told the chair of the Republican Party in Indiana, John D. Defrees, that popular sovereignty would ignite "filibustering for all South of us." In the new year, he was still at it, exhorting Seward that the territorial solutions being proposed would "put us again on the high-road to a slave empire" and warning a Republican congressman from Pennsylvania that surrendering Republican principles would be a horrible mistake: "A year will not pass, till we shall have to take Cuba as a condition upon which they will stay in the Union," Lincoln predicted. Nor did he convey this message only to Republicans and northerners. To North Carolina congressman John A. Gilmer, under consideration for a cabinet position, Lincoln explained on December 15 that he would never propose abolishing the domestic slave trade or slavery in the District of Columbia to Congress; nor would he consciously appoint Republicans or nonslaveholders to office in the South. But his conciliation stopped there: "On the territorial question, I am inflexible.... On that, there is a difference between you and us; and it is the only substantial difference. You think slavery is right and ought to be extended; we think it is wrong and ought to be restricted." Lincoln repeated these thoughts in the famous letter he sent off on December 22 to his old congressional friend future Confederate vice president, Alexander H. Stephens.[19]

[19] AL to Elihu B. Washburne, Dec. 13, 1860, AL to Lyman Trumbull, Dec. 17, 1860, AL to Thurlow Weed, Dec. 17, 1860, AL to John D. Defrees, Dec. 18, 1860, AL to Alexander H. Stephens, Dec. 22, 1860, AL to WHS, Feb. 1, 1861, AL to James T. Hale, Jan. 11, 1861, AL to John A. Gilmer, Dec. 15, 1860, CWAL, 4: 151, 153, 154, 155, 160, 183, 172, 152;

Not surprisingly given Lincoln's relentless messaging, which Harold Holzer labels an unprecedented "show of power and influence" by a U.S. president-elect, Republicans in Congress, many of whom instinctively loathed Crittenden's package anyway, turned it down repeatedly between December and February. On December 22 (while Seward was absent from the Committee of Thirteen because he had gone to Syracuse to meet with Weed and learn the results of the editor's consultations with Lincoln) Toombs, Davis, and Robert Hunter of Virginia reportedly announced in committee that they would support Crittenden's proposal if the committee's Republicans did likewise. But the Republicans declined, causing the southerners to join them in rejecting the hereafter clause 5–7. Days later, having learned from Weed that Lincoln was unreceptive to the hereafter proposal, Seward very purposely had his name recorded in committee as joining his Republican colleagues in rejecting the deal. On February 18, when Crittenden's hereafter clause was revived for consideration at the Washington Peace Conference, a specially called gathering to deal with the crisis, the delegates, voting for their states, rejected it 8–12, with all the northern states except New Jersey opposing it and not a single slave state turning it down.

Republicans in Pittsburgh so hated Crittenden's plan they literally invaded a public meeting called to endorse it. Seizing control of the stage, they drowned out a speaker, cursed the Kentuckian and his compromise, and then smashed seats and turned off the gas lighting to break up the meeting. Not only did Republican leaders reject Crittenden's proposal outright; some baited southern secessionists by turning the Caribbean issue on its head, warning that once secession occurred, the North rather than the South would take the Tropics. Republican senator Ben Wade taunted his southern colleagues three days before South Carolina left the Union that Mexicans, who were prejudiced against the South because of slavery and filibustering, eagerly anticipated secession; once the Union lacked slave states, "they would invite us to take a protectorate over them." William Seward, in a widely reported speech to the New England Society at the Astor House in New York, cautioned southerners that Canada and the Mexican states would rush into the Union the moment the slave states seceded, realizing the benefits of joining the North. Raymond, in his letters to Yancey, reminded the Alabamian that northerners were expansionists too. They would never surrender opportunities for "further accessions

David M. Potter, *Lincoln and His Party in the Secession Crisis* (1942; rpt., New Haven, 1965), 152.

from Mexico, Central America or the West India islands" to a "Slave Empire on the south." Raymond contended northerners were vested in the Southwest by virtue of their expenditures for annexing Texas, fighting the Mexican War, and making the Gadsden Purchase.[20]

On December 24, when it became evident that Crittenden's proposal would fail of passage in the Committee of Thirteen, Douglas presented the Senate with a different package of suggested constitutional amendments, which were printed and referred to the Committee of Thirteen on his request. Douglas's plan incorporated Crittenden's suggestions regarding fugitive slave legislation and slavery in the nation's capital. It also imposed a complex formula to determine the status of slavery in the nation's current territories, prohibited African Americans in states and territories from getting the vote or holding office, allowed for colonizing free blacks at federal expense in South America and Africa, and most importantly prevented the nation from acquiring new territories unless by treaty or by endorsement of the acquisition with a two-thirds vote by each branch of Congress. Since treaties also required a two-thirds vote for Senate passage, Douglas's measures ruled out the kind of joint resolution by majority vote that admitted Texas in 1845 and offered a virtual veto to both the North and South over acquisitions favoring the other's labor system, possibly sacrificing for the Union his beloved Manifest Destiny. Further, Douglas stipulated that settlers in a newly acquired territory could not change the status of slavery until the territory reached a population of 50,000 residents, assuaging southern apprehensions that Yankee free-soilers could rush to a new acquisition, dominate it during its early settlement, and quickly prohibit slavery before southerners could colonize it. Like Crittenden's proposal, however, Douglas's failed in both the committee and the full Senate. When the Senate finally voted as a

[20] Holzer, *Lincoln President-Elect*, 158; Archibald Williams to AL, Dec. 19, 1861, William B. Thomas to AL, Feb. 6, 1861, Carl Schurz to AL, Jan. 31, 1861, Oliver P. Morton to AL, Jan. 29, 1861, AL Papers, Series 1, LC; CG, 36 Cong. 2 Sess., 104, 1392; *Sen. Reports*, 36 Cong., 2 Sess., No. 288: 5; *New York Herald*, Dec. 24, 26, 1860; L. E. Chittenden, *Report of the Debates and Proceedings in the Secret Sessions of the Conference Convention, for Proposing Amendments to the Constitution of the United States, Held at Washington, D. C., in February, A. D. 1861* (New York, 1864), 80, 82; Pittsburgh correspondent of the *Louisville Courier* in the *Macon Daily Telegraph*, Jan. 31, 1861; *New York Commercial Advertiser*, Dec. 24, 1860; Report from Washington, DC correspondent in *Charleston Mercury*, Dec. 25, 1860; *Washington (DC) Constitution*, Dec. 27, 1860; *Milwaukee Daily Sentinel*, Dec. 31, 1860; Henry J. Raymond to William L. Yancey, Dec. 19, 1860, in Raymond, *Disunion and Slavery*, 19; Nevins, *Emergence of Lincoln*, 2: 396–97, 411. A number of states, including the entire Deep South, already in the Confederacy, boycotted the Washington Peace Conference.

body on the Crittenden Compromise on the very last day of Congress before Lincoln's inauguration, Republicans voted unanimously against its passage.[21]

There can be little doubt that revulsion at the hereafter clause lay at the heart of the Republicans' dissent against Crittenden's plan, though Crittenden's other concessions to slaveholders also displeased them. Possibly Republicans in Congress would have turned on the program with near-unanimity even had Lincoln *not* indicated his own feelings, given their apocalyptic interpretations of Crittenden's proposal. Republicans had bitter memories of southern efforts to spread slavery to the Tropics and were bent on purifying the government of their vestiges. Thus James Doolittle urged Lincoln to appoint "the glorious old Commodore" Hiram Paulding as secretary of the navy in his administration because he had done "his duty so well in seizing the Fillibusters" on Nicaragua's coast. Few Republicans of any stripe would countenance proposals inviting new slave state initiatives southward. Crittenden's geographical mandate, warned Francis P. Blair Sr., reversed laws against slavery below the border, guaranteeing slavery in "all that may be acquired hereafter, from Mexico." Besides, the compromise would not even keep the cotton states in the Union because their secessionists sought "conquest & slave empire" through independence, not by the nation's perpetuity. Conditioned by a decade of southern aggressions against Mexico, Central America, and Spain's rule in Cuba, the *Chicago Tribune* predicted,

filibustering would at once begin. New and more powerful expeditions would be fitted out for the rich and fertile States of Central America. Predatory bands would swarm on the Texas frontier, ready upon a word of encouragement to crowd over into Mexico, and, upon the plea of protecting the Border from the ravages of the Indians, seize upon and hold as many provinces as they could occupy. Sonora and Lower California would be overrun and by and by annexed; and wherever, south of the division line between freedom and slavery, an inch could be gained, that inch would be had. Agitation for Cuba would at once begin.

The *Tribune* added that the South would have already taken Mexico but for the expectation that northerners would prevent slavery there. Crittenden's proposal, by *mandating* slavery in an acquired Mexico, would end such restraint. Explaining his party's stance, Representative Justin S. Morrill of Vermont bluntly asserted that Republicans were unconcerned with slavery getting a foothold in the New Mexican

[21] CG, 36 Cong., 2 Sess., 183; Johannsen, *Douglas*, 836–37; Wells, *Douglas*, 270–71, 277n; Nichols, *Disruption of American Democracy*, 433, 481.

Territory under the plan; rather, they worried that the hereafter provision envisioned the United States acquiring new territory where "slavery of the African race" would be recognized. To a Republican representative from Indiana, Crittenden's proposal amounted to "'devilish enginery'" by guaranteeing slavery where it "may hereafter exist" as well as in its current footholds.[22]

Observers at the time, including many of Crittenden's informants, had little trouble connecting the congressional Republicans' rejection of the entire Crittenden package with the hereafter clause. Democratic Party leader August Belmont informed Douglas in a letter marked "Private" that Republican leaders had told him "they will not vote for Crittenden's amendments, because they will not accept the Missouri line for future acquisitions of Territory. They say this would be holding out a premium for filibustering against Mexico & Cuba, in order to make new slave states." A Washington-based reporter of a Philadelphia paper observed after Republican senators voted down the Crittenden Compromise on January 16, "their chief objection was to the part which proposed to divide the territory which may hereafter be acquired." After the Civil War, *New York Tribune* editor Horace Greeley explained he had preferred disunion to feeling "guilt" by "complicity in Slavery extension" southward by means of Crittenden's scheme. Crittenden, he remembered, had enticed southerners with prospects of "a few hundred thousand miles" of additional slave territory, including "Cuba, Mexico &c." – something he and other Republicans could not countenance despite the benefits of access to cheaper supplies of cotton and sugar if the annexations occurred.[23]

Of course, Douglas, who had always welcomed American territorial growth and never expressed strong inhibitions about slavery being allowed in it, felt otherwise. In a major Senate speech on January 3 asking Republicans belatedly to accept Crittenden's proposal, his own December 24 plan, or an alternate settlement, Douglas not only reiterated his willingness to forsake popular sovereignty for the Kentuckian's

---

[22] James R. Doolittle to AL, Jan. 10, 1861, Francis P. Blair Sr. to AL, Jan. 14, 1861, N. Ewing to AL, Jan. 19, 1861, AL Papers, Series 1, LC; *Chicago Daily Tribune*, Dec. 20, 24, 1860; CG, 36 Cong., 2 Sess., 1392; Shearer Davis Bowman, *At the Precipice: Americans North and South during the Secession Crisis* (Chapel Hill, 2010), 268–69.

[23] August Belmont to SAD, Dec. 31, 1860, SAD Papers, UC; *Sen. Reports*, 36 Cong., 2 Sess., No. 288: 5; *New York Herald*, Dec. 24, 1860; dispatch dated January 17 in *Philadelphia Public Ledger*, Jan. 18, 1861; Horace Greeley, *Recollections of a Busy Life* (New York, 1868), 397; J. P. Ogden to John J. Crittenden, Jan. 19, 1861, John Van Buren to Crittenden, Feb. 14, 1861, John J. Crittenden Papers, LC; H. Chrisman to William C. Rives, Feb. 4, 1861, William C. Rives Papers, LC.

scheme but also strongly hinted at his own thinking about slavery to the south. Arguing the nation would have benefited had the original Missouri Compromise line been extended in the 1840s through Texas to "every new acquisition, whenever we enlarged our territorial possessions *in that direction*," Douglas endorsed Crittenden's reviving the 36°30' line and chided Republicans for not going along. How could they oppose restoring the Missouri Compromise solution when its eradication had been Republicans' gripe against his own Kansas-Nebraska Act? "You have sung paens enough to its praise, and uttered imprecations enough on my head for its repeal," Douglas noted ironically, "one would think, to justify you now in claiming a triumph in its reestablishment." Yet, Douglas all but conceded slavery would penetrate the Tropics if given the opportunity in arguing that politicians were unwise to contest slavery's extension since everything should be left to the laws of "climate, health, and productions" – a resolution best achieved by his own popular sovereignty formula. Southerners could never establish slavery where it was "physically impossible to sustain it." Northerners were foolish to seek slavery's elimination in "countries where the white man cannot endure the climate and cultivate the soil." Surely these last remarks suggest Douglas's tolerance of slavery spreading through tropical domains where "physical geography" invited it, confirming longtime Republican suspicions about his intentions in the Caribbean. Perhaps no agent of the Slave Power, Douglas remained a fellow traveler on its southward course, even if most southern politicians and voters failed to see him that way. Lincoln and his party, it would seem, had been right about the Little Giant all along.[24]

Ironically, Lincoln and his Republicans displayed more willingness to compromise on slavery in the West than on slavery in the Caribbean, as they reacted to a scheme of Charles Francis Adams, a Republican on the House Committee of Thirty-three, to stop the Upper South states from joining the Deep South in secession. Adams, who worked with Congressman Henry Winter Davis of Maryland on this initiative, hoped to please Upper South states with the possibility that New Mexico might gain admission as a new slave state despite Republican policy against slavery in the West. After days of caucusing in late December, committee Republicans agreed 9–6 to a resolution that would have admitted New Mexico to statehood without any stipulation banning slavery. Since

[24] CG, 36 Cong., 2 Sess., Appendix, 41, 36. The italics are mine.

the New Mexico Territory at the time included today's Arizona and had territorial limits ranging from 35 to 165 miles *above* the 36°30' line at different parts of its northern border, the resolution (which passed the whole committee 13–11) represented a remarkable concession for a party pledged to stopping slave territory from growing an inch. Further, though Lincoln disliked allowing slavery a foothold in New Mexico, he sent word through Seward to congressional Republicans in late February that he cared little about New Mexico if it was not a prelude to other extensions of slavery.[25]

Ultimately, though, Republicans did more to prevent the New Mexico measure's passage than facilitate it, and there is considerable evidence that Adams never really favored it in the first place but saw it mainly as a stalling tactic. Probably House Republicans gave Adams's measure what procedural support they provided partly because it entailed no concessions by them of the principle that Congress had the *right* to ban slavery in a territory. Besides, it seemed unlikely that even under a slave code the peculiar institution would become embedded in New Mexico. The territory's aridity was unsuited to plantation labor. The few black slaves there already – a number possibly as low as ten (and no more than fifty) – labored almost entirely as house domestics for U.S. government officials and army officers. Still, there remained the possibility that New Mexican mining operations could profitably utilize slave labor, so when an actual statehood bill came before the full House on March 1, Republicans voted 76–26 for a motion that carried to table the proposition, in effect consigning New Mexico to continued territorial status. The majority of Republicans apparently felt similarly to the *Chicago Tribune*, which argued that slavery was feasible in New Mexico's agricultural and mining areas and that it was no time for Republicans to surrender to "the powers of darkness" their long-standing principles against slavery's expansion.

Still, Republicans demonstrated more flexibility on New Mexico than on Crittenden's hereafter clause because the latter had Caribbean implications. Partly for the same reason, of the slave state representatives on

---

[25] Potter, *Lincoln and His Party*, 290–94; Mark J. Stegmaier, "A Law That Would Make Caligula Blush? New Mexico Territory's Unique Slave Code, 1859–1861," *New Mexico Historical Review* 87 (Spring 2012): 209–42; Nevins, *Emergence of Lincoln*, 2: 408–409; Richard H. Sewell, *Ballots for Freedom: Antislavery Politics in the United States, 1837–1860* (New York, 1976), 297–98. Shearer Davis Bowman hypothesizes that Lincoln may have been willing to compromise on slavery in New Mexico as a legitimate fulfillment of the already enacted Compromise of 1850. Bowman, *At the Precipice*, 271.

the House Committee of Thirty-three voting on Adams's scheme, only two from states remaining in the Union (Maryland and Kentucky) supported it. All other slave state men on the committee either abstained or opposed New Mexico statehood despite the territorial slave code. Two of them stated explicitly that what they wanted was slavery in future acquisitions below 36°30' and that they would cease voting in committee if that concession was off the table. Crittenden's implied Caribbean hereafter clause, in other words, offered the South more than Adams's New Mexico measure. In the final March 1 vote on New Mexico, southern representatives split nearly evenly, voting by a slim majority of two to table. On the other hand, southern representatives voted overwhelmingly for Crittenden's measure when they belatedly were afforded an opportunity to cast votes on it on March 2.[26]

By rejecting Crittenden's scheme outright, Lincoln and the Republicans took a consequential step that strengthened the secessionists' appeal throughout Dixie in the wake of South Carolina's withdrawal on December 20. Tennessee's governor, Isham G. Harris, told his state's legislature that he would consider Tennessee's rights "reasonably secure" and the Union worth preserving with the hereafter provision enacted, and Tennessee's state senate specifically endorsed Crittenden's hereafter clause by an overwhelming 56–7 vote. Missouri's state convention was even more decisive, endorsing the hereafter provision 90–4 and voting 88–0 for a resolution thanking both Crittenden and Douglas for their "patriotic" efforts to reach a settlement, with considerable speech making on the hereafter clause's Caribbean implications. A Kentuckian told Douglas that "disunionism" was increasing in his state "since the news of the Blk republicans refusing to vote for the Crittenden Compromise." Former U.S. president John Tyler of Virginia, who favored the hereafter clause and served as presiding officer of the Washington Peace Conference before promoting disunion at Virginia's secession convention, warned the latter gathering that the South would "never get Cuba" from Lincoln. A southern newspaper columnist deemed as shameful the Republicans' rejection of the hereafter clause, blaming it on their desire

---

[26] McClintock, *Lincoln and the Decision for War*, 101, 103, 118; Potter, *Lincoln and His Party*, 294–302; Stegmaier, "Law That Would Make Caligula Blush?" 224–25; *Chicago Daily Tribune*, Feb. 15, 1861. For additional factors defeating the New Mexico measure, see Mark J. Stegmaier, "New Mexico's Delegate in the Secession Winter Congress, Part 1: Two Newspaper Accounts of Miguel Otero in 1861," *New Mexico Historical Review* 86 (Summer 2011): 385–92.

to deprive the South of the very annexations it sought in Mexico and Central America.[27]

Whether or not Republican acquiescence in Crittenden's compromise or any other settlement in play could have saved the Union at the last moment and averted the Civil War remains one of the unknowns of American history. An argument can be constructed that the Deep South had never been united behind a Caribbean agenda in the first place, and therefore tropical concessions would have made little difference. Many southerners opposed Caribbean acquisitions since they would introduce multitudes of dark-skinned Catholic people into the Union as citizens. There were also economic and demographic factors tamping down southern desires for Caribbean lands. Admitting Cuba, for instance, meant extra market competition for Louisiana sugar producers while offering nothing to the many southerners who worried that high slave reproduction rates were causing a regional demographic disaster, since Cuba's slave density nearly matched Alabama's already; sending excess slaves to an annexed Cuba would relieve racial congestion in one corner of the South but exacerbate it in another.[28]

Certainly the case can be made that the Deep South's secession and the creation of a southern nation were irreversible by the winter of 1860–61 and that southerners never would have rallied to Crittenden's plan even had it passed Congress. Jefferson Davis wanted the Committee of Thirteen to adopt his own slave code doctrine – not Crittenden's compromise – and he tried without success to persuade the committee to endorse it. Douglas heard from a correspondent in New Orleans who believed Crittenden's plan acceptable, "the Proposition would have been promptly rejected by the Cotton States even though it had recd the support of every Republican in Congress." There is not even conclusive evidence that secessionists in the four Upper South states, including Virginia, which withdrew from the Union after Lincoln's call for troops after Fort

---

[27] *Senate Journal of the Extra Session of the Thirty-third General Assembly of the State of Tennessee* (Nashville, 1861), 13, 126; *Journal and Proceedings of the Missouri State Convention Held at Jefferson City and St. Louis, March 1861* (St. Louis, 1861), 36, 47, 30, 86, 120, 215, 231–32; Stephen R. Mallory to James H. Hammond, Dec. 27, 1860, James H. Hammond Papers, LC; V. B. Young to SAD, Dec. 29, 1860, Felix Zollicoffer to SAD, Dec. 31, 1860, SAD Papers, UC; Edward P. Crapol, *John Tyler: The Accidental President* (Chapel Hill, 2006), 262, 264; "Telamon" in *Nashville Daily Union and American*, Apr. 14, 1861.

[28] *Charleston (SC) Mercury*, Feb. 26, 1858; John Ashworth, *Slavery, Capitalism, and Politics in the Antebellum Republic.* vol. 2: *The Coming of the Civil War, 1850–1861* (New York, 2007), 49–53, 149.

Sumter, would have changed course had Crittenden's proposition passed. The radical *Richmond Enquirer* announced in January it lacked any confidence that new constitutional amendments would do the South any substantive good, taking the position that since the northern states had failed to adhere faithfully to the old Constitution there was little reason to expect them to treat new amendments any better.[29]

Had Committee members quickly passed the compromise promise to slavery of future southern territorial gains with Republican support, however, they might have interrupted the rhythm of secessionism beyond South Carolina, possibly halting the movement in some or all of the other Deep South states. This, indeed, was Crittenden's hope. On December 6, he told the Kentucky Whig politician and editor Orlando Brown that although South Carolina was a lost cause, he might "by conciliatory measures" ward off "other states" from following its "bad example." Instead, expansionist-inclined Deep South politicians learned from the compromise's fate that any hopes of territorial growth southward depended on secession. In a speech at the Alabama Secession Convention on January 25, delegate Lewis M. Stone envisioned a healthy Confederacy embracing Cuba, Mexico, Central America, and Arizona, allowing it to preempt control of the "trade of all tropical America" and monopolize the production of tropical fruits, tobacco, coffee, sugar, cotton, and rice.[30]

Conceivably, had the Senate committee's Republicans embraced Crittenden's proposal, Davis and Toombs, both longtime Caribbean expansionists, would have cooperated, making it unlikely any of the other committee members would have dissented. This would have sent the plan to the full Senate, bearing the committee's unanimous imprimatur. Possibly the measure could have subsequently passed Congress, forcing the Deep South states other than South Carolina to consider the deal as their secession conventions began. William J. Cooper, Davis's biographer, contends that Jefferson Davis arrived in Washington hopeful for a settlement and bluntly argues that had Crittenden's plan passed the Committee of Thirteen, radical secessionists would have been thwarted

[29] Jefferson Davis to John J. Pettus, Dec. 26, 1860, Jefferson Davis Papers, Mississippi Department of Archives and History; J. O. Harrison to SAD, Jan. 31, 1861, SAD Papers, UC; William Y. Thompson, *Robert Toombs of Georgia* (Baton Rouge, 1966), 151; *Richmond (VA) Enquirer*, Jan. 29, 1861; May, *Southern Dream*, 190–205; William W. Freehling, *The Reintegration of American History: Slavery and the Civil War* (New York, 1994), 166–72.
[30] John J. Crittenden to Orlando Brown, Dec. 6, 1860, Orlando Brown Papers, Filson Historical Society, Louisville; William R. Smith, ed., *The History and Debates of the Convention of the People of Alabama* ... (Montgomery, AL, 1861), 236–37.

in all Deep South states but South Carolina because their citizens were not yet fully committed to leaving the Union.

It hardly needs adding, moreover, that had the Deep South remained in the Union because of Crittenden's measures, the Upper South would have done the same. In a disunion speech in the House on January 16, Representative Muscoe R. H. Garnett of Virginia explained that the reason impending Republican rule so frightened southerners was that the current Union had territory enough for twenty additional states and that the nation could expect "large acquisitions from Mexico." If the North controlled all this territory, over a period of decades, it would accrue the political power to extinguish slavery, reducing a racially amalgamated South to the degradation of Haiti and Jamaica in the way that freedom had ruined the British West Indies. Garnett believed it was too late, by then, to preserve the Union, but that earlier the South would have accepted constitutional amendments protecting slavery had Republicans been willing to offer them. As late as January 25, a Tennessee representative still thought that if Crittenden's propositions passed both houses of Congress, possibly all the southern states but South Carolina would be satisfied.[31]

One can take the position that Davis and Toombs were so thoroughly committed to secession by December that their willingness even to serve on the Committee of Thirteen and consider legislative propositions was a kind of public relations charade to demonstrate their own reasonableness and lay on the Republicans responsibility for disunion. Seward told Lincoln on December 26 that it was hopeless even to think of enticing Georgia, Alabama, Mississippi, and Louisiana to stay in the Union and suggested that when "persons acting for" them claimed restoring the Missouri line would stop secession, they did so assuming Republicans would never concur. Why not cast full blame for the Union's destruction on the Republicans? Still, a Charleston newspaper's correspondent in Washington reported on December 22 that Davis agreed belatedly to serve on the committee because he genuinely wished to "contribute anything in his power to an adjustment of the pending difficulties," and that the application of the Missouri Compromise line to all present and future territory represented the "*sine qua non*" for not only Davis but all the

---

[31] Stampp, *And the War Came*, 166; William J. Cooper Jr., "The Critical Signpost on the Journey toward Secession," *Journal of Southern History* 77 (Feb. 2011): 3–16; CG, 36 Cong., 2 Sess., 412–14, Appendix, 107. William Freehling argues the Union was still salvageable in mid-December but by other means than Crittenden's plan since there were no hopes of Republicans' embracing it. Freehling, *Road to Disunion*, 2: 464, 470–75.

southern members of the committee. Toombs in a January 7 speech said he had informed the Committee of Thirteen he would have accepted the extension of 36°30′ "for the sake of peace – permanent peace" and was still willing to accept it, if it was paired with "other satisfactory provisions." To Toombs, it was crucial "that the whole continent to the north pole shall be settled upon the one rule, and to the south pole under the other." On March 2, 1861, northern Democratic senator George Pugh claimed that just before resigning from Congress to join the Confederacy, Davis had confided he would have accepted Crittenden's package had "the other side of this chamber" gone along with it. Douglas not only immediately confirmed Pugh's statement but added it applied to Toombs too. Moreover, in reminiscences published in 1885, northern Democratic congressman Samuel Sullivan Cox claimed he had "talked frequently" with Crittenden while the Committee of Thirteen was in session, and Crittenden had confirmed privately the comments Toombs, Douglas, and Pugh had been making in public. Both Toombs and Davis would have acceded to the package's passage, though Toombs emphasized that it only barely met his minimal demands.[32]

Following the adjournment of the Senate on March 28 and the outbreak of the Civil War at Fort Sumter on April 12, Stephen Douglas returned to Illinois. Before leaving Washington, however, he called on Lincoln at the White House as a demonstration of national solidarity across party lines in the face of crisis. In a nearly two-hour conversation on April 14 (the day Fort Sumter surrendered to the Confederates) widely reported in the press, Douglas promised to back Lincoln's efforts to put down the Confederacy and apparently urged Lincoln to deploy far more troops to do so than the president intended. A few days later, Douglas informed a St. Louis editor that though deprecating war he stood with his country "under all circumstances." Then Douglas left the capital, hoping to rally his party in the Old Northwest behind the president's war effort, traveling by rail with his wife and nearly suffering arrest when his train crossed Virginia, which was then in the process of joining the Confederacy.[33]

[32] WHS to AL, Dec. 26, 1860, AL Papers, Series 1, LC; correspondent's report of December 22, in *Charleston Daily Courier*, Dec. 27, 1860; CG, 36 Cong., 2 Sess., 270, 1390, 1391; S. S. Cox, *Union-Disunion-Reunion: Three Decades of Federal Legislation* (Providence, 1885), 77.

[33] Johannsen, *Douglas*, 858–64; SAD to James L. Faucett, Apr. 17, 1861, Robert W. Johannsen, ed., *The Letters of Stephen A. Douglas* (Urbana, 1961), 510.

Arriving in Springfield on April 25, Douglas spent part of the day consulting other politicians and at night made his way to the Illinois statehouse, where, on invitation of the two houses, he gave one of his last public addresses. Douglas used this opportunity, in the spirit of his recent conversation with Lincoln, to urge fellow northern Democrats to suspend partisanship and support their government's war preparations. To make his case, he emphasized the danger the nation faced from enemy invasion and threats to interrupt commerce on the Mississippi River. Urging fellow citizens to protect the nation from the Confederacy's "piratical flag," he reflected on Mexican history to make his point. According to his "reading" of Mexico's past, not one of its presidents had completed a full term in office without being forced to abdicate by a defeated rival or turned out of office by bayonet. Douglas challenged his listeners: "Are we to inaugurate this Mexican system in the United States of America?" Responses of "No! never!" indicated that Douglas's argument struck a receptive cord.[34]

Presumably, many of the cries of agreement were from Republican legislators. After years of fighting Republicans about the Gulf-Caribbean Basin, Douglas had struck a tropical theme that resonated with many of his political opponents, including his greatest rival. Lincoln had announced in January that if the secessionists got their way, the U.S. government would be reduced to "the existing disorganized state of affairs in Mexico." Similarly, the *Chicago Tribune*'s correspondent in Washington asserted that the South could not be allowed to leave the Union, lest "anarchy" overrun the country, reducing it to "the horrible condition of Mexico." Republican Carl Schurz, too, worried (according to his later account) that "a step might be taken that would – to use a term current at that time – 'Mexicanize' our government." For William Seward, however, a better model of tropical declension was the Central American isthmus, where states had undergone endemic revolutionary turmoil. Warning the South that the North could not afford to allow even a single state to secede lest it ignite a process of continuing withdrawals, Seward told his Astor House listeners that such a process would reduce the United States to "the condition of Central America." Individual "republican States" represented "sheaves in the harvest field; put them up singly, and every gust blows them down; stack them together and they defy the winds of heaven."[35] As war erupted in North America in 1861, Douglas and his

[34] Johannsen, *Douglas*, 864–65; *Speech of Senator Douglas, before the Legislature of Illinois, April 25, 1861* (n.p., n.d.), 2.
[35] AL remarks c. Jan. 19–21, 1861, in CWAL, 3:358, 4: 176, 176n; report of Dec. 31, 1860 in *Chicago Daily Tribune*, Jan. 3, 1861; Schurz, *Reminiscences of Carl Schurz*, vol. 2, 212;

political enemies found themselves citing shared Latin American models of instability to rationalize their rejection of disunion.

Had the Little Giant lived longer, he and Lincoln might have found other common ground on Latin America, since in one of the most surprising twists of his long political career Douglas renounced Manifest Destiny toward the end of his life. Douglas did so in late February during Senate debate on the Morrill bill, a Republican measure to raise tariff duties that passed because many of the bill's likely opponents – southern Democratic senators – had resigned their seats to join the Confederacy. That Douglas, representing the traditionally antitariff Democratic Party, would oppose the Morrill measure is unremarkable, but his logic for doing so repudiated his longtime doctrine that expansion was good. Belatedly, he seemed to grasp something Lincoln had understood more than fifteen years earlier – that territorial growth endangered the Union by repeatedly recycling the slavery extension dispute.

In remarks foreshadowing the North American Free Trade Agreement (NAFTA) of 1994, Douglas referenced the German Zollverein, a customs union among German states, to propose that the United States would be better served by a continental, commercial union with uniform customs duties – and eventually free trade – than by protective tariffs. Douglas envisioned Britain's provinces in Canada, Mexico, Cuba, and the Central American states all joining his tariff-free nation and argued that Congress would only provoke southerners and reinforce their determination to persist in disunion if it raised tariff rates. A customs union opening a market of nine million Mexicans to southern agricultural productions, on the other hand, might undermine secessionism. Further, by securing new markets for the industrial and agricultural goods of all Americans, his experiment would improve hemispheric relations by ending "the jealousies and hostilities which have been engendered by lawless fillibustering expeditions, and put an end to all outrages of that kind in the future." Then, in a moment truly verging on confession, Douglas predicted that substituting a customs union for expansion would also improve domestic harmony by averting the kind of "difficulties we have had, growing out of this slavery question and the continual annexation of countries adjoining us." All but blaming the *issue* of slavery's expansion for disunion, Douglas ended his remarks by observing that his proposal would

New York Commercial Advertiser, Dec. 24, 1860; Montgomery Blair to Gustavus Fox, Jan. 31, 1861, *Confidential Correspondence of Gustavus Vasa Fox, Assistant Secretary of the Navy, 1861–1865* (1920; rpt., Freeport, NY, 1972), 4.

neutralize the "disturbing elements" dissolving the Union of the Founding Fathers.[36]

Physically used up and emotionally exhausted from his fight to preserve the Union over the winter and spring, Douglas contracted a serious ailment diagnosed as acute rheumatism soon after his return to Illinois. After about a month of suffering from fever, throat pain, constipation, and other debilities, Douglas died in Chicago on June 3, 1865. Reportedly, his last words instructed his wife to ensure that their two sons supported the U.S. Constitution.[37]

[36] CG, 36 Cong., 2 Sess., 1051–52.
[37] Johannsen, *Douglas*, 870–72.

6

Freedom in the Tropics

In the spring of 1864, just before General Ulysses S. Grant began the campaign that crushed southern hopes for independence, a Union embarrassment off Haiti's southwestern coast gave Confederates a rare late Civil War propaganda bonanza. A year earlier, as part of President Abraham Lincoln's colonization program, four hundred and fifty-three African Americans had boarded the brig *Ocean Ranger* at Union-held Fortress Monroe on Virginia's coast, bound for Haiti's Île-à-Vache, or Cow Island.[1] Nothing had gone right for the emigrants on ship or on the island. Now, a press report of their fate played into Confederate hands (Figure 6.1).

Lincoln's embarrassment originated in the machinations of a sleazy entrepreneur named Bernard Kock, who in August 1862 signed a contract with Haiti's government leasing Île-à-Vache for ten years. According to the deal, Kock would deliver 35.25 percent of all timber cut during his lease to Haitian authorities and he would have the work performed by imported laborers "of the African or Indian Race" who would gain Haitian citizenship upon their arrival and later get land. During September and October, Kock had lobbied the Union government to back the scheme. He submitted to Lincoln a synopsis of his contract, a proposal to colonize 5,000 African Americans on the island, and a request that Union authorities provide them with transportation there and subsistence until

[1] Affidavit of Charles K. Tuckerman, dated Fort Monroe, Apr. 12, 1863; affidavit of U.S. Vice Consul George C. Ross, Aux Cayes, Haiti, July 7, 1863; list of emigrants, all enclosed in Paul S. Forbes and Tuckerman to John P. Usher, July 7, 1863, RG 48, Roll 9; "Honduras and Hayti," *African Repository* 39 (Nov. 1863): 344. Contemporary documents alluded to the island also as 'vache Island," "a' vache Island," "Ile A' Vache," and "Lavache."

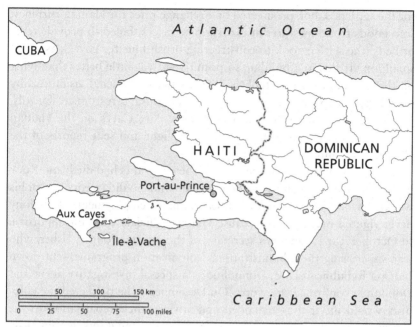

FIGURE 6.1 Île-à-Vache.
Note: This map shows the locale of the Lincoln administration's black colony off Haiti's southwestern coast.

the immigrants could harvest a crop. On New Year's Eve, Lincoln gave a short-lived endorsement to Kock's proposal, changing his mind after Secretary of State William Seward received a negative report about Kock's character and intentions. On January 6, 1863, Lincoln instructed Seward to withhold the official U.S. seal from the document. Kock then worked around the administration's displeasure. On March 30, he transferred his contract to Wall Street financiers Paul S. Forbes and Charles K. Tuckerman, and Lincoln approved the scaled-back agreement, which provided the capitalists with $50 per emigrant in federal funds to colonize 500 former slaves.

Nothing went right. Forbes and Tuckerman were required to secure Haiti's consent before implementing their plan. Instead, to save on expenses, they dispatched the expedition without explicit Haitian clearance. Worse, they sent Kock, a con artist par excellence, to supervise the colony. En route, Kock confiscated the emigrants' money for phony bank bills he had printed before sailing. Once at the island, the self-proclaimed "Governor" subjected his wards to horrific deprivations. He paid little for the settlers' labor, profiteered on exchange rates for Haitian currency, sold goods from his stores at extortionate prices, failed to provide tents or beds (the settlers took to constructing brush huts for cover), assigned smallpox victims to a building so primitive it was little better than lying on the beach, failed to establish courts, strictly restricted visitations by outsiders, and posted armed guards to discourage resistance. Luckily, James De Long, the U.S. consul at nearby Aux Cayes on the Haitian mainland, took a strong interest in their plight and sent reports of the abuses to Washington.[2]

By midsummer 1863, some forty of the emigrants had died, and Kock had abandoned the colony for Haiti's mainland. So did twenty-one of his workers, who went to Aux Cayes, searching for employment. The colony never righted itself, partly because Haitian officials were unsupportive. In October 1863, Lincoln's secretary of the interior John P. Usher, who was supervising the administration's colonization programs, sent down Indiana Republican D. C. Donnohue as a special investigative agent and Donnohue confirmed the worst. On December 6, he predicted the colonists would die if they remained and advised their repatriation to the United States. Learning from Donnohue that the emigrants unanimously wanted to return, Usher asked Union Secretary of War Edwin M. Stanton to detach a transport for that purpose. Fearing "embarrassment from any quarter" over the rescue, Usher asked Donnohue to make the rescue as publicity-free as possible.[3]

[2] J. R. S. Van Vleet to AL, Oct. 4, 1862 with synopsis of contract, WHS to AL, Jan. 3, 1863, Charles K. Tuckerman to AL, Mar. 31, 1863, AL Papers, Series 1, LC; Bernard Kock to Caleb B. Smith, Sept. 27 (1862), John P. Usher, Jan. 8, 1863, with translated, certified copy of Kock's Aug. 8 contract with the government of Haiti, B. F. Whidden to WHS, Mar. 21, 1863, RG48, Roll 9, John P. Usher to Paul S. Forbes and Tuckerman, Apr. 3, 1863, with enclosures, Usher to John J. Cisco, Apr. 3, 1863 (letterbook copy), Usher to Forbes and Tuckerman, Apr. 13, 1863 (letterbook copy), Usher to Tuckerman, Apr. 17, 1863 (letterbook copy), Forbes and Tuckerman contract with Usher, Apr. 6, 1863 (copy), Usher to Leonard W. Jerome, Dec. 14, 1863, RG48, Roll 1; James De Long to Henry Conard, June 25, 1863 (copy) in Whidden to WHS, July 30, 1863, De Long to Conard, July 8, 1863 and Tilton Cook affidavit, July 27, 1863, enclosed in Whidden to WHS, Aug. 21, 1863, RG48, Roll 9; AL to WHS, Jan. 6, 1863, CWAL, 6: 41–42, 42n; Eric Foner, *The Fiery Trial: Abraham Lincoln and American Slavery* (New York, 2010), 239–40, 259; Michael Burlingame, *Abraham Lincoln: A Life*, 2 vols. (Baltimore, 2008), 2: 395–96; James D. Lockett, "Abraham Lincoln and Colonization: An Episode That Ends in Tragedy at L'Ile à Vache, Haiti, 1863–1864," *Journal of Black Studies* 21 (June 1991): 436–38. On April 16, 1863, Lincoln issued a proclamation cancelling his earlier signature on Kock's contract. AL Proclamation, Apr. 16, 1863, CWAL, 6: 178–79.

[3] James De Long to Henry Conard, June 27, July 6, 1863, enclosed in B. F. Whidden to WHS, Aug. 21, 1863, De Long to WHS, Oct. 3, 1863, John P. Usher to D. C. Donnohue,

Stanton's relief ship arrived on February 29 and boarded more than four hundred surviving emigrants the next day. Three weeks later, the vessel took them to Alexandria, Virginia, whereupon federal authorities had them carried by wagon to "Freedman's Village" – a camp for freed slaves that had been established earlier in the year at Robert E. Lee's Arlington estate across the Potomac from Washington. The famous escaped slave Harriet Jacobs went to the Alexandria docks on a snowy March 22 to greet and help the emigrants, whom she described as barefoot, hatless, and virtually in rags. When she went out to Freedman's Village the next day to check up on them, she learned that three had died during their first night there. Days afterward, a *New York Tribune* reporter journeyed to the settlement to interview the returnees and wrote a wrenching account about their deprivations on the island and health problems afterward that appeared in the *Tribune*'s April 2 number. Many, he said, still suffered from smallpox or "Haytiañ fever" (likely malaria). Though writing for a notoriously antislavery newspaper, he nonetheless judged that the emigrants had "tasted a more bitter and blithing slavery than any of them ever experienced in their own country." He even claimed they had unanimously informed him they would prefer enslavement to "the hardest of American masters" over returning to Haiti.[4]

The damning column was bound to fall into Confederate hands given the *Tribune*'s wide circulation, and when it did, southern newspapers had a field day luxuriating in Lincoln's embarrassment. A North Carolina newspaper ran the heading "AN EXPLODED YANKEE HUMBUG." In the Confederate capital, the *Richmond Dispatch* cynically exploited what

Oct. 9, 17, Dec. 19, 1863, Jan. 14, Feb. 2, 1864, Usher to Henry T. Raymond, Oct. 15, 1863, Donnohue to Usher, Oct. 16, 1863, Andrew A. Ripka to Donnohue, Dec. 5, 1863, Donnohue to Hallet Kilbourn, Dec. 6, 1863, Usher to Paul S. Forbes and Charles K. Tuckerman, Dec. 18, 19, 1863, De Long to Usher, Dec. 28, 1863, Ripka to Usher, Jan. 9, 1864, Tuckerman to Usher, Jan. 9, 1864, Usher to WHS, Jan. 25, Feb. 5,1864, Usher to Edwin M. Stanton, Feb. 1, 1864, Usher to Kilbourn, Feb. 5, 1864, RG48, Roll 9.

[4] D. C. Donnohue to John P. Usher, Mar. 1, 1864, RG48, Roll 9; Elizabeth Brown Pryor, *Reading the Man: A Portrait of Robert E. Lee through His Private Letters* (New York, 2007), 303, 309; Harriet Jacobs and Louisa Matilda Jacobs to Lydia Maria Child, Mar. 26, 1864, *The Harriet Jacobs Family Papers*, ed. Jean Fagan Yellin (2 vols.; Chapel Hill, 2008), 2: 561; *New-York Daily Tribune*, Apr. 2, 1864; Ira Berlin, Steven F. Miller, Joseph P. Reidy, and Leslie S. Rowand, ed., *Freedom: A Documentary History of Emancipation, 1861–1867*, Series 1, vol. 2: *The Wartime Genesis of Free Labor: The Upper South* (New York, 1993), 253–55, 257–58. The *Tribune* noted that among the returnees were survivors of 116 colonists who had left Alexandria for Haiti in June 1862. Presumably these other returnees were emigrants sent to Haiti by James Redpath's Haitian Emigration Bureau. See John McKivigan, *Forgotten Firebrand: James Redpath and the Making of Nineteenth-Century America* (Ithaca, 2008), 76, 81–82.

the escapade revealed about the intentions of "humane philanthropic, negro-loving Yankees." Describing the black emigrants as "stolen" by Union soldiers from Maryland and Virginia planters, the *Dispatch* accused Lincoln's administration of subjecting the settlers to worse conditions than were common in the African slave trade. By the time the colonists returned to U.S. soil, the article declared, the onetime emigrants were so filthy that anyone approaching them was nauseated. At Freedman's Village, they walked about barefoot in clothing so ragged it amounted to "indecent exposure." To the *Dispatch*, the episode legitimated longtime southern claims that their own slave labor system was humane. Similarly, an account appearing in both the *Augusta Constitutionalist* in Georgia and the *Charleston Mercury* in South Carolina construed the story as evidence of the "utter incapacity of the Yankees to promote the welfare or happiness of the black peasantry of the South." Rarely did Confederates find anything so satisfying to crow about.[5]

What do we make of this dismaying tale? On one level, it evidences Lincoln's racism, his preference for exporting African Americans abroad as colonists rather than assimilating them into American society. Lincoln had long favored Liberian colonization schemes; his Haitian project marked a change of destination, not principle. On the other hand, it reflected Lincoln's hope that African Americans, free and slave alike, could achieve in the Tropics the equality and freedom that eluded them in his own country. Lincoln's Haitian experiment, however ill conceived, attested to an important shift in U.S. foreign policy from expanding slavery to growing the domain of free labor. Just as Republican policy demanded the American West for free white laborers, now America's sixteenth president wanted pockets of Latin America preserved for U.S. free black laborers. It would become one of the ironies of Lincoln's presidency that his colonization program failed partly because of Latin American suspicions that Lincoln's black emigrants would morph into Manifest Destiny's latest agents. In reality, few U.S. presidents in the nineteenth century expended less effort on growing the American empire than Lincoln.

If we can take at face value a letter he sent to a South American official, during the Civil War, Abraham Lincoln regarded "the interests of the Spanish American Republics with no common concern."[6] Although

[5] *Fayetteville (NC) Observer*, Apr. 18, 1864; *Richmond (VA) Daily Dispatch*, Apr. 14, 1864; *Augusta (GA) Daily Constitutionalist*, Apr. 19, 1864; *Charleston Mercury*, Apr. 16, 1864.
[6] AL to Pedro Diez Canseco, May 13, 1863, CWAL, 6: 212–13.

Latin America was a secondary priority for an overtaxed wartime administration, the president gave more attention to affairs in the Southern Hemisphere than is commonly recognized. Even before inauguration day, Lincoln briefly turned his attention to Latin American affairs. On Christmas Day 1860, Mexican liberal forces captured Mexico City from its conservative occupiers, conferring a temporary peace on Mexico after years of civil strife. Desiring good relations with Lincoln's incoming administration in Washington, Mexico's liberal president Benito Juárez instructed Matías Romero, his chargé d'affaires in Washington, to meet with Lincoln. Securing an interview with the president-elect in Springfield on January 19, 1861, Romero told Lincoln that Mexico "rejoiced" over the Republicans' election triumph because Lincoln was expected to be friendlier than his Democratic predecessors, who "stooped to take territory from Mexico in order to extend slavery." As they talked, Romero affirmed that Juárez was committed to progressive development and would protect U.S. commercial interests in his country, and Lincoln promised his administration would treat Mexico fairly and with sympathy. Lincoln also, however, took the opportunity to criticize Mexican peonage, a system of debt servitude that was similar in many ways to slavery and was endemic below the Rio Grande (Figure 6.2).[7]

Though Lincoln never categorically opposed U.S. territorial growth southward, he probably would have presided over a nonexpansionist administration even if the Civil War had not absorbed his attention and Union resources. Twelve days before the Confederate attack on Fort Sumter, Lincoln revealed his instinctive disinterest in military adventurism abroad. On April 1, Secretary of State Seward gave Lincoln a remarkable memorandum entitled "Some thoughts for the President's consideration," a stratagem to buy time and reunite the nation before warfare with the Confederacy erupted. Arguing that Lincoln was too consumed by decisions on federal appointments to develop any defined "policy either domestic or foreign," Seward warned that further policy delays would endanger the country. Regarding domestic affairs, Seward made several suggestions, including that Lincoln surrender Fort Sumter to the

[7] Matías Romero Diary, quoted in Robert Ryal Miller, "Matías Romero: Mexican Minister to the United States during the Juárez-Maximilian Era," *Hispanic American Historical Review* 45 (May 1965): 230; Donathon C. Olliff, *Reforma Mexico and the United States: A Search for Alternatives to Annexation, 1854–1861* (University, AL, 1981), 149; Thomas Schoonover, *Dollars over Dominion: The Triumph of Liberalism in Mexican–United States Relations, 1861–1867* (Baton Rouge, 1978), 1–2; Harold Holzer, *Lincoln, President-Elect: Abraham Lincoln and the Great Secession Winter, 1860–1861* (New York, 2008), 229–30.

FIGURE 6.2 Matías Romero. Courtesy of National Archives.

Confederates. Respecting foreign matters, Seward urged a potpourri of aggressive initiatives, mostly in Latin America, on the assumption that Confederates would patriotically rejoin the Union if the administration provoked a foreign crisis or war. Seward explained that Lincoln needed a "safe means for changing the issue" from slavery and party politics.

Seward's most striking recommendation, though ambiguous, was that Lincoln should "demand explanations from *Spain* and France." Almost certainly, Seward's allusion to Spain referenced its pending takeover of the Dominican Republic, a country that traded more with the United States than with any other power.[8] For some time, a faction in the Dominican

[8] WHS, "Some thoughts for the President's consideration" (in the hand of Frederick W. Seward), Apr. 1, 1861, AL to WHS, Apr. 1, 1861, CWAL, 4: 317n, 316; Wayne H. Bowen, *Spain and the American Civil War* (Columbia, MO, 2011), 87.

Republic had been promoting a European protectorate for the country, partly to avert a feared invasion by Haiti, which bordered it to the west. Several times since gaining independence in 1821 the Dominican Republic had been occupied by its neighbor. Although European powers had previously declined accepting protectorates over the Dominicans, Spain was in a position to respond favorably after Dominican president Pedro Santana, faced with national insolvency and spiraling inflation, sent a letter to Spain's Queen Isabel II in April 1860 requesting Spain's reannexation of its onetime colony. Taking advantage of their nation's temporarily improved finances, Spanish leaders responded positively. On March 18, 1861, Santana announced the results of a rigged plebiscite favoring Spanish rule, and Spain in May dispatched occupation troops from Cuba. Formal approval of reannexation from Spain's legislative assembly, the Cortes, followed on December 16. It is hard to conceive of Seward's April 1 allusion to Spain as meaning anything other than its Dominican scheme.[9]

The secretary's reference to France likely applied to Mexico, which faced possible European intervention over its defaulted loans. Mexico did not actually suspend payments on its international debt obligations until July 17, months after Seward's memo, and France did not join Britain and Spain in a concrete Mexican interventionist policy until even later. On October 31, the three powers signed the Tripartite Treaty of London authorizing European intervention to gain reparations from Mexico.[10] Seward's memorandum, however, almost certainly anticipated French intervention against Benito Juárez's government. By coupling France and Spain, Seward seems to have conceived the militant defense of the Monroe Doctrine in Latin America that Stephen Douglas had incessantly championed. And that was not all. Seward also wanted Lincoln to "seek explanations from Great Britain and Russia" (again failing to allege the precise sins he had in mind) and dispatch "agents into *Canada, Mexico* and *Central America*, to rouse a vigorous continental *spirit of independence* on this continent against European intervention." If Lincoln was inadequate to prosecuting such a bold program, Seward suggested he assign it to someone in his cabinet. Trying to strike a non-ambitious tone in what rings as a power grab, Seward added he would

[9] Dexter Perkins, *A History of the Monroe Doctrine* (1941; rpt., Boston, 1963), 138–39; Bowen, *Spain and the American Civil War*, 48–50, 84–89; Linda S. Hudson, *Mistress of Manifest Destiny: A Biography of Jane McManus Storm Cazneau, 1807–1878* (Austin, 2001), 170–71.
[10] Bowen, *Spain and the American Civil War*, 51; Howard Jones, *Blue and Gray Diplomacy: A History of Union and Confederate Foreign Relations* (Chapel Hill, 2010), 79.

not evade the responsibility if asked even though military affairs were not his specialty.[11]

Lincoln rejected Seward's summons to hemispheric interventionism. In a note drafted to the secretary that same day, Lincoln conceded that the news about "St. Domingo" introduced "a new item within the range of our foreign policy" but said nothing about demanding anything from Spain. He also rejected Seward's insinuation that the administration lacked a foreign policy, noting that it had been busily preparing diplomatic instructions for its representatives abroad, and gently rebuked Seward's offer to take charge. If any hard-line policy was required, Lincoln said, the responsibility was his, not a cabinet member's.[12]

Possibly, since the letter remained afterward in Lincoln's papers, Seward never received Lincoln's response. Lincoln may have had second thoughts about rebuking the most influential member of his administration. On March 2, Seward had made an aborted attempt to pull out of the cabinet, and Lincoln may have withheld his answer rather than risk losing Seward's service. Still, Lincoln's reaction suggests his prewar Whiggish caution about military interventionism southward persisted. When Lincoln boasted in his Second Annual Message to Congress (December 1, 1862) that the "independent States of our own continent," notably "Mexico, Nicaragua, Costa Rica, Honduras, Peru, and Chile," entertained "more friendly sentiments" toward the United States "than have heretofore existed," he implied their appreciation of his departure from prior U.S. aggressiveness in the hemisphere, without belaboring the point. Throughout his presidency, Lincoln articulated the implicitly antiexpansionist message that America's international influence depended upon its being a beacon of liberty for other countries to emulate, and he melded into his diplomatic messaging a commitment to republican and democratic institutions in Latin America. Although the United States sought friendship with all nations, he told Peru's minister in Washington, it had special regard for countries that "founded their institutions on the principle of the equal rights of men."[13]

[11] WHS, "Some thoughts for the President's consideration," CWAL, 4: 317n–318n. See Walter Stahr, *Seward: Lincoln's Indispensable Man* (New York, 2012), 269–70 regarding the allusion to Russia.

[12] AL to WHS, Apr. 1, 1861, CWAL, 4: 316–17; Schoonover, *Dollars over Dominion*, 17; D. P. Crook, *Diplomacy during the American Civil War* (New York, 1975), 155.

[13] CWAL, 4: 317n and AL to Federico Barreda, Mar. 4, 1862, *ibid.*, 5: 143; AL, Second Annual Message, Dec. 1, 1862, JRMP, 6: 128; Dean B. Mahin, *One War at a Time: The International Dimensions of the American Civil War* (Washington, DC, 1999), 264.

Lincoln's principles contrasted starkly with the proslavery expansionism of his Democratic predecessors, and his administration was appreciated on that basis in Latin America. As early as August 1862, Costa Rica's foreign minister perceived a dramatic policy transformation from Buchanan to Lincoln, though he worried about its possible impermanence. Writing to New Granada's foreign minister, Francisco M. Iglesias cautioned that moderate, "just and honest men, such as those who form the Lincoln administration" might not control power in the United States indefinitely and that Latin American nations should therefore not rush to the assumption that "vandalous filibustering expeditions" and other threats against their "territorial integrity" had entirely vanished. As time passed, Lincoln's image became even better in republican Latin America, especially after he identified his administration with the abolition of slavery.[14]

From the perspective of many Latin American observers, the Lincoln administration, if anything, intervened insufficiently in their part of the world, rather than excessively. Instead of defying Spain, Lincoln tolerated its new colony. On April 2, 1861, Seward warned Spain's minister that the U.S. government would consider Spanish rule in the "territory of Dominica" a threat to Mexico, Haiti, the independent former Spanish colonies in South America, and even onetime Spanish territory now within the United States. Seward also cautioned that Lincoln would regard a Spanish takeover as an "unfriendly" act and resist it. Upon receiving instructions from Seward, the Union chargé d'affaires in Madrid lodged a formal protest on June 19 asserting that Spain had violated the Monroe Doctrine. However, when Spain's government refused to back down, citing the takeover as invited and thus within the United States' principles of "popular sovereignty," Lincoln and Seward refrained from substantive steps to uproot the Spanish régime. Even after resistance to Spanish rule known as the "War of the Restoration" erupted in the Dominican Republic in 1863 and the U.S. consul in Santo Domingo City recommended intervention over destruction of American property, Lincoln and Seward remained passive. At one cabinet meeting, Lincoln announced his disinclination "to take any new trouble" by becoming committed there. When Spain pulled out of the Dominican Republic in 1865, it did so because of deadly yellow fever outbreaks among Spanish

---

[14] Francisco M. Iglesias to the foreign minister of Colombia, Aug. 14, 1862, *Documents on Inter-American Cooperation*, vol. 1, ed. Robert N. Burr and Roland D. Hussey (Philadelphia, 1955): 148–49; Alfred Jackson Hanna and Kathryn Abbey Hanna, *Napoleon III and Mexico: American Triumph over Monarchy* (Chapel Hill, 1971), 184, 186, 189, 193–94.

soldiers and resistance from the population there, not because of pressure from Washington.[15]

Lincoln never publicly invoked the Monroe Doctrine during his administration, not even against the French takeover in neighboring Mexico, though as his secretary of the treasury Salmon P. Chase observed, he never renounced it either.[16] On December 8, 1861, some six thousand troops debarked from Spanish ships lying off the Mexican port of Veracruz on the Gulf of Mexico, and within weeks they were followed by some thirty-two hundred British and French soldiers, in an effort to compel Mexico to resume payment on its outstanding foreign debts. When the French later marched on Mexico City, despite provisions in the London treaty precluding territorial conquest, Spain and Great Britain made their own separate settlements with Mexico's liberal government and withdrew from the operation, leaving French ambitions to follow their own brazen course. Emperor Napoleon III not only hoped to install the Austrian Archduke Ferdinand Maximilian as Mexico's ruler but harbored a "Grand Design" that included growing France's cultural sway and trade throughout Latin America while squeezing out U.S. influence in the region.

Early in 1862, Seward instructed the Union minister in Paris William Dayton to caution the French that they faced war with the United States once the Confederacy fell if they installed a monarchy in Mexico. Still, Lincoln and Seward showed marked restraint in regard to the French intervention. Montgomery Blair, Lincoln's postmaster general, explained to Romero in 1862 that the United States would not intervene before the war in the United States ended. Given a pass for the time being by Lincoln, the French persisted. In late May 1863, French forces took Mexico City,

---

[15] Perkins, *Monroe Doctrine*, 139–47; John Edwin Fagg, *Cuba, Haiti, and the Dominican Republic* (Englewood Cliffs, NJ, 1965), 149–50. William G. W. Jaeger to WHS, Dec. 27, 1863, Despatches from United States Consuls in Santo Domingo, T56, Roll 4, National Archives; Gideon Welles Diary, Feb. 2, 1864, *Diary of Gideon Welles: Secretary of the Navy under Lincoln and Johnson*, ed. Howard K. Beale (3 vols.; New York, 1960), 1: 519. When in 1864 Spanish warships seized the guano-rich Chincha Islands, located some thirteen miles off Peru's Pacific Coast, during a dispute with Peru over claims and anti-Spanish incidents (Chincha Islands War of 1864–66), Lincoln and Seward yet again resisted intervention beyond a vague warning. Perkins, *Monroe Doctrine*, 145–46; James W. Cortada, *Two Nations over Time: Spain and the United States, 1776–1977* (Westport, CT, 1978), 87–88; Bowen, *Spain and the American Civil War*, 105; Nathan L. Ferris, "The Relations of the United States with South America during the American Civil War," *Hispanic American Historical Review* 21 (Feb. 1941): 69–70.

[16] Jay Sexton, *The Monroe Doctrine: Empire and Nation in Nineteenth-Century America* (New York, 2011), 148; Salmon P. Chase to Joshua Leavitt, Jan. 24, 1864, *The Salmon P. Chase Papers*, ed. John Niven (5 vols.; Kent, OH, 1993–98), 4: 262.

compelling Juárez's liberals to flee the capital. Subsequently the Juárez government moved between northern urban centers, including El Paso del Norte on the border with Texas, to elude the French. After considerable delay, Maximilian arrived at Mexico City in June 1864 to assume the throne the intervention had created for him.

This is not to suggest that the administration was totally passive. Seward recalled Thomas Corwin, the Union's minister in Mexico, once the French were embedded in Mexico, and Lincoln continued to receive Juárez's envoy Romero as Mexico's legitimate representative at Washington. In 1863 and 1864, Lincoln endorsed the launching of Union military operations into Confederate Texas and western Louisiana partly as a cautionary signal to the French. Lincoln's private secretary John Hay observed that the president was "very anxious that Texas should be occupied and firmly held in view of French possibilities." Romero, however, wanted much more, and Lincoln's restraint also troubled Treasury Secretary Chase and a number of Republicans in Congress. Frustrated by the pressure, Lincoln told Hay that war with France over Mexico would be a serious error because it would drive Britain and France into an anti-Union alliance at a time when it was to his great advantage to keep them divided.[17]

Even assurances of Latin American cooperation against the European powers proved insufficient to reverse Washington's caution. In 1862, Seward rebuffed a Peruvian initiative proposing that various South American countries join the United States, Mexico, and all the Central American republics in a convention that would mutually guarantee the signers' independence. When Latin American ministers in Washington asked that the Union government send representation to a hemispheric conference in Panama on January 1, 1863, to oppose the escalating European interventionism, Seward declined U.S. participation. The meeting, after a

---

[17] AL to Matías Romero, Oct. 29, 1863, CWAL, 6: 548–49; Thomas Schoonover, "Napoleon Is Coming! Maximilian Is Coming?" in *The Union, the Confederacy, and the Atlantic Rim*, ed. Robert E. May (West Lafayette, IN, 1995), 101; Miller, "Matías Romero," 231–32; Bowen, *Spain and the American Civil War*, 50–51; Jones, *Blue and Gray Diplomacy*, 127–28; Schoonover, *Dollars over Dominion*, 76, 106–109, 115–17, 142–43; Mahin, *One War at a Time*, 220–22; Sexton, *Monroe Doctrine*, 140–41; John Hay Diary, Aug. 9, 1863, June 24, 1864, *Inside Lincoln's White House: The Complete Civil War Diary of John Hay*, ed. Michael Burlingame and John R. Turner (Carbondale, 1997), 71, 211; Salmon Chase to George Wilkes, Aug. 27, 1863, Niven, ed., *Salmon P. Chase Papers*, 4: 262; Crook, *Diplomacy*, 155–59, 163; Henry Blumenthal, *France and the United States: Their Diplomatic Relations, 1789–1914* (Chapel Hill, 1970), 109–11, 109n; Burlingame, *Abraham Lincoln*, 2: 740–41.

considerable delay, finally convened in November 1864 without a Union delegation.[18]

If Lincoln and Seward saw eye to eye on relaxing the Monroe Doctrine in wartime, they may have differed over colonizing the hemisphere's southern latitudes with America's black population. Francis B. Carpenter, the youthful portraitist who stayed in the White House in 1864 (while painting his famous *First Reading of the Emancipation Proclamation of Abraham Lincoln before the Cabinet*), claimed that Seward confided to a third party that colonization was his only substantive wartime disagreement with Lincoln about "public policy." In contrast to the president, who favored black resettlement abroad, Seward preferred establishing equal rights for African Americans on their own soil. Carpenter's account gains credence from C. K. Tuckerman of the Île-à-Vache debacle, who claimed that Seward once described the Haitian colonization scheme to him as the president's "child."[19]

According to New Yorker Elisha Crosby, Lincoln began promoting black colonization in Latin America as soon as he became president. Crosby, who could speak Spanish, was appointed U.S. minister to Guatemala in March 1861, around the time that colonizationist Montgomery Blair assumed his duties in Lincoln's cabinet. The *Times of London* reporter William Howard Russell described Blair as a deliberate speaker with "rat-like" deep-set eyes after meeting him at a White House function the same month and expressed concern that the postmaster general had undue influence in the administration. Crosby's memoirs tell us that before sailing to Central America he met with Lincoln, and the president gave him "secret instructions" to carry out Francis P. Blair Sr.'s plan to colonize the slave states' free blacks in "a neighboring country" where they could establish themselves "under a free government, similar to the colony of Liberia." According to Crosby, Blair thought colonization southward would facilitate a political compromise "by which the rebellion then impending" in the United States could be either "modified" or warded off entirely since it would undermine the slavery problem at the root of secession. Significant numbers of southern whites would

[18] Schoonover, *Dollars over Dominion*, 154–56; Sexton, *Monroe Doctrine*, 148; Hanna and Hanna, *Napoleon III and Mexico*, 185.
[19] F. B. Carpenter, *Six Months at the White House with Abraham Lincoln: The Story of a Picture* (New York, 1866), 290–91; C. K. Tuckerman to WHS, Jan. 13, 1864, RG48, Roll 9.

divest themselves of slaves once they gained confidence that emancipated laborers would leave the country.[20]

Very soon after he arrived in Guatemala, Crosby brought up with its president Rafael Carrera – as Crosby subsequently recounted to Blair's ally Senator James R. Doolittle of Wisconsin – the "Colonization scheme of which we used to speak." In July, Carrera offered Crosby his own Pacific Coast hacienda with thousands of acres for an initial colonization site, suggesting the program could be expanded if the experiment went well. Crosby told Doolittle that he had alerted Blair that it would be good if fifty or one hundred black families were dispatched quickly to Guatemala to capitalize on the opening. He also said that Carrera would provide each emigrant family a town lot, as much farmland as they could tend, and the right to cut timber for fences and buildings and would see that they were paid if they desired to work for others.[21]

Guatemala, however, was not the only spot of colonization interest to the early Lincoln administration. In June 1861, Montgomery Blair approached Matías Romero with a suggestion Romero assumed was Lincoln's that U.S. blacks would be well suited for agricultural colonies in Tehuantepec and Yucatán, areas in southern Mexico starved for laborers. Romero responded encouragingly, believing such colonies were appropriate for his country given Mexico's lack of race prejudice and that the black emigrants would be fleeing "a country which considers them as an inferior race ... reduced to slavery." Whether Lincoln prompted Blair's feeler to Romero is unclear, but resettlement of blacks seems to have been on the president's mind. According to his Illinois friend Orville Browning, Lincoln discussed "the negro question" with him on July 8, emphasizing that no slaves who fled to Union armies during the war would be reenslaved. Instead, Lincoln explained, they would have to fend for themselves until they might be colonized once the war ended.[22]

[20] William Howard Russell Diary, Mar. 28, 1861, in William Howard Russell, *My Diary North and South*, ed. Eugene H. Berwanger (New York, 1988), 48, 50; William C. Harris, *Lincoln and the Border States: Preserving the Union* (Lawrence, 2011), 31; Barker, ed., *Memoirs of Elisha Oscar Crosby*, x, xii, 75–76, 87; Mary Patricia Chapman, "The Mission of Elisha O. Crosby to Guatemala, 1861–1864," *Pacific Historical Review* 24 (Aug. 1955): 276.
[21] E. O. Crosby to James R. Doolittle, Nov. 20, 1861, James R. Doolittle File, Miscellaneous Personal Names, Manuscripts and Archives Division, New York Public Library.
[22] Thomas Schoonover, "Misconstrued Mission: Expansion and Black Colonization in Mexico and Central America during the Civil War," *Pacific Historical Review* 49 (Nov. 1980): 611–12; Orville Hickman Browning Diary, July 8, 1861, *The Diary of Orville Hickman Browning*, ed. Theodore Calvin Pease and James G. Randall (2 vols.; Springfield, IL, 1925–33), 477.

It was significant that Lincoln mentioned blacks in Union army lines and colonization in the same context. So did Crosby, who promoted colonization in Guatemala with the proposition that "persons who are 'contraband' in the U.S. become citizens here." There was nothing careless about Crosby's use of the term "contraband," which usually denotes goods in neutral hands liable to seizure by a warring power because they might help the military effort of an enemy. By the time Crosby wrote to Doolittle, the word had a new application. When three male slave field hands arrived at the Union's Fortress Monroe shortly after the outbreak of the Civil War, the fort's commander, General Benjamin Butler, rejected Confederate demands that they be returned to bondage. Needing legal grounds for disregarding the Fugitive Slave Act of 1850 and federal policy dating to the origins of the Republic, Butler justified retaining black escapees from slavery and putting them to work for the Union army as paid laborers on the logic they represented captured "contrabands of war." Had he not kept them, they would certainly have helped the Confederate war effort; they told him they had been on the verge of being sent to North Carolina for work on enemy fortifications. Gradually, the term "contraband" gained currency for thousands of escaped slaves in federal hands, reflecting their liminal legal status between slavery and freedom prior to the Union's adoption of emancipation policies.[23]

Encouraged by what he had learned from Crosby, Francis Blair Sr. pressed colonization in a November 16 letter to Lincoln. Blair asked Lincoln to back not only the Guatemalan project but also Ambrose Thompson's scheme to use colonists to develop lands in Chiriqui, a province of New Granada (today's Colombia) farther south on the Central American isthmus. A native of Pennsylvania and entrepreneur, Thompson had secured an appointment in August as an assistant quartermaster in the U.S. Army at the rank of captain, and he was using his new position to promote his project.[24]

In May 1859, Thompson's Chiriqui Improvement Company, which reportedly held title to coal-rich land on the Caribbean coast between

---

[23] E. O. Crosby to James R. Doolittle, Nov. 20, 1861, James R. Doolittle File, New York Public Library; Ervin L. Jordan, Jr., *Black Confederates and Afro-Yankees in Civil War Virginia* (Charlottesville, 1995), 82–84; John David Smith, "Let Us All Be Grateful That We Have Colored Troops That Will Fight," in Smith, ed., *Black Soldiers in Blue: African American Troops in the Civil War Era* (Chapel Hill, 2002), 11–12, 17; Foner, *Fiery Trial*, 167, 169–70.

[24] Francis P. Blair Sr. to AL, Nov. 16, 1861, AL Papers, LC, Series 1; Francis B. Heitman, comp., *Historical Register and Dictionary of the United States Army, from Its Organization, September 29, 1789, to March 2, 1903* (2 vols.; Washington, DC, 1903), 1: 955.

Costa Rica's southern border and today's Panama Canal, had negotiated an agreement with the Buchanan administration's naval department. By the draft contract, which required congressional approval to take effect, the U.S. government would pay Thompson's company $300,000 for 5,000 acres of land for naval depots and stations, the right of free transit along a road Thompson would construct from Chiriqui to the Pacific, naval visitation rights in company waters, and the right to all coal needed for U.S. naval purposes (at merely ten cents per ton tax to cover the company's mining and delivery costs). Since Congress withheld approval at the time, the matter remained pending when Lincoln took office.[25]

Showing interest in Thompson's project, Lincoln asked his financially challenged brother-in-law Ninian W. Edwards, whom he appointed as a Union commissary officer on August 8, 1861, to review its paper trail and assess its merits. Edwards, a lawyer who had held public office, reported on August 9 that the Buchanan administration's investigations had verified Chiriqui's naval and transit potential. Edwards also confirmed the legitimacy of Thompson's company contract for land and coal mines, considered the implications under international law of the U.S. gaining sovereignty over lands within other countries, and noted that Thompson's company was willing to lease parts of its holdings for "colonization purposes" to the U.S. government. Lincoln subsequently conditionally approved Thompson's contract, but, on the recommendation of his secretary of the navy, Gideon Welles, withheld final consent while Secretary of the Interior Caleb Smith determined whether the contract was legally valid. In relaying this assignment to Smith, Lincoln implied his own interest in Chiriqui largely lay in its colonization potential. Lincoln told the interior secretary that if Congress were to modify an 1819 U.S. statute for the suppression of the African slave trade, federal authorities could send slaves confiscated from slaving vessels to Central America instead of returning them to Africa at much less expense. An added bonus, Lincoln noted, might be "the removal of negroes from this country" to Central America. Lincoln also assigned Treasury Secretary Chase to do a feasibility study. On November 12, Chase reported that after spending much of the day studying "the Chiriqui business," he was

[25] Contract summarized in Annual Report of the Secretary of the Navy for the Year 1859, Dec. 2, 1859, in *New York Herald*, Dec. 28, 1859; John H. Schroeder, *Shaping a Maritime Empire: The Commercial and Diplomatic Role of the American Navy, 1829–1861* (Westport, CT, 1985), 135.

impressed enough to give it his preliminary endorsement, pending more thorough analysis.[26]

Francis P. Blair Sr.'s November 16 letter, therefore, addressed two separate colonization prospects under consideration. He assured Lincoln that so many "freedmen of African blood" would flock to Guatemala when the Union won the Civil War that they would upstage English settlement in Central America, given their "superior intelligence" and particular skills in the cultivation of cotton. Arguing that it would be "superfluous" to elaborate the benefits of "removing" the people who had convulsed American politics and caused the Civil War, Blair elaborated regarding Thompson's scheme that the time had arrived when, as Thomas Jefferson had predicted, the "African race" in the United States would be either deported or exterminated. Blair must have been confirmed in his views on receiving a November 17 letter from Thompson hyping his scheme. In a burst of excessive boosterism, Thompson claimed that by merely laboring five days a month in "the Switzerland of Central America" cultivating cotton, tobacco, sugar, and cochineal, black colonists could achieve economic independence and then some in Chiriqui. Blair sent the letter on to Lincoln.[27]

Given the countervailing pressures Lincoln was under, it is not surprising he took Blair's newest recommendations seriously. Since the beginning of the war, radical antislavery elements had been pressuring him to use hostilities with the South as a golden opportunity to attack slavery. No sooner did news of the Confederate attack on Fort Sumter reach Washington than the radical antislavery senator Charles Sumner of Massachusetts rushed to the White House, where he pressured Lincoln to free the slaves under the war powers granted the executive branch under the U.S. Constitution. When abolitionist Wendell Phillips rendered a

[26] Paul J. Scheips, "Lincoln and the Chiriqui Colonization Project," *Journal of Negro History* 37 (Oct. 1952): 418–19; AL to Ninian W. Edwards, June 19, 1861 and editor's note, AL to Caleb B. Smith, Oct. 23[?], 24, 1861, CWAL, 4: 412, 412n, 561; 5: 2–3; Edwards to AL, Aug. 9, 1861, Salmon P. Chase to AL, Nov. 12, 1861, AL Papers, LC, Series 1. Section 2 of "An Act in addition to the Acts prohibiting the slave trade," enacted March 3, 1819, authorized the president to appoint "a proper person or persons, residing upon the coast of Africa, as agent or agents for receiving the negroes, mulattoes, or persons of colour, delivered from on board vessels, seized in the prosecution of the slave trade, by commanders of the United States' armed vessels." *Statutes at Large*, 15 Cong., 2 Sess., 532–33.

[27] Francis P. Blair Sr. to AL, Nov. 16, 1861, Ambrose W. Thompson to Blair Sr., Nov. 17, 1861, AL Papers, Series 1, LC. Some documents call Thompson's company the American Improvement Company. Thompson cited Panama's clear mountainous streams in making his Switzerland analogy.

rousing emancipation speech in Boston, it was republished and sold some
200,000 copies. Black journalist and orator Frederick Douglass, who
recently had reconsidered his longtime opposition to black expatriation
and taken to promoting Haiti as a destination for dissatisfied African
Americans, now saw hope at home and canceled a planned trip to the
black republic. Douglass editorialized that the Lincoln administration should recruit both free blacks and slaves for a "liberating army"
to march southward and emancipate slaves. Neither the Union's loss in
the war's first major battle at Bull Run in July 1861 nor the failure of
Union authorities to mount a credible threat against the Confederate capital at Richmond before the end of the year lessened this crescendo for
abolitionizing the war. If anything, such losses and growing indications
that peaceful reconstruction of the Union was impossible strengthened
the argument to assault slavery, for the obvious reason that slave labor
helped free white southern men to fight.[28]

Lincoln knew, however, that almost all northern Democrats, some
of his leading generals, and even conservatives in his own party either
opposed federally imposed emancipation in principle or believed that
acting against slavery would divide the North at a time when unity was
required for victory. Equally worrisome, Lincoln recognized that fla-
grant abolitionism would antagonize slave owners and their allies in four
slave states that so far had not seceded – Delaware, Maryland, Kentucky,
and Missouri – possibly driving three of them (only Delaware lacked a
strong secessionist element) into joining the Confederacy, something he
could hardly afford. These "border" states, plus the part of Virginia that
seceded from it early in the war and in 1863 became the new Union state
of West Virginia, produced 37 percent of the South's corn crop. They also
held 30 percent of the South's livestock, about 28 percent of its population, and a whopping 52 percent of its industrial capacity.

If Lincoln had any doubts about these stakes, he was disabused of them
when he received a letter in early September 1861 from his old Kentucky
friend Joshua Speed. Speed had learned that Union general and former
Republican presidential candidate John C Frémont, then commanding
the Union's Department of the West in St. Louis, had issued a proclamation on August 30 declaring freedom for the slaves of Missourians

[28] James M. McPherson, *The Struggle for Equality: Abolitionists and the Negro in the Civil War and Reconstruction* (1967; rpt., Princeton, 1972), 47–66, 75–80; David W. Blight, *Frederick Douglass' Civil War: Keeping Faith in Jubilee* (Baton Rouge, 1989), 131–34, 148–49.

supporting the Confederacy. Speed told Lincoln he was so upset he was
unable to sleep or eat. Observing that Kentucky public opinion was as rig-
idly opposed to "freeing negroes & allowing negroes to be emancipated
& remain among us" as northern opinion would be if Lincoln were to
end freedom of religion or the right to educate children, Speed cautioned
that Frémont's decree, unless reversed, would destroy Union feeling in
his state and possibly lead to a race war in which Kentucky's blacks
would be virtually exterminated. Obviously alarmed by Speed's warning,
Lincoln wrote to Orville Browning that it would amount to losing "the
whole game" if Kentucky were alienated since Missouri and Maryland
would surely follow in Kentucky's track. In a message ordering Frémont
to modify his proclamation, Lincoln warned the general his policy, if
allowed to stand, would turn southern Unionists against the administration and "perhaps ruin our rather fair prospect for Kentucky."[29]

Given Lincoln's predicament, tropical colonization potentially represented a way to thread the needle between competing interests and
address the very slavery and racial issues that had helped cause the war.
After all, Speed had indicated that Kentuckians were appalled at the
prospect of blacks staying in their state after gaining their freedom, not
with the idea of emancipation itself. On December 1, 1861, Lincoln told
Browning he had great hopes of inducing Delaware, Kentucky, Maryland,
and Missouri to emancipate their slaves gradually if the federal government would reimburse them $500 per slave with the understanding "that
there should be connected with it a scheme of colonizing the blacks some
where on the American Continent." Several months later, Lincoln heard
from Montgomery Blair that a program he had proposed in the interim
for compensated emancipation by Delaware state action depended for
its acceptance on "providing homes for such of them in a neighboring
country as would voluntarily emigrate." Delaware's nonslaveholders,
Blair reported, were anxious "to get the negroes from among them." As
the historian William C. Harris argues, only the possibility of colonizing emancipated slaves made Lincoln's compensation program – eventually proposed for all the border slave states as well as occupied parts of

[29] William W. Freehling, *The Reintegration of American History: Slavery and the Civil War* (New York, 1994), 233; Stephanie McCurry, *Confederate Reckoning: Power and Politics in the Civil War South* (Cambridge, MA, 2010), 65–67, 75–76; Paludan *People's Contest*, 86–88; Mark E. Neely, *The Last Best Hope of Earth: Abraham Lincoln and the Promise of America* (1993; rpt., 1995), 96–98; Joshua F. Speed to AL, Sept. 3, 1861, AL Papers, Series 1, LC; AL to Orville H. Browning, Sept. 22, 1861, AL to John C. Frémont, Sept. 2, 11, 1861, CWAL, 4: 532, 506, 517–18; McPherson, *Struggle for Equality*, 67.

Tennessee and western Virginia – remotely palatable to resistant politicians and public opinion in those places.[30]

Starting with his First Annual Message to Congress on December 3, 1861, Lincoln publicly promoted programs anticipating black colonization in the Tropics along the lines that Crosby and the Blairs wanted. Saying the moment had come for overdue recognition of Liberia and Haiti, two countries that had never enjoyed official relations with the United States, Lincoln asked Congress to appropriate funds for appointment of a U.S. chargé d'affaires to both countries – a recommendation with colonization implications because both had previously taken in U.S. black emigrants and because of what Lincoln added later in the message. As he neared its end, Lincoln cited a congressional enactment passed earlier in the war dubbed the "First Confiscation Act" that allowed the U.S. government to confiscate Confederate property, including slaves used for hostile purposes; he also obliquely referenced his initiative in Delaware to persuade the four loyal southern border states to undertake emancipation at the state level in the expectation of federal compensation for forfeited slaves. Embracing the "isothermal" theories believed by many contemporaries that blacks were physiologically predestined to live and labor in tropical places, Lincoln suggested Congress relocate both "classes" of slaves (meaning the confiscated and border state slaves) to "some place or places in a climate congenial to them." Further, he wished Congress to include "the free colored people already in the United States" and encouraged the lawmakers to appropriate funds for territory purchased to resettle blacks abroad. Noting that such a policy would free up "additional room" in the United States for "white men remaining or coming here," Lincoln dramatically ended the colonization section of his message by warning that the Union might not survive without black resettlement.[31]

By the Civil War's first winter, Lincoln was vested in tropical colonization. As the *New York Times* observed, the scheme represented Lincoln's

---

[30] Orville Hickman Browning Diary, Dec. 1, 1861, Pease and Randall, ed., *Diary of Orville Hickman Browning*, 512; Montgomery Blair to AL, March 5 [1862?], AL Papers, Series 1, LC; Harris, *Lincoln and the Border States*, 170, 173, 179–80; Patience Essah, *A House Divided: Slavery and Emancipation in Delaware, 1638–1865* (Charlottesville, 1996), 162–75; H. Clay Reed, "Lincoln's Compensated Emancipation Plan and Its Relation to Delaware," *Delaware Notes* 7 (1931): 28–29, 37.

[31] AL, First Annual Message, Dec. 3, 1861, JRMP, 6: 47, 54; "An Act to Confiscate Property Used for Insurrectionary Purposes," Aug. 6, 1861, *Statutes at Large*, 37 Cong., 1 Sess., 319; CG, 36 Cong., 1 Sess., 1629, 2 Sess., 104, 37 Cong., 2 Sess., Appendix, 83; Mark E. Neely Jr., "Colonization and the Myth That Lincoln Prepared the People for Emancipation," *Lincoln's Proclamation: Emancipation Reconsidered*, ed. William A. Blair and Karen Fisher Younger (Chapel Hill, 2009), 64–65.

fusing of Blair's ideas with Henry Clay's "ancient ground" regarding slavery. If Lincoln read the influential and Democratic-leaning *New York Herald* the day after submitting his message, he would have been very encouraged. Although the *Herald* disapproved of establishing official relations with Haiti, it lauded Lincoln's plans for "contraband negroes" as the best way to turn emancipation "to any good account." Further, the *Herald* endorsed Haiti as the best place to send them.[32]

Lincoln's message put compensation, colonization, and recognition of Haiti squarely on Congress's agenda, and on January 16, 1862, Frank Blair Jr. introduced a colonization petition from 242 free black Californians in the House asking for resettlement in Africa or Central America. Congress, however, deferred action until spring, when it addressed slavery in the nation's capital. On April 11, Congress acted to end slavery in the District of Columbia and granted loyal masters up to $300 per liberated slave. It also included a provision drafted by Senator Doolittle, appropriating $100,000 to be expended at presidential discretion for resettling blacks abroad, stipulating that no more than $100 be expended per emigrant with eligibility limited to free blacks living in Washington at the time as well as district slaves liberated under the new law. The law anticipated the resettlement of such blacks in "the Republics of Hayti or Liberia," or any other foreign country "as the President may determine."

Lincoln signed the measure on April 16, telling Congress he was gratified that it incorporated the "two principles" of colonization and compensation he had been promoting. He also put implementation of colonization under the auspices of Interior Secretary Smith, though the formalization of this role occurred months later. On April 25, Smith asked U.S. Marshal Robert Henry in New York City to investigate costs for sending emigrants from Fortress Monroe, Virginia, on a first-class vessel to Chiriqui, Haiti, and Liberia, including food, medicines, and the hiring of at least one doctor. The next day, Smith cited Congress's colonization legislation and bluntly asked Ambrose Thompson, whose project had just gained the final imprimatur of the Department of the Treasury, whether he was prepared to colonize blacks on the landholdings of the Chiriqui Improvement Company.[33]

[32] *New-York Times*, Dec. 4, 1861; *New York Herald*, Dec. 4, 1861. For Lincoln's prioritizing of Latin America over Liberia, see Benjamin Quarles, *Lincoln and the Negro* (New York, 1962), 110–11.
[33] CG, 37 Cong., 2 Sess., 365; *House Miscellaneous Doc.* 31, 37 Cong., 2 Sess., 1–2; *New-York Times*, Jan. 19, 1862; *Statutes at Large*, 37 Cong., 2 Sess., 376–78, 421; *Sen.*

Meanwhile, Charles Sumner and other Republicans steered legislation enacting Lincoln's recommended recognition of Haiti and Liberia through Congress, and, on June 5 Lincoln signed a measure authorizing him to appoint representatives at the rank of "commissioner and consul-general" to both nations. This establishment of official relations with countries governed by blacks challenged racial prejudices in the Union while encouraging pro-Union sentiment in English antislavery circles. When Haiti's representative in Washington, the mulatto Ernest Roumain, was received by the Lincoln administration in early 1863, Mexican minister Romero could only marvel at the policy change given the "profoundly deep-rooted prejudices" Americans harbored against dark-skinned peoples. Romero could have been reading Cara Kasson's thoughts. The Iowa Republican congressman's wife, a southerner by birth, barely restrained herself after Roumain and his secretary turned up at a Washington party and circulated openly at an event also attended by cabinet members, other diplomats, and Union generals. Voicing her discomfort to a Des Moines paper, Kasson explained,

And who else [was there] do you suppose? Guess, and guess again! Not right yet? Well! who indeed but the Haytien Embassy!! It is so, I tell you; there they were, guests and honored guests, and unmistakably *colored* at that. ... I felt queerly, as though I were having a very funny dream. Two elegant colored gentlemen, white kid gloves, Parisian Toilet, conversing in Spanish, French and English, yet most unmistakably darkey! Col. Romaine, the Haytien Charge d'Affairs, is tall, very fine looking and bright copper colored. ... His Secretary is a regular colored representative and no mistake. The hair of this gentleman kinks! ... I confess I stared more at them than was quite polite, and I found it a little hard to keep my face straight.

Yet, Mrs. Kasson reported that as a "good Abolitionist" she was able to contain her prejudices and treat the "dignitaries" with respect.[34]

Journal, Apr. 16, 1862, 37 Cong., 2 Sess., 402; Foner, *Fiery Trial*, 198–200; Caleb B. Smith to Robert Henry, Apr. 25, 1862, Smith to Ambrose W. Thompson, Apr. 26, 1862, RG48, Roll 1; Burlingame, *Abraham Lincoln*, 2: 54; Scheips, "Lincoln and the Chiriqui Colonization Project," 424.

34 Charles H. Wesley, "The Struggle for the Recognition of Haiti and Liberia as Independent Republics," *Journal of Negro History* 2 (Oct. 1917): 380–82. [Owen Lovejoy], *His Brother's Blood: Speeches and Writings*, ed. William F. Moore and Jane Ann Moore (Urbana, 2004), 281; Matías Romero to the Mexican Ministry of Foreign Relations," *A Mexican View of America in the 1860s: A Foreign Diplomat Describes the Civil War and Reconstruction*, trans. and ed. Thomas Schoonover (Rutherford, NJ, 1991): 146; "Miriam" to the (Des Moines) *Iowa State Register*, Mar. 18, 1863, "Source Material of Iowa History: An Iowa Woman in Washington, D.C., 1861–1865," *Iowa Journal of History* 52 (Jan. 1954): 77–78; *London Anti-Slavery Reporter*, Jan. 1, 1862; *London Daily News*, Jan. 30, 1863.

Lincoln's colonization program, with its congressional stamp of approval, gained traction throughout the spring of 1862. On April 21, Frank Blair Jr. returned to the House of Representatives with a new colonization petition, this one obviously drafted with the April 16 act in mind. The petition had the signatures of forty free blacks living in the District of Columbia asking for help in emigrating to Central America and obtaining short-term protection once there; the petitioners intended to raise staple crops that would benefit U.S. commerce without undermining the jobs of white laborers in the Union. On May 5, Secretary Smith advised Lincoln that the program's implementation required "the services of an efficient agent familiar with the subject" and suggested that James Mitchell (whom Lincoln already knew from his earlier involvement in African colonization) was just the person to do it.[35] Smith also investigated whether the U.S. government could gain sovereignty over whatever place was selected for black colonization abroad, an inquiry prompted by a clause in Congress's April 16 act. On May 16, he reported to Lincoln that Ambrose Thompson, whose Chiriqui program was still pending, could not promise such a cession since New Granada's constitution prohibited the alienation of national territory. Smith believed that trying to circumvent the ban would so delay colonization as to ruin the program, and he also discouraged Lincoln from pursuing outlets in Mexico's Yucatán Peninsula or the island of Cozumel off its coast, two other locales of interest in Washington. Smith considered the population of the peninsula too primitive (and the land too poor) for successful colonization, and he thought Cozumel too small to accommodate the numbers of emigrants the administration anticipated. Smith felt Lincoln's best bet was Thompson's Chiriqui Improvement Company minus a cession if the government could verify that Chiriqui truly had sufficient coal supplies to benefit the navy's steam vessels.[36]

With Washington all abuzz, as Lincoln's secretary William O. Stoddard put it, over the "disposal of the contrabands," the president made Mitchell his colonization agent on June 3, a position formalized in

[35] *House Journal*, 37 Cong., 2 Sess., 578; "Joseph Enoch Williams et al. to the Honorable the Senate and House of Representatives," in Berlin, Miller, Reidy and Rowland, ed., *Freedom ... Wartime Genesis*, 263–65; Caleb B. Smith to AL, May 5, 1862 (letterbook copy), AL Papers, Series 1, LC. The April petition was referred to the House Select Committee on Emigration and Colonization including Blair and many border state members. Eric Foner, "Lincoln and Colonization," in *Our Lincoln: New Perspectives on Lincoln and His World*, ed. Eric Foner (New York, 2008), 152; *Statutes at Large*, 37 Cong., 2 Sess., 589–92.
[36] Caleb B. Smith to AL, May 16, 1862 (letterbook copy), AL Papers, Series 1, LC.

an August 4 commission appointing Mitchell "in connection with" the Department of the Interior, to execute the current Congress's colonization laws. Lincoln's commission used the plural "laws" because on July 17 he had signed a new and more punitive law confiscating Confederate property, which broadened the government's colonization program by including blacks living beyond Washington, D.C. The act deemed all Confederate slaves coming under Union control "forever free of their servitude" – regardless of whether they had been used for enemy military purposes – and declared that the president could employ any of them he wanted in putting down the rebellion. He also could colonize them. Section 12 declared:

That the President ... is hereby authorized to make provision for the transportation, colonization and settlement, in some tropical country beyond the limits of United States, of such persons of the African race, made free by the provisions of this act, as may be willing to emigrate, having first obtained the consent of the government of said country to their protection and settlement ... with all the rights and privileges of freemen.[37]

Further, Congress gifted Lincoln with a fivefold increase in colonization funding. On July 15, three days after Lincoln told border state congressmen at a private meeting that there was ample space in South America for resettling freed blacks if they accepted his compensated emancipation plan, Congress enacted an appropriations measure – approved by Lincoln on the sixteenth – that anticipated the "probable passage" of Congress's pending confiscation bill. It gave Lincoln an additional $500,000 for colonization and provided that the money should be repaid to the U.S. Treasury from confiscated Confederate property. On July 21, Lincoln briefly mentioned the "colonization of negroes in some tropical country" in a cabinet meeting.[38]

---

[37] Dispatch signed "Illinois" [William O. Stoddard], May 12, 1862 in the *New York Examiner*, May 15, 1862, *Dispatches from Lincoln's White House: The Anonymous Civil War Journalism of Presidential Secretary William O. Stoddard*, ed. Michael Burlingame (Lincoln, 2002), 79; James Mitchell to John P. Usher, Jan. 21, 1864, Commission of Emigration Agency signed by Abraham Lincoln (copy), Aug. 4, 1862, RG48, Roll 8. Mitchell's salary was set, in December 1862, at $1,800 a year.

[38] AL, "Appeal to Border State Representatives to Favor Compensated Emancipation," July 12, 1862, CWAL, 5: 318; "An Act making supplemental Appropriations for sundry Civil Expenses of the Government ...," *Statutes at Large*, 37 Cong., 2 Sess., 582; *House Journal*, 37 Cong., 2 Sess., 1092; Salmon P. Chase Diary, July 21, 22, *Diary and Correspondence of Salmon P. Chase: July 21, 1861 to October 12, 1862* (*Annual Report of the American Historical Association for the Year 1902*) (2 vols.; Washington, DC, 1903), 2: 46, 48.

What tropical country would wind up taking Lincoln's colonists? Although Lincoln's secretary William O. Stoddard was convinced they were bound for railroad work in Mexico, whose climate was matched "to the peculiar constitution of the race,"[39] for much of 1862 it appeared that many foreign colonies and independent governments in Central and South America and the Caribbean would vie for emigrants. Month by month, Lincoln and his cabinet sorted through proposals and reports to determine what tropical destinations most deserved federal funding.

Even before Congress enacted the Washington, D.C., emancipation act with its associated colonization funding, the New York merchant Aaron Columbus Burr and his lobbyist Anna Carroll promoted a so-called Lincoln Colony in British Honduras for liberated slaves. Carroll submitted a formal project to the administration a week after passage of the legislation and offered 175 square miles there for $75,000. Emigrants, Burr promised, could labor in British Honduras cutting and shipping mahogany. Also in early 1862, Costa Rica's president asked his nation's Congress to set aside land for former U.S. slaves, and Costa Rica's foreign minister instructed his country's minister to the United States about colonization negotiations with Washington. By springtime, Secretary of the Interior Smith was telling Lincoln about a New York City consortium's application to take free black emigrants to Spain's new Dominican Republic colony for $20 apiece with the promise that each emigrant would receive five acres of land and guaranteed work. Smith also noted that Denmark's minister had applied for emigrants to labor on the sugar estates of its St. Croix colony in the West Indies with the stipulation that they be contrabands freed by Union armies rather than blacks from the District of Columbia since the latter presumably would lack the desired agricultural labor experience. From Honduras, U.S. Consul William C. Burchard informed Seward that Honduras's chief executive wanted colonists to develop his country's vacant land. Down in Brazil (the only nation in South America to declare neutrality in the American Civil War officially), Union minister James Watson Webb nonetheless enthusiastically promoted settling freed U.S. slaves because of its climate's similarities to the southern United States. In July 1862, Brazil's government expressed interest in Webb's idea of a joint-stock company, with him as president, to carry out the project.

[39] Dispatch signed "Illinois" [William O. Stoddard], May 12, 1862, published in the *New York Examiner*, May 15, 1862, Burlingame, ed., *Dispatches from Lincoln's White House*, 79–80.

In the fall of 1862, a Honduran envoy in Guatemala alerted Elisha Crosby that he soon expected to conduct a mission to Washington to facilitate black colonization of Honduras's eastern coast. Around the same time, Lincoln learned from Smith that a former U.S. consul in the French Caribbean island of Guadeloupe wanted sixty thousand to eighty thousand "contraband negroes" for Guadeloupe and the nearby French island colony of Martinique, offering to take them without funding for various concessions. By that time, Smith had received an inquiry from the Netherlands' envoy in the United States about the feasibility of a Dutch-U.S. contract to resettle freed blacks in Dutch Surinam (today an independent country usually spelled "Suriname") on the north coast of South America. Meanwhile, Britain's government considered settling U.S. blacks in British Guiana on the same coastline.[40]

Thompson's Chiriqui scheme, too, remained in the mix and through early October 1862, Lincoln considered Chiriqui the most promising colonization destination. Seward discouraged Webb's advocacy of Brazil, instructing, "The President is ardently for Central American colonization, as near at hand & more likely to take with the blacks," likely alluding to Brazil's continuing slave labor system. According to a September 1862 entry in Navy Secretary Welles's diary, Lincoln had considered Chiriqui the place "to send the negroes out of the country" for some time. On August 2, Assistant Secretary of the Interior John P. Usher had recommended that Lincoln approve a revised Thompson contract on the basis of recent concessions that Thompson had offered the government, predicting that the government would recoup its expenses in coal supplies. Usher reasoned that black colonization of Chiriqui would undercut northern fears about blacks liberated by war and induce southerners to make peace before their "cherished property" was entirely removed from their control.[41]

---

[40] Caleb B. Smith to J. W. Fabens, May 1, 1862, Smith to AL, May 9, 1862, Smith to Charles William Kimball, Sept. 20, 1862, Smith to Roest van Limburg, Sept. 22, 1862, RG48, Roll 8; Janet L. Coryell, "The Lincoln Colony: Aaron Columbus Burr's Proposed Colonization of British Honduras," *Civil War History* 43 (Mar. 1997): 5–16; Schoonover, 'Misconstrued Mission," 613; Gerald Horne, *The Deepest South: The United States, Brazil, and the African Slave Trade* (New York, 2007), 175–79; Ferris, "Relations," 54; Hudson, *Mistress of Manifest Destiny*, 177–78; William Javier Nelson, *Almost a Territory: America's Attempt to Annex the Dominican Republic* (Newark, 1990), 48–49.

[41] WHS to James Watson Webb quoted in Horne, *Deepest South*, 183; Gideon Welles Diary, Sept. 26, 1862, *Diary of Gideon Welles*, 150; AL to Caleb B. Smith, Oct. 23[?], 1861, CWAL, 4: 561; John P. Usher to AL, Aug. 2, 1862, AL Papers, Series 1, LC; Paul D. Escott, *"What Shall We Do with the Negro?,"* 53.

Lincoln wound up accepting an offer from the antislavery U.S. senator from Kansas, Samuel C. Pomeroy – who had opposed the colonization provision of the District of Columbia Emancipation Act – to serve as an unpaid "colonization agent" to identify a suitable initial site in Chiriqui and lead five hundred black emigrants there. This curious matching of man and job has caused speculation that the Kansan accepted the assignment to discredit colonization and convert Lincoln to a full-fledged emancipation program. Evidence suggests, however, that Pomeroy was awarded the mission because he convinced Lincoln of his sincerity. On September 11, 1862, Lincoln told Smith he now approved the Thompson contract; a few days later, Smith alerted a U.S. marshal in New York City that Lincoln wanted to know the legal status of a confiscated Confederate vessel that was earmarked for transporting the Chiriqui emigrants. Everything seemed full speed ahead. On October 11, Lincoln's friend Orville Browning noted that Pomeroy and his wife were in Quincy, Illinois, en route to New York City, and he intended "to embark for New Granada, with a Colony of blacks." Pomeroy, Browning reported, had become "thoroughly and earnestly" procolonization despite his earlier opposition. Meanwhile, on September 11, Lincoln had authorized Smith to finalize the Chiriqui contract with Thompson. On October 3, Smith explained to James Mitchell, "The President has not settled [on] any plan for the expenditure of the appropriations except the authority to Senator Pomeroy to colonize in New Granada," but he had other places under contemplation.[42]

Lincoln did more than unleash the Chiriqui project; he also tried his hand at recruitment for it. In early July, while the Chiriqui scheme remained on hold, Lincoln requested his colonization czar James Mitchell to assemble members of the capital's black community to hear his pitch. On August 14, Mitchell presented the project before a group of African Americans representing several black churches when they gathered at the Union Bethel African Methodist Church in the capital's downtown.

---

[42] Sheips, "Lincoln and the Chiriqui Colonization Project," 422; Samuel C. Pomeroy to Usher, Feb. 4, 1864, Roll 8, Caleb B. Smith to Robert Murray, Sept. 16, 1862, Smith to Pomeroy, Sept. 20, 1862, Smith to James Mitchell, Oct. 3, 1862, Roll 1, RG48; Neely, "Colonization," 64; AL [to Caleb B. Smith], Sept. 11, 1862, CWAL, 5, 414; Orville Hickman Browning Diary, Oct. 11, 1862, Pease and Randall, ed., *Diary of Orville Hickman Browning,* 577. Usher became secretary of the interior on January 8, 1863 following Smith's confirmation as a federal judge on December 22. CWAL, 4: 492n. For additional evidence Pomeroy was genuinely committed to colonization, see Samuel C. Pomeroy to James Doolittle, Oct. 20, 1862, *Publications of the Southern History Association* 9 (Nov. 1905): 401–402.

The attendees selected a delegation of five to hear what the president had to say; three of them were affiliated with Washington's Social, Civil and Statistical Association, a society that drew its membership mostly from the city's black elite. Mitchell then accompanied the delegation, chaired by Edward M. Thomas, president of a black society called the Anglo-African Institute for the Encouragement of Industry and Art, to the White House for an afternoon meeting with the president.[43]

Once the delegates were introduced and seated, Lincoln told them that Congress had placed funds for colonization at his disposal and that he had "for a long time" been inclined "to favor that cause." Making his case for black emigration on racial grounds, Lincoln argued that differences distinguishing blacks and whites were "broader" than those "between almost any two other races," and he sidestepped the issue of whether racial barriers were "right or wrong" by emphasizing instead the negative effects on both races of coexistence. "Your race suffer very greatly ... by living among us," he observed, "while ours suffer from your presence." Calling for realism from his listeners, he conceded that blacks suffered "the greatest wrong inflicted on any people" but cautioned that they had no chance of equality in the United States. Ruminating ambiguously that he lacked ability to change racial inequality in the United States "if I would," he then all but put the onus on blacks for the Civil War. Without slavery and "the colored race as a basis," he declared, white men would not be "cutting one another's throats." Colonization represented the obvious solution, but would blacks emigrate? Anticipating that long-time free blacks like the ones he was addressing, given their relatively comfortable lifestyles as compared to slaves, might reject colonization abroad, Lincoln challenged his listeners to benefit their race by unselfishly departing. If blacks like the "intelligent colored men" before him did this, they would make a great humanitarian contribution. Prejudiced whites worried about blacks' remaining "with us" would then have cause to emancipate many of their slaves. Trying to nudge the delegates into assent, Lincoln remarkably equated George Washington's personal sacrifices in the cause of American independence from England with what

[43] Kate Masur, *An Example for All the Land: Emancipation and the Struggle over Equality in Washington, D.C.* (Chapel Hill, 2010), 34–35; Foner, "Lincoln and Colonization," 155; Phillip S. Paludan, "Greeley, Colonization, and a 'Deputation of Negroes': Three Considerations on Lincoln and Race," *Lincoln Emancipated: The President and the Politics of Race* (DeKalb, 2007), 41–42; James Oakes, *The Radical and the Republican: Frederick Douglass, Abraham Lincoln, and the Triumph of Antislavery Politics* (New York, 2007), 191; CWAL, 5: 370n–71n.

he was asking of his black visitors. He also told his guests they would be going to Central America, a superior destination to Liberia, since it only took seven days travel to sail there, one-fourth the time it would take to reach Africa. Without mentioning Chiriqui by name, Lincoln praised his Central American site for its "great natural resources" and strategic location astride a natural transit route across the isthmus. Coal deposits there, moreover, would provide "immediate employment" for emigrants. Though Lincoln conceded the problematic nature of Central America's "political affairs" (presumably an allusion to endemic civil strife in the region), he argued that the racial equality Central American governments promised offered an overriding advantage to emigrants. Saying that he hoped to launch his experiment with one hundred black men and their families but would settle for "twenty-five able bodied men, with a mixture of women and children," he charged the delegates, whom he considered "men ... capable of thinking as white men," to think over his proposal at their leisure and get back to him.[44]

Whether Lincoln's remarks, recorded by a stenographer and reprinted in many papers over the following days, would produce colonization converts remained to be seen. On August 16, delegation spokesman Thomas wrote to Lincoln that although he and his companions had been "entirely hostile" to colonization before the meeting, they had been won over by the president's able presentation and assumed that "the leading minds of our people" in Boston, Philadelphia, and New York would react similarly once they familiarized themselves with the project. Thomas was so certain of this that he requested Lincoln to send two or more of the five delegates along with a letter of presidential support to the cities mentioned, paying their expenses from Congress's colonization fund. If Lincoln did so, the delegates could raise the desired recruits within two weeks of their departures from Washington.[45]

Many blacks, however, were aghast at Lincoln's sentiments. Within days, a meeting of African Americans in Long Island, New York, published a rejoinder that affirmed the unity of races ("God has made of one blood all nations that dwell on the face of the earth"), suggested that Lincoln had played into the hands of racist white mobs, and reported that their white enemies were already citing Lincoln's remarks to pressure them to leave the country. In a searing commentary, Frederick Douglass

[44] *New-York Times*, Aug. 15, 1862.
[45] Foner, "Lincoln and Colonization," 155; Edward M. Thomas to AL, Aug. 16, 1862, AL Papers, Series 1, LC.

attacked the "contempt for Negroes" and "canting hypocrisy" revealed by Lincoln's White House remarks. Douglas lambasted the absurdity of blaming the presence of blacks in the United States for the war – noting that many races lived peaceably together in South America, Mexico, and Central America – and predicted that Lincoln's comments would trigger "outrages" against blacks by "ignorant and base" whites who only needed encouragement from people in authority to follow their racist instincts. Further, Douglass interpreted Lincoln's whole colonization program as evidence of Lincoln's desire to maintain slavery as a means of conciliating the Border South. Many blacks protested that they were too American to want to move abroad. It also became apparent very quickly that frustration with Lincoln's comments crossed racial and party lines. Republican secretary of the treasury Chase, who was stridently antislavery, expressed dismay upon reading in a Washington paper about Lincoln's pontificating at the meeting, exclaiming, "Saw in 'Republican' account of interview invited by President with colored people, and his talk to them on Colonization. How much better would be a manly protest against prejudice, against color! and a wise effort to give Freemen homes in America!" Even more vehemently, the former Polish revolutionary Adam Gurowsky, serving the Lincoln administration as a State Department translator, condemned Lincoln's pronouncements on racial incompatibility as "clap-trap" and "bosh" and judged the Chiriqui scheme impractical since the Central American states would never allow an "independent community" as envisioned by Lincoln to be established in their midst. Lincoln's address drew ridicule from the satirist "Orpheus C. Kerr" (pen name for Robert Newell) and even failed to rally the very northern politicians and newspapers most likely to support a program based on racist premises. Opposition Democrats and their newspapers were wary of funding the eventual resettlement abroad of four million freed slaves and skeptical that blacks would wish to emigrate in significant numbers.[46] It remained to be seen whether Lincoln could overcome the resistance, gather his emigrants, and actually launch his program.

[46] Statement of meeting at Newtown, Long Island, Aug. 20, 1862 (abridged) and other documents and author's comments in James M. McPherson, *The Negro's Civil War: How American Negroes Felt and Acted during the War for the Union* (1965; rpt., Urbana, 1982), 92–95; Frederick Douglass, "The President and His Speeches," *Douglass' Monthly* 5 (Sept. 1862), 707; Richard Blackett, "Lincoln and Colonization," *OAH Magazine of History*, 21 (Oct. 2007): 22; Salmon P. Chase Diary, Aug. 15, 1862, *Diary and Correspondence of Salmon P. Chase*, 2: 59; Adam Gurowsky Diary, "August, 1862," in Gurowsky, *Diary, from March 4, 1861, to November 12, 1862* (Boston, 1862), 251; Neely, "Colonization," 54–57.

Even after Lincoln brandished his Preliminary Emancipation Proclamation on September 22, 1862, he remained committed to colonization. Considerable evidence exists that Lincoln, under increasing pressure to convert the war for Union into a crusade for emancipation, had been considering such a step since late May or early June, just waiting for the right opportunity. Further, it seems clear he regarded colonization and emancipation as a two-edged sword to deal with America's race and slavery problems rather than as mutually exclusive. Although there is no definitive evidence that the politically savvy Lincoln promoted colonization primarily as an expedient to reconcile doubters to emancipation, he left hints by the timing of his colonization decisions that he considered emancipation a hard sell in the North and the slave border states without the connected suggestion that liberated blacks might leave the country.[47]

Lincoln previously had postponed issuing an emancipation declaration, for fear that critics, especially overseas, might pounce on it as a sign of Union weakness – a desperate attempt to turn a losing war around by encouraging slaves to rebel at a time when the Union military was having difficulty in the field. After Union forces stopped a Confederate invasion of Maryland at the Battle of Antietam on September 17, however, he had more flexibility on emancipation. Even though Union and Confederate casualties were roughly comparable at Antietam, the battle had the aura of Yankee success since Confederate forces retreated to Virginia two days afterward. The September 22 proclamation's most important provision gave Confederate states until January 1 to rejoin the Union with elected representatives sitting in Congress. On that date, Lincoln would issue a declaration freeing all slaves in states or designated parts of states still in rebellion against federal authorities. Significantly, though, Lincoln preceded his emancipation wording with an announcement of his intention to continue efforts "to colonize persons of African descent" either "upon this continent, or elsewhere" and persuade Congress to provide financial help to states voluntarily enacting emancipation. Though Lincoln's final January 1 proclamation lacked colonization language, it neither repudiated his colonization program nor implied the prior program was defunct.[48]

[47] John Hope Franklin, *The Emancipation Proclamation* (1963; rpt., Wheeling, IL, 1995), 31–33; Michael Vorenberg, Abraham Lincoln and the Politics of Black Colonization," *Journal of the Abraham Lincoln Association* 14 (Summer 1993): 24–25, 31–33, 37, 40.

[48] AL Proclamations Sept. 22, 1862, Jan. 1, 1863, JRMP, 6: 96–98, 157–67; Grady McWhiney and Perry D. Jamieson, *Attack and Die: Civil War Military Tactics and the Southern Heritage* (University, AL, 1982), 8; Howard Jones, *Abraham Lincoln and a New*

Lincoln made his strongest effort to commit his cabinet to colonization at the very moment when he was announcing emancipation to the country. Lincoln's reading of the preliminary proclamation to his cabinet on September 22 caused Seward to propose that the draft colonization wording be revised to clarify that emigrants had to agree to their removal and that the country of their destination must consent to their immigration. Two days later, Lincoln called a special cabinet meeting to take up two matters, one of them being – in the spirit of Seward's reservations – whether his administration should seek treaties with foreign nations that would specifically authorize black colonies. During the discussion that followed, Seward recommended such treaties but expressed little enthusiasm in principle for colonization. Postmaster General Blair, unsurprisingly, argued lengthily for colonization, and he and Attorney General Edward Bates thought that blacks should be deported abroad since they were unlikely to leave voluntarily. Treasury Secretary Chase disfavored treaties as a colonization tool, recommending instead, "simple arrangements ... by which any person who might choose to emigrate, would be secured in such advantages as might be offered them by other States or Governments." Secretary of the Navy Welles believed it best simply to let blacks, like white people, cut their best emigration deals with foreign governments and move on their own to "where there were the best inducements." Faced with diverse advice, Lincoln emphasized that compulsory emigration was out of the question, but he thought Britain, Denmark, and other countries would take in voluntary black emigrants. He wished his advisers, as Chase remembered, "to think of the subject, and be ready to express our opinions when we next come together." That "next" gathering occurred four days later, with Seward speaking on the issue and Bates reading a formal paper to the cabinet endorsing colonization treaties. Lincoln made it clear that he now thought treaties were the right approach (Figure 6.3).[49]

Not long after Lincoln held his White House colonization meeting with black leaders and even before the Chiriqui project was finalized, Pomeroy issued an appeal "To the Free Colored People of the United States" for

Birth of Freedom: The Union and Slavery in the Diplomacy of the Civil War (Lincoln, NE, 1999), 86–87.

[49] Diary of Samuel P. Chase, Sept. 22, 24, 1862, *Diary and Correspondence of Samuel P. Chase*, 89, 92–93; Edward Bates Diary, Sept. 25, 1862, *Diary of Edward Bates*, 262–63; Gideon Welles Diary, Sept. 26, 1862, *Diary of Gideon Welles*, 150–53.

FIGURE 6.3 Lincoln at Antietam.

Courtesy of Library of Congress (USZ62–2276).

Note: This famous photograph shows Lincoln visiting Union general George B. McClellan (facing Lincoln) after McClellan's repulse at the Battle of Antietam of the invasion of Maryland by Robert E. Lee's Confederate Army of Northern Virginia. It was around the time that this photograph was taken that Lincoln was most enthusiastic about colonizing freed slaves in Latin America.

emigrants. The call, which appeared in media outlets throughout the North beginning August 26, expressed Pomeroy's intention to depart for Chiriqui on October 1 with one hundred "colored men" – preferably laborers and mechanics – and their families, noting pointedly that any of these colonization "pioneers" who were formerly slaves would put so much distance between them and their former masters that they would be "free and independent beyond the reach of the power that has oppressed you." Pomeroy opened a colonization office in Washington, hired a clerk, held a recruitment meeting with blacks in the Washington, D.C., area, and visited New York to gather supplies and get a transport steamer for the emigrants. On September 24, the U.S. Treasury Department authorized a reimbursement of $20,000 to Pomeroy for his expenses (Figure 6.4).[50]

Pomeroy's emigrants never left, paradoxically in part because of suspicions abroad that Lincoln's project represented a new iteration of Manifest Destiny. And, in a way, it did. Although Lincoln conceived of emigrant communities as opportunities for black freedom, some of his advisers believed black colonists would extend U.S. influence in the Tropics. At the least, Lincoln's plan, because it envisioned removing a population unwanted by many U.S. whites, seemed to represent what some modern scholars dub "social imperialism" – the dumping of a country's "social woes" on foreign places: by exporting the inequities of its own political economy, a nation potentially can defuse explosive situations at home.[51] Yet territorial imperialism also cast a shadow over the program. In 1861, the former Cuba filibuster collaborator Robert W. Shufeldt, serving as U.S. consul at Havana, promoted the creation of a black settlement on Mexico's Tehuantepec isthmus because he thought it would enhance U.S. control over a key commercial route. Secretary of the Interior Smith told Lincoln that colonization in Chiriqui by "Colored Americans whose Sympathies would naturally be with this country would ultimately establish" there "such an influence as would most probably secure to us the absolute control of the country." Presumably by "country" Smith only

[50] Samuel C. Pomeroy, "To the Free Colored People of the United States," Aug. 25, 1862, in *New York Herald*, Aug. 26, 1862, *Boston Daily Advertiser*, Aug. 27, 1862, *Washington (DC) Daily National Intelligencer*, Aug. 27, 1862, *Milwaukee Daily Sentinel*, Aug. 29, 1862, and *Worcester Massachusetts Spy*, Sept. 3, 1862; Caleb B. Smith to S. C. Pomeroy, Sept. 25, 1862, RG48, Roll 1, Pomeroy to John P. Usher, Feb. 4, 1864, RG48, Roll 8; Scheips, "Lincoln and the Chiriqui Colonization Project," 437.
[51] Schoonover, "Napoleon Is Coming!" 103–104, 115–16; Sharon Hartman Strom, "Labor, Race, and Colonization: Imagining a Post-Slavery World in the Americas," *The Problem of Evil: Slavery, Freedom, and the Ambiguities of American Reform*, ed. Steven Mintz and John Stauffer (Amherst, 2007), 262.

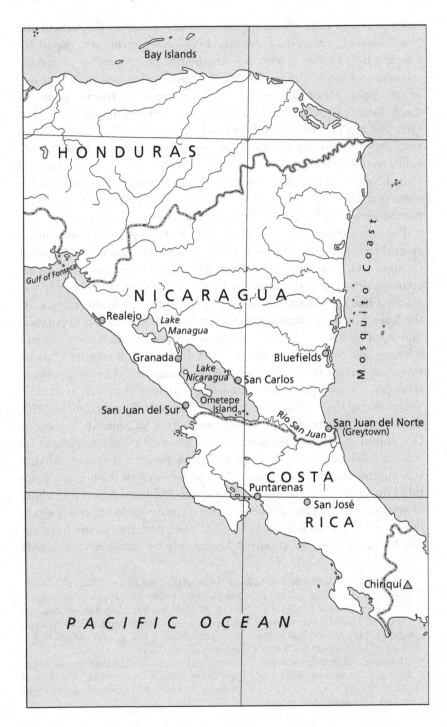

meant Chiriqui, but maybe he anticipated a broader slice of Central America. After all, Secretary of the Treasury Chase, whose instincts were mostly against colonization, told the cabinet that the only advantage to colonization would be "as a means of getting a foothold in Central America."[52]

Though Latin American diplomats and leaders would not have been privy to the Lincoln administration's internal deliberations, they harbored suspicions of colonization's expansionist potential. Matías Romero initially welcomed the idea of colonizing parts of Mexico with U.S. blacks, but he also harbored concerns about possible territorial ambitions lurking behind such proposals. Central American leaders expressed similar reservations about U.S. intentions soon after it became evident that their region was in play for Lincoln's program, partly because Costa Rica claimed some of the land embraced within the intended colony. Elisha Crosby recalled later that from the moment he broached the subject of black colonization to Guatemalan leaders, the presidents of Guatemala and Honduras expressed concerns about "considerable" numbers of "English speaking negroes" endangering the region's "Spanish forms and customs." Nicaragua's official newspaper editorialized that colonization might be filibustering in another form, and Costa Rica's foreign minister explained in a diplomatic dispatch that it would be advisable to decline all North American colonization projects given North American expansionist proclivities and the difficulties of self-defense against a large influx of immigrants. In September, 1861, Luis Molina, officially representing Nicaragua and Honduras as well as Costa Rica in Washington, lodged a protest with Seward about colonization in the three countries

---

FIGURE 6.4 Lincoln's Chiriqui Project.

Note: This map shows the Chiriqui region of Panama, the focus of one of Lincoln's most important black colonization projects during the Civil War. The map also indicates the Mosquito Coast and the Bay Islands, areas of Central America under British control that greatly concerned Stephen Douglas throughout the 1850s. The Clayton-Bulwer Treaty of 1850 angered Douglas because it allowed Britain to keep its protectorate while preventing U.S. territorial expansion in the region. Britain surrendered its claims to the Mosquito Coast in treaties with Honduras and Nicaragua in 1859 and 1860, respectively.

[52] Schoonover, "Misconstrued Mission," 610, 617; Caleb Smith to AL, May 16, 1862, RG48, Roll 1; Samuel P. Chase Diary, Sept. 24, 1862, *Diary and Correspondence of Salmon P. Chase,* 93; Robert E. May, *John A. Quitman: Old South Crusader* (Baton Rouge, 1985), 282, 285.

and warned that Central Americans would identify the movement with filibustering if the administration kept promoting it. El Salvador's official newspaper warned that Lincoln could not prevent a future Pierce-type administration from capitalizing territorially from such colonies, and Guatemala's minister to the United States feared that black colonies would repeat Texas's history of seceding from Mexico. New Granada, where Pomeroy's colonists were supposedly bound, demanded that the emigrants formally forsake U.S. protection in advance and that the U.S. government confirm this revocation. The cumulative protests and obstructions, plus British concerns that settlements of U.S. blacks would violate the Clayton-Bulwer Treaty's provision against new colonies in Central America, jeopardized the probability that the Chiriqui project would ever be launched.[53]

Given the barrage of protests from Central American states and his own decision that colonization depended upon formal treaty authorization, Lincoln had no realistic option other than to rein in the Thompson project even though the government was vested in it through prior reimbursements to Pomeroy. On October 7, 1862, Usher notified Pomeroy that the president was suspending the program temporarily, a decision that dismayed the Kansan. On October 20, Pomeroy wrote to Senator Doolittle that he had applications from 13,700 blacks who wished to go and he had already selected 500 of them for his "pioneer party." Blaming the suspension on Seward and claiming that neither New Granada's government nor its people had protested the scheme, Pomeroy urged Doolittle to have the policy reversed.[54]

Pomeroy may not have been dissembling about having a pool of willing black emigrants or New Granada's interest in getting them. The *New York Herald* published a November 2, 1862, report that a delegation of

---

[53] *London Daily News*, Oct. 15, 1862; Schoonover, "Miscontrued Mission," 612, 618; Caleb B. Smith to S. C. Pomeroy, Sept. 27, 1862, RG48, Scheips, "Lincoln and the Chiriqui Colonization Project," 443–44; Barker, ed., *Memoirs of Elisha Oscar Crosby,* 89–90; William Stuart to Lord Russell, Oct. 18, 1862, *The American Civil War through British Eyes, Dispatches from British Diplomats*, vol. 2: *April 1862–February 1863*, ed. James J. Barnes and Patience P. Barnes (Kent, OH, 2005), 212; Horne, *Deepest South,* 180, 182.

[54] William Stuart to Lord Russell, Oct. 18, 1862, in Barnes and Barnes, ed., *American Civil War through British Eyes,* 2: 212; Samuel C. Pomeroy to James Doolittle, Oct. 20, 1862, *Publications of the Southern History Association* 9 (Nov. 1905): 401–402; John P. Usher to S. C. Pomeroy, Oct. 7, 1862, RG48, Roll 1; Phillip W. Magness and Sebastian N. Page, *Colonization after Emancipation: Lincoln and the Movement for Black Resettlement* (Columbia, MO,, 2011), 32, 46, 48.

Washington, D.C., blacks had recently sought a meeting with Lincoln to protest the suspension of the project, and they had submitted a formal letter to him making their case. According to the *Herald*, they claimed many blacks in the federal district had sold their homes and furniture in preparation for leaving and were facing poverty come winter unless the expedition departed. Praising Pomeroy for his dedication to the project, they told Lincoln it was inconceivable that he would raise false hopes and then leave them in such an exposed position. Lincoln answered that he remained "anxious" for their departure and hoped to meet personally with the delegation. Black interest in Central American colonization continued through at least 1863, when the African Civilization Society, an emigration organization headed by the fiery abolitionist minister Henry Highland Garnet (who had returned from Jamaica and was presiding over the Shiloh Presbyterian Church in New York City) investigated colonization opportunities in British Honduras. In November, the society dispatched a delegation of officers to meet with Lincoln. In the spring of 1864, New Granada, now officially Colombia, informed Washington that it approved of colonization and that landowners had the legal right to settle emigrants on their property.[55]

Lincoln informed the whole country of his continuing commitment to colonization when he delivered his Second Annual Message to Congress on December 1, 1862, exactly one month before he issued the final Emancipation Proclamation. His address promoted a colonization amendment he wished incorporated within the U.S. Constitution, authorizing Congress to "appropriate money and otherwise provide for colonizing free colored persons with their own consent at any place or places without the United States." In his elaboration of the draft amendment, Lincoln dismissed fears that free blacks threatened the jobs of U.S. workers but nonetheless reiterated his support for black emigration: "I can not make it better known than it already is that I strongly favor colonization." Further, he argued that Congress should receive his proposed colonization amendment as "unobjectionable ... inasmuch as it comes to nothing unless by the mutual consent of the people to be deported and the American voters, through their representatives in Congress."[56]

[55] *New York Herald,* Nov. 3, 1862; William Cheek and Aimee Lee Cheek, *John Mercer Langston and the Fight for Black Freedom, 1829–1865* (Urbana, 1989), 427; Magness and Page, *Colonization after Emancipation,* 46, 86; Francisco Párraga to Ambrose W. Thompson, Apr. 4, 1864, in Scheips, "Lincoln and the Chiriqui Colonization Project," 447–48.
[56] AL, Second Annual Message, Dec. 1, 1862, JRMP, 6: 136, 140.

Although some scholars have argued that Lincoln ditched colonization after his final Emancipation Proclamation on January 1, 1863, that seems not to have been the case – and not just because his ill-fated expedition to the Haitian island of Île-à-Vache sailed after this date. Even in the wake of the proclamation, the Lincoln administration continued to receive colonization proposals and take them seriously, though it increasingly restricted recruitment to blacks living around Washington, D.C. When, in April 1863, the Interior Department considered a proposal from the American West India Company, a New York City concern, to take blacks to the Dominican Republic to cultivate cotton, John P. Usher (who had replaced Smith as interior secretary) encouraged the idea as long as the emigrants were drawn from the capital's free blacks. Usher emphasized that it might prove impossible to get authorization from Union military commanders in occupied parts of the South for emigrants to leave their lines. In a letter written a few weeks later, Usher attributed the military interference with colonization to Union secretary of war, Edwin Stanton. Stanton had no interest in helping male ex-slaves who might enlist in the Union military to leave the country.[57]

Lincoln's continuing interest in colonization is further revealed in a January 27 message to his government from Lord Lyons, Britain's minister to the United States. Lyons recounted a conversation he had with Lincoln the day before. Noting that the president had summoned him to the meeting, he said that no sooner had he arrived than Lincoln said "he had been for some time anxious to speak to me in an informal and unofficial manner on ... emigration of coloured people ... to the British [Latin American] colonies." Sensitive to Britain's neutrality in the Civil War, Lincoln clarified that he would not expect Britain to accept any blacks still claimed as slaves by Confederates, but he wanted to know whether blacks who had been freeborn or who had been voluntarily emancipated by their owners might be welcomed. A long discussion ensued, during which Lyons expressed his understanding that British colonies were indeed "anxious to obtain a supply of coloured laborers" from the United States and Lincoln asked whether Britain were willing to cut a formal deal to get them. The conversation revolved around the necessity of rules to protect black emigrants during and after their voyages, with Lyons saying he had already raised such matters with colonization agent

---

[57] John P. Usher to WHS, Apr. 22, 1863, Usher to Hiram Ketchum, President, American West India Company, Apr. 24, 1863, Usher to John Hodge, May 11, 1863, RG48, Roll 1; Hudson, *Mistress of Manifest Destiny*, 178.

Mitchell. When Lyons said his primary concern was that there would not be a large enough potential supply of emigrants to justify dispatching recruiting agents to the Union, Lincoln conceded that recruitment remained problematic and directed Lyons to consult Seward further on these matters.[58]

A significant colonization effort in British Honduras might have ensued had it not been for Stanton's obstruction. In April, Secretary Usher met with John Hodge, a landowning merchant and officer of the British Honduras Company, which wanted a large influx of black laborers. Stanton, however, blocked Hodge's access to potential emigrants in contraband camps in Virginia. Hodge's reaction offers further evidence of Lincoln's continuing interest in black emigration. Observing that he would have to "abstain for the present from exercising the permission which was so readily ... accorded to me by His Excellency the President, and other Members of the Government" to make emigration inquiries at the camps and in Washington, D.C., as well, Hodge registered disappointment and asked whether he instead could just raise two hundred or three hundred laborers among blacks who would be "unsuitable" for military duty since they had families dependent on them. In a separate note, Hodge told Usher that he had just had several applications from U.S. free blacks who were neither district inhabitants nor contrabands and wished to go to British Honduras. Around the same time, Mitchell urged Stanton to reconsider his interference, partly on the basis of the argument that by so doing he would "sustain the long cherished policy of the President." Mitchell also suggested that once the war ended, former slaves could be colonized in an occupied Texas, which not only would help the government keep an eye on French activities in Mexico but also pave the way for their eventual emigration to Mexico's southern reaches. On June 13 Lincoln endorsed Mitchell's permission to Hodge and his associate S. R. Dickson for unobstructed "canvassing for emigrants" and Mitchell's request that U.S. officials assist them in their quest.[59]

Lincoln's hemispheric colonization interests after Emancipation Day transcended Haiti and British Honduras, and his administration seriously

[58] Lord Lyons to Lord Russell, Jan. 27, 1863, in Barnes and Barnes, ed., *The American Civil War through British Eyes*, 307–308.

[59] Magness and Page, *Colonization after Emancipation*, 19; Foner, "Lincoln and Colonization," 160–62; John Hodge to John P. Usher, May 14, 20, 1863, Usher to John Hodge, May 11, 1863, "A. Lincoln" endorsement, June 13, 1863 on James Mitchell to John Hodge and S. R. Dickson, June 14, 1862 [1863], copies with Mitchell to Lincoln, Nov. 25, 1863 (copy), RG48, Roll 8; Mitchell to Edwin M. Stanton, May 28, 1863, Records of the Secretary of War, Letters Received, Irregular Series, RG 107, M31, NA.

considered a "second wave" of tropical projects that embraced places like British Guiana and Dutch Surinam. Throughout the spring of 1863, officials in Demarara, British Guiana, and British agents in Washington investigated the possibility of importing free black laborers from the United States for the colony's labor-short sugar plantations. Furthermore, Lincoln did not simply leave these post-Emancipation colonization projects in commissioner Mitchell's hands. In June 1863, Lincoln met with Hodge at the White House and reiterated his determination to proceed with black emigration, giving Hodge's mission a signed endorsement. On another occasion, Lincoln reportedly lost his temper when he was informed of Stanton's continuing obstruction of colonization. Probably, Lincoln encouraged Seward's negotiation that year of a draft convention with the Hague for colonization in Surinam.[60]

No project other than Haiti materialized, though the reasons varied by locale. What deserves emphasis is that Lincoln kept pursuing the notion of resettling blacks in the Tropics until the summer of 1864, when his secretary John Hay, who considered colonization "a hideous and barbarous humbug" promoted by crooks, exulted on July 1 that "the President has sloughed off that idea of colonization." The very next day, Lincoln signed off on a congressional appropriations measure with a provision cutting off colonization funding other than reimbursement of disbursements already made. As Eric Foner observes, Lincoln's own racial prejudices were now softening, in part because he appreciated the profound contribution enlisted blacks were making to the Union's war effort. Probably, too, Lincoln was swayed by Secretary Usher's observation in December 1863 that there seemed to be no evidence of a "greater disposition ... among the colored persons" to emigrate than there had been when Lincoln made his colonization remarks to Congress a year earlier.[61]

Of course, neither Hay's observation nor Lincoln's signature on a complex appropriations measure amounts to conclusive proof that the president had given up entirely on colonization. After all, Lincoln remained an instinctive moderate concerning slavery's eradication, even after issuing his Emancipation Proclamation. In March 1864, when slavery's

[60] Magness and Page, *Colonization after Emancipation*, 10, 20–21, 25–26, 39–40, 57, 78–79.

[61] John Hay Diary, July 1, 1864, Burlingame and Turner, ed., *Inside Lincoln's Cabinet*, 217; "An Act making Appropriations for sundry Civil Expenses of the Government for the Year ending the Thirtieth of June, eighteen hundred and sixty-five ...," *Statutes at Large*, 38 Cong., 1 Sess., 352; John P. Usher to AL, Dec. 5, 1863, *House Exec. Doc.*, 38 Cong., 1 Sess., # 1, xviii; Foner, *Fiery Trial*, 256–57.

continuing legality in Maryland (a state exempt from the proclamation since it never seceded) was an issue, Lincoln privately expressed his preference for that state to end slavery gradually.[62] The American constitutional system, moreover, provided no line-item-veto authority that would have enabled Lincoln to register dissent at Congress's cutting off colonization funding. He would have had to veto the entire appropriations bill, an action that would have been very disruptive as Congress was nearing adjournment.

Many years later, Benjamin F. Butler claimed he spoke to Lincoln in early 1865 and that Lincoln still remained emphatically a colonizationist. It is hard to accept Butler's account verbatim, since he quoted Lincoln at length some thirty-seven years after the fact, apparently without any notes or diary entry to guide him. Recent detective work by historian Phillip Magness, however, discredits claims that Butler could not have met with Lincoln in early 1865 since the chronology Butler gave for their meeting is inconsistent with Lincoln's whereabouts at the time. Magness demonstrates the two men did meet at the White House on April 11, three days before Lincoln's assassination.

If Butler even remotely captured the essence of Lincoln's remarks, Lincoln remained reluctant to surrender colonization to his death. As Butler tells the story, Lincoln was worried about integrating into American society the 150,000 or so blacks whom the Union had already armed during the war and believed race war would erupt if they returned to the South once the Civil War ended. Lincoln wanted Butler to study the "figures" as to "whether the negroes can be transported" and said it would be best "to export them all to some fertile country with a good climate, which they could have to themselves." Butler claimed that two days afterward he called on the president, reported that the United States lacked sufficient shipping to transport all of the South's blacks safely to San Domingue ("the nearest place that can be found fit for them") because the voyages could never offset the numbers of black children born in the United States, and advised that the smartest course would be for government to employ its enlisted former slaves in digging a Central American canal.[63]

---

[62] AL to John A. J. Creswell, Mar. 7, 1864, CWAL, 7: 226–27.

[63] Benjamin F. Butler, *Butler's Book: Autobiographic and Personal Reminiscences of Major-General Benj F Butler* (Boston, 1892), 902–907; Phillip W. Magness, "Benjamin Butler's Colonization Testimony Reevaluated," *Journal of the Abraham Lincoln Association* 29 (No. 1, 2008): 1–11.

What are we to make of Lincoln's pursuit of colonization phantoms? In hindsight, Lincoln's program demands censure on many counts, most obviously its disturbing premise that blacks should leave the country. Decades after the program died, Lincoln's colonization czar James Mitchell told an interviewer that the president thought that racial amalgamation threatened his nation and that whites and blacks had better separate for the country's good. In fact, Mitchell attributed Lincoln's disinterest in Latin American annexations to his certainty that the mixed races already inhabiting the Tropics held "anti-republican" values. Possibly Mitchell distorted Lincoln's discussions with him, but there is no denying that in pursuing policies promoted by the Blairs, Lincoln followed the lead of an indisputably racist family nervous that the war might release one-time slaves into American society. Frank Blair Jr., after all, kept a horse named "Nigger," and when British journalist William Howard Russell met Montgomery Blair, he was struck by the postmaster general's "peculiar notions with reference to the black and white races." Colonization mastermind Blair Sr. undoubtedly fostered his sons' bigotry. Late in the war, Blair Sr. fretted that federal emancipation policy was tending toward "negro citizenship & equality as the means of destroying our Democratic Institutions."[64]

Had no white Americans advocated equal rights for blacks at the time, Lincoln's colonization program might seem less reprehensible. Mark Neely rightly censures Lincoln for lagging behind more enlightened northern public opinion when it came to incorporating blacks within American society. Eric Foner observes Lincoln's difficulty in even imagining his country "as a biracial society" and suggests that publication of the president's White House remarks on colonization helped ignite mob violence against northern blacks during that summer of 1862. Yet another scholar reflects caustically that at his death Lincoln was prepared to offer defeated Confederates "magnanimous" terms, while "for black Americans, the rights of full citizenship seemed a long way off except, of course, in a different country."[65] From this perspective, the best case

---

[64] James Mitchell interview published in the *St. Louis Daily Globe-Democrat*, Aug. 26, 1894, quoted in Michael Lind, *What Lincoln Believed: The Values and Convictions of America's Greatest President* (2004; rpt., New York, 2006), 113; Frank Blair Jr. to Francis P. Blair Sr., Apr. 30, 1864, Blair Sr. to Blair Jr., Dec. 23, 1863, Blair Family Papers, LC, Roll 2; William Howard Russell Diary, Mar. 28, 1861, Berwanger, ed., *My Diary North and South*, 50.

[65] Neely, "Colonization," 56; Foner, *Fiery Trial*, 128, 156–57; James N. Leiker, "The Difficulties of Understanding Abe: Lincoln's Reconciliation of Racial Inequality and Natural Rights," in *Lincoln Emancipated: The President and the Politics of Race*, ed.

for Lincoln's program rests on its genesis as a tactical maneuver to pre-
pare the public mind for general emancipation and its realistic assessment
of the racial attitudes of the overwhelming majority of whites living in
the United States at the time. Anticipating that racial prejudices would
remain embedded in American culture, Lincoln embraced colonization as
an end run around the problem.[66]

Still, it deserves emphasis that Lincoln's conception of colonization
was dualistic. On the one hand, colonization promised to alleviate white
America's racial paranoia by draining its black population southward.
On the other, Lincoln seems to have envisioned colonization as enriching
the lives of its black participants and extending freedom in the hemisphere. Noteworthy, in this respect, are the Lincoln administration's
related dramatic steps to end the African slave trade to the Caribbean.
Although the United States had outlawed the African slave trade back
in 1808, its subsequent efforts to suppress the traffic had been irregular,
hampered by an insufficiency of naval vessels and by an unwillingness of
U.S. leaders to authorize British naval officers to board suspected slaving
vessels flying U.S. flags. Lincoln was so eager to suppress the slave trade
that he was willing to work with the British. In early 1862, Nathaniel
Gordon became the first slave trader the U.S. government had ever executed for that crime after Lincoln refrained from commuting his sentence.
Two months later, with Lincoln's strong backing, Seward signed a treaty
with British minister Lord Lyons that allowed both nations to search
merchant vessels flying each other's flags off Africa and Cuba. The next
year, the administration strengthened the treaty by adding waters within
thirty leagues of the islands of Hispaniola, Puerto Rico, and Madagascar
to its coverage. Although it is true, as Howard Jones emphasizes, that
agreeing to the treaty was smart diplomacy, as it lessened the likelihood
that the antislavery British would intervene in the Civil War to help the
Confederacy, it also suggests Lincoln's commitment to black freedom in
the Caribbean basin. It is telling that after the Senate's unanimous ratification of the initial pact with Britain in 1862, Seward congratulated
Lincoln on the completion of "the most important act of your life and of
mine" in a private letter.[67]

Brian R. Dirck (DeKalb, 2007), 79; Blackett, "Lincoln and Colonization," 22; Lerone
Bennett Jr., *Forced into Glory: Abraham Lincoln's White Dream* (Chicago, 2000), 149.

[66] Paludan, "Greeley, Colonization," 41; Escott, "What Shall We Do with the
Negro?" 222–24.

[67] William Lee Miller, *President Lincoln: The Duty of a Statesman* (New York, 2008), 298;
Betty Fladeland, *Men and Brothers: Anglo-American Antislavery Cooperation* (Urbana,

Had Lincoln's sole purpose in colonization been to rid his country of blacks, he would have made it compulsory rather than voluntary, something he never considered. He hoped, rather, that his first emigrants would achieve such striking and reported success and happiness abroad that other African Americans would wish to follow their lead. Some of Lincoln's advisers spoke of "deporting blacks"; during late 1862, when emancipation and colonization were under discussion in Lincoln's cabinet, Postmaster General Blair and Attorney General Bates both argued for compulsory emigration. Blair said, according to Secretary of the Navy Welles, that it "would be necessary to rid the country of its black population." Bates argued that "deportation, by force if necessary, should go with emancipation." Welles also reported that in private conversation Pomeroy talked about "deporting slaves and colored people to Chiriqui." Certainly the concept of forced emigration was discussed.[68]

Lincoln dismissed talk of draconian roundups, and his emigration agents knew he wanted a voluntary program. When talking about colonization in his First Annual Message, Lincoln noted that southern slaves already liberated by the war were now "dependent on the United States," and he also anticipated that slaves who might in the future be liberated by voluntary state action would be "thrown upon" those states "for disposal." When he then said that "steps" should be taken to colonize them abroad, however, he said nothing about compulsory emigration. Surely this omission was purposeful, since when he commissioned James Mitchell as emigration agent he specified Mitchell should colonize African Americans "who, by their own free consent may desire to migrate to countries beyond the limits of the United States." In a wartime letter about funding for emigrants to Liberia, Interior Secretary Smith said that the government needed to discern "the number of free Colored persons ... *willing* to emigrate." According to Welles, moreover, when Bates urged deportation during cabinet deliberations, Lincoln "objected unequivocally to compulsion. Their emigration must be voluntary and without expense to themselves."

1972), 340; Phillip E. Myers, *Caution and Cooperation: The American Civil War in British-American Relations* (Kent, OH, 2008), 209–12; "Additional Article to the Treaty for the Suppression of the African Slave-Trade ...," *Statutes at Large*, 38 Cong., 1 Seess., 645; Jones, *Abraham Lincoln and a New Birth of Freedom*, 65–66; WHS to AL, Apr. 24, 1862, AL Papers, LC, Series 1.

[68] Gideon Welles Diary, Oct. 1, Sept. 10, 1862, Beale, ed., *Diary of Gideon Welles*, 1: 158, 123.

Lincoln's primary reservations about the program derived from its very voluntary essence. Would blacks *want* to go? As the president put it to Britain's minister, the only way to know whether blacks would emigrate would be "to hold out sufficient inducements to the coloured people" and launch "the experiment." Only African Americans anticipating better prospects in Latin America than in the United States, in other words, would choose to leave.[69]

Whether Lincoln ever genuinely thought the program would generate a mass migration remains unknown. In a published 1862 report, Mitchell asserted the necessity of maintaining a "homogeneous population" in the United States as a means of preserving the nation's republican institutions.[70] It is risky, however, conflating Mitchell's thinking with Lincoln's. One wonders whether Lincoln believed the United States had the shipping capacity to take a significant fraction of its black population abroad. In an 1862 editorial entitled "What To Do with the Negroes," *Harper's Weekly* calculated it would require control of the entire world's fleet of large sailing ships for two years to take some four million slaves abroad. Even if Lincoln thought the shipping capacity sufficient, he surely recognized the limits of Congress's funding. Its initial $100,000 colonization appropriation would have funded the resettlement abroad of less than 10 percent of the District of Columbia's black population if that aid-per-emigrant were limited to $100 for the fourteen thousand African Americans residing there. Secretary of the Interior Caleb Smith specifically pointed to the one-thousand-person limitation in his May 1862 colonization letter to the president, noting the law would fund fewer than one thousand settlers since it did not cover contingent expenses. Further, the administration, adhering to Congress's legislation, rejected applications for emigration assistance from blacks already free in 1862 other than those living in Washington, D.C. It is hard to believe that Lincoln thought mass numbers of free blacks living elsewhere in the North would

[69] AL, First Annual Message, Dec. 3, 1861, JRMP, 6: 54; Commission of Emigration Agency signed by AL (copy), Aug. 4, 1862, RG48, Roll 8; Caleb B. Smith to William McLain, Apr. 23, 1862, RG48, Roll 1 (emphasis mine); Gideon Welles Diary, Sept. 26, 1862, Beale, ed., *Diary of Gideon Welles*, 1: 152; Lord Lyons to Lord Russell, Jan. 27, 1863, Barnes and Barnes, ed., *American Civil War through British Eyes*, 2: 308; Walter A. Payne, "Lincoln's Caribbean Colonization Plan," *Pacific Historian* 7 (May 1963): 71.

[70] James Mitchell, *Letters on the Relation of the White and African Races of the United States, Showing the Necessity of the Colonization of the Latter: Addressed to the President of the U.S.*, quoted in Michael Lind, *What Lincoln Believed: The Values and Convictions of America's Greatest President* (New York: Anchor Books, 2004), 196–200.

be so inspired by a cohort of Washington, D.C., blacks exiting the country that they would voluntarily fund their own removal.[71]

Possibly we should pay closer attention to the ambiguity of scale in Lincoln's own colonization remarks. He told the border state congressmen during their White House audience in July 1862 that once "numbers" of black emigrants were at a "large enough" level, other freed people would "not be so reluctant to go." Speaking to his Washington, D.C., black listeners the next month, he explained that Congress's funding of colonization was designed to support the emigration of "the people, *or a portion of them, of African descent.*" Lincoln never specified how small a *portion* might capitalize on his program. Perhaps the anticipated percentage was lower than Lincoln's critics would have it.[72] Lincoln's colonization program deserves remembrance as a tropical variant of his own free-soil ideology reserving the West for "white settlers." In talking to the African American delegation who met him at the White House in 1862, he used language reminiscent of his remarks at Peoria in 1854 about how Kansas and Nebraska needed preservation as a place for "poor white people" to migrate to, make homes for themselves, and "better their condition."

Lincoln shared with his black listeners a vision that Stephen A. Douglas would certainly have rejected. The president expected free blacks "capable of thinking as white men" to lead liberated slaves southward, to lands without race discrimination where they could thrive economically and become so self-reliant they emerged "equals of the best."[73] As he had once wished the West reserved for white people back east hoping to better their own condition, he now envisioned the Tropics as a haven where African Americans could achieve the equality and progress that eluded them in the United States of America.

[71] *Harper's Weekly,* Apr. 5, 1862, p. 210; Foner, *Fiery Trial,* 200; Caleb B. Smith to AL, May 9, 1862, John P. Usher to James Hall, Colonization Agent of the Maryland Colonization Society, Oct. 11, 1862, RG48, Roll 1.
[72] AL, "Appeal to Border State Representatives," CWAL, 318; *New-York Times,* Aug. 15, 1862 (emphasis mine).
[73] *New-York Times,* Aug. 15, 1862; CWAL, 2: 268.

Coda

According to a report reaching New York from Panama, nothing had ever caused a reaction locally comparable to what occurred when the shocking news "flashed across the wires" on May 1, 1865, that Abraham Lincoln had been assassinated in Washington. As the information sank in, people stared at each other "in blank astonishment, and the expressions, 'It is incredible!' 'It is impossible!' were heard on all sides." Foreign and native residents seemed equally horrified and the whole isthmian community plunged into "gloom."[1]

When John Wilkes Booth shot President Lincoln at Ford's Theater on Good Friday, April 14, 1865, he committed an act that reverberated profoundly throughout Latin America. Word of Lincoln's death caused Argentina's Congress, for instance, to resolve that the country's national flag be flown at half-mast for three days and members don mourning garb during that period. In Valparaiso, Chile, officials called upon vessels in the harbor to droop their U.S. and Chilean flags at half-mast for eight days. At the capital, Santiago, flags on public and private buildings were lowered to half-mast, a salute was rendered from the local fort, and the Congress met in special session to receive a message from their president lamenting Lincoln's death. In Chihuahua, Mexico, liberal president Benito Juárez ordered flags set at half-mast on all public buildings and at all official functions and decreed that military and civil officials wear mourning dress for nine days. In Colombia, the paper *El Tiempo* railed at the "slavery spirit" that brought Lincoln down and the military of Bogota paraded in Lincoln's honor. Some sixty presidential

---

[1] "From Panama," report dated May 5, 1865, *New York Times*, May 16, 1865.

musicians in the city played "solemn dirges" before the U.S. legation. In remote Montevideo, Uruguay, authorities felt compelled to lower public flags to half-mast and fire cannons every half-hour for a full day in Lincoln's honor.[2]

Common people everywhere seemed as crestfallen as their leaders. U.S. minister C. N. Riotte informed the State Department from San José, Costa Rica, that a "real gloom" had settled on the "whole community." Guatemala's minister in Washington told Secretary Seward he had learned that the entire Guatemalan people "made with horror at the announcement of the terrible catastrophe." In the still slaveholding country of Brazil, U.S. minister James Watson Webb in Rio de Janeiro discerned a "universal horror and dismay" engulfing all "classes" in the city upon receipt of the "melancholy news." Similar laments erupted in Chilean cities; according to the U.S. minister resident, "men wandered about the streets weeping like children, and foreigners, unable to speak our language, manifested a grief almost as deep as our own."[3]

Most of the sadness in Latin America derived from Lincoln's dualistic image as a republican nationalist who preserved his nation's unity and democratic institutions under great duress and as an emancipationist who freed the slaves. In writing to Matías Romero about Lincoln's death, Benito Juárez, still engaged in a struggle to overthrow Maximilian's régime, cited Lincoln's "abnegation" in the pursuit of "nationality." Similarly, the influential Argentinean officeholder and diplomat Tomás Guido lamented Lincoln's passing "at a time when his sacred patriotism had gained its end." Argentinean Domingo Faustino Sarmiento, who became minister to the United States around the time of the assassination and whose quickly written, widely circulated, and reprinted biography of the president (*Vida de Lincoln*) helped define Lincoln for decades in the minds of Latin American readers, revered Lincoln's success in preserving and completing the United States as a nation. Lincoln's story held special meaning for Sarmiento, whose own country had become engulfed in civil strife in 1859 over the secession of its Buenos Aires Province a few years

[2] Marcos Paz to the United States Congress, June 3, 1865, with resolution (translations), Thomas H. Nelson to WHS, June 1, 15, 1865, Lerdo de Tejada Circular (translation), May 16, 1865, Allan A. Burton to WHS, July 31, 1865, Decree dated Montevideo, June 3, 1865 (translation), *The Assassination of Abraham Lincoln ... Expressions of Condolence and Sympathy Inspired by These Events* (Washington, DC, 1867), 10–11; 37, 39–40, 626, 811, 830; Stephen J. Randall, *Colombia and the United States: Hegemony and Interdependence* (Athens, GA, 2002), 52.

[3] Antonio José de Irisarri to WHS, June 26, 1865, J. Watson Webb to WHS, May 23, 1865, Thomas H. Nelson to WHS, June 1, 1865; *ibid.*, 788–89, 30, 37.

earlier. Many tributes to Lincoln celebrated him as an icon of liberty. As Colombia's president put it, Lincoln's name was "associated with the emancipation of four millions of men, and erasing the stigma of an odious institution."[4]

Lincoln's greatest gift to Latin America, however, may have been his reversal, though unfortunately it proved temporary, of decades of U.S. interventionism in the region and annexationist grabs in the Gulf-Caribbean Basin. One can only assume that U.S. policy there would have been far different had Lincoln's longtime rival, the expansionist Stephen Douglas, succeeded in his own ambitions for the presidency. José Martí, the late-nineteenth-century Cuban nationalist and writer, who greatly admired Lincoln, recalled in the prologue to his most famous collection of poetry how Latin Americans could never forget U.S. conquests in the Mexican War or "López and Walker," and how the American eagle had once "clutched all the flags of America in its talons." Lincoln had opposed the Mexican War and worked as president toward reciprocal respect with Latin American countries, consistently avoiding military interventionism or even advocating it. This was sufficient, in the thinking of later generations of Latin Americans, to recall Lincoln, as historian Nicola Miller puts it, as the one *americanista*, the exception among U.S. presidents, who genuinely promoted inter-American cooperation.[5]

In 1921, after two decades of persistent U.S. gunboat diplomacy and occupations in Latin America, Peru's ambassador to the United States expressed it well. Speaking at Lincoln's tomb in Springfield, Illinois, on the anniversary of Lincoln's birthday, Federico A. Pezet, the grandson of Peru's president at the time of the American Civil War, emphasized how different Lincoln's Latin American policies had been from those of his predecessors. Noting how Lincoln's predecessor James Buchanan had consistently championed the deployment of U.S. ground and naval forces in Central and South America, Pezet lauded the sixteenth U.S. president for seeing that relations could be different and for resolving disputes between

[4] Benito Juárez to Matías Romero, May 11, 1865, Tomas Guido to Robert C. Kirk, May 30, 1865, Manuel Murillo to Allan A. Burton, June 21, 1865; *ibid.*, 627, 13, 809; Nicola Miller, "'That Great and Gentle Soul': Images of Lincoln in Latin America," in *The Global Lincoln*, ed. Richard Carwardine and Jay Sexton (New York, 2011), 207–209; José Antonio Portuondo, "The Uncommon Man: Lincoln as Seen by His Latin American Contemporaries," *Americas* 11 (Jan. 1959): 21.

[5] José Martí quoted in *José Martí: Selected Writings*, ed. and trans. Esther Allen (New York, 2002), 270; Miller, "'Great and Gentle Soul,'" 214–15.

the Union and Peru through peaceful negotiations. Lincoln's "attitude toward Latin America," Pezet reflected, "showed the man's vision, his broadness of mind, and true sense of justice." Pezet could only wonder how many wars over the course of the history of the world might have been averted had other nations been led by statesmen like Lincoln.[6]

---

[6] *Lincoln and Peru: An Address by His Excellency Don Federico Pezet, Ambassador from the Republic of Peru, Delivered at Springfield, Illinois February 12, 1921 ...* (Washington, DC, 1921).

Index

Printed in the United States
By Bookmasters